Comfort Food
MAKEOVERS

RDA ENTHUSIAST BRANDS, LLC
MILWAUKEE, WI

Taste of Home

Reader's digest

A TASTE OF HOME/READER'S DIGEST BOOK
©2015 RDA Enthusiast Brands, LLC, 1610 N. 2nd St., Suite 102, Milwaukee WI 53212-3906. All rights reserved.
Taste of Home and Reader's Digest are registered trademarks of The Reader's Digest Association, Inc.

EDITORIAL

Editor-in-Chief: Catherine Cassidy
Creative Director: Howard Greenberg
Editorial Operations Director: Kerri Balliet

Managing Editor, Print & Digital Books: Mark Hagen
Associate Creative Director: Edwin Robles Jr.

Editor: Christine Rukavena
Associate Editor: Molly Jasinski
Art Director: Maggie Conners
Layout Designer: Nancy Novak
Editorial Production Manager: Dena Ahlers
Copy Chief: Deb Warlaumont Mulvey
Copy Editors: Dulcie Shoener, Mary-Liz Shaw
Contributing Copy Editor: Valerie Phillips
Editorial Intern: Michael Welch
Business Analyst, Content Tools: Amanda Harmatys
Content Operations Assistant: Shannon Stroud
Editorial Services Administrator: Marie Brannon

Food Editors: Gina Nistico; James Schend; Peggy Woodward, RD
Recipe Editors: Mary King; Jenni Sharp, RD; Irene Yeh

Test Kitchen & Food Styling Manager: Sarah Thompson
Test Cooks: Nicholas Iverson (lead), Matthew Hass, Lauren Knoelke
Food Stylists: Kathryn Conrad (senior), Leah Rekau, Shannon Roum
Prep Cooks: Bethany Van Jacobson (lead), Megumi Garcia, Melissa Hansen

Photography Director: Stephanie Marchese
Photographers: Dan Roberts, Jim Wieland
Photographer/Set Stylist: Grace Natoli Sheldon
Set Stylists: Melissa Franco, Stacey Genaw, Dee Dee Jacq
Photo Studio Assistant: Ester Robards

Editorial Business Manager: Kristy Martin
Editorial Business Associate: Samantha Lea Stoeger

BUSINESS

Vice President, Group Publisher: Kirsten Marchioli
Publisher: Donna Lindskog
General Manager, Taste of Home Cooking School: Erin Puariea
Executive Producer, Taste of Home Online Cooking School: Karen Berner

THE READER'S DIGEST ASSOCIATION, INC.

President and Chief Executive Officer: Bonnie Kintzer
Chief Financial Officer: Tom Callahan
Vice President, Chief Operating Officer, North America: Howard Halligan
Chief Revenue Officer: Richard Sutton
Chief Marketing Officer: Leslie Dukker Doty
Senior Vice President, Global HR & Communications: Phyllis E. Gebhardt, SPHR
Vice President, Digital Content & Audience Development: Diane Dragan
Vice President, Brand Marketing: Beth Gorry
Vice President, Financial Planning & Analysis: William Houston
Publishing Director, Books: Debra Polansky
Vice President, Chief Technology Officer: Aneel Tejwaney
Vice President, Consumer Marketing Planning: Jim Woods

For other **Taste of Home** books and products, visit us at **tasteofhome.com.**

For more **Reader's Digest** products and information,
visit **rd.com** (in the United States) or **rd.ca** (in Canada).

Library of Congress Number: 2015942761

International Standard Book Number: 978-1-61765-422-0

Cover Photographer: Jim Wieland
Set Stylist: Melissa Franco
Food Styling: Laurel Zimienski

Pictured on front cover: Light Linguine Carbonara, page 186.
Pictured on spine: Irish Cream Cupcakes, page 254.
Pictured on back cover: Zucchini Crust Pizza, page 242; Low-Fat Chocolate Cookies, page 278; Buffalo Turkey Burgers, page 164.

Printed in China.
1 3 5 7 9 10 8 6 4 2

LIKE US
facebook.com/tasteofhome

TWEET US
@tasteofhome

FOLLOW US
pinterest.com/taste_of_home

SHOP WITH US
shoptasteofhome.com

SHARE A RECIPE
tasteofhome.com/submit

57

120

10

256

84

44

CONTENTS

Dish up all the **comfort foods** you enjoy **without an ounce of guilt!**

155

The pros at *Taste of Home* received hundreds of requests to lighten up all-time comfort foods—and they did! Now they're sharing their best secrets in *Comfort Food Makeovers!*

About Our Nutritional Guidelines

All the recipes in **Taste of Home Comfort Food Makeovers** fit the lifestyles of health-conscious cooks and their families. The recipes represent a variety of foods that fit into any meal plan within the standards of the USDA's "MyPlate" recommendations for moderately active adults (see the Daily Nutrition Guide on page 5).

Nutrition Facts

- Nutrition Facts are based on one serving. For appetizers, cookies, rolls and other per-piece foods, serving information is based on one piece.
- Whenever a choice of ingredients is given in a recipe (such as ⅓ cup of plain yogurt or sour cream), the first ingredient listed is always the one calculated in the Nutrition Facts.
- When a range is given for an ingredient (such as 2 to 3 teaspoons), we calculate using the first amount.
- Only the amount of a marinade absorbed during preparation is calculated.
- Optional ingredients are not included in our calculations.

Diabetic Exchanges

All of the recipes in this book have been reviewed by a Registered Dietitian. Diabetic Exchanges are assigned to recipes in accordance with guidelines from the American Diabetic and American Dietetic associations. The majority of recipes in *Taste of Home Comfort Food Makeovers* are suitable for people with diabetes.

Inside, you will find:

- 50+ appetizers, dips, meatballs, beverages and other light bites perfect for parties

- 7 dozen sensible sweets so there's always room for dessert

- Useful icons highlighting recipes that are fast, freezer-friendly, slow-cooked or made with just five or fewer ingredients

- A handy Clip & Keep Substitution Chart on the back flap to help you lighten up your own dishes

- Secrets from our Test Kitchen pros throughout

248

173

56

268

The Inside Scoop

Here's a sampling of the savvy makeover tricks you'll discover in this cookbook. Apply them to your family's own favorite recipes for tasty results that get good nutrition marks, too!

Remember that we first eat with our eyes. Nancy Langrock's lightened-up **Stovetop Macaroni and Cheese** holds back some cheese so a generous amount can be sprinkled on top. Use this handy trick to make bacon, sour cream or any other indulgent ingredient go further. **Page 248**

Bulk up dishes with healthy veggies. Kari Kelley's **Vermont Turkey Loaf** packs in a hearty ½ cup of vegetables per serving. The healthy results? A larger serving size (which is visually satisfying), a flavorful loaf that is lower in fat, and 2 grams added fiber per serving. **Page 173**

Use bold doses of herbs and spices to create big flavor with just a few calories. Judith Foreman's **Tomatoes with Buttermilk Vinaigrette** piles on the chives and tarragon—and just ¾ teaspoon oil per serving—to deliver summer-fresh flavor at its best for only 79 calories. **Page 56**

Hold on to some fat to ensure rich texture. Diane Roth's **Light Cheesecake** uses both reduced-fat and fat-free cream cheese along with light sour cream to create a tender, melt-in-your-mouth cheesecake—better than the results of using all fat-free ingredients. **Page 268**

DAILY NUTRITION GUIDE

	WOMEN 25-50	WOMEN OVER 50	MEN 50-65
Calories	2,000	1,800	2,400
Fat	67 g or less	60 g or less	80 g or less
Saturated Fat	22 g or less	20 g or less	27 g or less
Cholesterol	300 mg or less	300 mg or less	360 mg or less
Sodium	2,400 mg or less	2,400 mg or less	2,400 mg or less
Carbohydrates	300 g	270 g	360 g
Fiber	20-30 g	20-30 g	20-30 g
Protein	50 g	45 g or less	60 g

This chart is only a guide. Calorie requirements vary, depending on age, weight, height and amount of activity. Children's dietary needs vary as they grow.

TRISHA KRUSE'S
CHICKEN SALAD PARTY
SANDWICHES *PAGE 24*

Appetizers & Snacks

Don't be late to the party! Cook up something **quick, nutritious and tasty** for your next **get-together,** and leave guests asking for your **healthy secrets.**

**STACY MULLENS'
MEDITERRANEAN EGGPLANT DIP**

PAGE 13

**MARILYN MCSWEEN'S
BRIE CHERRY PASTRY CUPS**

PAGE 19

**SUSAN HINTON'S
BLUE CHEESE DATE WRAPS**

PAGE 33

SLOW-COOKED SALSA

Cheesy Bean Dip

This reworked version of a favorite Mexican party dip has all the great taste of the classic, but it uses lower-fat ingredients to advantage.
—**TASTE OF HOME** TEST KITCHEN

START TO FINISH: 30 MIN.
MAKES: 4 CUPS

- 1½ cups (6 ounces) shredded reduced-fat Mexican cheese blend
- 1½ cups (6 ounces) shredded reduced-fat cheddar cheese
- 1 can (16 ounces) fat-free refried beans
- 1 can (10 ounces) diced tomatoes and green chilies
- 1 package (8 ounces) reduced-fat cream cheese, cubed
- ½ cup reduced-fat sour cream
- 1 tablespoon taco seasoning
  Tortilla chips and assorted fresh vegetables

1. In a large bowl, combine cheeses; set aside 1 cup for topping. Add the beans, tomatoes, cream cheese, sour cream and taco seasoning to the remaining cheeses; stir until blended. Transfer the mixture to a greased 2-qt. baking dish; sprinkle with the reserved cheeses.
2. Bake, uncovered, at 350° for 20-25 minutes or until bubbly around the edges. Serve warm with chips and vegetables.
PER SERVING *2 tablespoons dip equals 61 cal., 3 g fat (2 g sat. fat), 10 mg chol., 177 mg sodium, 4 g carb., 1 g fiber, 5 g pro.* **Diabetic Exchanges:** *½ starch, ½ lean meat.*

(5) INGREDIENTS SLOW COOKER
Slow-Cooked Salsa
I love the fresh taste of homemade salsa, but as a working mother, I don't have much time to make it. So I came up with this slow-cooked version that practically makes itself!
—**TONI MENARD** LOMPOC, CA

PREP: 15 MIN. • **COOK:** 2½ HOURS + COOLING
MAKES: ABOUT 2 CUPS

- 10 plum tomatoes
- 2 garlic cloves
- 1 small onion, cut into wedges
- 2 jalapeno peppers
- ¼ cup cilantro leaves
- ½ teaspoon salt, optional

1. Core tomatoes. Cut a small slit in two tomatoes; insert a garlic clove into each slit. Place tomatoes and onion in a 3-qt. slow cooker.
2. Cut stems off jalapenos; remove seeds if a milder salsa is desired. Place jalapenos in the slow cooker.
3. Cover and cook on high for 2½-3 hours or until vegetables are softened (some may brown slightly); cool.
4. In a blender, combine the tomato mixture, cilantro and, if desired, salt; cover and process until blended. Refrigerate leftovers.
NOTE *Wear disposable gloves when cutting hot peppers; the oils can burn skin. Avoid touching your face.*
PER SERVING *¼ cup (calculated without salt) equals 24 cal., trace fat (0 sat. fat), 0 chol., 9 mg sodium, 5 g carb., 0 fiber, 1 g pro.* **Diabetic Exchange:** *1 vegetable.*

seeds. Serve warm, or cool before storing in an airtight container.

NOTE *This recipe was tested in a 1,100-watt microwave.*

PER SERVING *¼ cup equals 87 cal., 5 g fat (1 g sat. fat), 0 chol., 191 mg sodium, 9 g carb., 1 g fiber, 3 g pro.* **Diabetic Exchanges:** *1 fat, ½ starch.*

⑤ INGREDIENTS **FAST FIX**

Tomato Basil Snackers

Fresh basil, summer-ripe tomatoes and melted mozzarella cheese top toasted English muffins in this fabulous afternoon pick-me-up.

—*TASTE OF HOME* TEST KITCHEN

START TO FINISH: 15 MIN.
MAKES: 4 SERVINGS

- 2 **English muffins, split and toasted**
- 2 **tablespoons fat-free mayonnaise**
- 3 **plum tomatoes, cut into ¼-inch slices**
- 6 **fresh basil leaves, thinly sliced**
- ⅛ **teaspoon pepper**
- ½ **cup shredded part-skim mozzarella cheese**

Place English muffin halves on an ungreased baking sheet; spread with mayonnaise. Top with the tomatoes, basil, pepper and cheese. Broil 4 in. from the heat for 3-4 minutes or until cheese is melted.

PER SERVING *1 serving equals 118 cal., 3 g fat (2 g sat. fat), 9 mg chol., 261 mg sodium, 17 g carb., 1 g fiber, 6 g pro.* **Diabetic Exchanges:** *1 starch, ½ fat.*

TOP TIP

Awesome recipe...and so easy to make. I used fresh avocado instead of mayonnaise.

—STARSHIP71 TASTEOFHOME.COM

⑤ INGREDIENTS **FAST FIX**

Garlic Pumpkin Seeds

What to do with all those leftover pumpkin seeds after carving your jack-o'-lantern? Try this microwave-easy recipe. It works well with butternut or acorn squash seeds, too.

—**IOLA EGLE** BELLA VISTA, AR

START TO FINISH: 25 MIN.
MAKES: 2 CUPS

- 1 **tablespoon canola oil**
- ½ **teaspoon celery salt**
- ½ **teaspoon garlic powder**
- ½ **teaspoon seasoned salt**
- 2 **cups fresh pumpkin seeds**

1. In a small bowl, combine the oil, celery salt, garlic powder and seasoned salt. Add pumpkin seeds; toss to coat. Spread a quarter of the seeds in a single layer on a microwave-safe plate. Microwave, uncovered, on high for 1 minute; stir.

2. Microwave 2-3 minutes longer or until seeds are crunchy and lightly browned, stirring after each minute. Repeat with remaining pumpkin

TOMATO BASIL SNACKERS

Saucy Asian Meatballs

This meatball recipe originally called for beef and pork and a different combination of seasonings. I used ground turkey and altered the seasonings to create a healthy, fresh-flavored variation.

—**LISA VARNER** EL PASO, TX

PREP: 20 MIN. • **BAKE:** 20 MIN.
MAKES: ABOUT 3 DOZEN

- 1 **pound lean ground turkey**
- 2 **garlic cloves, minced**
- 1 **teaspoon plus ¼ cup reduced-sodium soy sauce, divided**
- ½ **teaspoon ground ginger**
- ¼ **cup rice vinegar**
- ¼ **cup tomato paste**
- 2 **tablespoons molasses**
- 1 **teaspoon hot pepper sauce**

1. Preheat oven to 350°. Place turkey in a large bowl. Sprinkle with garlic, 1 teaspoon soy sauce and ginger; mix lightly but thoroughly. Shape into 1-in. balls; place in a 15x10x1-in. baking pan. Bake 20-25 minutes or until meatballs are cooked through.
2. In a large saucepan, combine vinegar, tomato paste, molasses, pepper sauce and remaining soy sauce; cook and stir over medium heat 3-5 minutes. Add meatballs; heat through, stirring gently to coat.
PER SERVING *1 meatball equals 26 cal., 1 g fat (trace sat. fat), 10 mg chol., 87 mg sodium, 2 g carb., trace fiber, 2 g pro.*

FAST FIX

Mini Bacon Quiches

This lightened-up recipe is loved by friends and family—and it tastes so indulgent with ½ pound of bacon! *Taste of Home* slashed the calories, fat and sodium in my dish, but not one bit of real bacon flavor.

—**JULIE HIEGGELKE** GRAYSLAKE, IL

START TO FINISH: 30 MIN.
MAKES: 2½ DOZEN

- 1 **large egg, lightly beaten**
- ½ **pound sliced bacon, cooked and crumbled**
- ½ **cup reduced-fat ricotta cheese**
- ½ **cup shredded part-skim mozzarella cheese**
- ½ **cup shredded reduced-fat cheddar cheese**
- 1 **small onion, finely chopped**
- ¼ **teaspoon garlic powder**
  Dash cayenne pepper
  Dash pepper
- 2 **packages (1.9 ounces each) frozen miniature phyllo tart shells**

1. In a small bowl, combine the first nine ingredients. Place tart shells on an ungreased baking sheet; fill each with 2 teaspoons mixture.
2. Bake at 350° for 8-10 minutes or until filling is set and shells are lightly browned. Serve warm.
PER SERVING *1 appetizer equals 54 cal., 3 g fat (1 g sat. fat), 13 mg chol., 77 mg sodium, 3 g carb., trace fiber, 3 g pro.*

SAUCY ASIAN MEATBALLS

Spicy Tomato Juice

People love the spicy taste of this zesty juice all year-round. It's a delicious mixer, too.

—MARTHA PHILBECK LA FONTAINE, IN

PREP: 45 MIN. • **COOK:** 20 MIN. + CHILLING
MAKES: 15 SERVINGS (1 CUP EACH)

- 12 **pounds tomatoes**
- 9 **dried ancho chilies**
- 3 **medium onions, chopped**
- 1 **celery rib, chopped**
- ¼ **cup chopped seeded jalapeno pepper**
- ½ **cup sugar**
- 1 **tablespoon Worcestershire sauce**
- 2 **teaspoons salt**
- ¼ **teaspoon pepper**

1. Fill a Dutch oven two-thirds full with water; bring to a boil. Score an X on the bottom of each tomato. Using a slotted spoon, place tomatoes, one at a time, in boiling water for 30-60 seconds. Remove tomatoes and immediately plunge into ice water. Discard peel; chop tomatoes and place in a stockpot.
2. Add the chilies, onions, celery and jalapenos. Bring to a boil. Reduce heat; simmer, uncovered, for 20-25 minutes or until vegetables are tender. Cool slightly. In a food processor, process juice in batches until blended. Strain and discard seeds and pulp. Place puree in a Dutch oven.
3. Stir in the remaining ingredients; heat through. Cool. To serve, refrigerate until chilled or transfer to storage containers. May be refrigerated for up to 3 days or frozen for up to 3 months.
NOTE *Wear disposable gloves when cutting hot peppers; the oils can burn skin. Avoid touching your face.*
PER SERVING *1 cup equals 134 cal., 2 g fat (trace sat. fat), 0 chol., 351 mg sodium, 29 g carb., 7 g fiber, 5 g pro. Diabetic Exchange: 2 starch.*

AVOCADO SHRIMP SALSA

FAST FIX ▶ Avocado Shrimp Salsa

Salsa gets a deluxe twist when you add avocado and shrimp. It's delicious scooped up with tortilla chips, spooned over grilled chicken breasts or pork chops, or served as a fresh side salad alongside your favorite entree.

—MARIA RIVIOTTA-SIMMONS
SAN TAN VALLEY, AZ

START TO FINISH: 25 MIN.
MAKES: 6 CUPS

- 1 **pound peeled and deveined cooked shrimp, chopped**
- 2 **medium tomatoes, seeded and chopped**
- 2 **medium ripe avocados, peeled and chopped**
- 1 **cup minced fresh cilantro**
- 1 **medium sweet red pepper, chopped**
- ¾ **cup thinly sliced green onions**
- ½ **cup chopped seeded peeled cucumber**
- 3 **tablespoons lime juice**
- 1 **jalapeno pepper, seeded and chopped**
- 1 **teaspoon salt**
- ¼ **teaspoon pepper**
  Tortilla chips

In a large bowl, combine the first 11 ingredients. Serve with tortilla chips.
NOTE *Wear disposable gloves when cutting hot peppers; the oils can burn skin. Avoid touching your face.*
PER SERVING *¼ cup (calculated without chips) equals 52 cal., 3 g fat (trace sat. fat), 33 mg chol., 133 mg sodium, 3 g carb., 1 g fiber, 5 g pro. Diabetic Exchanges: 1 lean meat, ½ fat.*

ORIGINAL	MAKEOVER
62 Calories	**35** Calories
4g Fat	**1**g Fat
146mg Sodium	**87**mg Sodium

MAKEOVER STUFFED POTATOES

4. Place in a 15x10x1-in. baking pan. Sprinkle with the remaining bacon. Bake the potatoes, uncovered, at 400° for 15-20 minutes or until heated through.

PER SERVING *1 stuffed potato half equals 35 cal., 1 g fat (1 g sat. fat), 4 mg chol., 87 mg sodium, 4 g carb., trace fiber, 2 g pro.*

THE SKINNY

Makeover Stuffed Potatoes use fat-free cream cheese and reduced-fat sour cream in slightly lesser quantities than the original. They also call for less bacon and salt, but they keep the same amount of flavorful cheeses.

Makeover Stuffed Potatoes

We tried this makeover version of an all-time favorite, and my friends and I loved it. We barely noticed the difference! Best of all, we kept all of the cheeses in the original.

—**SONYA LABBE** WEST HOLLYWOOD, CA

PREP: 45 MIN. + COOLING • **BAKE:** 15 MIN.
MAKES: 40 APPETIZERS

- 20 **baby Yukon Gold potatoes (2 pounds)**
- 6 **ounces fat-free cream cheese**
- ¾ **cup reduced-fat sour cream**
- 6 **bacon strips, cooked and crumbled**
- ¼ **cup shredded Monterey Jack cheese**
- ¼ **cup shredded sharp cheddar cheese**
- 2 **green onions, chopped**
- ½ **teaspoon salt**
- ½ **teaspoon pepper**

1. Place potatoes in a Dutch oven and cover with water. Bring to a boil. Reduce heat; cover and cook for 8-10 minutes or just until tender. Drain.
2. When cool enough to handle, cut each potato in half lengthwise. Scoop out the pulp, leaving thin shells. Remove ⅓ cup pulp (discard or save for another use).
3. In a large bowl, mash the remaining pulp with cream cheese. Add sour cream and half of the bacon. Stir in the cheeses, green onions, salt and pepper; spoon into potato shells.

⑤INGREDIENTS FAST FIX
Crisp Finger Sandwich

I love snacking on this delicious sandwich with its crisp English cucumber. I have also made batches of these for parties and showers, using a small party loaf of whole wheat or sourdough bread.

—**MELISSA SELIN** BOTHELL, WA

START TO FINISH: 10 MIN.
MAKES: 1 SERVING

- 1 **slice whole wheat bread, toasted**
- 2 **tablespoons reduced-fat spreadable garden vegetable cream cheese**
- ⅓ **cup thinly sliced English cucumber**
- 3 **tablespoons alfalfa sprouts**
  Dash coarsely ground pepper

Spread toast with cream cheese. Top with cucumber, sprouts and pepper.
PER SERVING *1 sandwich equals 136 cal., 6 g fat (3 g sat. fat), 15 mg chol., 323 mg sodium, 13 g carb., 2 g fiber, 7 g pro.* **Diabetic Exchanges:** *1 starch, 1 fat.*

FAST FIX ▶ Deviled Eggs

This lighter version of a classic uses only half of the egg yolks of the original recipe and calls for soft bread crumbs to firm up the filling. We replaced the mayo with fat-free mayonnaise and reduced-fat sour cream. These contain ⅓ fewer calories than the original and half the fat.
—*TASTE OF HOME* TEST KITCHEN

START TO FINISH: 10 MIN.
MAKES: 16 SERVINGS

- 8 hard-cooked large eggs
- ¼ cup fat-free mayonnaise
- ¼ cup reduced-fat sour cream
- 2 tablespoons soft bread crumbs
- 1 tablespoon prepared mustard
- ¼ teaspoon salt
  Dash white pepper
- 4 pimiento-stuffed olives, sliced

Slice eggs in half lengthwise and remove yolks; refrigerate eight yolk halves for another use. Set whites aside. In a small bowl, mash remaining yolks. Stir in the mayonnaise, sour cream, bread crumbs, mustard, salt and pepper. Stuff or pipe into egg whites. Garnish with olives.
PER SERVING *1 stuffed egg half equals 50 cal., 3 g fat (1 g sat. fat), 95 mg chol., 133 mg sodium, 1 g carb., trace fiber, 3 g pro.*

Mediterranean Eggplant Dip

I love Mediterranean food, and the flavors in this dip are so vibrant.
—STACY MULLENS
GRESHAM, OR

PREP: 20 MIN. • **BAKE:** 40 MIN.
MAKES: 4 CUPS

- 1 large eggplant (about 1½ pounds), peeled
- 1 small onion, coarsely chopped
- 6 garlic cloves, peeled
- 3 tablespoons olive oil
- 2 cups (16 ounces) reduced-fat sour cream
- 4 teaspoons lemon juice
- ¾ teaspoon salt
- ½ teaspoon pepper
- 10 drops liquid smoke, optional
  Minced fresh parsley
  Optional ingredients: naan flatbread wedges or miniature pitas, cherry tomatoes, celery sticks, julienned red pepper, baby carrots and Greek olives

1. Preheat oven to 400°. Cut eggplant crosswise into 1-in. slices; place on a greased 15x10x1-in. baking pan. Top with chopped onion and the garlic cloves. Drizzle with oil.
2. Roast 40-45 minutes or until eggplant is very soft, turning and stirring vegetables once. Cool slightly.
3. Place mixture in a food processor; process until blended. Transfer to a large bowl; stir in sour cream, lemon juice, salt, pepper and, if desired, liquid smoke.
4. Sprinkle with parsley. Serve with flatbread and vegetables as desired.
PER SERVING *¼ cup (calculated without optional ingredients) equals 77 cal., 5 g fat (2 g sat. fat), 10 mg chol., 132 mg sodium, 5 g carb., 2 g fiber, 3 g pro.*

MEDITERRANEAN
EGGPLANT DIP

Rosemary Walnuts

This recipe is from my Aunt Mary, who always had a batch ready for us. Cayenne adds an unexpected zing. When you need a housewarming or hostess gift, double the ingredients and save half for yourself.

—**RENEE CIANCIO** NEW BERN, NC

START TO FINISH: 20 MIN
MAKES: 2 CUPS

- 2 **cups walnut halves**
  Cooking spray
- 2 **teaspoons dried rosemary, crushed**
- ½ **teaspoon kosher salt**
- ¼ **to ½ teaspoon cayenne pepper**

1. Place walnuts in a small bowl. Spritz with cooking spray. Add the seasonings; toss to coat. Place in a single layer on a baking sheet.
2. Bake nuts at 350° for 10 minutes. Serve warm, or cool completely and store in an airtight container.
PER SERVING ¼ *cup equals 166 cal., 17 g fat (2 g sat. fat), 0 chol., 118 mg sodium, 4 g carb., 2 g fiber, 4 g pro. Diabetic Exchange: 3 fat.*

Crab Appetizer Spread

The delicate flavors of crab and green onion come through in each bite of this elegant appetizer. It's smart for parties because you can make it the day before.

—**KATHI MULCHIN** WEST VALLEY CITY, UT

PREP: 30 MIN. + CHILLING
MAKES: 4½ CUPS

- 1 **envelope unflavored gelatin**
- 3 **tablespoons cold water**
- 1 **can (10¾ ounces) reduced-fat reduced-sodium condensed cream of mushroom soup, undiluted**
- 1 **package (8 ounces) reduced-fat cream cheese, cubed**
- 1 **cup fat-free mayonnaise**
- 2 **cans (6 ounces each) crabmeat, drained, flaked and cartilage removed**
- 2 **celery ribs, finely chopped**
- 3 **green onions, finely chopped**
  Assorted crackers

1. In a small microwave-safe bowl, sprinkle gelatin over cold water; let stand for 1 minute. Microwave, uncovered, on high for 20 seconds. Stir; let stand for 1 minute or until gelatin is completely dissolved.
2. In a large saucepan, combine the soup, cream cheese, mayonnaise and gelatin. Cook and stir over medium heat for 5-7 minutes or until smooth. Remove from the heat; stir in the crab, celery and onions.
3. Transfer to a 5-cup ring mold coated with cooking spray. Cover and refrigerate for 4 hours or until set. Unmold onto a serving platter; serve with crackers.
PER SERVING ¼ *cup (calculated without crackers) equals 72 cal., 4 g fat (2 g sat. fat), 28 mg chol., 294 mg sodium, 4 g carb., trace fiber, 6 g pro. Diabetic Exchanges: 1 lean meat, ½ fat.*

Tex-Mex Popcorn

Spicy Southwest seasoning makes this snackin'-good popcorn ideal for any fiesta.

—**KATIE ROSE** PEWAUKEE, WI

START TO FINISH: 15 MIN.
MAKES: 4 QUARTS

- ½ **cup popcorn kernels**
- 3 **tablespoons canola oil**
- ½ **teaspoon cumin seeds**
  Refrigerated butter-flavored spray
- ¼ **cup minced fresh cilantro**
- 1 **teaspoon salt**
- 1 **teaspoon chili powder**
- ½ **teaspoon garlic powder**
- ⅛ **teaspoon smoked paprika**

1. In a Dutch oven over medium heat, cook the popcorn kernels, oil and cumin seeds until oil begins to sizzle. Cover and shake for 2-3 minutes or until popcorn stops popping.
2. Transfer to a large bowl; spritz with butter-flavored spray. Add remaining ingredients and toss to coat. Continue spritzing and tossing until popcorn is coated.
PER SERVING *1 cup equals 44 cal., 3 g fat (trace sat. fat), 0 chol., 150 mg sodium, 5 g carb., 1 g fiber, 1 g pro. Diabetic Exchanges: ½ starch, ½ fat.*

BBQ CHICKEN PIZZA ROLL-UP

BBQ Chicken Pizza Roll-Up

Snack on this fab, flavorful appetizer without the guilt. No one will guess these slices are low-cal! You'd better make two; they disappear fast.

—TRACEY BIRCH QUEEN CREEK, AZ

PREP: 15 MIN. • **BAKE:** 15 MIN. + COOLING
MAKES: 2 DOZEN

- 1 **tube (13.8 ounces) refrigerated pizza crust**
- ¼ **cup honey barbecue sauce**
- 1½ **cups (6 ounces) shredded part-skim mozzarella cheese**
- 1½ **cups shredded cooked chicken breast**
- 1 **small red onion, finely chopped**
- ¼ **cup minced fresh cilantro**
- 1 **teaspoon Italian seasoning, optional**
- 1 **large egg white**
- 1 **tablespoon water**
- ¼ **teaspoon garlic powder**

1. On a lightly floured surface, roll crust into a 12x9-in. rectangle; brush with barbecue sauce. Layer with the cheese, chicken, onion, cilantro and, if desired, Italian seasoning.

2. Roll up jelly-roll style, starting with a long side; pinch seams to seal. Place seam side down on a baking sheet coated with cooking spray.

3. Beat egg white and water; brush over top. Sprinkle with garlic powder. Bake at 400° for 15-20 minutes or until lightly browned. Cool for 10 minutes before slicing.

PER SERVING *1 slice equals 81 cal., 2 g fat (1 g sat. fat), 11 mg chol., 177 mg sodium, 9 g carb., trace fiber, 6 g pro.*
Diabetic Exchanges: *1 lean meat, ½ starch.*

CORDON BLEU APPETIZERS

and oil. Crumble turkey over mixture and mix well.

2. Place 1 tablespoon turkey mixture in the center of a wonton wrapper. (Keep remaining wrappers covered with a damp paper towel until ready to use.) Moisten edges with water. Fold one corner diagonally over filling and press edges to seal.

3. Line a steamer basket with three lettuce leaves. Arrange a third of the dumplings 1 in. apart over lettuce; place in a large saucepan over 1 in. of water. Bring to a boil; cover and steam dumplings for 10-12 minutes or until a thermometer reads 165°. Discard the lettuce. Repeat twice.

4. Combine sauce ingredients; serve with dumplings.

PER SERVING *1 dumpling with ¾ teaspoon sauce equals 52 cal., 2 g fat (trace sat. fat), 10 mg chol., 208 mg sodium, 6 g carb., trace fiber, 3 g pro. Diabetic Exchange: ½ starch.*

FAST FIX
Cordon Bleu Appetizers

Looking for a cheesy snack with mass appeal? Adults and kids alike love this satisfying cheese toast.

—SUSAN MELLO JACKSON HEIGHTS, NY

START TO FINISH: 30 MIN.
MAKES: 1½ DOZEN

- 4 ounces cream cheese, softened
- 1 teaspoon Dijon mustard
- 1 cup (4 ounces) shredded Swiss cheese
- ¾ cup diced fully cooked ham
- ½ cup minced chives, divided
- 18 slices French bread (½ inch thick)

1. In a small bowl, beat cream cheese and mustard until smooth. Stir in the Swiss cheese, ham and ¼ cup chives. Spread 1 tablespoon mixture over each bread slice; place bread on an ungreased baking sheet.

2. Bake at 350° for 12-15 minutes or until lightly browned. Sprinkle with remaining chives.

PER SERVING *1 appetizer equals 86 cal., 5 g fat (3 g sat. fat), 16 mg chol., 185 mg sodium, 7 g carb., trace fiber, 4 g pro. Diabetic Exchanges: 1 fat, ½ starch.*

Steamed Turkey Dumplings

This appetizer tastes wonderful but will not make you feel as though you've eaten an entire meal. The dumplings are easy to make and a joy to serve—try them at your next party!

—DONNA BARDOCZ HOWELL, MI

PREP: 30 MIN. • **COOK:** 10 MIN./BATCH
MAKES: 20 APPETIZERS (⅓ CUP SAUCE)

- 2 green onions, thinly sliced
- 2 tablespoons cornstarch
- 2 tablespoons minced fresh gingerroot
- 1 tablespoon reduced-sodium soy sauce
- 1 teaspoon sesame oil
- ½ pound lean ground turkey
- 20 wonton wrappers
- 9 lettuce leaves

DIPPING SAUCE
- ¼ cup reduced-sodium soy sauce
- 1½ teaspoons finely chopped green onion
- 1½ teaspoons sesame oil
- 1 garlic clove, minced

1. In a large bowl, combine the green onions, cornstarch, ginger, soy sauce

PER SERVING *1 cup equals 3 cal., trace fat (0 sat. fat), 0 chol., 1 mg sodium, trace carb., trace fiber, trace pro.* **Diabetic Exchange:** *Free food.*

`SLOW COOKER`

Creamy Artichoke Dip

Folks are sure to gather around this fabulous dip whenever it's placed on the buffet table. It's a lightened-up take on a treasured family favorite.

—**MARY SPENCER** GREENDALE, WI

PREP: 20 MIN. • **COOK:** 1 HOUR
MAKES: 5 CUPS

- 2 **cans (14 ounces each) water-packed artichoke hearts, rinsed, drained and coarsely chopped**
- 1 **package (8 ounces) reduced-fat cream cheese, cubed**
- ¾ **cup (6 ounces) plain yogurt**
- 1 **cup (4 ounces) shredded part-skim mozzarella cheese**
- 1 **cup reduced-fat ricotta cheese**
- ¾ **cup shredded Parmesan cheese, divided**
- ½ **cup shredded reduced-fat Swiss cheese**
- ¼ **cup reduced-fat mayonnaise**
- 2 **tablespoons lemon juice**
- 1 **tablespoon chopped seeded jalapeno pepper**
- 1 **teaspoon garlic powder**
- 1 **teaspoon seasoned salt**
  Tortilla chips

1. In a 3-qt. slow cooker, combine the artichokes, cream cheese, yogurt, mozzarella cheese, ricotta, ½ cup Parmesan cheese, Swiss cheese, mayonnaise, lemon juice, jalapeno, garlic powder and seasoned salt.

2. Cover and cook on low for 1 hour or until heated through.

3. Sprinkle with remaining Parmesan cheese. Serve with tortilla chips.

NOTE *Wear disposable gloves when cutting hot peppers; the oils can burn skin. Avoid touching your face.*

PER SERVING *¼ cup (calculated without chips) equals 104 cal., 6 g fat (3 g sat. fat), 20 mg chol., 348 mg sodium, 5 g carb., trace fiber, 7 g pro.* **Diabetic Exchanges:** *1 fat, ½ starch.*

`5 INGREDIENTS`

Iced Lemon Tea

I stir sugar-free lemonade into iced tea. It not only tastes cool and refreshing, but it also cuts out extra calories.

—**DAWN LOWENSTEIN** HATBORO, PA

PREP: 10 MIN. • **COOK:** 10 MIN. + COOLING
MAKES: 12 SERVINGS (1 CUP EACH)

- 3½ **teaspoons Crystal Light lemonade drink mix**
- 4 **cups cold water**
- 8 **cups water**
- 8 **individual decaffeinated tea bags**
- 1 **mint-flavored black tea bag**
  Ice cubes
  Fresh mint leaves and lemon slices, optional

1. In a large pitcher, combine the lemonade mix and the cold water. Refrigerate until chilled.

2. Meanwhile, in a large saucepan, bring water to a boil. Remove from the heat; add tea bags. Cover and steep for 3-5 minutes. Discard tea bags. Cool; stir into lemonade mixture. Serve over ice, with mint and lemon if desired.

CREAMY ARTICHOKE DIP

GRILLED NECTARINE &
CHEESE CROSTINI

Grilled Nectarine & Cheese Crostini

At our house, we love the summery taste of sweet grilled nectarines and fresh basil over goat cheese. I can usually find all the ingredients at the farmers market.

—BRANDY HOLLINGSHEAD GRASS VALLEY, CA

START TO FINISH: 25 MIN.
MAKES: 1 DOZEN

- ½ **cup balsamic vinegar**
- 1 **tablespoon olive oil**
- 12 **slices French bread baguette (¼ inch thick)**
- 2 **medium nectarines, halved and pitted**
- ¼ **cup fresh goat cheese, softened**
- ¼ **cup loosely packed basil leaves, thinly sliced**

1. In a small saucepan, bring vinegar to a boil; cook 10-15 minutes or until liquid is reduced to 3 tablespoons. Remove from heat.

2. Brush oil over both sides of the baguette slices. Grill, uncovered, over medium heat until golden brown on both sides. Grill the nectarines for 45-60 seconds on each side or until tender and lightly browned. Cool slightly.

3. Spread goat cheese over toasts. Cut nectarines into thick slices; arrange over cheese. Drizzle with balsamic syrup and sprinkle with basil. Serve immediately.

PER SERVING *1 appetizer equals 48 cal., 2 g fat (1 g sat. fat), 5 mg chol., 55 mg sodium, 6 g carb., trace fiber, 1 g pro.* **Diabetic Exchange:** *½ starch.*

BRIE CHERRY PASTRY CUPS

Brie Cherry Pastry Cups

Golden brown and flaky, these bite-size pastries with Brie and sweet cherry preserves could double as a dessert.

—MARILYN MCSWEEN MENTOR, OH

START TO FINISH: 30 MIN.
MAKES: 3 DOZEN

- 1 **sheet frozen puff pastry, thawed**
- ½ **cup cherry preserves**
- 4 **ounces Brie cheese, cut into ½-inch cubes**
- ¼ **cup chopped pecans or walnuts**
- 2 **tablespoons minced chives**

1. Unfold the puff pastry; cut into 36 squares. Gently press squares onto the bottoms of 36 greased miniature muffin cups.

2. Bake at 375° for 10 minutes. Using the end of a wooden spoon handle, make a ½-in.-deep indentation in the center of each. Bake 6-8 minutes longer or until golden brown. With spoon handle, press squares down again.

3. Spoon a rounded ½ teaspoonful of preserves into each cup. Top with cheese; sprinkle with nuts and chives. Bake for 3-5 minutes or until cheese is melted.

PER SERVING *1 appetizer equals 61 cal., 3 g fat (1 g sat. fat), 3 mg chol., 42 mg sodium, 7 g carb., 1 g fiber, 1 g pro.* **Diabetic Exchanges:** *½ starch, ½ fat.*

tomato mixture. Refrigerate salsa until serving.

PER SERVING *¼ cup equals 41 cal., 4 g fat (trace sat. fat), 0 chol., 53 mg sodium, 3 g carb., 1 g fiber, trace pro.*

FAST FIX

Little Mexican Pizzas

These little pizzas are perfect for lunch, snacks or parties. Whole wheat English muffins offer more fiber than regular pizza crust. You can really get creative making these with your favorite toppings.
—LINDA EGGERS ALBANY, CA

START TO FINISH: 25 MIN.
MAKES: 1 DOZEN

- 1 **package (13 ounces) whole wheat English muffins, split**
- ¾ **cup fat-free refried beans**
- ¾ **cup salsa**
- ⅓ **cup sliced ripe olives**
- 2 **green onions, chopped**
- 2 **tablespoons canned chopped green chilies**
- 1½ **cups (6 ounces) shredded part-skim mozzarella cheese**

1. Spread cut sides of muffins with refried beans; top with salsa, olives, onions, chilies and cheese.
2. Place on baking sheets; broil 4-6 in. from the heat for 2-3 minutes or until cheese is melted.

PER SERVING *1 pizza equals 129 cal., 3 g fat (2 g sat. fat), 8 mg chol., 368 mg sodium, 17 g carb., 2 g fiber, 7 g pro. Diabetic Exchanges: 1 starch, 1 lean meat.*

⑤ INGREDIENTS FAST FIX

Strawberry Salsa

Here's a sweet and tangy salsa that's miles away from the spicy version people expect. Serve it as an appetizer with tortilla chips for scooping, or make it part of the main event and spoon it over white meat.
—AMY HINKLE TOPEKA, KS

START TO FINISH: 25 MIN.
MAKES: 6 CUPS

- 2 **pints cherry tomatoes, quartered**
- 1 **pint fresh strawberries, chopped**
- 8 **green onions, chopped**
- ½ **cup minced fresh cilantro**
- 6 **tablespoons olive oil**
- 2 **tablespoons balsamic vinegar**
- ½ **teaspoon salt**

In a large bowl, combine tomatoes, strawberries, green onions and cilantro. In a small bowl, whisk the oil, vinegar and salt; gently stir into

LITTLE MEXICAN PIZZAS

Sparkling Party Punch

This has been my go-to punch recipe for years. It's sparkly, fruity, frothy (if you add the sherbet) and so simple!

—**JAN WITTEVEEN** NORBORNE, MO

START TO FINISH: 5 MIN.
MAKES: 17 SERVINGS (¾ CUP EACH)

- 1 can (46 ounces) unsweetened pineapple juice, chilled
- 3 cups apricot nectar or juice, chilled
- 1 liter diet lemon-lime soda, chilled
  Pineapple sherbet, optional

In a punch bowl, combine the pineapple juice, apricot nectar and soda. Top with scoops of sherbet if desired. Serve immediately.

PER SERVING *¾ cup (calculated without sherbet) equals 66 cal., trace fat (trace sat. fat), 0 chol., 9 mg sodium, 16 g carb., trace fiber, trace pro.* **Diabetic Exchange:** *1 fruit.*

Margarita Granita with Spicy Shrimp

While tinkering and tuning up recipes for my spring menu, I came up with a snazzy little appetizer that's exactly right for Cinco de Mayo. It features two all-time favorites: shrimp and margaritas!

—**NANCY BUCHANAN** COSTA MESA, CA

PREP: 20 MIN. + FREEZING • **GRILL:** 5 MIN.
MAKES: 8 SERVINGS

- 1 cup water
- ½ cup sugar
- ½ cup lime juice
- 3 tablespoons tequila
- 3 tablespoons Triple Sec
- 4½ teaspoons grated lime peel, divided
- 1 teaspoon ground cumin
- 1 teaspoon smoked paprika
- 1 teaspoon ground oregano
- ½ teaspoon salt

MARGARITA GRANITA WITH SPICY SHRIMP

- ¼ teaspoon ground chipotle pepper
- 16 uncooked medium shrimp, peeled and deveined

1. In a large saucepan, bring water and sugar to a boil. Cook and stir until sugar is dissolved. Remove from heat; stir in lime juice, tequila, Triple Sec and 3 teaspoons lime peel.

2. Transfer to an 11x7-in. dish; cool to room temperature. Freeze 1 hour; stir with a fork. Freeze 4-5 hours longer or until completely frozen, stirring every 30 minutes.

3. In a small bowl, combine cumin, paprika, oregano, salt and chipotle pepper; add shrimp, tossing to coat.

Thread shrimp onto eight soaked wooden appetizer skewers.

4. Moisten a paper towel with cooking oil; using long-handled tongs, lightly coat grill rack. Grill shrimp, covered, over medium heat or broil 4 in. from heat 3-4 minutes on each side or until shrimp turn pink.

5. Stir granita with a fork just before serving; spoon into small glasses. Top with remaining lime peel; serve with the shrimp.

PER SERVING *¼ cup granita with 2 shrimp equals 110 cal., 1 g fat (trace sat. fat), 31 mg chol., 180 mg sodium, 17 g carb., trace fiber, 4 g pro.*

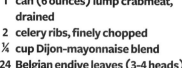

Shrimp Salad Appetizers

This crisp, refreshing hors d'oeuvre has gained a big following since a friend shared her family's recipe with me. My 7-year-old son says it best: The celery and shrimp are so good together.

—SOLIE KIMBLE KANATA, ON

START TO FINISH: 15 MIN.
MAKES: 2 DOZEN

- 1 **pound peeled and deveined cooked shrimp, chopped**
- 1 **can (6 ounces) lump crabmeat, drained**
- 2 **celery ribs, finely chopped**
- ¼ **cup Dijon-mayonnaise blend**
- 24 **Belgian endive leaves (3-4 heads) or small butterhead lettuce leaves**

In a large bowl, combine shrimp, crab and celery. Add the mayonnaise blend; toss to coat. To serve, top each leaf with about 2 tablespoons shrimp mixture.

PER SERVING *1 appetizer equals 31 cal., trace fat (trace sat. fat), 35 mg chol., 115 mg sodium, 1 g carb., trace fiber, 5 g pro.*

SHRIMP SALAD APPETIZERS

Indian Snack Mix

I love curry, so I added it to a snack mix. It disappeared quickly on a camping trip with friends. So yummy! For a less spicy flavor, use only 1½ teaspoons of curry powder.

—NOELLE MYERS GRAND FORKS, ND

PREP: 15 MIN. • **BAKE:** 45 MIN. + COOLING
MAKES: ABOUT 3 QUARTS

- 4 **cups Corn Chex**
- 4 **cups Rice Chex**
- 3 **cups miniature pretzels**
- 1 **cup slivered almonds**
- ⅓ **cup butter, melted**
- 3 **tablespoons Louisiana-style hot sauce**
- 4½ **teaspoons Worcestershire sauce**
- 2½ **teaspoons curry powder**
- 1 **teaspoon onion powder**
- 1 **teaspoon seasoned salt**
- ¼ **teaspoon ground chipotle pepper**
- 1 **cup golden raisins**

1. In a large bowl, combine the cereals, pretzels and almonds. In a small bowl, combine the butter, hot sauce, Worcestershire sauce and seasonings. Drizzle over cereal mixture; toss to coat.

2. Transfer to two 15x10x1-in. baking pans coated with cooking spray. Bake at 250° for 45 minutes or until golden brown, stirring every 15 minutes. Stir in raisins. Cool completely on wire racks. Store in airtight containers.

PER SERVING *¾ cup equals 172 cal., 7 g fat (3 g sat. fat), 9 mg chol., 360 mg sodium, 26 g carb., 2 g fiber, 3 g pro.* *Diabetic Exchanges: 1½ starch, 1 fat.*

SOUTHWEST PRETZELS

Southwest Pretzels

These fun pretzels with mild Southwest spices are a winning snack while you watch the game. And they score just as high with kids as they do with the adults!

—CATHY TANG REDMOND, WA

PREP: 30 MIN. + STANDING • **BAKE:** 25 MIN.
MAKES: 16 PRETZELS

- 4 **cups all-purpose flour**
- 1 **tablespoon sugar**
- 1 **package (¼ ounce) quick-rise yeast**
- 1½ **teaspoons salt**
- 1 **teaspoon dried minced onion**
- ½ **teaspoon chili powder**
- ¼ **teaspoon ground cumin**
- ¼ **teaspoon cayenne pepper**
- 1½ **cups warm water (120° to 130°)**
- 1 **large egg, lightly beaten**
  Coarse salt
  Salsa con queso dip

1. In a large bowl, combine 2 cups flour, sugar, yeast, salt, minced onion and spices. Add water. Beat just until moistened. Stir in enough remaining flour to form a soft dough.

2. Turn onto a floured surface; knead until smooth and elastic, about 4-6 minutes. Cover and let rest for 10 minutes. Divide dough into 16 equal portions; roll each into a 15-in. rope. Cover and let rest 10 minutes longer.

3. Twist into pretzel shapes. Place on greased baking sheets; brush with egg. Bake at 350° for 15 minutes. Brush again with egg; sprinkle with coarse salt. Bake 10-13 minutes longer or until golden brown. Remove to wire racks. Serve pretzels warm with dip.

PER SERVING *1 pretzel (calculated without coarse salt and dip) equals 120 cal., trace fat (trace sat. fat), 4 mg chol., 224 mg sodium, 25 g carb., 1 g fiber, 4 g pro.* **Diabetic Exchange:** *1½ starch.*

Smoked Trout Pate

This recipe is versatile, so feel free to substitute your own favorite smoked fish. It has only about half the calories and fat of traditional smoked goose liver pate.

—JUDY WALLE TOLEDO, OH

START TO FINISH: 15 MIN.
MAKES: 2⅔ CUPS

- 1 **pound flaked smoked trout**
- 3 **ounces reduced-fat cream cheese, softened**
- ½ **cup half-and-half cream**
- 1 **tablespoon horseradish sauce**
- 1 **tablespoon lemon juice**
- ⅛ **teaspoon pepper**
- 2 **teaspoons minced fresh parsley**
  Assorted crackers

Place the first seven ingredients in a food processor; cover and process until blended. Transfer to a small bowl. Chill until serving. Serve pate with crackers.

PER SERVING *2 tablespoons pate (calculated without crackers) equals 55 cal., 3 g fat (1 g sat. fat), 16 mg chol., 174 mg sodium, 1 g carb., trace fiber, 5 g pro.* **Diabetic Exchanges:** *1 lean meat, ½ fat.*

HOW TO

SHAPE PRETZELS

Shape the dough into balls; roll each into a 15-in. rope. Curve ends of rope to form a circle; twist ends once and lay over opposite side of circle, pinching the ends to seal. Proceed as directed in the recipe.

CHICKEN SALAD PARTY
SANDWICHES

FAST FIX ▶ Chicken Salad Party Sandwiches

My famous chicken salad arrives at the party chilled in a plastic container. When it's time to set out the food, I stir in the pecans and assemble the sandwiches. They're ideal for buffet-style potlucks.

—**TRISHA KRUSE** EAGLE, ID

START TO FINISH: 25 MIN.
MAKES: 15 SERVINGS

- 4 cups cubed cooked chicken breast
- 1½ cups dried cranberries
- 2 celery ribs, finely chopped
- 2 green onions, thinly sliced
- ¼ cup chopped sweet pickles
- 1 cup fat-free mayonnaise
- ½ teaspoon curry powder
- ¼ teaspoon coarsely ground pepper
- ½ cup chopped pecans, toasted
- 15 whole wheat dinner rolls
  Torn leaf lettuce

1. In a large bowl, combine the first five ingredients. In a small bowl, combine the mayonnaise, curry and pepper. Add to chicken mixture; toss to coat. Chill until serving.

2. Stir pecans into chicken salad. Serve on rolls lined with lettuce.
PER SERVING *1 sandwich equals 235 cal., 6 g fat (1 g sat. fat), 30 mg chol., 361 mg sodium, 33 g carb., 4 g fiber, 14 g pro.*

FAST FIX ▶ Asian Tuna Bites with Dijon Dipping Sauce

Quick, easy and fresh with big, bold and bright flavors, this healthy dish is a snap to make and beautiful to serve. You can make it up to 8 hours in advance, which is convenient for entertaining.

—**JAMIE BROWN-MILLER** NAPA, CA

START TO FINISH: 30 MIN.
MAKES: 2½ DOZEN (½ CUP SAUCE)

- 3 tablespoons Dijon mustard
- 2 tablespoons red wine vinegar
- 2 tablespoons reduced-sodium soy sauce
- 1 tablespoon sesame oil
- 1 teaspoon hot pepper sauce
- 1 pound tuna steaks, cut into thirty 1-inch cubes
  Cooking spray
- ¼ cup sesame seeds
- ½ teaspoon salt
- ¼ teaspoon pepper
- 2 green onions, finely chopped

1. In a small bowl, whisk the first five ingredients; set aside. Spritz tuna with cooking spray. Sprinkle with sesame seeds, salt and pepper. In a large nonstick skillet, brown tuna on all sides in batches until medium-rare or slightly pink in the center; remove from the skillet.

2. On each of 30 wooden appetizer skewers, thread one tuna cube. Arrange on a serving platter. Garnish with onions. Serve with sauce.
PER SERVING *1 appetizer with ¾ teaspoon sauce equals 29 cal., 1 g fat (trace sat. fat), 7 mg chol., 123 mg sodium, 1 g carb., trace fiber, 4 g pro.*

Makeover Veggie Pizza Squares

This attractive pizza, loaded with crunchy veggies, will bring oohs and aahs from even the most traditional pizza lovers.

—SANDRA SHAFER MOUNTAIN VIEW, CA

PREP: 30 MIN. + CHILLING
MAKES: 2 DOZEN

- 2 tubes (8 ounces each) refrigerated reduced-fat crescent rolls
- 1 package (8 ounces) reduced-fat cream cheese
- 1 package (8 ounces) fat-free cream cheese
- ½ cup plain yogurt
- ⅓ cup reduced-fat mayonnaise
- ¼ cup fat-free milk
- 1 tablespoon dill weed
- ½ teaspoon garlic salt
- 1 cup shredded carrots
- 1 cup fresh cauliflowerets, chopped
- 1 cup fresh broccoli florets, chopped
- 1 cup julienned green pepper
- 1 cup sliced fresh mushrooms
- 2 cans (2¼ ounces each) sliced ripe olives, drained
- ¼ cup finely chopped sweet onion

1. Unroll both tubes of crescent dough and pat into an ungreased 15 x10x1-in. baking pan; seal all perforations and seams. Bake at 375° for 10-12 minutes or until golden brown. Cool crust completely on a wire rack.

2. In a small bowl, beat the cream cheeses, yogurt, mayonnaise, milk, dill and garlic salt until smooth. Spread over crust. Sprinkle with carrots, cauliflower, broccoli, green pepper, mushrooms, olives and onion. Chill at least 1 hour. Cut into squares.

PER SERVING *1 piece equals 128 cal., 7 g fat (2 g sat. fat), 9 mg chol., 365 mg sodium, 11 g carb., 1 g fiber, 4 g pro. Diabetic Exchanges: 1 starch, 1 fat.*

THE SKINNY

The original Veggie Pizza Squares used 1 pound full-fat cream cheese, ¾ cup mayonnaise and ¼ cup of heavy cream. The lighter version subs in milk and yogurt, plus a lower-fat crust, and it keeps all the crisp veggie toppings.

ORIGINAL	MAKEOVER
212 Calories	128 Calories
18g Fat	7g Fat
7g Sat. Fat	2g Sat. Fat

MAKEOVER VEGGIE PIZZA SQUARES

Flank Steak Crostini

Perfect for gatherings or holidays or as a Sunday football snack, this crostini is a beloved favorite of my friends and family. You can substitute butter for olive oil and use any kind of steak.

—DONNA EVARO CASPER, WY

PREP: 25 MIN. • **GRILL:** 15 MIN.
MAKES: 3 DOZEN

- 1 **beef flank steak (1½ pounds)**
- ½ **teaspoon salt**
- ½ **teaspoon pepper**
- 3 **tablespoons olive oil**
- 3 **garlic cloves, minced**
- 1 **teaspoon dried basil**
- 1 **French bread baguette (10½ ounces), cut into 36 slices**
- ½ **cup finely chopped fresh portobello mushrooms**
- ¼ **cup shredded part-skim mozzarella cheese**
- 2 **tablespoons grated Parmesan cheese**
- 1 **tablespoon minced chives**

1. Sprinkle steak with salt and pepper. Grill steak, covered, over medium heat or broil 4 in. from the heat for 6-8 minutes on each side or until the beef reaches desired doneness (for medium-rare, a thermometer should read 145°; medium, 160°; well-done, 170°). Let stand for 5 minutes. Thinly slice across the grain.

2. Meanwhile, in a small bowl, combine the oil, garlic and basil; brush over baguette slices. Place on baking sheets. Bake at 400° for 5 minutes. Top with mushrooms and mozzarella cheese. Bake 2-3 minutes longer or until cheese is melted.

3. Top with sliced steak, Parmesan cheese and chives. Serve immediately.

PER SERVING *1 appetizer equals 63 cal., 3 g fat (1 g sat. fat), 10 mg chol., 105 mg sodium, 5 g carb., trace fiber, 5 g pro.*

(5) INGREDIENTS Buffalo Chicken Meatballs

I like to make these game-day appetizer meatballs with blue cheese or ranch salad dressing for dipping. If I prepare them for a meal, I often skip the dressing and serve the meatballs with blue cheese polenta on the side. Yum!

—AMBER MASSEY ARGYLE, TX

PREP: 15 MIN. • **BAKE:** 20 MIN.
MAKES: 2 DOZEN

- ¾ **cup panko (Japanese) bread crumbs**
- ⅓ **cup plus ½ cup Louisiana-style hot sauce, divided**
- ¼ **cup chopped celery**
- 1 **large egg white**
- 1 **pound lean ground chicken Reduced-fat blue cheese or ranch salad dressing, optional**

1. Preheat oven to 400°. In a large bowl, combine bread crumbs, ⅓ cup hot sauce, celery and egg white. Add chicken; mix lightly but thoroughly.

2. Shape into twenty-four 1-in. balls. Place on a greased rack in a shallow baking pan. Bake 20-25 minutes or until cooked through.

3. Toss meatballs with remaining hot sauce. If desired, drizzle with salad dressing just before serving.

PER SERVING *1 meatball equals 35 cal., 1 g fat (trace sat. fat), 14 mg chol., 24 mg sodium, 2 g carb., trace fiber, 4 g pro.*

FLANK STEAK CROSTINI

BUFFALO CHICKEN MEATBALLS

in plastic wrap. Refrigerate for 1 hour or until firm.

2. Unwrap and cut into scant 1-in. slices. Serve with salsa if desired.

PER SERVING *1 piece (calculated without salsa) equals 40 cal., 1 g fat (trace sat. fat), 3 mg chol., 103 mg sodium, 5 g carb., 1 g fiber, 2 g pro.* **Diabetic Exchange:** *½ starch.*

Spinach Dip-Stuffed Mushrooms

Here's a lighter version of classic spinach dip, stuffed inside juicy mushrooms and baked. You can also prepare these stuffed mushrooms on the grill. Just be sure to use a grill pan so they don't slip through the grate.

—ASHLEY PIERCE BRANTFORD, ON

PREP: 25 MIN. • **BAKE:** 15 MIN.
MAKES: 16 APPETIZERS

- **16 large fresh mushrooms**
- **2 cups fresh baby spinach, coarsely chopped**
- **1 tablespoon olive oil**
- **2 garlic cloves, minced**
- **½ cup reduced-fat sour cream**
- **3 ounces reduced-fat cream cheese**
- **⅓ cup shredded part-skim mozzarella cheese**
- **3 tablespoons grated Parmesan cheese**
- **¼ teaspoon salt**
- **¼ teaspoon cayenne pepper**
- **¼ teaspoon pepper**

1. Preheat oven to 400°. Remove stems from mushrooms and set caps aside; discard the stems or save for another use. In a small skillet, saute spinach in oil until wilted. Add garlic; cook 1 minute longer.

2. In a small bowl, combine sour cream, cream cheese, mozzarella, Parmesan, salt, cayenne, pepper and spinach mixture. Stuff into mushroom caps.

3. Place in a 15x10x1-in. baking pan coated with cooking spray. Bake, uncovered, 12-15 minutes or until mushrooms are tender.

PER SERVING *1 stuffed mushroom equals 48 cal., 3 g fat (2 g sat. fat), 8 mg chol., 94 mg sodium, 2 g carb., trace fiber, 3 g pro.*

DID YOU KNOW?

Using baby spinach saves prep time because you don't have to remove the tough stems of mature spinach. Some people prefer baby spinach's tender texture in salads.

Mexican Pinwheels

Chopped green chilies give these cool bite-size snacks the right amount of zip. They're a real crowd-pleaser.

—LEIGH THOMAS HAHIRA, GA

PREP: 25 MIN. + CHILLING
MAKES: ABOUT 4 DOZEN

- **1 package (8 ounces) fat-free cream cheese**
- **1 cup (8 ounces) fat-free sour cream**
- **1 cup (4 ounces) shredded reduced-fat cheddar cheese**
- **1 can (4 ounces) chopped green chilies, drained**
- **4 green onions, chopped**
- **1 can (4¼ ounces) chopped ripe olives, drained**
- **1 teaspoon garlic powder**
- **5 flour tortillas (10 inches), room temperature**
  Salsa, optional

1. In a small bowl, combine the first seven ingredients. Spread over tortillas. Roll up tightly and wrap

(5) INGREDIENTS | FAST FIX ▶

Asparagus with Horseradish Dip

This is a terrific hot-weather party dip. Serve asparagus on a decorative platter with lemon wedges on the side for garnish. For a flavor variation, use chopped garlic in place of the horseradish.

—**MILDRED LYNN CARUSO** BRIGHTON, TN

START TO FINISH: 15 MIN.
MAKES: 16 APPETIZERS

- 32 **fresh asparagus spears (about 2 pounds), trimmed**
- 1 **cup reduced-fat mayonnaise**
- ¼ **cup grated Parmesan cheese**
- 1 **tablespoon prepared horseradish**
- ½ **teaspoon Worcestershire sauce**

1. Place asparagus spears in a steamer basket; place in a large saucepan over 1 in. of water. Bring to a boil; cover and steam for 2-4 minutes or until crisp-tender. Drain and immediately place in ice water. Drain and pat dry.
2. In a small bowl, combine the remaining ingredients. Serve with the asparagus.
PER SERVING *2 asparagus spears with 1 tablespoon dip equals 63 cal., 5 g fat (1 g sat. fat), 6 mg chol., 146 mg sodium, 3 g carb., trace fiber, 1 g pro.*
***Diabetic Exchange:** 1 fat.*

FAST FIX ▶ # Shrimp Spread

People will never know that you used lower-fat ingredients in this tasty spread that's always a winner at parties.

—**NORENE WRIGHT** MANILLA, IN

START TO FINISH: 15 MIN.
MAKES: 20 SERVINGS (3¾ CUPS)

- 1 **package (8 ounces) reduced-fat cream cheese**
- ½ **cup reduced-fat sour cream**
- ¼ **cup reduced-fat mayonnaise**
- 1 **cup seafood cocktail sauce**
- 2 **cups (8 ounces) shredded part-skim mozzarella cheese**
- 1 **can (6 ounces) small shrimp, rinsed and drained**
- 3 **green onions, sliced**
- 1 **medium tomato, finely chopped Sliced Italian bread or assorted crackers**

1. In a small bowl, beat the cream cheese, sour cream and mayonnaise until smooth. Spread onto a 12-in. round serving plate; top with cocktail sauce. Sprinkle with cheese, shrimp, onions and tomato.
2. Chill until serving. Serve with bread or crackers.
PER SERVING *3 tablespoons spread (calculated without bread or crackers) equals 93 cal., 6 g fat (3 g sat. fat), 35 mg chol., 312 mg sodium, 4 g carb., trace fiber, 6 g pro.*

SHRIMP SPREAD

Grilled Shrimp Appetizer Kabobs

The combination of pineapple, onion and marinated shrimp has turned me into a fan of these appetizers. Their prepare-ahead convenience is wonderful for parties.

—**MICHELE TUNGETT** ROCHESTER, IL

PREP: 15 MIN. + MARINATING • **GRILL:** 5 MIN.
MAKES: 10 SERVINGS

- ⅓ cup tomato sauce
- ⅓ cup olive oil
- 3 tablespoons minced fresh basil
- 3 tablespoons red wine vinegar
- 5 garlic cloves, minced
- ¾ teaspoon salt
- ½ teaspoon cayenne pepper
- 10 uncooked jumbo shrimp, peeled and deveined (8-10 ounces)
- 10 fresh pineapple chunks
- 1 small onion, cut into 1-inch chunks

1. In a large bowl, whisk first seven ingredients until blended. Reserve ¼ cup marinade for basting. Add shrimp to remaining marinade; toss to coat. Refrigerate, covered, 30 minutes.
2. On each of 10 metal or soaked wooden appetizer skewers, alternately thread one shrimp, one pineapple chunk and an onion chunk. Grill, covered, over medium heat or broil 4 in. from heat for 4-6 minutes or until shrimp turn pink, turning occasionally and basting with reserved marinade during the last 2 minutes.

PER SERVING *1 kabob equals 68 cal., 4 g fat (1 g sat. fat), 31 mg chol., 138 mg sodium, 4 g carb., trace fiber, 4 g pro.* **Diabetic Exchanges:** *1 lean meat, ½ fat.*

GRILLED SHRIMP APPETIZER KABOBS

FAST FIX ▶ Crab Rangoon

Bite into these golden appetizers and you'll find a creamy crab filling that rivals restaurant fare. Best of all, these are baked and not fried, so you don't have to feel guilty about enjoying them.

—*TASTE OF HOME* TEST KITCHEN

START TO FINISH: 25 MIN.
MAKES: 14 APPETIZERS

- 3 ounces reduced-fat cream cheese
- ⅛ teaspoon garlic salt
- ⅛ teaspoon Worcestershire sauce
- ½ cup lump crabmeat, drained
- 1 green onion, chopped
- 14 wonton wrappers

1. In a small bowl, combine the cream cheese, garlic salt and Worcestershire sauce until smooth. Stir in crab and onion. Place 2 teaspoonfuls in the center of each wonton wrapper. Moisten edges with water; bring corners to center over filling and press edges together to seal.
2. Place on a baking sheet coated with cooking spray. Lightly spray wontons with cooking spray. Bake at 425° for 8-10 minutes or until golden brown.

PER SERVING *2 appetizers equals 83 cal., 3 g fat (2 g sat. fat), 19 mg chol., 248 mg sodium, 10 g carb., trace fiber, 4 g pro.* **Diabetic Exchanges:** *1 starch, ½ fat.*

FAST FIX ▸

Spiced Party Peanuts

Seasoned nuts have just the right blend of spices, sugar and heat to liven up a party. They also make a welcome holiday gift.

—CYNTHIA DEVOL PATASKALA, OH

START TO FINISH: 30 MIN.
MAKES: 3 CUPS

- 1 large egg white
- 1 teaspoon water
- 3 cups unsalted dry roasted peanuts
- 1 tablespoon sugar
- 1 teaspoon ground cinnamon
- ½ teaspoon cayenne pepper
- ¼ teaspoon salt
- ¼ teaspoon ground cumin
- ¼ teaspoon ground coriander

1. In a large bowl, beat egg white and water until frothy. Stir in peanuts. Combine sugar and spices; add to peanut mixture, stirring gently to coat.
2. Transfer mixture to an ungreased 15x10x1-in. baking pan. Bake at 325° for 20-25 minutes or until lightly browned, stirring twice. Cool on a wire rack. Store in an airtight container.
PER SERVING *¼ cup equals 220 cal., 18 g fat (3 g sat. fat), 0 chol., 56 mg sodium, 9 g carb., 3 g fiber, 9 g pro. Diabetic Exchange: 3 fat.*

GARBANZO-STUFFED MINI PEPPERS

⑤INGREDIENTS FAST FIX ▸

Garbanzo-Stuffed Mini Peppers

Pretty mini peppers are naturally sized for a two-bite snack. They have all the crunch of a pita chip—but without the unwanted calories.

—CHRISTINE HANOVER LEWISTON, CA

START TO FINISH: 20 MIN.
MAKES: 32 APPETIZERS

- 1 teaspoon cumin seeds
- 1 can (15 ounces) garbanzo beans or chickpeas, rinsed and drained
- ¼ cup fresh cilantro leaves
- 3 tablespoons water
- 3 tablespoons cider vinegar
- ¼ teaspoon salt
- 16 miniature sweet peppers, halved lengthwise
    Additional fresh cilantro leaves

1. In a dry small skillet, toast cumin seeds over medium heat 1-2 minutes or until aromatic, stirring frequently. Transfer to a food processor. Add the garbanzo beans, cilantro, water, vinegar and salt; pulse until blended.
2. Spoon into pepper halves. Top with additional cilantro. Refrigerate until serving.
PER SERVING *1 appetizer equals 15 cal., trace fat (trace sat. fat), 0 chol., 36 mg sodium, 3 g carb., 1 g fiber, 1 g pro.*

CHILLED PEA SOUP SHOOTERS

FAST FIX

Tomato-Basil Bruschetta

It's easy to double this enticing recipe for a crowd. You can make the tomato topping ahead, and keep it simpler yet by serving it as a dip alongside the French bread. Add a jar of olive tapenade to create instant, effort-free variety.

—**MARIE COSENZA** CORTLANDT MANOR, NY

START TO FINISH: 25 MIN.
MAKES: ABOUT 2 DOZEN

- 3 plum tomatoes, chopped
- ⅓ cup thinly sliced green onions
- 4 tablespoons olive oil, divided
- 1 tablespoon minced fresh basil or 1 teaspoon dried basil
- 1 tablespoon red wine vinegar
- ½ teaspoon dried oregano
- ¼ teaspoon salt
- ⅛ teaspoon pepper
- 1 loaf (1 pound) French bread, cut into ½-inch slices
- 2 garlic cloves, peeled and halved

1. In a small bowl, combine the tomatoes, onions, 2 tablespoons oil, basil, vinegar, oregano, salt and pepper; set aside.
2. Lightly brush both sides of bread slices with remaining oil. Arrange on ungreased baking sheets. Broil 3-4 in. from the heat for 2-3 minutes on each side or until golden brown.
3. Rub garlic over toast. With a slotted spoon, top each slice with some of the tomato mixture.
PER SERVING *1 piece equals 84 cal., 3 g fat (trace sat. fat), 0 chol., 162 mg sodium, 12 g carb., 1 g fiber, 3 g pro. Diabetic Exchange: 1 starch.*

Chilled Pea Soup Shooters

Enjoy pea soup in a whole new way! The tasty garnish is curried crab, which will catch everyone by surprise.

—*TASTE OF HOME* TEST KITCHEN

PREP: 20 MIN. + CHILLING
MAKES: 2 DOZEN

- 1 package (16 ounces) frozen peas, thawed
- 1 cup chicken broth
- ¼ cup minced fresh mint
- 1 tablespoon lime juice
- 1 teaspoon ground cumin
- ¼ teaspoon salt
- 1½ cups plain yogurt

CURRIED CRAB

- 2 tablespoons minced fresh mint
- 4 teaspoons lime juice
- 4 teaspoons canola oil
- 2 teaspoons red curry paste
- ⅛ teaspoon salt
- 1 cup lump crabmeat, drained

1. Place the peas, broth, mint, lime juice, cumin and salt in a blender. Cover and process until smooth. Add yogurt; process until blended. Refrigerate for at least 1 hour.
2. Meanwhile, in a small bowl, whisk the mint, lime juice, oil, curry paste and salt. Add crabmeat; toss gently to coat. Chill until serving.
3. To serve, pour soup into shot glasses; garnish with crab mixture.
PER SERVING *1 serving equals 40 cal., 1 g fat (trace sat. fat), 20 mg chol., 216 mg sodium, 4 g carb., 1 g fiber, 3 g pro. Diabetic Exchange: ½ starch.*

Sweet 'n' Salty Popcorn

This popcorn is a family favorite on movie nights, thanks to the classic salty and sweet flavors. The secret ingredient is pudding mix!

—**HILARY KERR** HAWKS, MI

PREP: 10 MIN. • **BAKE:** 25 MIN. + COOLING
MAKES: 10 CUPS

- 10 **cups air-popped popcorn**
- 1 **tablespoon butter**
- 5 **tablespoons instant vanilla pudding mix**
- ⅓ **cup light corn syrup**
- 1 **teaspoon vanilla extract**
  Dash salt

1. Place popcorn in a large bowl. In a small microwave-safe bowl, melt butter; whisk in the pudding mix, corn syrup, vanilla and salt until smooth.
2. Microwave mixture, uncovered, for 45 seconds or until bubbly. Pour over popcorn; toss to coat. Spread in two 15x10x1-in. baking pans coated with cooking spray.

3. Bake at 250° for 25-30 minutes or until crisp, stirring once. Remove popcorn from pans to waxed paper to cool. Break into clusters. Store in airtight containers.
NOTE *This recipe was tested in a 1,100-watt microwave.*
PER SERVING *1 cup equals 91 cal., 2 g fat (1 g sat. fat), 3 mg chol., 83 mg sodium, 19 g carb., 1 g fiber, 1 g pro.* **Diabetic Exchange:** *1 starch.*

Blue Cheese Date Wraps

My friends and I used to make the traditional bacon-wrapped jalapenos at cookouts. I decided to sweeten them up a bit with dates and apricots.

—**SUSAN HINTON** APEX, NC

PREP: 25 MIN. • **BAKE:** 10 MIN.
MAKES: 3 DOZEN

- 12 **bacon strips**
- 36 **pitted dates**
- ⅔ **cup crumbled blue cheese**

1. Cut each bacon strip into thirds. In a large skillet, cook bacon in batches over medium heat until partially cooked but not crisp. Remove to paper towels to drain; keep warm.
2. Carefully cut a slit in the center of each date; fill with blue cheese. Wrap a bacon piece around each stuffed date; secure with wooden toothpicks.
3. Place on ungreased baking sheets. Bake at 375° for 10-12 minutes or until bacon is crisp.
PER SERVING *1 appetizer equals 44 cal., 2 g fat (1 g sat. fat), 4 mg chol., 84 mg sodium, 6 g carb., 1 g fiber, 2 g pro.* **Diabetic Exchanges:** *½ starch, ½ fat.*

BLUE CHEESE DATE WRAPS

GWEN NELSON'S
ZESTY CHICKEN
SOUP *PAGE 50*

Soups

Warm yourself with a steaming bowl of **comforting soup** that you can feel good about serving. Each **health-conscious** choice on the following pages delivers **classic flavor** and **satisfying appeal,** with fewer calories, less fat and decreased sodium.

BILLY HENSLEY'S CHUNKY BEEF & VEGETABLE SOUP

PAGE 51

VICKI KERR'S VEGGIE CHOWDER

PAGE 43

SHERYL OLENICK'S LASAGNA SOUP

PAGE 39

Hearty Chipotle Chicken Soup

Sweet corn and cool sour cream help tame the smoky hot flavor of chipotle pepper. This zesty soup is perfect for a chilly night.

—SONALI RUDER NEW YORK, NY

PREP: 15 MIN. • **COOK:** 30 MIN.
MAKES: 8 SERVINGS (3¼ QUARTS)

- 1 large onion, chopped
- 1 tablespoon canola oil
- 4 garlic cloves, minced
- 4 cups reduced-sodium chicken broth
- 2 cans (15 ounces each) pinto beans, rinsed and drained
- 2 cans (14½ ounces each) fire-roasted diced tomatoes, undrained
- 3 cups frozen corn
- 2 chipotle peppers in adobo sauce, seeded and minced
- 2 teaspoons adobo sauce
- 1 teaspoon ground cumin
- ¼ teaspoon pepper
- 2 cups cubed cooked chicken breast
- ½ cup fat-free sour cream
- ¼ cup minced fresh cilantro

1. In a Dutch oven, saute onion in oil until tender. Add garlic; cook 1 minute longer. Add the broth, beans, tomatoes, corn, chipotle peppers, adobo sauce, cumin and pepper. Bring to a boil. Reduce heat; simmer, uncovered, for 20 minutes.

2. Stir in chicken; heat through. Garnish with sour cream; sprinkle with cilantro.

PER SERVING *1⅔ cups with 1 tablespoon sour cream equals 287 cal., 4 g fat (1 g sat. fat), 29 mg chol., 790 mg sodium, 42 g carb., 7 g fiber, 21 g pro.* **Diabetic Exchanges:** *2 starch, 2 lean meat, 2 vegetable.*

HEARTY CHIPOTLE CHICKEN SOUP

Shrimp Gazpacho

Here's a refreshing take on the classic chilled tomato soup. Our twist features shrimp, lime and plenty of avocado.

—TASTE OF HOME TEST KITCHEN

PREP: 15 MIN. + CHILLING
MAKES: 12 SERVINGS (ABOUT 3 QUARTS)

- 6 cups spicy hot V8 juice
- 2 cups cold water
- 1 pound peeled and deveined cooked shrimp (31-40 per pound)
- 2 medium tomatoes, seeded and diced
- 1 medium cucumber, seeded and diced
- 2 medium ripe avocados, diced
- ½ cup lime juice
- ½ cup minced fresh cilantro
- ½ teaspoon salt
- ¼ to ½ teaspoon hot pepper sauce

In a large bowl, combine all of the ingredients. Cover and refrigerate for 1 hour. Serve cold.

NOTE *This recipe is best served the same day it's made.*

PER SERVING *1 cup equals 128 cal., 6 g fat (1 g sat. fat), 57 mg chol., 551 mg sodium, 10 g carb., 2 g fiber, 10 g pro.* **Diabetic Exchanges:** *2 vegetable, 1 lean meat, 1 fat.*

Lentil-Tomato Soup

Double the recipe and share this fabulous soup with friends and neighbors on cold winter nights. With corn bread for dunking, it's even more irresistible.

—**MICHELLE CURTIS** BAKER CITY, OR

PREP: 15 MIN. • **COOK:** 30 MIN.
MAKES: 6 SERVINGS

- 4½ **cups water**
- 4 **medium carrots, sliced**
- 1 **medium onion, chopped**
- ⅔ **cup dried lentils, rinsed**
- 1 **can (6 ounces) tomato paste**
- 2 **tablespoons minced fresh parsley**
- 1 **tablespoon brown sugar**
- 1 **tablespoon white vinegar**
- 1 **teaspoon garlic salt**
- ½ **teaspoon dried thyme**
- ¼ **teaspoon dill weed**
- ¼ **teaspoon dried tarragon**
- ¼ **teaspoon pepper**

1. In a large saucepan, bring water, carrots, onion and lentils to a boil.

2. Reduce heat; cover and simmer for 20-25 minutes or until vegetables and lentils are tender. Stir in the remaining ingredients; return to a boil. Reduce the heat; simmer soup, uncovered, for 5 minutes to allow flavors to blend.

ZESTY HAMBURGER SOUP

PER SERVING *¾ cup equals 138 cal., trace fat (trace sat. fat), 0 chol., 351 mg sodium, 27 g carb., 9 g fiber, 8 g pro.* **Diabetic Exchanges:** *1 starch, 1 lean meat, 1 vegetable.*

FREEZE IT | **FAST FIX**

Zesty Hamburger Soup

This recipe offers comforting warmth on those very cold winter days. I serve it with hot garlic bread or crusty French bread.

—**KELLY MILAN** LAKE JACKSON, TX

START TO FINISH: 30 MIN.
MAKES: 10 SERVINGS (3¾ QUARTS)

- 1 **pound ground beef**
- 2 **cups sliced celery**
- 1 **cup chopped onion**
- 2 **teaspoons minced garlic**
- 4 **cups water**
- 2 **medium red potatoes, peeled and cubed**
- 2 **cups frozen corn**
- 1½ **cups uncooked small shell pasta**
- 4 **pickled jalapeno slices**
- 4 **cups V8 juice**
- 2 **cans (10 ounces each) diced tomatoes with green chilies**
- 1 **to 2 tablespoons sugar**

1. In a Dutch oven, cook beef, celery and onion over medium heat until meat is no longer pink. Add garlic; cook 1 minute longer. Drain. Stir in the water, potatoes, corn, pasta and jalapeno.

2. Bring to a boil. Reduce heat; cover and simmer 10-15 minutes or until pasta is tender. Stir in the remaining ingredients; heat through.

PER SERVING *1½ cups equals 221 cal., 5 g fat (2 g sat. fat), 22 mg chol., 548 mg sodium, 33 g carb., 4 g fiber, 13 g pro.* **Diabetic Exchanges:** *2 vegetable, 1½ starch, 1 lean meat.*

FREEZE OPTION *Cool soup and transfer to freezer containers. Freeze up to 3 months. To use, thaw in the refrigerator overnight. Transfer to a saucepan. Cover and cook over medium heat until heated through.*

TURKEY GNOCCHI SOUP

Summer Squash Soup

Delicate and lemony, this squash soup would set the stage for a memorable ladies luncheon. It's the best of late summer in a bowl.

—**HEIDI WILCOX** LAPEER, MI

PREP: 35 MIN. • **COOK:** 15 MIN.
MAKES: 8 SERVINGS (2 QUARTS)

- **2 large sweet onions, chopped**
- **1 medium leek (white portion only), chopped**
- **2 tablespoons olive oil**
- **6 garlic cloves, minced**
- **6 medium yellow summer squash, seeded and cubed (about 6 cups)**
- **4 cups reduced-sodium chicken broth**
- **4 fresh thyme sprigs**
- **¼ teaspoon salt**
- **2 tablespoons lemon juice**
- **⅛ teaspoon hot pepper sauce**
- **1 tablespoon shredded Parmesan cheese**
- **2 teaspoons grated lemon peel**

1. In a large saucepan, saute onions and leek in oil until tender. Add garlic; cook 1 minute longer. Add squash; saute 5 minutes. Stir in the broth, thyme and salt. Bring to a boil. Reduce heat; cover and simmer the mixture for 15-20 minutes or until squash is tender.

2. Discard thyme sprigs. Cool slightly. In a blender, process soup in batches until smooth. Return all to the pan. Stir in lemon juice and hot pepper sauce; heat through. Sprinkle each serving with cheese and lemon peel.

PER SERVING *1 cup equals 90 cal., 4 g fat (1 g sat. fat), trace chol., 377 mg sodium, 12 g carb., 3 g fiber, 4 g pro.* **Diabetic Exchanges:** *1 starch, ½ fat.*

FREEZE IT
Turkey Gnocchi Soup

While trying to find a creative use for leftover turkey, we decided to add gnocchi instead of noodles. My 8-year-old daughter always asks for more. If you don't have leftover turkey, a rotisserie chicken works just as well.

—**AMY BABINES** VIRGINIA BEACH, VA

PREP: 15 MIN. • **COOK:** 25 MIN.
MAKES: 6 SERVINGS (2 QUARTS)

- **1 tablespoon butter**
- **3 medium carrots, chopped**
- **4 garlic cloves, minced**
- **6 cups water**
- **3 teaspoons reduced-sodium chicken base**
- **¾ teaspoon Italian seasoning**
- **1 package (16 ounces) potato gnocchi**
- **2 cups cubed cooked turkey breast**
- **1 cup frozen peas**
- **½ teaspoon pepper**
- **½ cup shredded Parmesan cheese**

1. In a Dutch oven, heat butter over medium heat. Add carrots; cook and stir 8-10 minutes or until crisp-tender. Add garlic; cook 1 minute longer.

2. Stir in water, chicken base and Italian seasoning; bring to a boil. Add gnocchi. Reduce heat; simmer, uncovered, 3-4 minutes or until gnocchi float. Stir in turkey, peas and pepper; heat through. Top servings with cheese.

FREEZE OPTION *Freeze cooled soup in freezer containers. To use, partially thaw in refrigerator overnight. Heat through in a saucepan, stirring occasionally and adding a little water if necessary.*

PER SERVING *1⅓ cups soup with 4 teaspoons cheese equals 307 cal., 6 g fat (3 g sat. fat), 55 mg chol., 782 mg sodium, 39 g carb., 4 g fiber, 24 g pro.* **Diabetic Exchanges:** *3 lean meat, 2 starch, ½ fat.*

FAST FIX ▶

Lasagna Soup

All the traditional flavors of lasagna come together in this heartwarming meal-in-a-bowl. Better yet, it's just 30 minutes away.

—**SHERYL OLENICK** DEMAREST, NJ

START TO FINISH: 30 MIN.
MAKES: 8 SERVINGS (2¾ QUARTS)

- 1 pound lean ground beef (90% lean)
- 1 large green pepper, chopped
- 1 medium onion, chopped
- 2 garlic cloves, minced
- 2 cans (14½ ounces each) diced tomatoes, undrained
- 2 cans (14½ ounces each) reduced-sodium beef broth
- 1 can (8 ounces) tomato sauce
- 1 cup frozen corn
- ¼ cup tomato paste
- 2 teaspoons Italian seasoning
- ¼ teaspoon pepper
- 2½ cups uncooked spiral pasta
- ½ cup shredded Parmesan cheese

1. In a large saucepan, cook beef, green pepper and onion over medium heat 6-8 minutes or until meat is no longer pink, breaking up beef into crumbles. Add garlic; cook 1 minute longer. Drain.

2. Stir in tomatoes, broth, tomato sauce, corn, tomato paste, Italian seasoning and pepper. Bring to a boil. Stir in pasta. Return to a boil. Reduce heat; simmer, covered, 10-12 minutes or until pasta is tender. Serve with cheese.

PER SERVING *1⅓ cups soup with 1 tablespoon cheese equals 280 cal., 7 g fat (3 g sat. fat), 41 mg chol., 572 mg sodium, 35 g carb., 4 g fiber, 20 g pro.* **Diabetic Exchanges:** *2 lean meat, 2 vegetable, 1½ starch.*

New England Clam Chowder

In the Pacific Northwest, we dig our own razor clams and grind them for chowder. Since those aren't readily available, canned clams are perfectly acceptable.

—**SANDY LARSON** PORT ANGELES, WA

PREP: 20 MIN. • **COOK:** 35 MIN.
MAKES: 5 SERVINGS

- 4 center-cut bacon strips
- 2 celery ribs, chopped
- 1 large onion, chopped
- 1 garlic clove, minced
- 3 small potatoes, peeled and cubed
- 1 cup water
- 1 bottle (8 ounces) clam juice
- 3 teaspoons reduced-sodium chicken bouillon granules
- ¼ teaspoon white pepper
- ¼ teaspoon dried thyme
- ⅓ cup all-purpose flour
- 2 cups fat-free half-and-half, divided
- 2 cans (6½ ounces each) chopped clams, undrained

1. In a Dutch oven, cook bacon over medium heat until crisp. Remove to paper towels to drain; set aside. Saute celery and onion in the drippings until tender. Add garlic; cook 1 minute longer. Stir in the potatoes, water, clam juice, bouillon and seasonings. Bring to a boil. Reduce heat; simmer, uncovered, for 15-20 minutes or until potatoes are tender.

2. Combine flour and 1 cup half-and-half until smooth; gradually stir into soup. Bring to a boil; cook and stir for 1-2 minutes or until thickened.

3. Stir in clams and the remaining half-and-half; heat through (do not boil). Crumble the bacon; sprinkle over each serving.

PER SERVING *1⅓ cups equals 260 cal., 4 g fat (1 g sat. fat), 22 mg chol., 788 mg sodium, 39 g carb., 3 g fiber, 13 g pro.* **Diabetic Exchanges:** *2½ starch, 1 lean meat.*

NEW ENGLAND CLAM CHOWDER

Colorado Lamb Chili

This hearty and flavorful chili is wonderful with fresh rolls and your favorite green salad.

—KAREN GORMAN GUNNISON, CO

PREP: 20 MIN. • **COOK:** 1½ HOURS
MAKES: 6 SERVINGS (2¼ QUARTS)

- 1 **pound lamb stew meat, cut into 1-inch pieces**
- 2 **tablespoons canola oil, divided**
- 1 **large onion, chopped**
- 1 **large sweet yellow pepper, chopped**
- 4 **garlic cloves, minced**
- 1 **can (30 ounces) black beans, rinsed and drained**
- 1 **can (28 ounces) diced tomatoes, undrained**
- 1 **can (14½ ounces) reduced-sodium beef broth**
- 1 **tablespoon dried oregano**
- 1 **tablespoon chili powder**
- 1 **tablespoon brown sugar**
- 2 **teaspoons Worcestershire sauce**
- 1 **teaspoon ground cumin**
- ½ **teaspoon fennel seed, crushed**
  Sliced green onions, chopped tomatoes and corn chips, optional

1. In a Dutch oven, brown lamb in 1 tablespoon oil. Remove and set aside.
2. In the same pan, saute onion and pepper in remaining oil until tender. Add the garlic; cook 1 minute longer. Add the beans, tomatoes, beef broth, oregano, chili powder, brown sugar, Worcestershire sauce, cumin and fennel. Return lamb to the pan.
3. Bring to a boil. Reduce heat; cover and simmer for 1¼-1½ hours or until lamb is tender. Garnish each serving with green onions, tomatoes and corn chips if desired.

PER SERVING *1½ cups equals 325 cal., 9 g fat (2 g sat. fat), 51 mg chol., 646 mg sodium, 36 g carb., 9 g fiber, 25 g pro.* **Diabetic Exchanges:** *3 lean meat, 2 starch, 1 vegetable, 1 fat.*

Turkey-Sweet Potato Soup

My satisfying soup has a nostalgic feel and heartwarming flavors to remind you of happy times. It makes the whole house smell cozy.

—RADINE KELLOGG FAIRVIEW, IL

PREP: 20 MIN. • **COOK:** 30 MIN.
MAKES: 4 SERVINGS

- 2 **medium sweet potatoes, peeled and cubed**
- 2 **cups water**
- 2 **teaspoons sodium-free chicken bouillon granules**
- 1 **can (14¾ ounces) cream-style corn**
- 1 **tablespoon minced fresh sage**
- ¼ **teaspoon pepper**
- 1 **tablespoon cornstarch**
- 1 **cup 2% milk**
- 2 **cups cubed cooked turkey breast**

1. In a large saucepan, combine potatoes, water and bouillon; bring to a boil. Reduce heat; cook, covered, 10-15 minutes or until potatoes are tender.
2. Stir in corn, sage and pepper; heat through. In a small bowl, mix the cornstarch and milk until smooth; stir into soup. Bring to a boil; cook and stir 1-2 minutes or until thickened. Stir in turkey and heat through.

PER SERVING *1½ cups equals 275 cal., 3 g fat (1 g sat. fat), 65 mg chol., 374 mg sodium, 39 g carb., 3 g fiber, 26 g pro.* **Diabetic Exchanges:** *3 lean meat, 2½ starch.*

COLORADO LAMB CHILI

Makeover Chicken Enchilada Soup

Even though there are many other delicious dishes on the menu, I always find myself ordering Chicken Enchilada Soup from Chili's. I asked *Taste of Home* to create a lightened-up version I could enjoy at home.

—TRACI CAMPBELL SAGINAW, TX

PREP: 30 MIN. • **COOK:** 25 MIN.
MAKES: 6 SERVINGS

- 2 **corn tortillas (6 inches)**
- ½ **teaspoon canola oil**
- ½ **teaspoon chili powder**
- ⅛ **teaspoon salt**
- ⅛ **teaspoon cayenne pepper**

SOUP

- 1 **medium onion, chopped**
- 1 **tablespoon canola oil**
- 1 **garlic clove, minced**
- 5 **cups water, divided**
- 2 **teaspoons reduced-sodium chicken base**
- 1 **teaspoon chili powder**
- ½ **teaspoon ground cumin**
- ¼ **teaspoon ground coriander**
- ⅛ **teaspoon cayenne pepper**
- ⅓ **cup masa harina**
- 8 **ounces reduced-fat process cheese (Velveeta), cubed**
- 2 **cups cubed cooked chicken breast**
- ¾ **cup pico de gallo**
- 6 **tablespoons shredded Colby-Monterey Jack cheese**

1. Cut each tortilla lengthwise into thirds; cut widthwise into ¼-in. strips. Place strips and oil in a resealable plastic bag; shake to coat. Combine chili powder, salt and cayenne. Add to bag; shake to coat.

2. Arrange strips on a baking sheet coated with cooking spray. Bake at 400° for 6-8 minutes or until crisp, stirring once. Cool on paper towels.

3. Meanwhile, in a Dutch oven, saute onion in oil until tender. Add garlic; cook 1 minute longer. Stir in 4 cups water, chicken base, chili powder, cumin, coriander and cayenne. Whisk masa harina and remaining water until smooth; stir into pan. Bring to a boil; cook and stir for 2 minutes or until slightly thickened.

4. Reduce heat. Stir in process cheese until melted. Add cubed chicken; heat through. Ladle soup into bowls. Top with pico de gallo, shredded cheese and tortilla strips.

ORIGINAL	MAKEOVER
380 Calories	**266** Calories
24g Fat	**11g** Fat
9g Sat. Fat	**4g** Sat. Fat

MAKEOVER CHICKEN ENCHILADA SOUP

PER SERVING *1 cup equals 266 cal., 11 g fat (4 g sat. fat), 56 mg chol., 866 mg sodium, 19 g carb., 2 g fiber, 24 g pro.*

DID YOU KNOW?

Masa harina is a corn flour commonly used in Latin American cuisines. It's the base of corn tortillas and tamale fillings. Use cornmeal or a corn tortilla finely ground in a food processor if you don't have masa harina.

SLOW-COOKED CHICKEN CHILI

Slow-Cooked Chicken Chili

Lime gives this zesty chili a cool twist, while canned tomatoes and beans make preparation a snap. Instead of preparing the toasted tortilla strips, you could serve the chili with corn muffins.

—**DIANE RANDAZZO** SINKING SPRING, PA

PREP: 25 MIN. • **COOK:** 4 HOURS
MAKES: 6 SERVINGS (2 QUARTS)

- 1 medium onion, chopped
- 1 each medium sweet yellow, red and green peppers, chopped
- 2 tablespoons olive oil
- 3 garlic cloves, minced
- 1 pound ground chicken
- 2 cans (14½ ounces each) diced tomatoes, undrained
- 1 can (15 ounces) white kidney or cannellini beans, rinsed and drained
- ¼ cup lime juice
- 1 tablespoon all-purpose flour
- 1 tablespoon baking cocoa
- 1 tablespoon ground cumin
- 1 tablespoon chili powder
- 2 teaspoons ground coriander
- 1 teaspoon grated lime peel
- ½ teaspoon salt
- ½ teaspoon garlic pepper blend
- ¼ teaspoon pepper
- 2 flour tortillas (8 inches), cut into ¼-inch strips
- 6 tablespoons reduced-fat sour cream

1. In a large skillet, saute the onion and peppers in oil for 7-8 minutes or until crisp-tender. Add garlic; cook 1 minute longer. Add the ground chicken; cook and stir over medium heat for 8-9 minutes or until the meat is no longer pink.

2. Transfer to a 3-qt. slow cooker. Stir in the tomatoes, beans, lime juice, flour, cocoa, cumin, chili powder, coriander, lime peel, salt, garlic pepper and pepper.

3. Cover and cook on low for 4-5 hours or until heated through.

4. Place tortilla strips on a baking sheet coated with cooking spray. Bake at 400° for 8-10 minutes or until crisp. Serve over chili with sour cream.

PER SERVING *1¼ cups equals 356 cal., 14 g fat (3 g sat. fat), 55 mg chol., 644 mg sodium, 39 g carb., 8 g fiber, 21 g pro.*

Veggie Chowder

Packed with potatoes, carrots and corn, this soup is a smart healthy dinner choice. Because it's not too heavy, it makes a nice light partner for a sandwich.

—**VICKI KERR** PORTLAND, ME

START TO FINISH: 30 MIN.
MAKES: 7 SERVINGS (1¾ QUARTS)

- 2 cups cubed peeled potatoes
- 2 cups reduced-sodium chicken broth
- 1 cup chopped carrots
- ½ cup chopped onion
- 1 can (14¾ ounces) cream-style corn
- 1 can (12 ounces) fat-free evaporated milk
- ¾ cup shredded reduced-fat cheddar cheese
- ½ cup sliced fresh mushrooms
- ¼ teaspoon pepper
- 2 tablespoons bacon bits

1. In a large saucepan, combine potatoes, broth, carrots and onion; bring to a boil. Reduce heat; simmer, uncovered, 10-15 minutes or until vegetables are tender.

2. Add the corn, milk, cheese, mushrooms and pepper; cook and stir 4-6 minutes longer or until heated through. Sprinkle with bacon bits.

PER SERVING *1 cup equals 191 cal., 5 g fat (2 g sat. fat), 15 mg chol., 505 mg sodium, 29 g carb., 2 g fiber, 11 g pro.*
Diabetic Exchanges: *2 starch, ½ fat.*

VEGGIE CHOWDER

FAST FIX ▶
30-Minute Chicken Noodle Soup

Perfect for a cold, blustery day, this truly fuss-free soup is my favorite thing to eat when I'm under the weather. It makes me feel so much better.

—LACEY WAADT PAYSON, UT

START TO FINISH: 30 MIN.
MAKES: 6 SERVINGS (2¼ QUARTS)

- 4 cups water
- 1 can (14½ ounces) chicken broth
- 1½ cups cubed cooked chicken breast
- 1 can (10¾ ounces) condensed cream of chicken soup, undiluted
- ¾ cup sliced celery
- ¾ cup sliced carrots
- 1 small onion, chopped
- 1½ teaspoons dried parsley flakes
- 1 teaspoon reduced-sodium chicken bouillon granules
- ¼ teaspoon pepper
- 3 cups uncooked egg noodles

In a Dutch oven, combine the first 10 ingredients. Bring to a boil. Reduce heat; cover and simmer for 10 minutes or until vegetables are crisp-tender. Stir in noodles; cook 5-7 minutes longer or until noodles and vegetables are tender.

PER SERVING *1½ cups equals 196 cal., 5 g fat (1 g sat. fat), 49 mg chol., 759 mg sodium, 22 g carb., 2 g fiber, 15 g pro. **Diabetic Exchanges:** 2 lean meat, 1 starch, ½ fat.*

FREEZE IT
Apple Squash Soup

I add a little ginger and sage to apples and squash to make this creamy soup. My family loves it when autumn rolls around.

—CRYSTAL RALPH-HAUGHN
BARTLESVILLE, OK

PREP: 10 MIN. • **COOK:** 35 MIN.
MAKES: 5 SERVINGS

- 2 tablespoons butter
- 1 large onion, chopped
- ½ teaspoon rubbed sage
- 1 can (14½ ounces) chicken or vegetable broth
- 2 medium tart apples, peeled and finely chopped
- ¾ cup water
- 1 package (12 ounces) frozen cooked winter squash, thawed
- 1 teaspoon ground ginger
- ½ teaspoon salt
- ½ cup fat-free milk

1. In a large saucepan, heat butter over medium-high heat. Add onion and sage; cook and stir 2-4 minutes or until tender. Add broth, apples and water; bring to a boil. Reduce heat; simmer, covered, 12 minutes.

2. Add squash, ginger and salt; return to a boil. Reduce heat; simmer, uncovered, 10 minutes to allow the flavors to blend. Remove from heat; cool slightly.

3. Process in batches in a blender until smooth; return to pan. Add milk; heat through, stirring occasionally (do not allow to boil).

FREEZE OPTION *Freeze cooled soup in freezer containers. To use, partially thaw in refrigerator overnight. Heat through in a saucepan, stirring occasionally and adding a little broth if necessary.*

PER SERVING *1 cup equals 142 cal., 6 g fat (3 g sat. fat), 13 mg chol., 647 mg sodium, 22 g carb., 2 g fiber, 3 g pro. **Diabetic Exchanges:** 1 starch, 1 fat, ½ fruit.*

APPLE SQUASH SOUP

Hearty Vegetable Split Pea Soup

My secret weapon on busy days is this slow-cooked soup. It's delicious served with oyster crackers that have been tossed in a bit of melted butter and herbs and then lightly toasted in the oven.
—**WHITNEY JENSEN** SPRING LAKE, MI

PREP: 10 MIN. • **COOK:** 7 HOURS
MAKES: 8 SERVINGS (2 QUARTS)

- 1 **package (16 ounces) dried green split peas, rinsed**
- 1 **large carrot, chopped**
- 1 **celery rib, chopped**
- 1 **small onion, chopped**
- 1 **bay leaf**
- 1½ **teaspoons salt**
- ½ **teaspoon dried thyme**
- ½ **teaspoon pepper**
- 6 **cups water**

In a 3- or 4-qt. slow cooker, combine all ingredients. Cook, covered, on low 7-9 hours or until peas are tender. Stir before serving. Discard bay leaf.
FREEZE OPTION *Freeze cooled soup in freezer containers. To use, partially thaw in the refrigerator overnight. Heat through in a saucepan, stirring occasionally and adding a little water if necessary.*
PER SERVING *1 cup equals 202 cal., 1 g fat (trace sat. fat), 0 chol., 462 mg sodium, 36 g carb., 15 g fiber, 14 g pro. Diabetic Exchanges: 2 starch, 1 lean meat.*

TOP TIP

Hearty Vegetable Split Pea Soup is a meatless recipe. You could stir in ¼ pound of extra-lean turkey ham at the end of cooking, for an increase of 8 calories and 128 mg sodium per serving. Decrease the salt if desired.

WHITE BEAN
SOUP WITH ESCAROLE

White Bean Soup with Escarole

This winter warmer has become a standby because it uses kitchen staples, it's packed with healthy ingredients, and it's a cinch to prepare. If I can't find escarole, I sub fresh spinach at the very end of cooking.
—**GINA SAMOKAR** NORTH HAVEN, CT

PREP: 15 MIN. • **COOK:** 35 MIN.
MAKES: 8 SERVINGS (2 QUARTS)

- 1 **tablespoon olive oil**
- 1 **small onion, chopped**
- 5 **garlic cloves, minced**
- 3 **cans (14½ ounces each) reduced-sodium chicken broth**
- 1 **can (14½ ounces) diced tomatoes, undrained**
- ½ **teaspoon Italian seasoning**
- ¼ **teaspoon crushed red pepper flakes**
- 1 **cup uncooked whole wheat orzo pasta**
- 1 **bunch escarole or spinach, coarsely chopped (about 8 cups)**
- 1 **can (15 ounces) white kidney or cannellini beans, rinsed and drained**
- ¼ **cup grated Parmesan cheese**

1. In a Dutch oven, heat oil over medium heat. Add onion and garlic; cook and stir until tender. Add the broth, tomatoes, Italian seasoning and pepper flakes; bring to a boil. Reduce heat; simmer, uncovered, 15 minutes.
2. Stir in orzo and escarole. Return to a boil; cook 12-14 minutes or until orzo is tender. Add the beans; heat through, stirring occasionally. Sprinkle the servings with cheese.
FREEZE OPTION *Freeze cooled soup in freezer containers. To use, partially thaw in refrigerator overnight. Heat through in a saucepan, stirring occasionally and adding a little broth if necessary.*
PER SERVING *1 cup equals 174 cal., 3 g fat (1 g sat. fat), 2 mg chol., 572 mg sodium, 28 g carb., 8 g fiber, 9 g pro. Diabetic Exchanges: 1 starch, 1 lean meat, 1 vegetable, ½ fat.*

ORIGINAL	MAKEOVER
195 Calories	**106** Calories
12g Fat	**3**g Fat
8g Sat. Fat	**2**g Sat. Fat

MAKEOVER CAULIFLOWER SOUP

Makeover Cauliflower Soup

Creamy soups are soul-warming and satisfying, and this cauliflower one is no exception. The *Taste of Home* Test Kitchen made a healthier version of this recipe that I received from a friend.

—DORIS WATT DAVIS HELLERTOWN, PA

PREP: 30 MIN. • **COOK:** 30 MIN.
MAKES: 11 SERVINGS (2¾ QUARTS)

- 2 **celery ribs, chopped**
- 1 **small onion, chopped**
- 1 **medium carrot, chopped**
- 2 **tablespoons butter**
- 1 **large head cauliflower (2 pounds), cut into florets**
- 6 **cups reduced-sodium chicken broth**
- ½ **cup all-purpose flour**
- 2 **cups 2% milk**
- ¾ **cup fat-free half-and-half**
- 1 **tablespoon minced fresh parsley**
- 1 **teaspoon salt**
- 1 **teaspoon dill weed**
- ¼ **teaspoon white pepper**

1. In a Dutch oven, saute celery, onion and carrot in butter for 3-5 minutes or until crisp-tender. Stir in cauliflower and broth; bring to a boil. Reduce heat; cover and simmer for 15-20 minutes or until tender. Cool slightly.
2. In a blender, process vegetable mixture in batches until smooth. Return all to the pan. Heat over medium heat.
3. In a small bowl, whisk flour and milk until smooth; stir into puree. Bring to a boil; cook and stir for 2 minutes or until thickened. Reduce heat; stir in the half-and-half, parsley, salt, dill and pepper. Heat through.
PER SERVING *1 cup equals 106 cal., 3 g fat (2 g sat. fat), 9 mg chol., 641 mg sodium, 14 g carb., 3 g fiber, 6 g pro.* **Diabetic Exchanges:** *1 vegetable, ½ starch, ½ fat.*

> **THE SKINNY**
>
> Makeover Cauliflower Soup keeps its rich texture with 2% milk and fat-free half and half. The original recipe was thickened with a homemade cream sauce using ½ cup of butter and full-fat dairy products.

FAST FIX
Chicken Tortellini Soup

Tortellini and herbs give an Italian twist to a chicken soup that's beyond special— and it's easy, too.

—JEAN ATHERLY RED LODGE, MT

START TO FINISH: 30 MIN.
MAKES: 8 SERVINGS (ABOUT 2 QUARTS)

- 2 **cans (14½ ounces each) chicken broth**
- 2 **cups water**
- ¾ **pound boneless skinless chicken breasts, cut into 1-inch cubes**
- 1½ **cups frozen mixed vegetables**
- 1 **package (9 ounces) refrigerated cheese tortellini**
- 2 **celery ribs, thinly sliced**
- 1 **teaspoon dried basil**
- ½ **teaspoon garlic salt**
- ½ **teaspoon dried oregano**
- ¼ **teaspoon pepper**

1. In a large saucepan, bring broth and water to a boil; add chicken. Reduce heat; cook for 10 minutes.
2. Add the remaining ingredients; cook 10-15 minutes longer or until chicken is no longer pink and vegetables are tender.
PER SERVING *1 cup equals 170 cal., 4 g fat (2 g sat. fat), 37 mg chol., 483 mg sodium, 20 g carb., 3 g fiber, 14 g pro.* **Diabetic Exchanges:** *2 lean meat, 1 starch.*

Carrot Broccoli Soup

This soup is a beloved staple at our house. Excellent for lunch with a hot sandwich, it's fast and filled to the brim with carrots and broccoli.

—**SANDY SMITH** LONDON, ON

PREP: 15 MIN. • **COOK:** 20 MIN.
MAKES: 4 SERVINGS

- 1 medium onion, chopped
- 2 medium carrots, chopped
- 2 celery ribs, chopped
- 1 tablespoon butter
- 3 cups fresh broccoli florets
- 3 cups fat-free milk, divided
- ¾ teaspoon salt
- ½ teaspoon dried thyme
- ⅛ teaspoon pepper
- 3 tablespoons all-purpose flour

1. In a large saucepan coated with cooking spray, cook the onion, carrots and celery in butter for 3 minutes. Add broccoli; cook 3 minutes longer. Stir in 2¾ cups milk, salt, thyme and pepper.
2. Bring to a boil. Reduce heat; cover and simmer for 5-10 minutes or until vegetables are tender. Combine the flour and the remaining milk until smooth; gradually stir into the soup. Bring to a boil; cook 2 minutes longer or until thickened.
PER SERVING *1¼ cups equals 168 cal., 4 g fat (3 g sat. fat), 14 mg chol., 633 mg sodium, 24 g carb., 4 g fiber, 10 g pro.* **Diabetic Exchanges:** *2 vegetable, 1 fat-free milk, ½ fat.*

Hearty Navy Bean Soup

Use thrifty dried beans and a ham hock to create this comfort-food classic. Bean soup is a family favorite that I make often.
—**MILDRED LEWIS** TEMPLE, TX

PREP: 30 MIN. + SOAKING • **COOK:** 1¾ HOURS
MAKES: 10 SERVINGS (2½ QUARTS)

- 3 cups (1½ pounds) dried navy beans
- 1 can (14½ ounces) diced tomatoes, undrained
- 1 large onion, chopped
- 1 meaty ham hock or 1 cup diced cooked ham
- 2 cups chicken broth
- 2½ cups water
  Salt and pepper to taste
  Minced fresh parsley

1. Rinse and sort beans; soak according to package directions.
2. Drain and rinse beans, discarding liquid. Place in a Dutch oven. Add tomatoes, onion, ham hock, broth, water, salt and pepper. Bring to a boil. Reduce heat; cover and simmer until beans are tender, about 1½ hours.
3. Add more water if necessary. Remove ham hock and let stand until cool enough to handle. Remove meat from bone; discard bone. Cut meat into bite-size pieces; set aside. (For a thicker soup, cool slightly, then puree beans in a food processor or blender and return to pan.) Return ham to soup and heat through. Garnish with parsley.
PER SERVING *1 cup equals 245 cal., 2 g fat (trace sat. fat), 8 mg chol., 352 mg sodium, 42 g carb., 16 g fiber, 18 g pro.* **Diabetic Exchanges:** *3 starch, 2 lean meat.*

HEARTY NAVY BEAN SOUP

Couscous Meatball Soup

This soup is easy, healthy and full of flavor. It chases the shivers away on a wintry day, especially with fresh, warm crusty bread.

—**JONATHAN PACE** SAN FRANCISCO, CA

PREP: 25 MIN. • **COOK:** 40 MIN.
MAKES: 10 SERVINGS (2½ QUARTS)

- 1 **pound lean ground beef (90% lean)**
- 2 **teaspoons dried basil**
- 2 **teaspoons dried oregano**
- ½ **teaspoon salt**
- 1 **large onion, finely chopped**
- 2 **teaspoons canola oil**
- 1 **bunch collard greens, chopped (8 cups)**
- 1 **bunch kale, chopped (8 cups)**
- 2 **cartons (32 ounces each) vegetable stock**
- 1 **tablespoon white wine vinegar**
- ½ **teaspoon crushed red pepper flakes**
- ¼ **teaspoon pepper**
- 1 **package (8.8 ounces) pearl (Israeli) couscous**

1. In a small bowl, combine the beef, basil, oregano and salt. Shape into ½-in. balls. In a large nonstick skillet coated with cooking spray, brown meatballs; drain. Remove meatballs and set aside.

2. In the same skillet, brown onion in oil. Add greens and kale; cook 6-7 minutes longer or until wilted.

3. In a Dutch oven, combine the greens mixture, meatballs, stock, vinegar, pepper flakes and pepper. Bring to a boil. Reduce heat; cover and simmer for 10 minutes. Return to a boil. Stir in couscous. Reduce heat; cover and simmer for 10-15 minutes or until couscous is tender, stirring once.

PER SERVING *1 cup equals 202 cal., 5 g fat (2 g sat. fat), 28 mg chol., 583 mg sodium, 26 g carb., 2 g fiber, 13 g pro.* **Diabetic Exchanges:** *1½ starch, 1 lean meat, 1 vegetable.*

⑤INGREDIENTS

Cool as a Cucumber Soup

Chilled soup makes a wonderfully refreshing first course or side. In this one, bright bursts of dill provide a pleasant contrast to the milder flavor of cucumber.

—**DEIRDRE COX** KANSAS CITY, MO

PREP: 15 MIN. + STANDING
MAKES: 5 SERVINGS

- 1 **pound cucumbers, peeled, seeded and sliced**
- ½ **teaspoon salt**
- 1½ **cups fat-free plain yogurt**
- 1 **green onion, coarsely chopped**
- 1 **garlic clove, minced**
- 4½ **teaspoons snipped fresh dill**
  Additional chopped green onion and snipped fresh dill

1. In a colander set over a bowl, toss cucumbers with salt. Let stand for 30 minutes. Squeeze and pat dry.

2. Place the cucumbers, yogurt, onion and garlic in a food processor; cover and process until smooth. Stir in dill. Serve immediately in chilled bowls. Garnish with additional onion and dill.

PER SERVING *⅔ cup soup equals 40 cal., trace fat (trace sat. fat), 2 mg chol., 279 mg sodium, 8 g carb., 1 g fiber, 3 g pro.* **Diabetic Exchange:** *½ fat-free milk.*

COUSCOUS MEATBALL SOUP

Tuscan Turkey Soup

Transform leftover turkey into a uniquely flavored pumpkin soup that's sure to satisfy family and friends. It's so easy, even a beginner in the kitchen can pull this one off.

—**MARIE MCCONNELL** SHELBYVILLE, IL

START TO FINISH: 30 MIN.
MAKES: 8 SERVINGS (2 QUARTS)

- 2 **tablespoons olive oil**
- 1 **cup chopped onion**
- 1 **cup chopped celery**
- 2 **garlic cloves, minced**
- 2 **cans (14½ ounces each) reduced-sodium chicken broth**
- 1 **can (15 ounces) solid-pack pumpkin**
- 1 **can (15 ounces) white kidney or cannellini beans, rinsed and drained**
- 2 **cups cubed cooked turkey**
- ½ **teaspoon salt**
- ½ **teaspoon dried basil**
- ¼ **teaspoon pepper**
  Grated Parmesan cheese, optional

1. In a large saucepan, heat oil over medium-high heat. Add onion and celery; cook and stir until tender. Add garlic; cook 1 minute longer.

2. Stir in broth, pumpkin, beans, turkey, salt, basil and pepper. Bring to a boil. Reduce the heat; simmer, uncovered, 10-15 minutes to allow flaovrs to blend, stirring occasionally. If desired, serve with cheese.

PER SERVING *1 cup (calculated without cheese) equals 167 cal., g fat (1 g sat. fat), 27 mg chol., 549 mg sodium, 14 g carb., 5 g fiber, 15 g pro.* **Diabetic Exchanges:** *2 lean meat, 1 starch, 1 fat.*

Jumpin' Espresso Bean Chili

Chili is a hearty dish I love experimenting with. This meatless version I created is low in fat but high in flavor. Everyone tries to guess the secret ingredient, but no one ever thinks it's coffee.

—**JESSIE APFE** BERKELEY, CA

PREP: 15 MIN. • **COOK:** 35 MIN.
MAKES: 7 SERVINGS

- 3 **medium onions, chopped**
- 2 **tablespoons olive oil**
- 2 **tablespoons brown sugar**
- 2 **tablespoons chili powder**
- 2 **tablespoons ground cumin**
- 1 **tablespoon instant coffee granules**
- 1 **tablespoon baking cocoa**
- ¾ **teaspoon salt**
- 2 **cans (14½ ounces each) no-salt-added diced tomatoes**
- 1 **can (15 ounces) black beans, rinsed and drained**
- 1 **can (15 ounces) kidney beans, rinsed and drained**
- 1 **can (15 ounces) garbanzo beans or chickpeas, rinsed and drained Sour cream, thinly sliced green onions, shredded cheddar cheese and pickled jalapeno slices, optional**

1. In a Dutch oven, saute the onions in oil until tender. Add the brown sugar, chili powder, cumin, coffee granules, cocoa and salt; cook and stir for 1 minute.

2. Stir in tomatoes and beans. Bring to a boil. Reduce heat; cover and simmer for 30 minutes to allow flavors to blend. Serve with sour cream, onions, cheese and jalapeno slices if desired.

PER SERVING *1 cup (calculated without optional ingredients) equals 272 cal., 6 g fat (1 g sat. fat), 0 chol., 620 mg sodium, 45 g carb., 12 g fiber, 12 g pro.* **Diabetic Exchanges:** *2½ starch, 2 vegetable, 1 lean meat.*

JUMPIN' ESPRESSO BEAN CHILI

ZESTY CHICKEN SOUP

3. Garnish with cheese and tortilla chips if desired. Soup may be frozen for up to 3 months.

PER SERVING *1½ cups (calculated without cheese and tortilla chips) equals 152 cal., 3 g fat (1 g sat. fat), 31 mg chol., 518 mg sodium, 16 g carb., 5 g fiber, 14 g pro.* **Diabetic Exchanges:** *2 vegetable, 1 lean meat, ½ starch.*

⑤INGREDIENTS

Garlic Fennel Bisque

I usually serve this soup in the spring as a wonderful side dish or first course. The fennel in the bisque is so refreshing.

—**JANET ONDRICH** THAMESVILLE, ON

PREP: 30 MIN. • **COOK:** 40 MIN.
MAKES: 14 SERVINGS

- 4 **cups water**
- 2½ **cups half-and-half cream**
- 24 **garlic cloves, peeled and halved**
- 3 **medium fennel bulbs, cut into ½-inch pieces**
- 2 **tablespoons chopped fennel fronds**
- ½ **teaspoon salt**
- ⅛ **teaspoon pepper**
- ½ **cup pine nuts, toasted**

1. In a Dutch oven, bring the water, cream and garlic to a boil. Reduce heat; cover and simmer for 15 minutes or until garlic is very soft. Add fennel and fennel fronds; cover and simmer 15 minutes longer or until fennel is very soft.

2. Cool slightly. In a blender, process soup in batches until blended. Return all to the pan. Season with salt and pepper; heat through. Sprinkle each serving with pine nuts.

PER SERVING *½ cup equals 108 cal., 7 g fat (3 g sat. fat), 21 mg chol., 133 mg sodium, 8 g carb., 2 g fiber, 4 g pro.* **Diabetic Exchanges:** *1½ fat, 1 vegetable.*

Zesty Chicken Soup

My spicy chicken soup is chock-full of chicken and vegetables. Best of all, it freezes nicely, making a second meal with little effort!

—**GWEN NELSON** CASTRO VALLEY, CA

PREP: 25 MIN. • **COOK:** 40 MIN.
MAKES: 10 SERVINGS (3¾ QUARTS)

- 1¼ **pounds boneless skinless chicken breasts**
- 4 **cups water**
- 1 **medium onion, chopped**
- 2 **celery ribs, chopped**
- 4 **garlic cloves, minced**
- 1 **tablespoon canola oil**
- 1 **can (14½ ounces) Mexican diced tomatoes**
- 1 **can (14½ ounces) diced tomatoes**
- 1 **can (8 ounces) tomato sauce**
- 1 **cup medium salsa**
- 3 **medium zucchini, halved and sliced**
- 2 **medium carrots, sliced**
- 1 **cup frozen white corn**
- 1 **can (4 ounces) chopped green chilies**
- 3 **teaspoons ground cumin**
- 2 **teaspoons chili powder**
- 1 **teaspoon dried basil**
  Shredded cheddar cheese and tortilla chips, optional

1. Place chicken in a Dutch oven; add water. Bring to a boil. Reduce heat; cover and simmer for 10-15 minutes or until chicken juices run clear. Remove the chicken and cut into ½-in. cubes; set aside.

2. In a large skillet, saute onion, celery and garlic in oil until tender; add to cooking juices in the Dutch oven. Stir in the tomatoes, tomato sauce, salsa, zucchini, carrots, corn, chilies, cumin, chili powder and basil. Bring to a boil. Reduce heat; cover and simmer for 20-25 minutes or until vegetables are tender. Add chicken; heat through.

Lentil & Chicken Sausage Stew

This healthy stew will warm your family right down to their toes! Serve with rolls to soak up every last morsel.

—**JAN VALDEZ** CHICAGO, IL

PREP: 15 MIN. • **COOK:** 8 HOURS
MAKES: 6 SERVINGS

- 1 carton (32 ounces) reduced-sodium chicken broth
- 1 can (28 ounces) diced tomatoes, undrained
- 3 fully cooked spicy chicken sausage links (3 ounces each), cut into ½-inch slices
- 1 cup dried lentils, rinsed
- 1 medium onion, chopped
- 1 medium carrot, chopped
- 1 celery rib, chopped
- 2 garlic cloves, minced
- ½ teaspoon dried thyme

In a 4- or 5-qt. slow cooker, combine all of the ingredients. Cover and cook on low for 8-10 hours or until lentils are tender.

PER SERVING *1½ cups equals 231 cal., 4 g fat (1 g sat. fat), 33 mg chol., 803 mg sodium, 31 g carb., 13 g fiber, 19 g pro.* **Diabetic Exchanges:** *2 lean meat, 2 vegetable, 1 starch.*

Chunky Beef & Vegetable Soup

Nothing cures the winter blahs like wonderful soup, including this hearty one I first cooked up on a snowy day. It makes a satisfying meal with crusty bread.

—**BILLY HENSLEY** MOUNT CARMEL, TN

PREP: 25 MIN. • **COOK:** 2¾ HOURS
MAKES: 8 SERVINGS (3 QUARTS)

- 1½ pounds beef stew meat, cut into ½-inch pieces
- 1 teaspoon salt, divided
- 1 teaspoon salt-free seasoning blend, divided
- ¾ teaspoon pepper, divided
- 2 tablespoons olive oil, divided
- 4 large carrots, sliced
- 1 large onion, chopped
- 1 medium sweet red pepper, chopped
- 1 medium green pepper, chopped
- 2 garlic cloves, minced
- 1 cup Burgundy wine or additional reduced-sodium beef broth
- 4 cups reduced-sodium beef broth
- 1 can (14½ ounces) diced tomatoes, undrained
- 2 tablespoons tomato paste
- 2 tablespoons Worcestershire sauce
- 1 bay leaf
- 4 medium potatoes (about 2 pounds), cut into ½-inch cubes

1. Sprinkle beef with ½ teaspoon each salt, seasoning blend and pepper. In a Dutch oven, heat 1 tablespoon oil over medium heat. Brown beef in batches. Remove from pan.

2. In same pan, heat remaining oil over medium heat. Add carrots, onion and peppers; cook and stir until carrots are crisp-tender. Add garlic; cook 1 minute longer.

3. Add wine, stirring to loosen browned bits from pan. Stir in the broth, tomatoes, tomato paste, Worcestershire sauce, bay leaf and remaining seasonings. Return beef to pan; bring to a boil. Reduce heat; simmer, covered, 2 hours.

4. Add potatoes; cook 30-40 minutes longer or until beef and potatoes are tender. Skim fat and discard bay leaf.

PER SERVING *1½ cups equals 312 cal., 10 g fat (3 g sat. fat), 55 mg chol., 695 mg sodium, 31 g carb., 5 g fiber, 21 g pro.* **Diabetic Exchanges:** *2 starch, 2 lean meat, ½ fat.*

CHUNKY BEEF & VEGETABLE SOUP

**JANNINE FISK'S
TUSCAN-STYLE ROASTED ASPARAGUS**
PAGE 69

Sides, Salads & Breads

These **heartwarming** hot side dishes, **cool, crisp** salads and **hearty** breads will perfectly complement any meal **without breaking the calorie bank.** This chapter **proves** you don't even have to skip the bread just because **you're eating healthy.**

**AMY LOGAN'S
ROASTED HARVEST VEGETABLES**

PAGE 74

**ARLENE BUTLER'S
HONEY-OAT PAN ROLLS**

PAGE 63

**LAURA POUNDS'
KIWI-STRAWBERRY SPINACH SALAD**

PAGE 79

EASY BEANS & POTATOES WITH BACON

SLOW COOKER
Honey-Butter Peas and Carrots

Classic peas and carrots are even better when you add a handful of flavor enhancers. Slow cooking allows the flavors to meld for maximum richness. These are perfect for a holiday gathering.

—**THERESA KREYCHE** TUSTIN, CA

PREP: 15 MIN. • **COOK:** 5¼ HOURS
MAKES: 12 SERVINGS (½ CUP EACH)

- 1 pound carrots, sliced
- 1 large onion, chopped
- ¼ cup water
- ¼ cup butter, cubed
- ¼ cup honey
- 4 garlic cloves, minced
- 1 teaspoon salt
- 1 teaspoon dried marjoram
- ⅛ teaspoon white pepper
- 1 package (16 ounces) frozen peas

In a 3-qt. slow cooker, combine the first nine ingredients. Cook, covered, on low 5 hours. Stir in peas. Cook, covered, on high 15-25 minutes or until vegetables are tender.
PER SERVING *½ cup equals 106 cal., 4 g fat (2 g sat. fat), 10 mg chol., 293 mg sodium, 16 g carb., 3 g fiber, 3 g pro. Diabetic Exchanges: 1 starch, 1 fat.*

(5)INGREDIENTS SLOW COOKER
Easy Beans & Potatoes with Bacon

I love the combination of green beans with bacon, so I created this recipe. It's great for when you have company because you can start the side dish in the slow cooker and continue preparing the rest of your dinner.

—**BARBARA BRITTAIN** SANTEE, CA

PREP: 15 MIN. • **COOK:** 6 HOURS
MAKES: 10 SERVINGS

- 8 bacon strips, chopped
- 1½ pounds fresh green beans, trimmed and cut into 2-inch pieces (about 4 cups)
- 4 medium potatoes, peeled and cut into ½-inch cubes
- 1 small onion, halved and sliced
- ¼ cup reduced-sodium chicken broth
- ½ teaspoon salt
- ¼ teaspoon pepper

1. In a large skillet, cook bacon over medium heat until crisp, stirring occasionally. Remove to paper towels with a slotted spoon; drain, reserving 1 tablespoon drippings. Cover and refrigerate bacon until serving.
2. In a 5-qt. slow cooker, combine the remaining ingredients; stir in reserved drippings. Cover and cook on low for 6-8 hours or until potatoes are tender. Stir in bacon; heat through.
PER SERVING *¾ cup equals 116 cal., 4 g fat (1 g sat. fat), 8 mg chol., 256 mg sodium, 17 g carb., 3 g fiber, 5 g pro. Diabetic Exchanges: 1 starch, 1 fat.*

Popeye Corn

The Sailor Man himself would approve of this spinach-rich side, which gets a bit of heat from a splash of pepper sauce.

—**STACEY CHRISTENSEN** WEST VALLEY CITY, UT

START TO FINISH: 15 MIN.
MAKES: 6 SERVINGS

- 1 package (16 ounces) frozen corn
- 1 package (10 ounces) frozen chopped spinach, thawed and squeezed dry
- ¾ cup sour cream
- ¾ teaspoon salt
- ½ teaspoon hot pepper sauce

Combine all ingredients in a 1½-qt. microwave-safe dish. Microwave, uncovered, on high for 5 minutes. Stir; cook 2-3 minutes longer or until heated through.

NOTE *This recipe was tested in a 1,100-watt microwave.*
PER SERVING *⅔ cup equals 138 cal., 6 g fat (4 g sat. fat), 20 mg chol., 345 mg sodium, 19 g carb., 3 g fiber, 5 g pro.* *Diabetic Exchanges: 1 starch, 1 fat.*

Honey Spice Bread

The texture of this bread is light and cakelike, so I usually serve slices of it for dessert. The loaf looks so festive with the glaze drizzled on top.

—**GAYE O'DELL** BINGHAMTON, NY

PREP: 20 MIN. • **BAKE:** 55 MIN. + COOLING
MAKES: 1 LOAF (12 SLICES)

- ⅔ cup packed brown sugar
- ⅓ cup 2% milk
- 2 cups all-purpose flour
- 1½ teaspoons baking powder
- ½ teaspoon ground cinnamon
- ½ teaspoon ground nutmeg
- ⅛ teaspoon ground cloves
- 2 large eggs
- ½ cup honey
- ⅓ cup canola oil

GLAZE
- ⅓ cup confectioners' sugar
- 2 teaspoons 2% milk

1. In a small saucepan, combine brown sugar and milk. Cook and stir over low heat until sugar is dissolved. Remove from heat.
2. In a large bowl, whisk flour, baking powder, cinnamon, nutmeg and cloves. In another bowl, whisk eggs, honey, oil and brown sugar mixture until blended. Add to flour mixture; stir just until moistened.
3. Transfer to a greased 8x4-in. loaf pan. Bake at 350° for 55-60 minutes or until a toothpick inserted in center comes out clean (cover top loosely with foil if needed to prevent overbrowning).
4. Cool loaf in pan for 10 minutes before removing to a wire rack to cool completely. In a small bowl, stir glaze ingredients until smooth; drizzle over bread.

FREEZE OPTION *Securely wrap and freeze cooled loaf in plastic wrap and foil. To use, thaw at room temperature. Glaze as directed.*
PER SERVING *1 slice equals 187 cal., 6 g fat (1 g sat. fat), 27 mg chol., 53 mg sodium, 33 g carb., 1 g fiber, 3 g pro.* *Diabetic Exchanges: 2 starch, 1 fat.*

HONEY SPICE BREAD

Tomatoes with Buttermilk Vinaigrette

I like to make the most of tomatoes when they are in season, and I love an old-fashioned homemade dressing with summery taste.

—**JUDITH FOREMAN** ALEXANDRIA, VA

START TO FINISH: 20 MIN.
MAKES: 12 SERVINGS (¾ CUP EACH)

- ¾ cup buttermilk
- ¼ cup minced fresh tarragon
- ¼ cup white wine vinegar
- 3 tablespoons canola oil
- 1½ teaspoons sugar
- ½ teaspoon ground mustard
- ¼ teaspoon celery salt
- ¼ teaspoon pepper
- 4 pounds cherry tomatoes, halved
- ⅓ cup minced fresh chives

1. In a small bowl, whisk the first eight ingredients until blended. Refrigerate, covered, until serving.
2. Just before serving, arrange tomatoes on a platter; drizzle with vinaigrette. Sprinkle with chives.
PER SERVING *¾ cup equals 79 cal., 4 g fat (trace sat. fat), 1 mg chol., 63 mg sodium, 10 g carb., 2 g fiber, 2 g pro.* **Diabetic Exchanges:** *1 vegetable, ½ starch, ½ fat.*

TOMATOES WITH BUTTERMILK VINAIGRETTE

Blueberry Corn Muffins

Sweet blueberries really jazz up an ordinary box of muffin mix. These are perfect for on-the-go snacking or as an addition to any summer potluck.

—**DIANE HIXON** NICEVILLE, FL

START TO FINISH: 25 MIN.
MAKES: 8 MUFFINS

- 1 package (8½ ounces) corn bread/muffin mix
- 1 tablespoon brown sugar
- 1 egg, lightly beaten
- ⅓ cup milk
- ½ cup fresh or frozen blueberries

1. In a large bowl, combine the muffin mix and brown sugar. Combine egg and milk; stir into dry ingredients just until moistened. Fold in blueberries.
2. Coat muffin cups with cooking spray or use paper liners. Fill half full with batter. Bake muffins at 400° for 12-15 minutes or until a toothpick inserted into muffin comes out clean. Cool for 5 minutes before removing from pan to a wire rack. Serve warm.
NOTE *If using frozen blueberries, use without thawing to avoid discoloring the batter.*
PER SERVING *1 muffin equals 146 cal., 4 g fat (1 g sat. fat), 33 mg chol., 264 mg sodium, 25 g carb., 1 g fiber, 3 g pro.* **Diabetic Exchanges:** *1½ starch, ½ fat.*

Basil Dill Coleslaw

I was introduced to basil when I married into an Italian family. I loved the fragrance and flavor of the herb and began to use it in everything. Along with dill, it adds a summer-fresh touch to slaw.

—JUNE CAPPETTO SEATTLE, WA

START TO FINISH: 10 MIN.
MAKES: 6 SERVINGS

- 6 **cups shredded cabbage or coleslaw mix**
- 3 **to 4 tablespoons chopped fresh basil or 1 tablespoon dried basil**
- 3 **tablespoons snipped fresh dill or 1 tablespoon dill weed**

DRESSING

- ½ **cup mayonnaise**
- 3 **tablespoons sugar**
- 2 **tablespoons cider vinegar**
- 2 **tablespoons half-and-half cream**
- 1 **teaspoon coarsely ground pepper**

In a large bowl, combine cabbage, basil and dill. In a small bowl, whisk dressing ingredients until blended. Drizzle over cabbage mixture; toss to coat. Refrigerate until serving.

PER SERVING *¾ cup equals 138 cal., 11 g fat (2 g sat. fat), 7 mg chol., 87 mg sodium, 8 g carb., 1 g fiber, 1 g pro. Diabetic Exchanges: 2 fat, 1 vegetable.*

SESAME TOSSED SALAD

Sesame Tossed Salad

Crisp, crunchy and slightly sweet, this nutritious salad is simply delightful. Feel free to double up on any of your favorite toss-ins.

—ELIZABETH PERKINS SOUTH RIDING, VA

START TO FINISH: 10 MIN.
MAKES: 4 SERVINGS

- 1 **package (5 ounces) spring mix salad greens**
- ½ **cup sliced fresh mushrooms**
- ½ **cup chopped cucumber**
- ½ **cup canned mandarin oranges**
- ¼ **cup sliced almonds, toasted**
- ¼ **cup shredded carrots**
- 2 **green onions, chopped**
- ⅓ **cup reduced-fat Asian toasted sesame salad dressing**

Combine the first seven ingredients in a large bowl. Drizzle with dressing; toss to coat. Serve immediately.

PER SERVING *1½ cups equals 87 cal., 5 g fat (trace sat. fat), 0 chol., 233 mg sodium, 9 g carb., 2 g fiber, 3 g pro. Diabetic Exchanges: 1 fat, ½ starch.*

ARTICHOKE BREAD

Artichoke Bread

A creamy, rich artichoke topping is spread over fresh-baked bread for a flavor that folks just love. You won't find a simpler or more delicious way to round out your menu. It's especially good with Italian food.

—SHERRY CAMPBELL ST. AMANT, LA

PREP: 30 MIN. + COOLING • **BAKE:** 15 MIN.
MAKES: 1 LOAF (12 SLICES)

- 1 tube (11 ounces) refrigerated crusty French loaf
- 1 can (14 ounces) water-packed artichoke hearts, rinsed, drained and chopped
- ½ cup seasoned bread crumbs
- ⅓ cup grated Parmesan cheese
- ⅓ cup reduced-fat mayonnaise
- 2 garlic cloves, minced
- 1 cup (4 ounces) shredded part-skim mozzarella cheese

1. Bake loaf according to package directions; cool. Cut bread in half lengthwise; place on an ungreased baking sheet.
2. In a small bowl, combine the artichokes, bread crumbs, Parmesan cheese, mayonnaise and garlic; spread evenly over cut sides of bread. Sprinkle with mozzarella cheese.
3. Bake at 350° for 15-20 minutes or until cheese is melted. Serve warm.
PER SERVING 1 slice equals 151 cal., 5 g fat (2 g sat. fat), 10 mg chol., 456 mg sodium, 18 g carb., 1 g fiber, 7 g pro. *Diabetic Exchanges: 1 starch, 1 fat.*

SLOW COOKER
Parsley Smashed Potatoes

I love potatoes, but I don't like the work involved in making mashed potatoes from scratch. I came up with this side dish that's really easy thanks to my slow cooker.

—KATIE HAGY BLACKSBURG, SC

PREP: 20 MIN. • **COOK:** 6 HOURS
MAKES: 8 SERVINGS

- 16 small red potatoes (about 2 pounds)
- 1 celery rib, sliced
- 1 medium carrot, sliced
- ¼ cup finely chopped onion
- 2 cups chicken broth
- 1 tablespoon minced fresh parsley
- 1½ teaspoons salt, divided
- 1 teaspoon pepper, divided
- 1 garlic clove, minced
- 2 tablespoons butter, melted
  Additional minced fresh parsley

1. Place potatoes, celery, carrot and onion in a 4-qt. slow cooker. In a small bowl, mix broth, parsley, 1 teaspoon salt, ½ teaspoon pepper and garlic; pour over vegetables. Cook, covered, on low for 6-8 hours or until the potatoes are tender.
2. Transfer potatoes from slow cooker to a 15x10x1-in. pan; discard cooking liquid and vegetables. Using the bottom of a measuring cup, flatten potatoes slightly. Transfer to a large bowl; drizzle with butter. Sprinkle with the remaining salt and pepper and toss to coat. Sprinkle with additional parsley.
PER SERVING 2 smashed potatoes equals 114 cal., 3 g fat (2 g sat. fat), 8 mg chol., 190 mg sodium, 20 g carb., 2 g fiber, 2 g pro. *Diabetic Exchanges: 1 starch, ½ fat.*

PARSLEY SMASHED POTATOES

⑤INGREDIENTS FAST FIX

Avocado Tomato Salad

This simple salad is terrific with any kind of Mexican food. It makes a super appetizer spooned over toasted baguette slices. The recipe combines fresh tomatoes with avocados, a source of healthy fat.

—**GINGER BUROW** FREDERICKSBURG, TX

START TO FINISH: 15 MIN.
MAKES: 6-8 SERVINGS

- **4 cups chopped tomatoes**
- **½ cup chopped green pepper**
- **¼ cup chopped onion**
- **½ teaspoon salt**
- **⅛ teaspoon pepper**
- **2 medium ripe avocados, peeled and cubed**
- **1 tablespoon lime juice**

In a large bowl, combine the tomatoes, green pepper, onion, salt and pepper. Place the avocados in another bowl; sprinkle with lime juice and toss gently to coat. Fold into tomato mixture. Serve immediately.

PER SERVING *¾ cup equals 134 cal., 10 g fat (2 g sat. fat), 0 chol., 215 mg sodium, 11 g carb., 5 g fiber, 2 g pro.* **Diabetic Exchanges:** *2 vegetable, 2 fat.*

CHOCOLATE CHIP-CRANBERRY SCONES

FREEZE IT FAST FIX

Chocolate Chip-Cranberry Scones

My daughter started making these as a healthier alternative to cookies, since we seem to like cookies of any kind. For a more citrusy flavor, use orange-flavored cranberries.

—**NICHOLE JONES** IDAHO FALLS, ID

START TO FINISH: 30 MIN.
MAKES: 1 DOZEN

- **2 cups all-purpose flour**
- **3 tablespoons brown sugar**
- **2 teaspoons baking powder**
- **1 teaspoon grated orange peel**
- **½ teaspoon salt**
- **½ teaspoon baking soda**
- **¼ cup cold butter**
- **1 cup (8 ounces) plain yogurt**
- **1 egg yolk**
- **½ cup dried cranberries**
- **½ cup semisweet chocolate chips**

1. Preheat oven to 400°. In a large bowl, whisk the first six ingredients. Cut in butter until mixture resembles coarse crumbs. In another bowl, whisk yogurt and egg yolk; stir into crumb mixture just until moistened. Stir in cranberries and chocolate chips.

2. Turn onto a floured surface; knead gently 10 times. Pat dough into an 8-in. circle. Cut into 12 wedges. Place wedges on a baking sheet coated with cooking spray. Bake 10-12 minutes or until golden brown. Serve warm.

FREEZE OPTION *Freeze cooled scones in resealable plastic freezer bags. To use, thaw at room temperature. Or, if desired, microwave each scone on high for 20-30 seconds or until heated through.*

PER SERVING *1 scone equals 189 cal., 7 g fat (4 g sat. fat), 28 mg chol., 264 mg sodium, 29 g carb., 1 g fiber, 3 g pro.* **Diabetic Exchanges:** *2 starch, 1 fat.*

⑤INGREDIENTS
Sour Cream Cucumbers

It's been a tradition at our house to serve this dish with the other Hungarian specialties my mom learned to make from the women at church. It's especially good during the summer with fresh-picked cucumbers from the garden.

—PAMELA EATON MONCLOVA, OH

PREP: 15 MIN. + CHILLING
MAKES: 8 SERVINGS

- ½ **cup sour cream**
- 3 **tablespoons white vinegar**
- 1 **tablespoon sugar**
  Pepper to taste
- 4 **medium cucumbers, peeled if desired and thinly sliced**
- 1 **small sweet onion, thinly sliced and separated into rings**

In a large bowl, whisk sour cream, vinegar, sugar and pepper until blended. Add cucumbers and onion; toss to coat. Refrigerate, covered, at least 4 hours. Serve with a slotted spoon.

PER SERVING *¾ cup equals 62 cal., 3 g fat (2 g sat. fat), 10 mg chol., 5 mg sodium, 7 g carb., 2 g fiber, 2 g pro. **Diabetic Exchanges:** 1 vegetable, ½ fat.*

GRILLED VEGETABLE PLATTER

Grilled Vegetable Platter

Here is the best of summer in one dish! These pretty veggies are pefect for entertaining. Grilling brings out their natural sweetness, and the simple marinade really perks up the flavor.

—HEIDI HALL NORTH ST. PAUL, MN

PREP: 20 MIN. + MARINATING • **GRILL:** 10 MIN.
MAKES: 6 SERVINGS

- ¼ **cup olive oil**
- 2 **tablespoons honey**
- 4 **teaspoons balsamic vinegar**
- 1 **teaspoon dried oregano**
- ½ **teaspoon garlic powder**
- ⅛ **teaspoon pepper**
  Dash salt
- 1 **pound fresh asparagus, trimmed**
- 3 **small carrots, cut in half lengthwise**
- 1 **large sweet red pepper, cut into 1-inch strips**
- 1 **medium yellow summer squash, cut into ½-inch slices**
- 1 **medium red onion, cut into wedges**

1. In a small bowl, whisk the first seven ingredients. Place 3 tablespoons marinade in a large resealable plastic bag. Add vegetables; seal bag and turn to coat. Marinate for 1½ hours at room temperature.

2. Transfer vegetables to a grilling grid; place grid on grill rack. Grill vegetables, covered, over medium heat 8-12 minutes or until crisp-tender, turning occasionally.

3. Place vegetables on a large serving plate. Drizzle with the remaining marinade.

NOTE *If you don't have a grilling grid, use a disposable foil pan. Poke holes in the bottom of the pan with a meat fork to allow liquid to drain.*

PER SERVING *1 serving equals 144 cal., 9 g fat (1 g sat. fat), 0 chol., 50 mg sodium, 15 g carb., 3 g fiber, 2 g pro. **Diabetic Exchanges:** 2 vegetable, 2 fat.*

FAST FIX ▶ Cranberry Spinach Salad with Bacon Dressing

Salads don't get any easier to make than this! It's a cinch to whip up the dressing, too.

—ELSIE HERZOG JACKSONVILLE, NC

START TO FINISH: 15 MIN.
MAKES: 8 SERVINGS (1 CUP DRESSING)

- 2 packages (6 ounces each) fresh baby spinach
- 1 cup dried cranberries
- 1 medium red onion, sliced and separated into rings
- ½ cup lime juice
- ½ cup honey
- 2 tablespoons Dijon mustard
- 4 bacon strips, cooked and crumbled

1. In a salad bowl, combine the spinach, cranberries and onion.
2. In a small microwave-safe bowl, whisk the lime juice, honey and mustard; stir in bacon. Microwave until warm. Serve with salad.
PER SERVING *1½ cups equals 153 cal., 2 g fat (1 g sat. fat), 4 mg chol., 198 mg sodium, 35 g carb., 2 g fiber, 3 g pro.*

BASIL CORN & TOMATO BAKE

Basil Corn & Tomato Bake

When sweet Jersey corn is in season, I turn to this luscious recipe. It's studded with tomatoes, zucchini and basil.

—ERIN CHILCOAT CENTRAL ISLIP, NY

PREP: 30 MIN. • **BAKE:** 45 MIN. + STANDING
MAKES: 10 SERVINGS

- 2 teaspoons olive oil
- 1 medium onion, chopped
- 2 eggs
- 1 can (10¾ ounces) reduced-fat reduced-sodium condensed cream of celery soup, undiluted
- 4 cups fresh or frozen corn
- 1 small zucchini, chopped
- 1 medium tomato, seeded and chopped
- ¾ cup soft whole wheat bread crumbs
- ⅓ cup minced fresh basil
- ½ teaspoon salt
- ½ cup shredded part-skim mozzarella cheese
  Additional minced fresh basil, optional

1. Preheat oven to 350°. In a small skillet, heat oil over medium heat. Add onion; cook and stir until tender. In a large bowl, whisk eggs and condensed soup until blended. Stir in vegetables, bread crumbs, basil, salt and onion. Transfer mixture to an 11x7-in. baking dish coated with cooking spray.
2. Bake, uncovered, 40-45 minutes or until bubbly. Sprinkle with cheese. Bake 5-10 minutes longer or until cheese is melted. Let stand 10 minutes before serving. If desired, sprinkle with additional basil.
NOTE *To make soft bread crumbs, tear bread into pieces and place in a food processor or blender. Cover and pulse until crumbs form. One slice of bread yields ½ to ¾ cup crumbs.*
PER SERVING *¾ cup equals 131 cal., 4 g fat (1 g sat. fat), 47 mg chol., 299 mg sodium, 20 g carb., 3 g fiber, 6 g pro.* **Diabetic Exchanges:** *1 starch, ½ fat.*

Mushroom Bean Medley

Fresh mushrooms, onion and a splash of white wine really dress up frozen veggies. This side dish is an ideal accompaniment to almost any entree.

—*TASTE OF HOME* TEST KITCHEN

START TO FINISH: 15 MIN.
MAKES: 4 SERVINGS

- ½ **pound sliced fresh mushrooms**
- 1 **small onion, halved and sliced**
- 2 **tablespoons reduced-fat butter**
- 1 **package (16 ounces) frozen waxed beans, green beans and carrots**
- ½ **cup white wine or chicken broth**
- ¼ **teaspoon salt**
- ¼ **teaspoon pepper**

Saute mushrooms and onion in butter in a large skillet until tender. Add vegetables and wine. Bring to a boil. Reduce heat; cover and simmer for 5 minutes or until vegetables are tender. Drain; sprinkle with salt and pepper.
PER SERVING *1 cup equals 104 cal., 3 g fat (2 g sat. fat), 10 mg chol., 190 mg sodium, 13 g carb., 4 g fiber, 4 g pro. Diabetic Exchanges: 2 vegetable, 1 fat.*

Honey-Oat Pan Rolls

You won't feel guilty reaching for a second helping of these tender rolls. Whole wheat flour and oats make them tasty and nutritious.

—**ARLENE BUTLER** OGDEN, UT

PREP: 45 MIN. + RISING • **BAKE:** 20 MIN.
MAKES: 2 DOZEN

- 2½ to 2¾ **cups all-purpose flour**
- ¾ **cup whole wheat flour**
- ½ **cup old-fashioned oats**
- 2 **packages (¼ ounce each) active dry yeast**
- 1 **teaspoon salt**
- 1 **cup water**
- ¼ **cup honey**
- 5 **tablespoons butter, divided**
- 1 **egg**

1. In a large bowl, mix 1 cup all-purpose flour, whole wheat flour, oats, yeast and salt. In a small saucepan, heat water, honey and 4 tablespoons butter to 120°-130°. Add to dry ingredients; beat on medium speed 2 minutes. Add egg; beat on high 2 minutes. Stir in enough remaining all-purpose flour to form a soft dough (dough will be sticky).
2. Turn dough onto a floured surface; knead until smooth and elastic, about 6-8 minutes. Place in a greased bowl, turning once to grease the top. Cover with plastic wrap and let rise in a warm place until doubled, about 1 hour.
3. Punch down dough. Turn onto a lightly floured surface; divide and shape into 24 balls. Place in a greased 13x9-in. baking pan. Cover with a kitchen towel; let rise in a warm place until doubled, about 30 minutes.
4. Preheat oven to 375°. Bake 20-22 minutes or until golden brown. Melt remaining butter; brush over rolls. Remove from pan to a wire rack.
PER SERVING *1 roll equals 103 cal., 3 g fat (2 g sat. fat), 15 mg chol., 126 mg sodium, 17 g carb., 1 g fiber, 3 g pro. Diabetic Exchanges: 1 starch, ½ fat.*

HONEY-OAT PAN ROLLS

(5) INGREDIENTS FAST FIX
Fresh Green Beans & Garlic

I am a firm believer that fresh is best. I developed this recipe to take advantage of our garden's bounty. It really shows off the full flavor of the green beans.

—CAROL MAYER SPARTA, IL

START TO FINISH: 25 MIN.
MAKES: 8 SERVINGS

- 2 tablespoons canola oil
- 2 tablespoons butter
- 4 garlic cloves, sliced
- 2 pounds fresh green beans
- 1 cup reduced-sodium chicken broth
- ½ teaspoon salt
- ¼ teaspoon pepper

1. In a Dutch oven, heat oil and butter over medium-high heat. Add garlic; cook and stir 45-60 seconds or until golden. Using a slotted spoon, remove garlic from pan; reserve. Add green beans to pan; cook and stir 4-5 minutes or until crisp-tender.

2. Stir in broth, salt and pepper. Bring to a boil. Reduce heat; simmer, uncovered, 8-10 minutes or just until beans are tender and broth is almost evaporated, stirring occasionally. Stir in reserved garlic.

PER SERVING *1 serving equals 91 cal., 6 g fat (2 g sat. fat), 8 mg chol., 245 mg sodium, 8 g carb., 3 g fiber, 2 g pro. **Diabetic Exchanges:** 1½ fat, 1 vegetable.*

FAST FIX
Glazed Sprouts and Carrots

Your veggies will garner big smiles with the addition of just a few tried-and-true staples. The hint of nutmeg may even remind you of the holidays.

—PAGE ALEXANDER BALDWIN CITY, KS

START TO FINISH: 20 MIN.
MAKES: 4 SERVINGS

- ½ cup water
- 1 cup halved fresh Brussels sprouts
- 2 medium carrots, sliced
- 1 teaspoon cornstarch
- ½ teaspoon sugar
- ¼ teaspoon salt
- ⅛ teaspoon ground nutmeg
- ⅓ cup orange juice

1. Bring water to a boil in a large saucepan over medium heat. Add vegetables. Cover and simmer for 6-8 minutes or until almost tender; drain and return to pan.

2. Combine the cornstarch, sugar, salt if desired, nutmeg and orange juice; stir until smooth. Pour over the vegetables. Bring to a boil; cook and stir for 2 minutes or until thickened.

PER SERVING *½ cup equals 37 cal., trace fat (trace sat. fat), 0 chol., 176 mg sodium, 8 g carb., 2 g fiber, 1 g pro. **Diabetic Exchange:** 1 vegetable.*

FRESH GREEN BEANS & GARLIC

FAST FIX

Colorful Corn and Bean Salad

This quick recipe couldn't be easier...the liquid from the corn relish makes the fuss-free dressing. And because there's no mayo, it's a perfect salad to bring along on summer outings.

—TERRYANN MOORE VINELAND, NJ

START TO FINISH: 15 MIN.
MAKES: 12 SERVINGS (½ CUP EACH)

- 1 **can (15 ounces) black beans, rinsed and drained**
- 1 **jar (13 ounces) corn relish**
- ½ **cup canned kidney beans**
- ½ **cup quartered cherry tomatoes**
- ½ **cup chopped celery**
- ¼ **cup chopped sweet orange pepper**
- ¼ **cup sliced pimiento-stuffed olives**
- 2 **teaspoons minced fresh parsley**

In a large bowl, combine all ingredients. Cover and refrigerate until serving.
PER SERVING *½ cup equals 80 cal., 1 g fat (trace sat. fat), 0 chol., 217 mg sodium, 16 g carb., 2 g fiber, 2 g pro. Diabetic Exchange: 1 starch.*

HOMEMADE PASTA

(5) INGREDIENTS

Homemade Pasta

Try your hand at homemade pasta with this easy-to-work-with spinach dough. You don't need a pasta maker or other special equipment.

—*TASTE OF HOME* TEST KITCHEN

PREP: 30 MIN. + STANDING
COOK: 10 MIN./BATCH
MAKES: 8 SERVINGS

- 1 **package (10 ounces) frozen chopped spinach, thawed and squeezed dry**
- ¼ **cup packed fresh parsley sprigs**
- 3½ **to 4 cups all-purpose flour**
- ½ **teaspoon salt**
- 4 **eggs**
- 3 **tablespoons water**
- 1 **tablespoon olive oil**
  Marinara sauce

1. Place spinach and parsley in a food processor; cover and process until finely chopped. Add 3½ cups flour and salt; process until blended. Add the eggs, water and oil. Process for 15-20 seconds or until the dough forms a ball.

2. Turn onto a floured surface; knead for 8-10 minutes or until smooth and elastic, adding remaining flour if necessary. Cover dough and let rest for 30 minutes. Divide into fourths.

3. On a floured surface, roll each portion of dough to ¹⁄₁₆-in. thickness. Dust top of dough with flour to prevent sticking; cut into ¼-in. slices. Separate the slices; allow noodles to dry on kitchen towels at least 1 hour before cooking.

4. To cook, fill a Dutch oven three-fourths full with water. Bring to a boil. Add noodles in batches; cook, uncovered, for 8-10 minutes or until tender. Drain. Serve with sauce.

PER SERVING *1 cup (calculated without sauce) equals 259 cal., 5 g fat (1 g sat. fat), 106 mg chol., 211 mg sodium, 43 g carb., 3 g fiber, 10 g pro.*

PER SERVING *¾ cup equals 136 cal., 5 g fat (3 g sat. fat), 15 mg chol., 292 mg sodium, 19 g carb., 1 g fiber, 5 g pro. Diabetic Exchanges: 1 starch, 1 fat.*

THE SKINNY

The makeover recipe decreased sodium by 54% by using reduced-sodium soup, ½ teaspoon salt instead of 1 teaspoon, and 1 cup sharp cheddar cheese instead of the original's 2 cups of regular cheddar.

ORIGINAL	MAKEOVER
259 Calories	136 Calories
12g Fat	5g Fat
8g Sat. Fat	3g Sat. Fat

MAKEOVER HASH BROWN CASSEROLE

(5) INGREDIENTS FAST FIX

Seasoned Broccoli Spears

Dressing up broccoli is a snap with this recipe. We flavored fresh spears with lemon-pepper, garlic salt and thyme.
—**TASTE OF HOME** TEST KITCHEN

START TO FINISH: 10 MIN.
MAKES: 6 SERVINGS

- 1½ **pounds fresh broccoli, cut into spears**
- ¼ **cup water**
- 2 **tablespoons butter**
- 1 **teaspoon lemon-pepper seasoning**
- ½ **teaspoon garlic salt**
- ½ **teaspoon dried thyme**

Place the broccoli in a microwave-safe bowl; add water. Cover and microwave on high for 4-5 minutes or until tender; drain. Stir in the remaining ingredients.
NOTE *This recipe was tested in a 1,100-watt microwave.*
PER SERVING *¾ cup equals 66 cal., 4 g fat (2 g sat. fat), 10 mg chol., 285 mg sodium, 6 g carb., 3 g fiber, 3 g pro. Diabetic Exchanges: 1 vegetable, 1 fat.*

Makeover Hash Brown Casserole

As a side for brunch or dinner, this lightened-up casserole is just as good with scrambled eggs as it is with your favorite roast. Kids especially love its cheesy flavor and crisp topping.
—**KELLY KIRBY** VICTORIA, BC

PREP: 15 MIN. • **BAKE:** 40 MIN.
MAKES: 12 SERVINGS

- 1 **package (30 ounces) frozen shredded hash brown potatoes, thawed**
- 1 **can (10¾ ounces) reduced-fat reduced-sodium condensed cream of chicken soup, undiluted**
- 1 **cup (4 ounces) shredded reduced-fat sharp cheddar cheese**
- ⅔ **cup reduced-fat sour cream**
- 1 **small onion, chopped**
- ½ **teaspoon salt**
- ½ **teaspoon pepper**
- ¼ **cup crushed cornflakes**
- 1 **tablespoon butter, melted**

1. Preheat oven to 350°. In a large bowl, mix the first seven ingredients. Transfer to a 13x9-in. or 3-qt. baking dish coated with cooking spray.
2. In a small bowl, toss the cornflakes with melted butter; sprinkle over the top. Bake for 40-45 minutes or until golden brown.

Cranberry Couscous

Here's a fabulous dish to serve alongside chicken, pork chops or even lamb. If you like, toss in some almonds or pistachios at the end for a little crunch.

—TASTE OF HOME TEST KITCHEN

START TO FINISH: 15 MIN.
MAKES: 6 SERVINGS

- 1 can (14½ ounces) chicken broth
- 1 tablespoon butter
- 1½ cups uncooked couscous
- ¼ cup dried cranberries, chopped
- 3 tablespoons chopped green onions

Bring broth and butter to a boil in a large saucepan. Stir in the couscous, cranberries and onions. Remove from the heat. Cover and let stand for 5 minutes or until broth is absorbed. Fluff with a fork.

PER SERVING *¾ cup equals 202 cal., 3 g fat (1 g sat. fat), 5 mg chol., 295 mg sodium, 39 g carb., 2 g fiber, 7 g pro.*

Authentic Boston Brown Bread

The rustic, old-fashioned flavor of this hearty bread is out of this world. Recipes like this remind me why I find cooking and baking not only fun, but very fulfilling.

—SHARON DELANEY-CHRONIS
SOUTH MILWAUKEE, WI

PREP: 20 MIN. • **COOK:** 50 MIN. + STANDING
MAKES: 1 LOAF (12 SLICES)

- ½ cup cornmeal
- ½ cup whole wheat flour
- ½ cup rye flour
- ½ teaspoon baking powder
- ½ teaspoon baking soda
- ¼ teaspoon salt
- 1 cup buttermilk
- ⅓ cup molasses
- 2 tablespoons brown sugar
- 1 tablespoon canola oil
- 3 tablespoons chopped walnuts, toasted
- 3 tablespoons raisins
  Cream cheese, softened, optional

1. In a large bowl, combine the first six ingredients. In another bowl, whisk the buttermilk, molasses, brown sugar and oil. Stir into the dry ingredients just until moistened. Fold in walnuts and raisins. Transfer to a greased 8x4-in. loaf pan; cover with foil.

2. Place pan on a rack in a boiling-water canner or other large, deep pot; add 1 in. of hot water to pot. Bring to a gentle boil; cover and steam for 45-50 minutes or until a toothpick inserted near the center comes out clean, adding more water to the pot as needed.

3. Remove pan from the pot; let stand for 10 minutes before removing bread from pan to a wire rack. Serve with cream cheese if desired.

PER SERVING *1 slice equals 124 cal., 3 g fat (trace sat. fat), 1 mg chol., 145 mg sodium, 23 g carb., 2 g fiber, 3 g pro.* **Diabetic Exchanges:** *1½ starch, ½ fat.*

AUTHENTIC BOSTON BROWN BREAD

SWISS BEER BREAD

Swiss Beer Bread

This recipe is a favorite because it isn't greasy like other cheese breads I have tried. It will not last long!

—DEBI WALLACE CHESTERTOWN, NY

PREP: 15 MIN. • **BAKE:** 50 MIN. + COOLING
MAKES: 1 LOAF (12 SLICES)

- 4 ounces Jarlsberg or Swiss cheese
- 3 cups all-purpose flour
- 3 tablespoons sugar
- 3 teaspoons baking powder
- 1½ teaspoons salt
- ½ teaspoon pepper
- 1 bottle (12 ounces) beer or nonalcoholic beer
- 2 tablespoons butter, melted

1. Divide cheese in half. Cut half of cheese into ¼-in. cubes; shred remaining cheese. In a large bowl, combine the flour, sugar, baking powder, salt and pepper. Stir beer into dry ingredients just until moistened. Fold in cheese.

2. Transfer to a greased 8x4-in. loaf pan. Drizzle with butter. Bake at 375° for 50-60 minutes or until a toothpick inserted near the center comes out clean. Cool the bread for 10 minutes before removing from pan to a wire rack.

PER SERVING *1 slice equals 182 cal., 5 g fat (3 g sat. fat), 11 mg chol., 453 mg sodium, 28 g carb., 1 g fiber, 6 g pro. Diabetic Exchanges: 2 starch, ½ fat.*

FAST FIX
Fresh Apple & Pear Salad

Crunchy apples and ripe, juicy pears are fantastic tossed with crisp, cool cukes and a spicy dressing. This lovely combination of ingredients comes together quickly in one flavorful dish.

—JEAN ECOS HARTLAND, WI

START TO FINISH: 20 MIN.
MAKES: 8 SERVINGS

- 4 medium apples, thinly sliced
- 2 medium pears, thinly sliced
- 1 medium cucumber, seeded and chopped
- 1 medium red onion, halved and thinly sliced
- ¼ cup apple cider or juice
- 1 tablespoon snipped fresh dill or minced fresh tarragon
- 1 tablespoon olive oil
- 1 tablespoon spicy brown mustard
- 2 teaspoons brown sugar
- ½ teaspoon salt
- ¼ teaspoon pepper

In a large bowl, combine apples, pears, cucumber and onion. In a small bowl, whisk remaining ingredients until blended. Pour over apple mixture and toss to coat. Refrigerate until serving.

PER SERVING *1 cup equals 96 cal., 2 g fat (trace sat. fat), 0 chol., 175 mg sodium, 20 g carb., 4 g fiber, 1 g pro. Diabetic Exchanges: 1 fruit, ½ fat.*

Tuscan-Style Roasted Asparagus

This is especially wonderful when locally grown asparagus is in season. It's easy for celebrations because you can serve it hot or cold.

—**JANNINE FISK** MALDEN, MA

PREP: 20 MIN. • **BAKE:** 15 MIN.
MAKES: 8 SERVINGS

- 1½ pounds fresh asparagus, trimmed
- 1½ cups grape tomatoes, halved
- 3 tablespoons pine nuts
- 3 tablespoons olive oil, divided
- 2 garlic cloves, minced
- 1 teaspoon kosher salt
- ½ teaspoon pepper
- 1 tablespoon lemon juice
- ⅓ cup grated Parmesan cheese
- 1 teaspoon grated lemon peel

1. Preheat oven to 400°. Place the asparagus, tomatoes and pine nuts on a foil-lined 15x10x1-in. baking pan. Mix 2 tablespoons oil, garlic, salt and pepper; add to asparagus and toss to coat.
2. Bake 15-20 minutes or just until asparagus is tender. Drizzle with remaining oil and the lemon juice; sprinkle with cheese and lemon peel. Toss to combine.

PER SERVING *1 serving equals 95 cal., 8 g fat (2 g sat. fat), 3 mg chol., 294 mg sodium, 4 g carb., 1 g fiber, 3 g pro. Diabetic Exchanges: 1½ fat, 1 vegetable.*

FAST FIX
Lemon Couscous with Broccoli

I combined two recipes to create this side with broccoli and pasta. The splash of lemon adds nice flavor. Instead of toasted almonds, you could also sprinkle servings with grated Parmesan cheese.

—**BETH DAUENHAUER** PUEBLO, CO

START TO FINISH: 25 MIN.
MAKES: 6 SERVINGS

- 1 tablespoon olive oil
- 4 cups fresh broccoli florets, cut into small pieces
- 1 cup uncooked whole wheat couscous
- 2 garlic cloves, minced
- 1¼ cups reduced-sodium chicken broth
- 1 teaspoon grated lemon peel
- 1 teaspoon lemon juice
- ½ teaspoon salt
- ½ teaspoon dried basil
- ¼ teaspoon coarsely ground pepper
- 1 tablespoon slivered almonds, toasted

1. In a large skillet, heat oil over medium-high heat. Add broccoli; cook and stir until crisp-tender.
2. Add couscous and garlic; cook and stir 1-2 minutes longer. Stir in broth, lemon peel, lemon juice and seasonings; bring to a boil. Remove from heat; let stand, covered, 5-10 minutes or until broth is absorbed. Fluff with a fork. Sprinkle with toasted almonds.

PER SERVING *⅔ cup equals 115 cal., 3 g fat (trace sat. fat), 0 chol., 328 mg sodium, 18 g carb., 4 g fiber, 5 g pro. Diabetic Exchanges: 1 starch, ½ fat.*

LEMON COUSCOUS WITH BROCCOLI

CRUSTY HOMEMADE BREAD

Crusty Homemade Bread

Crackling homemade bread makes an average day extraordinary. Enjoy this beautiful loaf as is, or stir in a few favorites like cheese, garlic, herbs or dried fruits. Now there's no need to go to a bakery.

—**MEGUMI GARCIA** MILWAUKEE, WI

PREP: 20 MIN. + RISING
BAKE: 50 MIN. + COOLING
MAKES: 1 LOAF (16 SLICES)

- 1½ teaspoons active dry yeast
- 1¾ cups water (70° to 75°)
- 3½ cups plus 1 tablespoon all-purpose flour, divided
- 2 teaspoons salt
- 1 tablespoon cornmeal or additional flour

1. In a small bowl, dissolve yeast in water. In a large bowl, mix 3½ cups flour and salt. Using a rubber spatula, stir in yeast mixture to form a soft, sticky dough. Do not knead. Cover with plastic wrap; let rise at room temperature 1 hour.

2. Punch down dough. Turn onto a lightly floured surface; pat into a 9-in. square. Fold square into thirds, forming a 9x3-in. rectangle. Fold rectangle into thirds, forming a 3-in. square. Turn dough over; place in a greased bowl. Cover with plastic wrap; let rise at room temperature until almost doubled, about 1 hour.

3. Punch down dough and repeat folding process. Return dough to bowl; refrigerate, covered, overnight.

4. Dust bottom of a disposable foil roasting pan with cornmeal. Turn dough onto a floured surface. Knead gently 6-8 times; shape into a 6-in. round loaf. Place in prepared pan; dust top with remaining 1 tablespoon flour. Cover pan with plastic wrap; let dough rise at room temperature until it expands to a 7½-in.-loaf, about 1¼ hours.

5. Preheat oven to 500°. Using a sharp knife, make a slash (¼ inch deep) across top of loaf. Cover pan tightly with foil. Bake on lowest oven rack 25 minutes.

6. Reduce oven setting to 450°. Remove foil; bake bread 25-30 minutes longer or until deep golden brown. Remove loaf to a wire rack to cool.

FOR CHEDDAR CHEESE BREAD
Prepare dough as directed. After refrigerating dough overnight, knead in 4 ounces diced sharp cheddar cheese before shaping.

FOR RUSTIC CRANBERRY & ORANGE BREAD *Prepare dough as directed. After refrigerating dough overnight, knead in 1 cup dried cranberries and 4 teaspoons grated orange peel before shaping.*

FOR GARLIC & OREGANO BREAD
Prepare dough as directed. After refrigerating dough overnight, microwave ½ cup peeled and quartered garlic cloves with ¼ cup 2% milk on high for 45 seconds. Drain garlic, discarding milk; knead garlic and 2 tablespoons minced fresh oregano into dough before shaping.

PER SERVING *1 slice (calculated without add-ins) equals 105 cal., trace fat (trace sat. fat), 0 chol., 296 mg sodium, 22 g carb., 1 g fiber, 3 g pro.*

FAST FIX

Feta Romaine Salad

My friend Cathy, who is of Greek heritage, prepared this simple salad for me. She served it with lamb chops and pitas to create a classic Mediterranean meal!

—**MICHAEL VOLPATT** SAN FRANCISCO, CA

START TO FINISH: 15 MIN.
MAKES: 6 SERVINGS

- 1 bunch romaine, chopped
- 3 plum tomatoes, seeded and chopped
- 1 cup (4 ounces) crumbled feta cheese
- 1 cup chopped seeded cucumber
- ½ cup Greek olives, chopped
- 2 tablespoons minced fresh parsley
- 2 tablespoons minced fresh cilantro
- 3 tablespoons lemon juice
- 2 tablespoons olive oil
- ¼ teaspoon pepper

In a large bowl, combine the first seven ingredients. In a small bowl, whisk the remaining ingredients. Drizzle over salad; toss to coat. Serve immediately.

PER SERVING *1⅓ cups equals 139 cal., 11 g fat (3 g sat. fat), 10 mg chol., 375 mg sodium, 6 g carb., 3 g fiber, 5 g pro.* **Diabetic Exchanges: 2 fat, 1 vegetable.**

CRANBERRY
QUICK BREAD

Cranberry Quick Bread

My mother loved to make cranberry bread. I usually stock up on cranberries when they're in season and freeze them just so I can enjoy this special recipe year-round.

—KAREN CZECHOWICZ OCALA, FL

PREP: 20 MIN. • **BAKE:** 45 MIN. + COOLING
MAKES: 1 LOAF (12 SLICES)

- 1½ **cups all-purpose flour**
- ¾ **cup sugar**
- 1 **teaspoon baking powder**
- ¼ **teaspoon salt**
- ¼ **teaspoon baking soda**
- 1 **large egg**
- ½ **cup orange juice**
- 2 **tablespoons butter, melted**
- 1 **tablespoon water**
- 1½ **cups fresh or frozen cranberries, halved**

1. Preheat oven to 350°. In a large bowl, combine first five ingredients. In a small bowl, whisk egg, orange juice, butter and water. Stir into dry ingredients just until moistened. Fold in cranberries.

2. Transfer to an 8x4-in. loaf pan coated with cooking spray and sprinkled with flour. Bake 45-50 minutes or until a toothpick inserted near the center comes out clean. Cool 10 minutes before removing from pan to a wire rack.

PER SERVING *1 slice equals 138 cal., 2 g fat (1 g sat. fat), 23 mg chol., 129 mg sodium, 27 g carb., 1 g fiber, 2 g pro. Diabetic Exchange: 2 starch.*

Roasted Green Vegetable Medley

Roasting vegetables like broccoli, green beans and Brussels sprouts is a great way to serve them, and almost any veggie combo works. So get creative.

—SUZAN CROUCH GRAND PRAIRIE, TX

PREP: 15 MIN. • **BAKE:** 20 MIN.
MAKES: 12 SERVINGS (¾ CUP EACH)

- 2 **cups fresh broccoli florets**
- 1 **pound thin fresh green beans, trimmed and cut into 2-inch pieces**
- 10 **small fresh mushrooms, halved**
- 8 **fresh Brussels sprouts, halved**
- 2 **medium carrots, cut into ¼-inch slices**
- 1 **medium onion, sliced**
- 3 **to 5 garlic cloves, thinly sliced**
- 4 **tablespoons olive oil, divided**
- ½ **cup grated Parmesan cheese**
- 3 **tablespoons julienned fresh basil leaves, optional**
- 2 **tablespoons minced fresh parsley**
- 2 **tablespoons lemon juice**
- 1 **tablespoon grated lemon peel**
- ¼ **teaspoon salt**
- ¼ **teaspoon pepper**

1. Preheat oven to 425°. Place the first seven ingredients in a large bowl; drizzle with 2 tablespoons oil and toss to coat. Divide between two 15x10x1-in. baking pans coated with cooking spray. Roast 20-25 minutes or until tender, stirring occasionally.

2. Transfer to a large serving bowl. In a small bowl, mix remaining oil with remaining ingredients; add to vegetables and toss to combine.

PER SERVING *¾ cup equals 80 cal., 5 g fat (1 g sat. fat), 3 mg chol., 63 mg sodium, 7 g carb., 2 g fiber, 3 g pro. Diabetic Exchanges: 1 vegetable, 1 fat.*

GRILLED POTATOES & PEPPERS

Smoky Cauliflower

The smoked Spanish paprika gives a simple side of cauliflower more depth of flavor. We're fans of roasted veggies of any kind, and this one is a definite favorite.

—**JULIETTE MULHOLLAND** CORVALLIS, OR

START TO FINISH: 30 MIN.
MAKES: 8 SERVINGS

- 1 **large head cauliflower, broken into 1-inch florets (about 9 cups)**
- 2 **tablespoons olive oil**
- 1 **teaspoon smoked paprika**
- ¾ **teaspoon salt**
- 2 **garlic cloves, minced**
- 2 **tablespoons minced fresh parsley**

1. Place cauliflower in a large bowl. Combine oil, paprika and salt. Drizzle over cauliflower; toss to coat. Transfer to a 15x10x1-in. baking pan. Bake at 450° for 10 minutes.
2. Stir in garlic. Bake 10-15 minutes longer or until cauliflower is tender and lightly browned, stirring occasionally. Sprinkle with parsley.
PER SERVING *¾ cup equals 58 cal., 4 g fat (trace sat. fat), 0 chol., 254 mg sodium, 6 g carb., 3 g fiber, 2 g pro. Diabetic Exchanges: 1 vegetable, ½ fat.*

Grilled Potatoes & Peppers

My husband, Matt, grills these potatoes for both breakfast and dinner gatherings. Besides the guests we share it with, this recipe is always one of the best parts of the meal!

—**SUSAN NORDIN** WARREN, PA

PREP: 20 MIN. • **GRILL:** 40 MIN.
MAKES: 10 SERVINGS

- 8 **medium red potatoes, cut into wedges**
- 2 **medium green peppers, sliced**
- 1 **medium onion, cut into thin wedges**
- 2 **tablespoons olive oil**
- 5 **garlic cloves, thinly sliced**
- 1 **teaspoon paprika**
- 1 **teaspoon steak seasoning**
- 1 **teaspoon Italian seasoning**
- ¼ **teaspoon salt**
- ¼ **teaspoon pepper**

1. In a large bowl, combine all ingredients. Divide between two pieces of heavy-duty foil (about 18 in. square). Fold foil around potato mixture and crimp edges to seal.
2. Grill, covered, over medium heat 40-45 minutes or until potatoes are tender. Open foil carefully to allow steam to escape.
PER SERVING *¾ cup equals 103 cal., 3 g fat (trace sat. fat), 0 chol., 134 mg sodium, 18 g carb., 2 g fiber, 2 g pro. Diabetic Exchanges: 1 starch, ½ fat.*

TOP TIP

Smoked paprika's rich, smoky and slightly sweet flavor adds complexity to dishes. The spice is especially good in lentil and bean soups and vegetable recipes, where it lends a robust, meaty flavor. You could also use it in recipes that call for ground chipotle pepper. Just add cayenne or chili powder to boost the heat if desired.

Roasted Harvest Vegetables

Here is my favorite side dish to serve whenever we have company. I like to pair it with any kind of roasted meat.

—AMY LOGAN MILL CREEK, PA

PREP: 20 MIN. • **BAKE:** 30 MIN.
MAKES: 9 SERVINGS

- 8 small red potatoes, quartered
- 2 small onions, quartered
- 1 medium zucchini, halved and sliced
- 1 medium yellow summer squash, halved and sliced
- ½ pound fresh baby carrots
- 1 cup fresh cauliflowerets
- 1 cup fresh broccoli florets
- ¼ cup olive oil
- 1 tablespoon garlic powder
- 1½ teaspoons dried rosemary, crushed
- ½ teaspoon dried thyme
- ¼ teaspoon salt
- ¼ teaspoon pepper

1. Place the vegetables in a large bowl. Combine the remaining ingredients; drizzle over the vegetables and toss to coat.

2. Transfer to two greased 15-in. x 10-in. x 1-in. baking pans. Bake at 400° for 30-35 minutes or until tender, stirring occasionally.

PER SERVING *¾ cup equals 114 cal., 6 g fat (1 g sat. fat), 0 chol., 97 mg sodium, 13 g carb., 3 g fiber, 2 g pro. Diabetic Exchanges: 1 vegetable, 1 fat, ½ starch.*

(5) INGREDIENTS FAST FIX

Grilled Corn Relish

This colorful relish is a great way to get kids to eat their veggies. It's an instant upgrade for hot dogs!

—ELLEN RILEY BIRMINGHAM, AL

START TO FINISH: 25 MIN.
MAKES: 2 CUPS

- 1 large sweet red pepper
- 2 medium ears sweet corn, husks removed
- 5 tablespoons honey Dijon vinaigrette, divided
- 2 green onions, thinly sliced
- ½ teaspoon coarsely ground pepper
- ¼ teaspoon salt

1. Cut red pepper lengthwise in half; remove seeds. Grill red pepper and corn, covered, over medium heat for 10-15 minutes or until tender, turning and basting occasionally with 3 tablespoons vinaigrette.

2. Remove corn from cobs and chop red pepper; transfer to a small bowl. Add green onions, pepper, salt and the remaining vinaigrette; toss to combine.

PER SERVING *¼ cup equals 42 cal., 1 g fat (trace sat. fat), 0 chol., 157 mg sodium, 8 g carb., 1 g fiber, 1 g pro. Diabetic Exchange: ½ starch.*

ROASTED HARVEST VEGETABLES

PUMPKIN DINNER FOLLS

⑤ INGREDIENTS FAST FIX

Colorful Broccoli Rice

I found this quick and simple recipe years ago. It's a favorite with many meals. The buttery flavor makes it a great side for all kinds of meats.

—GALE LALMOND DEERING, NH

START TO FINISH: 15 MIN.
MAKES: 2 SERVINGS

- ⅔ **cup water**
- 2 **teaspoons butter**
- 1 **teaspoon reduced-sodium chicken bouillon granules**
- 1 **cup coarsely chopped fresh broccoli**
- ½ **cup instant brown rice**
- 2 **tablespoons chopped sweet red pepper**

1. In a small microwave-safe bowl, combine the water, butter and bouillon. Cover and microwave on high for 1½ minutes; stir until blended. Stir in the broccoli, rice and red pepper. Cover and cook for 6-7 minutes or until rice is tender.
2. Let stand for 5 minutes. Fluff with a fork.
NOTE *This recipe was tested in a 1,100-watt microwave.*
PER SERVING *½ cup equals 136 cal., 5 g fat (2 g sat. fat), 10 mg chol., 197 mg sodium, 20 g carb., 2 g fiber, 3 g pro. Diabetic Exchanges: 1 starch, 1 fat.*

Pumpkin Dinner Rolls

Serve these spicy-sweet dinner rolls and get ready to hear a chorus of "yums" in your house!

—LINNEA REIN TOPEKA, KS

PREP: 20 MIN. + RISING • **BAKE:** 20 MIN.
MAKES: 20 ROLLS

- ¾ **cup milk**
- ⅓ **cup packed brown sugar**
- 5 **tablespoons butter, divided**
- 1 **teaspoon salt**
- 2 **packages (¼ ounce each) active dry yeast**
- ½ **cup warm water (110° to 115°)**
- 2 **to 2½ cups all-purpose flour**
- 1½ **cups whole wheat flour**
- ½ **cup canned pumpkin**
- ½ **teaspoon ground cinnamon**
- ¼ **teaspoon ground ginger**
- ¼ **teaspoon ground nutmeg**

1. In a small saucepan, heat the milk, brown sugar, 4 tablespoons butter and salt to 110°-115°; set aside.
2. In a large bowl, dissolve the yeast in warm water. Stir in the milk mixture. Add 1½ cups all-purpose flour, whole wheat flour, pumpkin, cinnamon, ginger and nutmeg. Beat until smooth. Add enough of the remaining all-purpose flour to form a soft dough.
3. Turn onto a floured surface; knead until dough is smooth and elastic, about 6-8 minutes. Place in a greased bowl, turning once to grease top. Cover and let rise in a warm place until doubled, about 1 hour.
4. Punch dough down. Divide into 20 pieces; shape into balls. Place in a greased 13x9-in. baking pan. Cover dough and let rise for 30 minutes or until doubled.
5. Preheat oven to 375°. Melt remaining butter; brush over dough. Bake 20-25 minutes or until golden brown. Remove from pan to a wire rack. Serve warm.
PER SERVING *1 roll equals 124 cal., 3 g fat (2 g sat. fat), 9 mg chol., 154 mg sodium, 21 g carb., 2 g fiber, 3 g pro. Diabetic Exchanges: 1½ starch, ½ fat.*

CORN AND BROCCOLI
IN CHEESE SAUCE

1½ **pounds red potatoes, cut into**
1-inch cubes
7½ **cups chopped cabbage**
8 **green onions, chopped**
1 **cup fat-free milk**
⅓ **cup reduced-fat butter**
¾ **teaspoon salt**
¼ **teaspoon pepper**

1. Place potatoes in a Dutch oven; cover with water. Bring to a boil. Cover and cook over medium heat for 12-15 minutes or until potatoes are almost tender, adding the cabbage during the last 5 minutes of cooking.

2. Meanwhile, in a small saucepan, combine green onions and milk. Bring to a boil. Reduce heat; simmer, uncovered, for 5-6 minutes or until onions are soft.

3. Drain potato mixture. Mash with milk mixture, butter, salt and pepper.

NOTE *This recipe was tested in a 1,100-watt microwave.*

PER SERVING *¾ cup equals 131 cal., 4 g fat (2 g sat. fat), 11 mg chol., 320 mg sodium, 22 g carb., 4 g fiber, 4 g pro.* **Diabetic Exchanges:** *1 starch, 1 vegetable, 1 fat.*

SLOW COOKER
Corn and Broccoli in Cheese Sauce

This popular side dish is a standby at our house. My daughter likes to stir leftover ham into it. No one will guess that it's lightened up!

—JOYCE JOHNSON UNIONTOWN, OH

PREP: 10 MIN. • **COOK:** 3 HOURS
MAKES: 8 SERVINGS

1 **package (16 ounces) frozen corn, thawed**
1 **package (16 ounces) frozen broccoli florets, thawed**
4 **ounces reduced-fat process cheese (Velveeta), cubed**
½ **cup shredded cheddar cheese**
1 **can (10¼ ounces) reduced-fat reduced-sodium condensed cream of chicken soup, undiluted**
¼ **cup fat-free milk**

1. In a 4-qt. slow cooker, combine the corn, broccoli and cheeses. In a small bowl, combine soup and milk; pour over vegetable mixture.

2. Cover and cook on low for 3-4 hours or until heated through. Stir before serving.

PER SERVING *¾ cup equals 148 cal., 5 g fat (3 g sat. fat), 16 mg chol., 409 mg sodium, 21 g carb., 3 g fiber, 8 g pro.* **Diabetic Exchanges:** *1 starch, 1 medium-fat meat.*

(5) INGREDIENTS FAST FIX
Easy Colcannon

This health-conscious version of traditional Irish comfort food is good any time of the year.

—PAM KENNEDY LUBBOCK, TX

START TO FINISH: 30 MIN.
MAKES: 8 SERVINGS

MAKEOVER NOODLE KUGEL

ORIGINAL	MAKEOVER
432 Calories	**271** Calories
19g Fat	**6g** Fat
11g Sat. Fat	**3g** Sat. Fat

Makeover Noodle Kugel

I make this dish along with other Jewish specialties for an annual Hanukkah/ Christmas party with our friends. And now that it's lighter, I feel great about serving it!

—CATHY TANG REDMOND, WA

PREP: 15 MIN. • **BAKE:** 45 MIN. + STANDING
MAKES: 15 SERVINGS

- 1 **package (12 ounces) yolk-free noodles**
- 2 **tablespoons butter, melted**
- 2 **cups (16 ounces) 1% cottage cheese**
- 1½ **cups sugar**
- 4 **eggs**
- 1 **cup egg substitute**
- 1 **cup (8 ounces) reduced-fat sour cream**
- 1 **cup reduced-fat ricotta cheese**

TOPPING
- ½ **cup cinnamon graham cracker crumbs (about 3 whole crackers)**
- 1 **tablespoon butter, melted**

1. Cook noodles according to package directions; drain. Toss with butter; set aside.

2. In a large bowl, beat the cottage cheese, sugar, eggs, egg substitute, sour cream and ricotta cheese until well blended. Stir in noodles. Transfer to a 13x9-in. baking dish coated with cooking spray. Combine cracker crumbs and butter; sprinkle over top.

3. Bake, uncovered, at 350° for 45-50 minutes or until a thermometer reads 160°. Let kugel stand for 10 minutes before cutting.

PER SERVING *1 piece equals 271 cal., 6 g fat (3 g sat. fat), 73 mg chol., 235 mg sodium, 41 g carb., 1 g fiber, 13 g pro. **Diabetic Exchanges:** 2½ starch, 1 lean meat, ½ fat.*

THE SKINNY

Switching to yolk-free noodles and swapping 1 cup egg substitute for 4 of the original recipe's 8 whole eggs helps to save 115 mg cholesterol per serving versus the original dish. That's a decrease of 61%.

Sausage Corn Bread Dressing

You wouldn't know from tasting it, but my holiday dressing has only 3 grams of fat per serving. Made with turkey sausage, herbs, fruit and veggies, it's a healthy alternative to traditional recipes.

—REBECCA BAIRD SALT LAKE CITY, UT

PREP: 30 MIN. • **BAKE:** 50 MIN.
MAKES: 16 SERVINGS

- 1 cup all-purpose flour
- 1 cup cornmeal
- ¼ cup sugar
- 3 teaspoons baking powder
- 1 teaspoon salt
- 1 cup buttermilk
- ¼ cup unsweetened applesauce
- 2 egg whites

DRESSING

- 1 pound turkey Italian sausage links, casings removed
- 4 celery ribs, chopped
- 1 medium onion, chopped
- 1 medium sweet red pepper, chopped
- 2 medium tart apples, chopped
- 1 cup chopped roasted chestnuts
- 3 tablespoons minced fresh parsley
- 2 garlic cloves, minced
- ½ teaspoon dried thyme
- ½ teaspoon pepper
- 1 cup reduced-sodium chicken broth
- 1 egg white

1. For corn bread, combine the first five ingredients in a large bowl. Combine the buttermilk, applesauce and egg whites; stir into dry ingredients just until moistened.

2. Pour into an 8-in.-square baking dish coated with cooking spray. Bake at 400° for 20-25 minutes or until a toothpick inserted near the center comes out clean. Cool on a wire rack.

3. In a large nonstick skillet, cook the sausage, celery, onion and red pepper over medium heat until meat is no longer pink; drain. Transfer to a large bowl. Crumble corn bread over mixture. Add the apples, chestnuts, parsley, garlic, thyme and pepper. Stir in broth and egg white.

4. Transfer to a 13x9-in. baking dish coated with cooking spray. Cover and bake at 325° for 40 minutes. Uncover; bake for 10 minutes longer or until lightly browned.

NOTE *Dressing can be prepared as directed and used to stuff a 10- to 12-pound turkey.*

PER SERVING *¾ cup equals 157 cal., 3 g fat (1 g sat. fat), 18 mg chol., 464 mg sodium, 24 g carb., 2 g fiber, 8 g pro.* **Diabetic Exchanges:** *1½ starch, 1 lean meat.*

Lemon Vinaigrette Potato Salad

I developed this recipe for a friend who wanted a potato salad without mayonnaise. I have substituted fresh thyme for the basil. Any fresh herb would be great!

—MELANIE CLOYD MULLICA HILL, NJ

PREP: 25 MIN. • **COOK:** 15 MIN.
MAKES: 12 SERVINGS (¾ CUP EACH)

- 3 pounds red potatoes, cut into 1-inch cubes
- ½ cup olive oil
- 3 tablespoons lemon juice
- 2 tablespoons minced fresh basil
- 2 tablespoons minced fresh parsley
- 1 tablespoon red wine vinegar
- 1 teaspoon grated lemon peel
- ¾ teaspoon salt
- ½ teaspoon pepper
- 1 small onion, finely chopped

1. Place potatoes in a large saucepan and cover with water. Bring to a boil. Reduce heat; cover and simmer for 10-15 minutes or until tender. Meanwhile, in a small bowl, whisk the oil, lemon juice, herbs, vinegar, lemon peel, salt and pepper.

2. Drain potatoes. Place in a large bowl; add onion. Drizzle with vinaigrette; toss to coat. Serve warm or chill until serving.

PER SERVING *¾ cup equals 165 cal., 9 g fat (1 g sat. fat), 0 chol., 155 mg sodium, 19 g carb., 2 g fiber, 2 g pro.* **Diabetic Exchanges:** *2 fat, 1 starch.*

(5) INGREDIENTS

Apricot Gelatin Mold

After my husband and I got married, he asked me to get this special holiday recipe from my mother. Mom prepared it for every family celebration, and now I make it for our family! You can substitute peach or orange gelatin if you prefer.

—SUZANNE HOLCOMB ST. JOHNSVILLE, NY

PREP: 25 MIN. + CHILLING
MAKES: 12 SERVINGS (½ CUP EACH)

- 1 **can (8 ounces) unsweetened crushed pineapple**
- 2 **packages (3 ounces each) apricot or peach gelatin**
- 1 **package (8 ounces) reduced-fat cream cheese**
- ¾ **cup grated carrots**
- 1 **carton (8 ounces) frozen fat-free whipped topping, thawed**

1. Drain the pineapple, reserving juice in a 2-cup measuring cup; add enough water to measure 2 cups. Set pineapple aside. Pour juice mixture into a small saucepan. Bring to a boil; remove from heat. Dissolve gelatin in juice mixture. Cool for 10 minutes.
2. In a large bowl, beat cream cheese until creamy. Gradually add gelatin mixture, beating until smooth. Refrigerate for 30-40 minutes or until slightly thickened.
3. Fold in pineapple and carrots, then whipped topping. Transfer to an 8-cup ring mold coated with cooking spray. Refrigerate until set. Unmold onto a serving platter.
PER SERVING *½ cup equals 144 cal., 4 g fat (3 g sat. fat), 13 mg chol., 128 mg sodium, 23 g carb., trace fiber, 3 g pro.* **Diabetic Exchanges:** *1½ starch, 1 fat.*

FAST FIX

Kiwi-Strawberry Spinach Salad

This pretty salad is always a hit when I serve it! The recipe came from a cookbook, but I personalized it with my own little changes. Sometimes even a simple change in ingredients can make a big difference.

—LAURA POUNDS ANDOVER, KS

START TO FINISH: 20 MIN.
MAKES: 12 SERVINGS (1 CUP EACH)

- ¼ **cup canola oil**
- ¼ **cup raspberry vinegar**
- ¼ **teaspoon Worcestershire sauce**
- ⅓ **cup sugar**
- ¼ **teaspoon paprika**
- 2 **green onions, chopped**
- 2 **tablespoons sesame seeds, toasted**
- 1 **tablespoon poppy seeds**
- 12 **cups torn fresh spinach (about 9 ounces)**
- 2 **pints fresh strawberries, halved**
- 4 **kiwifruit, peeled and sliced**

1. Place oil, vinegar, Worcestershire sauce, sugar and paprika in a blender; cover and process for 30 seconds or until blended. Transfer to a bowl; stir in the green onions, sesame seeds and poppy seeds.
2. In a salad bowl, combine the spinach, strawberries and kiwifruit. Drizzle with the dressing and toss to coat. Serve immediately.
PER SERVING *1 cup equals 121 cal., 6 g fat (trace sat. fat), 0 chol., 64 mg sodium, 16 g carb., 4 g fiber, 3 g pro.* **Diabetic Exchanges:** *1 vegetable, 1 fat, ½ fruit.*

KIWI-STRAWBERRY SPINACH SALAD

COCONUT-PECAN SWEET POTATOES

(5) INGREDIENTS
Oatmeal Bread

My bread-machine loaf has a slightly sweet flavor from molasses and a good, tender texture from oats.

—**RUTH ANDREWSON** LEAVENWORTH, WA

PREP: 10 MIN. • **BAKE:** 3 HOURS
MAKES: 1 LOAF (2 POUNDS, 20 SLICES)

- 1 **cup warm water (70° to 80°)**
- ½ **cup molasses**
- 1 **tablespoon canola oil**
- 1 **teaspoon salt**
- 3 **cups bread flour**
- 1 **cup quick-cooking oats**
- 1 **package (¼ ounce) active dry yeast**

1. In bread machine pan, place all ingredients in order suggested by manufacturer. Select basic bread setting. Choose crust color and loaf size if available.
2. Bake according to bread machine directions (check dough after 5 minutes of mixing; add 1 to 2 tablespoons of water or flour if needed).
PER SERVING *1 slice equals 105 cal., 1 g fat (trace sat. fat), 0 chol., 121 mg sodium, 22 g carb., 1 g fiber, 3 g pro.* **Diabetic Exchange:** *1½ starch.*

SLOW COOKER
Coconut-Pecan Sweet Potatoes

These sweet potatoes cook effortlessly in the slow cooker so you can tend to other things. Coconut gives this classic dish a new, mouthwatering flavor.

—**RAQUEL HAGGARD** EDMOND, OK

PREP: 15 MIN. • **COOK:** 4 HOURS
MAKES: 12 SERVINGS (⅔ CUP EACH)

- ½ **cup chopped pecans**
- ½ **cup flaked coconut**
- ⅓ **cup sugar**
- ⅓ **cup packed brown sugar**
- ½ **teaspoon ground cinnamon**
- ¼ **teaspoon salt**
- ¼ **cup reduced-fat butter, melted**
- 4 **pounds sweet potatoes (about 6 medium), peeled and cut into 1-inch pieces**
- ½ **teaspoon coconut extract**
- ½ **teaspoon vanilla extract**

1. In a small bowl, combine the first six ingredients; stir in melted butter. Place sweet potatoes in a 5-qt. slow cooker coated with cooking spray. Sprinkle with pecan mixture.
2. Cook, covered, on low 4 to 4½ hours or until potatoes are tender. Stir in extracts.
NOTE *This recipe was tested with Land O'Lakes light stick butter.*
PER SERVING *⅔ cup equals 211 cal., 7 g fat (3 g sat. fat), 5 mg chol., 103 mg sodium, 37 g carb., 3 g fiber, 2 g pro.*

Apple 'n' Pepper Saute

This nutritious side dish blends apple slices, red onion rings, sweet pepper strips and herbs with a touch of soy sauce.

—EMILY GUIDRY BREAUX BRIDGE, LA

START TO FINISH: 25 MIN.
MAKES: 6 SERVINGS

- 3 **medium sweet peppers, julienned**
- 1 **small red onion, sliced and separated into rings**
- 1 **medium apple, sliced**
- 2 **tablespoons olive oil**
- 1 **tablespoon reduced-sodium soy sauce**
- 2 **garlic cloves, minced**
- ¼ **teaspoon dried rosemary, crushed**
- ¼ **teaspoon dried basil**

Saute the peppers, onion and apple in oil in a large nonstick skillet until crisp-tender. Stir in the soy sauce, garlic, rosemary and basil. Cook and stir until heated through.

PER SERVING *⅔ cup equals 83 cal., 5 g fat (1 g sat. fat), 0 chol., 103 mg sodium, 10 g carb., 2 g fiber, 1 g pro. Diabetic Exchanges: 2 vegetable, 1 fat.*

HOW TO

SEED AND SLICE PEPPERS

Holding the pepper by the stem, slice from the top of the pepper down, using a chef's knife. Use this technique to slice around the seeds when a recipe calls for julienned or chopped peppers.

Black-Eyed Peas & Ham

We have these slow-cooked peas regularly at our house. They're supposed to bring good luck!

—DAWN FRIHAUF FORT MORGAN, CO

PREP: 20 MIN. + SOAKING • **COOK:** 5 HOURS
MAKES: 12 SERVINGS (¾ CUP EACH)

- 1 **package (16 ounces) dried black-eyed peas, rinsed and sorted**
- ½ **pound fully cooked boneless ham, finely chopped**
- 1 **medium onion, finely chopped**
- 1 **medium sweet red pepper, finely chopped**
- 5 **bacon strips, cooked and crumbled**
- 1 **large jalapeno pepper, seeded and finely chopped**
- 2 **garlic cloves, minced**
- 1½ **teaspoons ground cumin**
- 1 **teaspoon reduced-sodium chicken bouillon granules**
- ½ **teaspoon salt**
- ½ **teaspoon cayenne pepper**
- ¼ **teaspoon pepper**
- 6 **cups water**
  Minced fresh cilantro, optional
  Hot cooked rice

1. Rinse beans. Place in a Dutch oven; add water to cover by 2 in. Bring to a boil; boil 2 minutes. Remove from heat; let soak, covered, 1 to 4 hours. Drain and rinse beans, discarding the liquid.

2. In a 6-qt. slow cooker, combine the first 13 ingredients. Cover and cook on low for 5-7 hours or until peas are tender. Sprinkle with fresh cilantro if desired. Serve with rice.

NOTE *Wear disposable gloves when cutting hot peppers; the oils can burn skin. Avoid touching your face.*

PER SERVING *¾ cup (calculated without rice) equals 170 cal., 3 g fat (1 g sat. fat), 13 mg chol., 386 mg sodium, 24 g carb., 7 g fiber, 13 g pro. Diabetic Exchanges: 1½ starch, 1 lean meat.*

BLACK-EYED PEAS & HAM

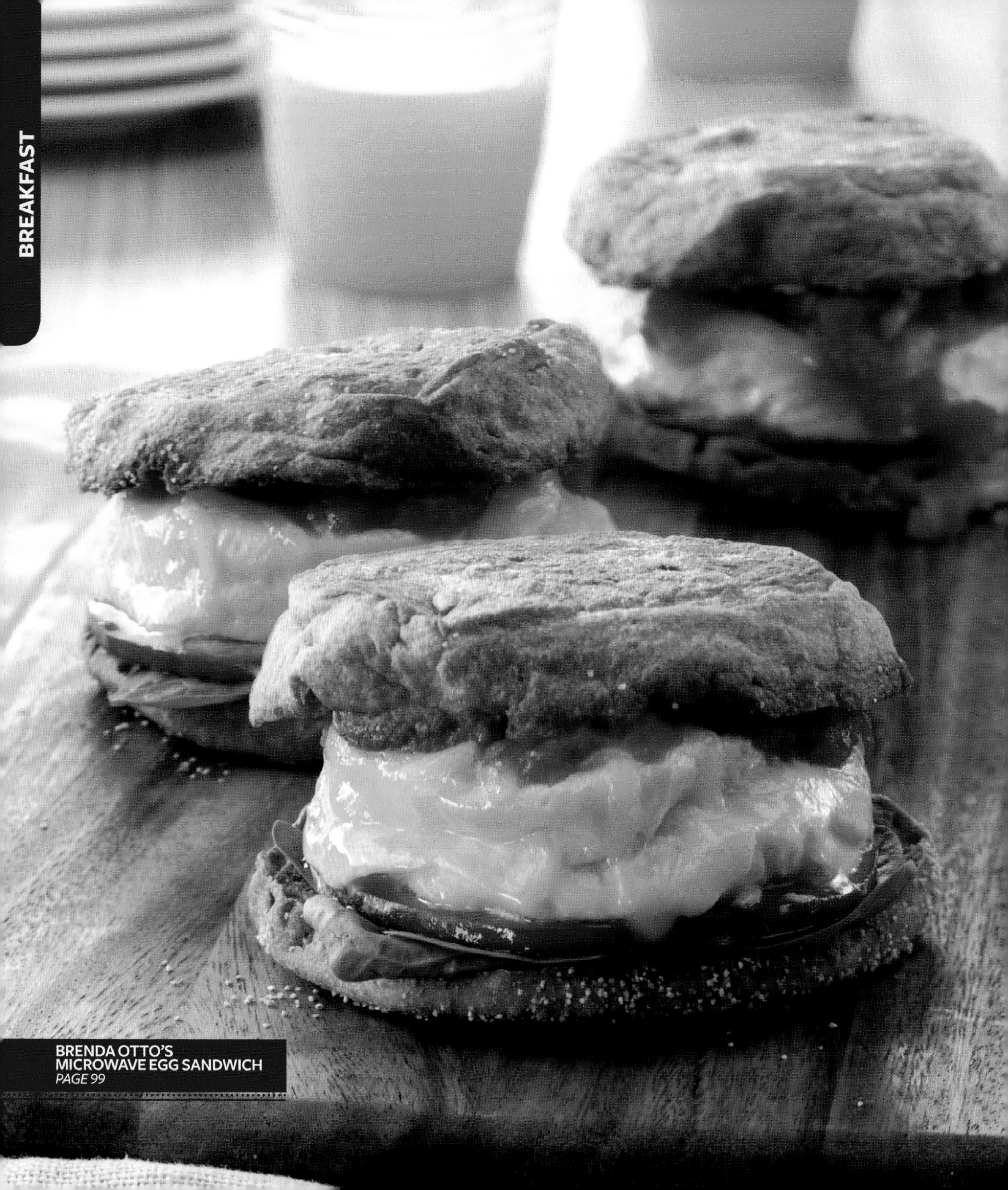

BRENDA OTTO'S
MICROWAVE EGG SANDWICH
PAGE 99

Breakfast

Start your day the **delicious and healthy way!** Whether you're looking for a **bite on the go** or a **special brunch dish,** these recipes give you the perfect reason to **savor the most important meal** of the day.

ANGELA SPENGLER'S BACON-MAPLE COFFEE CAKE
PAGE 96

JOAN HALLFORD'S MAKEOVER BLUEBERRY FRENCH TOAST *PAGE 87*

SUSAN WATT'S MINI HAM 'N' CHEESE FRITTATAS
PAGE 107

Slow Cooker Frittata Provencal

This slow cooker recipe means that a delectable meal is ready when I walk in the door. It makes an elegant holiday breakfast.

—**CONNIE EATON** PITTSBURGH, PA

PREP: 30 MIN. • **COOK:** 3 HOURS
MAKES: 6 SERVINGS

- ½ cup water
- 1 tablespoon olive oil
- 1 medium Yukon Gold potato, peeled and sliced
- 1 small onion, thinly sliced
- ½ teaspoon smoked paprika
- 12 large eggs
- 1 teaspoon minced fresh thyme or ¼ teaspoon dried thyme
- 1 teaspoon hot pepper sauce
- ½ teaspoon salt
- ¼ teaspoon pepper
- 1 log (4 ounces) fresh goat cheese, coarsely crumbled, divided
- ½ cup chopped soft sun-dried tomatoes (not packed in oil)

1. Layer two 24-in.-long pieces of aluminum foil; starting with a long side, fold up foil to create a 1-in.-wide strip. Shape strip into a coil to make a rack for bottom of a 6-qt. oval slow cooker. Add water to slow cooker; set foil rack in water.

2. In a large skillet, heat oil over medium-high heat. Add potato and onion; cook and stir 5-7 minutes or until potato is lightly browned. Stir in paprika. Transfer to a greased 1½-qt. baking dish (dish must fit in slow cooker).

3. In a large bowl, whisk eggs, thyme, pepper sauce, salt and pepper; stir in 2 ounces cheese. Pour over potato mixture. Top with tomatoes and remaining goat cheese. Place dish on foil rack.

4. Cook, covered, on low 3 hours or until eggs are set and a knife inserted near the center comes out clean.

NOTE *This recipe was tested with sun-dried tomatoes that are ready to use without soaking. When using other sun-dried tomatoes that are not oil-packed, cover with boiling water and let stand until soft. Drain before using.*

PER SERVING *1 wedge equals 245 cal., 14 g fat (5 g sat. fat), 385 mg chol., 338 mg sodium, 12 g carb., 2 g fiber, 15 g pro.* **Diabetic Exchanges:** *2 medium-fat meat, 1 starch, ½ fat.*

SLOW COOKER
FRITTATA PROVENCAL

---

5 INGREDIENTS

Tropical Muesli

This healthful combination of yogurt, oats, fruit and nuts is a delicious alternative to standard oatmeal. After sampling it at my sister's home, I had to have the recipe.

—**SUSANNE MELTON** MISSION VIEJO, CA

PREP: 10 MIN. + CHILLING
MAKES: 4 SERVINGS

- 2 cups (16 ounces) fat-free vanilla yogurt
- 1 cup quick-cooking oats
- 1 can (8 ounces) crushed pineapple, undrained
- ½ cup slivered almonds, toasted
- 2 medium firm bananas, sliced

In a bowl, combine the yogurt, oats, pineapple and almonds; cover and refrigerate overnight. Serve with sliced bananas.

PER SERVING *¾ cup equals 370 cal., 10 g fat (1 g sat. fat), 2 mg chol., 85 mg sodium, 58 g carb., 5 g fiber, 13 g pro.*

Cranberry Whole Wheat Bagels

The bagel recipes I saw in a magazine inspired me to try creating my own. I've been making them like crazy ever since! My whole wheat version dotted with sweet and tart dried cranberries is a favorite.

—**TAMI KUEHL** LOUP CITY, NE

PREP: 30 MIN. + RISING
BAKE: 15 MIN. + COOLING
MAKES: 1 DOZEN

- 1¼ cups water (70° to 80°)
- ⅓ cup honey
- 2 tablespoons butter, softened
- 1½ teaspoons salt
- 1 teaspoon dried orange peel
- ¼ teaspoon ground mace
- 2 cups all-purpose flour
- 1¼ cups whole wheat flour
- 2¾ teaspoons active dry yeast
- ½ cup dried cranberries
- 1 large egg white
- 1 tablespoon water

1. In bread machine pan, place first nine ingredients in order suggested by manufacturer. Select dough setting. Check dough after 5 minutes of mixing; add 1-2 tablespoons of water or flour if needed. Just before the final kneading (your machine may audibly signal this), add cranberries.

2. When cycle is completed, turn dough onto a lightly floured surface. Divide and shape into 12 balls. Push thumb through center of each, stretching and shaping to form an even ring with a 1½-in. hole. Place on a floured surface. Cover with kitchen towels; let rest 10 minutes. Flatten bagels slightly.

3. Fill a Dutch oven two-thirds full with water; bring to a boil. Drop bagels, two at a time, into boiling water. Cook 45 seconds; turn and cook 45 seconds longer. Remove bagels with a slotted spoon; drain well on paper towels.

4. Place 2 in. apart on parchment paper-lined baking sheets. Whisk the egg white and water; brush over bagels. Bake at 400° for 15-20 minutes or until golden brown. Remove from pans to wire racks to cool.

PER SERVING *1 bagel equals 184 cal., 2 g fat (1 g sat. fat), 5 mg chol., 315 mg sodium, 38 g carb., 3 g fiber, 5 g pro.*

CRANBERRY WHOLE WHEAT BAGELS

HOW TO

HOW TO MAKE BAGELS

❶ Shape dough into balls. Push your thumb through the center, forming a hole. Stretch and shape dough to form a ring.

❷ After boiling bagels, gently remove with a slotted spoon. Drain well on paper towels.

Cardamom Sour Cream Waffles

Sweet with just the right amount of baking spices, these easy waffles make it nearly impossible to skip your morning meal.

—**BARB MILLER** OAKDALE, MN

PREP: 15 MIN. • **COOK:** 5 MIN./BATCH
MAKES: 7 SERVINGS

- ¾ cup all-purpose flour
- ¾ cup whole wheat flour
- 1½ teaspoons baking powder
- 1 teaspoon ground cardamom
- ¾ teaspoon baking soda
- ½ teaspoon ground cinnamon
- ¼ teaspoon salt
- 2 large eggs
- 1 cup fat-free milk
- ¾ cup reduced-fat sour cream
- ½ cup packed brown sugar
- 1 tablespoon butter, melted
- 1 teaspoon vanilla extract

1. In a large bowl, combine the first seven ingredients. In another bowl, whisk the eggs, milk, sour cream, brown sugar, butter and vanilla. Stir into dry ingredients just until combined.

2. Bake in a preheated waffle iron according to manufacturer's directions until golden brown.

PER SERVING *2 waffles equals 235 cal., 6 g fat (3 g sat. fat), 74 mg chol., 375 mg sodium, 39 g carb., 2 g fiber, 8 g pro.* **Diabetic Exchanges:** *2½ starch, 1 fat.*

CARDAMOM SOUR CREAM WAFFLES

Garlic-Herb Mini Quiches

Looking for a wonderful little bite to dress up the brunch buffet? These delectable tartlets are irresistible.

—**JOSEPHINE PIRO** EASTON, PA

START TO FINISH: 25 MIN.
MAKES: 45 MINI QUICHES

- 1 package (6½ ounces) reduced-fat garlic-herb spreadable cheese
- ¼ cup fat-free milk
- 2 large eggs
- 3 packages (1.9 ounces each) frozen miniature phyllo tart shells
- 2 tablespoons minced fresh parsley
  Minced chives, optional

1. In a small bowl, beat the spreadable cheese, milk and eggs. Place tart shells on an ungreased baking sheet; fill each with 2 teaspoons mixture. Sprinkle with parsley.

2. Bake at 350° for 10-12 minutes or until filling is set and shells are lightly browned. Sprinkle with chives if desired. Serve warm.

PER SERVING *1 mini quiche equals 31 cal., 2 g fat (trace sat. fat), 12 mg chol., 32 mg sodium, 2 g carb., trace fiber, 1 g pro.*

Makeover Blueberry French Toast

With this luscious makeover from the test cooks at *Taste of Home*, I can enjoy all the decadent richness of my original French toast, but with less fat, calories and cholesterol. Bravo!

—JOAN HALLFORD NORTH RICHLAND HILLS, TX

PREP: 30 MIN. + CHILLING • **BAKE:** 55 MIN.
MAKES: 8 SERVINGS (1½ CUPS SAUCE)

- **6 whole wheat hamburger buns**
- **1 package (8 ounces) reduced-fat cream cheese**
- **1 cup fresh or frozen blueberries**
- **6 large eggs**
- **1 cup egg substitute**
- **2 cups fat-free milk**
- **⅓ cup maple syrup or honey**

SAUCE
- **½ cup sugar**
- **2 tablespoons cornstarch**
- **1 cup grape juice**
- **1 cup fresh or frozen blueberries**

1. Cut buns into 1-in. cubes; place half in a 13x9-in. baking dish coated with cooking spray. Cut cream cheese into 1-in. cubes; place over buns. Top with blueberries and the remaining bun cubes.

2. In a large bowl, beat the eggs and egg substitute. Add milk and syrup; mix well. Pour over bun mixture. Cover and refrigerate for 8 hours or overnight.

3. Remove from the refrigerator 30 minutes before baking. Cover and bake at 350° for 30 minutes. Uncover; bake 25-30 minutes longer or until golden brown and center is set.

4. Meanwhile, in a small saucepan, combine sugar and cornstarch; stir in juice until smooth. Bring to a boil over medium heat; cook and stir for 2 minutes. Stir in blueberries. Reduce heat; simmer, uncovered, for 8-10 minutes or until berries burst, stirring occasionally. Serve with French toast.

PER SERVING *1 piece with 3 tablespoons sauce equals 375 cal., 11 g fat (6 g sat. fat), 180 mg chol., 418 mg sodium, 54 g carb., 3 g fiber, 16 g pro.*

MAKEOVER BLUEBERRY FRENCH TOAST

ORIGINAL	MAKEOVER
530 Calories	**375** Calories
22g Fat	**11g** Fat
306mg Cholesterol	**180mg** Cholesterol

THE SKINNY

The original recipe used 12 slices of Texas toast. Our swap to whole wheat buns doubled the fiber in the dish while preserving a hearty texture because the buns are thicker and have more crust than regular whole wheat bread.

FLAXSEED OATMEAL PANCAKES

Overnight Yeast Waffles

These light, crispy waffles taste just like the higher-fat and -calorie version, but are so much healthier. Freeze the extras to munch on a hurried morning. A tasty breakfast like this makes it easy to start the day right.

—**MARY BALCOMB** FLORENCE, OR

PREP: 15 MIN. + CHILLING
COOK: 5 MIN./BATCH
MAKES: 10 SERVINGS

- 1 package (¼ ounce) active dry yeast
- ½ cup warm water (110° to 115°)
- 1 teaspoon sugar
- 2 cups warm fat-free milk (110° to 115°)
- 2 large eggs, separated
- 2 tablespoons butter, melted
- 1 tablespoon canola oil
- 1¾ cups all-purpose flour
- 1 teaspoon salt

1. In a large bowl, dissolve yeast in warm water. Add sugar; let stand for 5 minutes. Add the milk, egg yolks, butter and oil (refrigerate egg whites). Combine flour and salt; stir into milk mixture. Cover and refrigerate the batter overnight.
2. Let egg whites stand at room temperature for 30 minutes. In a small bowl, beat egg whites until stiff peaks form. Stir batter; fold in egg whites.
3. For each waffle, pour batter by ¼ cupfuls into a preheated waffle iron; bake according to manufacturer's directions until golden brown.
PER SERVING *2 waffles equals 148 cal., 5 g fat (2 g sat. fat), 50 mg chol., 298 mg sodium, 20 g carb., 1 g fiber, 5 g pro.* **Diabetic Exchanges:** *1 starch, 1 fat.*

FAST FIX ▸ Flaxseed Oatmeal Pancakes

I came up with this healthy and really tasty recipe because my husband loves pancakes. They have a pleasing texture and a delightful touch of cinnamon.

—**SHARON HANSEN** PONTIAC, IL

START TO FINISH: 20 MIN.
MAKES: 4 PANCAKES

- ⅓ cup whole wheat flour
- 3 tablespoons quick-cooking oats
- 1 tablespoon flaxseed
- ½ teaspoon baking powder
- ¼ teaspoon ground cinnamon
- ⅛ teaspoon baking soda
  Dash salt
- 1 large egg, separated
- ½ cup buttermilk
- 1 tablespoon brown sugar
- 1 tablespoon canola oil
- ½ teaspoon vanilla extract

1. In a large bowl, combine the first seven ingredients. In a small bowl, whisk the egg yolk, buttermilk, brown sugar, oil and vanilla; stir into dry ingredients just until moistened.
2. In a small bowl, beat egg white on medium speed until stiff peaks form. Fold into batter.
3. Pour batter by ¼ cupfuls onto a hot griddle coated with cooking spray; turn when bubbles form on top. Cook until the second side is golden brown.
PER SERVING *2 pancakes equals 273 cal., 13 g fat (2 g sat. fat), 108 mg chol., 357 mg sodium, 31 g carb., 5 g fiber, 10 g pro.* **Diabetic Exchanges:** *2 starch, 2 fat.*

Cantaloupe Banana Smoothies

This is one of my favorite flavor combinations for a smoothie. Cool and fruity, a full glass satisfies my evening munchies.

—JANICE MITCHELL AURORA, CO

START TO FINISH: 10 MIN.
MAKES: 3 SERVINGS

- ½ cup fat-free plain yogurt
- 4½ teaspoons orange juice concentrate
- 2 cups cubed cantaloupe
- 1 large firm banana, cut into 1-inch pieces and frozen
- 2 tablespoons nonfat dry milk powder
- 2 teaspoons honey

In a blender, combine all ingredients. Cover and process until blended. Pour into chilled glasses and serve immediately.

PER SERVING *1 cup equals 141 cal., 1 g fat (trace sat. fat), 2 mg chol., 60 mg sodium, 32 g carb., 2 g fiber, 5 g pro. Diabetic Exchanges: 1 starch, 1 fruit.*

Farm Girl Breakfast Casserole

I served this lightened-up breakfast casserole to my husband, Ken. He liked its fluffy texture—and said it was very good!

—NANCY ZIMMERMAN
CAPE MAY COURT HOUSE, NJ

PREP: 15 MIN. • **BAKE:** 35 MIN.
MAKES: 8 SERVINGS

- 4 large eggs
- 1½ cups egg substitute
- ½ cup all-purpose flour
- 1 teaspoon baking powder
- 2 cups (16 ounces) 1% cottage cheese
- 2 cups (8 ounces) shredded reduced-fat Monterey Jack cheese or reduced-fat Mexican cheese blend, divided
- 1 can (4 ounces) chopped green chilies

1. In a large bowl, beat the eggs and egg substitute on medium-high speed for 3 minutes or until light and lemon-colored. Combine flour and baking powder; gradually add to egg mixture and mix well. Stir in the cottage cheese, 1½ cups shredded cheese and chilies.

2. Pour into a 13x9-in. baking dish coated with cooking spray. Bake, uncovered, at 350° for 35-40 minutes or until a knife inserted near the center comes out clean. Sprinkle with the remaining cheese. Let stand for 5 minutes before serving.

PER SERVING *1 piece equals 210 cal., 9 g fat (4 g sat. fat), 128 mg chol., 665 mg sodium, 10 g carb., trace fiber, 24 g pro.*

FARM GIRL BREAKFAST CASSEROLE

HASH BROWN NESTS WITH PORTOBELLOS AND EGGS

FAST FIX ▸

Quick Crunchy Apple Salad

My simple salad pairs crunchy toppings with smooth vanilla yogurt for a combination everybody loves.

—KATHY ARMSTRONG POST FALLS, ID

START TO FINISH: 15 MIN.
MAKES: 5 SERVINGS

- 6 **tablespoons vanilla yogurt**
- 6 **tablespoons reduced-fat whipped topping**
- ¼ **teaspoon plus ⅛ teaspoon ground cinnamon, divided**
- 2 **medium red apples, chopped**
- 1 **large Granny Smith apple, chopped**
- ¼ **cup dried cranberries**
- 2 **tablespoons chopped walnuts**

In a large bowl, combine the yogurt, whipped topping and ¼ teaspoon cinnamon. Add apples and cranberries; toss to coat. Refrigerate until serving. Sprinkle with walnuts and the remaining cinnamon just before serving.

PER SERVING *¾ cup equals 116 cal., 3 g fat (1 g sat. fat), 1 mg chol., 13 mg sodium, 23 g carb., 3 g fiber, 2 g pro.* **Diabetic Exchanges:** *1 fruit, ½ starch, ½ fat.*

Hash Brown Nests with Portobellos and Eggs

Hash browns make a fabulous crust for individual egg quiches. They look fancy but are actually easy to make. The little nests have been a hit at holiday brunches and other special occasions.

—KATE MEYER BRENTWOOD, TN

PREP: 30 MIN. • **BAKE:** 15 MIN.
MAKES: 12 SERVINGS

- 3 **cups frozen shredded hash brown potatoes, thawed**
- 3 **cups chopped fresh portobello mushrooms**
- ¼ **cup chopped shallots**
- 2 **tablespoons butter**
- 1 **garlic clove, minced**
- ½ **teaspoon salt**
- ¼ **teaspoon pepper**
- 2 **tablespoons sour cream**
- 1 **tablespoon minced fresh basil**
  Dash cayenne pepper
- 7 **large eggs, beaten**
- ¼ **cup shredded Swiss cheese**
- 2 **bacon strips, cooked and crumbled Additional minced fresh basil, optional**

1. Preheat oven to 400°. Press ¼ cup hash browns onto the bottom and up the sides of each of 12 greased muffin cups; set aside.

2. In a large skillet, saute mushrooms and shallots in butter until tender. Add garlic, salt and pepper; cook 1 minute longer. Remove from heat; stir in sour cream, basil and cayenne.

3. Divide eggs among potato-lined muffin cups. Top with mushroom mixture. Sprinkle with the cheese and bacon.

4. Bake 15-18 minutes or until eggs are completely set. Garnish with additional basil if desired.

PER SERVING *1 nest equals 101 cal., 6 g fat (3 g sat. fat), 134 mg chol., 187 mg sodium, 5 g carb., 1 g fiber, 6 g pro.* **Diabetic Exchanges:** *1 medium-fat meat, ½ fat.*

Cherry Cobbler Smoothies

It's been said that breakfast is the most important meal of the day. I want to make it count, so I created this fruity and refreshing smoothie packed with good-for-you cherries and vanilla yogurt.

—SHERRY MOTE MARIETTA, GA

START TO FINISH: 10 MIN.
MAKES: 5 SERVINGS

- 2 **cups vanilla yogurt**
- ½ **cup orange juice**
- ¼ **cup honey**
- 1 **teaspoon vanilla extract**
- 1 **teaspoon almond extract**
- 2 **cups ice cubes**
- 2 **cups frozen pitted dark sweet cherries**
- 2 **teaspoons ground cinnamon**

In a blender, combine all ingredients; cover and process for 30 seconds or until smooth. Pour into chilled glasses; serve immediately.

PER SERVING *1 cup equals 197 cal., 2 g fat (1 g sat. fat), 5 mg chol., 66 mg sodium, 40 g carb., 2 g fiber, 6 g pro.*

Makeover Spinach-Bacon Quiche

This quiche is one of my husband's favorites, probably because it has bacon. Sometimes I saute sliced white or baby portobello mushrooms with the onions for an even meatier taste.

—RUBY HOCHSTETLER HOLLAND, MI

PREP: 15 MIN. • **BAKE:** 35 MIN. + STANDING
MAKES: 2 QUICHES (8 SERVINGS EACH)

- 1 **package (14.1 ounces) refrigerated pie pastry**
- 8 **bacon strips**
- 2 **large onions, chopped**
- 8 **large egg whites**
- 4 **large eggs**
- 3 **cups fat-free milk**
- 3 **cups (12 ounces) shredded part-skim mozzarella cheese**
- 1 **package (10 ounces) frozen chopped spinach, thawed and squeezed dry**
- ½ **cup chopped sun-dried tomatoes (not packed in oil)**
- 2 **tablespoons cornstarch**
- 1 **teaspoon dried basil**
- ½ **teaspoon pepper**

1. On a lightly floured surface, unroll pastry. Transfer to two 9-in. pie plates. Trim pastry to ½ in. beyond edge of plate; flute edges.

2. In a large nonstick skillet, cook bacon over medium heat until crisp. Remove to paper towels with a slotted spoon; drain and crumble. In the same skillet, saute onions until tender.

3. In a large bowl, whisk the egg whites, eggs, milk, cheese, spinach, onions, tomatoes, cornstarch, basil and pepper. Divide between pie plates. Sprinkle with bacon.

4. Bake at 375° for 35-40 minutes or until a knife inserted near the center comes out clean. Let stand for 10 minutes before cutting.

PER SERVING *1 piece equals 248 cal., 13 g fat (6 g sat. fat), 75 mg chol., 378 mg sodium, 20 g carb., 1 g fiber, 13 g pro.*

ORIGINAL	MAKEOVER
448 Calories	**248** Calories
28g Fat	**13**g Fat
13g Sat. Fat	**6**g Sat. Fat

MAKEOVER SPINACH-BACON QUICHE

PIGS IN A POOL

Pigs in a Pool

My kids love sausage and pancakes, but making them for breakfast on a busy weekday was out of the question. My homemade version of pigs in a blanket is a nice alternative to the packaged kind, and they freeze like a dream.

—LISA DODD GREENVILLE, SC

PREP: 45 MIN. • **BAKE:** 20 MIN.
MAKES: 4 DOZEN

- 1 **pound reduced-fat bulk pork sausage**
- 2 **cups all-purpose flour**
- ¼ **cup sugar**
- 1 **tablespoon baking powder**
- 1 **teaspoon salt**
- ½ **teaspoon ground cinnamon**
- ¼ **teaspoon ground nutmeg**
- 1 **large egg, lightly beaten**
- 2 **cups fat-free milk**
- 2 **tablespoons canola oil**
- 2 **tablespoons honey**
  Maple syrup, optional

1. Preheat oven to 350°. Coat mini-muffin cups with cooking spray.
2. Shape sausage into forty-eight ¾-in. balls. Place meatballs on a rack coated with cooking spray in a shallow baking pan. Bake 15-20 minutes or until cooked through. Drain on paper towels. In a large bowl, whisk flour, sugar, baking powder, salt and spices. In another bowl, whisk egg, milk, oil and honey until blended. Add to flour mixture; stir just until moistened.
3. Place a sausage ball into each mini-muffin cup; cover with batter. Bake 20-25 minutes or until lightly browned. Cool 5 minutes before removing from pans to wire racks. Serve warm with syrup if desired.

FREEZE OPTION *Freeze cooled muffins in resealable plastic freezer bags. To use, microwave each muffin on high for 20-30 seconds or until heated through.*
PER SERVING *4 mini muffins (calculated without syrup) equals 234 cal., 10 g fat (3 g sat. fat), 45 mg chol., 560 mg sodium, 26 g carb., 1 g fiber, 10 g pro.* **Diabetic Exchanges:** *1½ starch, 1 medium-fat meat, ½ fat.*

Delectable Granola

Here's a great make-ahead recipe! Be sure to remove the granola from the cookie sheets within 20 minutes, or it may stick to the pans.

—LORI STEVENS RIVERTON, UT

PREP: 20 MIN. • **BAKE:** 25 MIN. + COOLING
MAKES: 11 CUPS

- 8 **cups old-fashioned oats**
- 1 **cup finely chopped almonds**
- 1 **cup finely chopped pecans**
- ½ **cup flaked coconut**
- ½ **cup packed brown sugar**
- ½ **cup canola oil**
- ½ **cup honey**
- ¼ **cup maple syrup**
- 2 **teaspoons ground cinnamon**
- 1½ **teaspoons salt**
- 2 **teaspoons vanilla extract**
  Plain yogurt, optional

1. In a large bowl, combine the oats, almonds, pecans and coconut. In a small saucepan, combine brown sugar, oil, honey, maple syrup, cinnamon and salt. Cook for 3-4 minutes over medium heat until sugar is dissolved. Remove from the heat; stir in vanilla. Pour over the oat mixture; stir to coat.
2. Transfer to two 15x10x1-in. baking pans coated with cooking spray. Bake at 350° for 25-30 minutes or until crisp, stirring the granola every 10 minutes. Cool in pans on wire racks. Store in an airtight container. Serve with yogurt if desired.
PER SERVING *½ cup (calculated without yogurt) equals 288 cal., 15 g fat (2 g sat. fat), 0 chol., 170 mg sodium, 36 g carb., 4 g fiber, 6 g pro.* **Diabetic Exchanges:** *2½ starch, 2 fat.*

DELECTABLE GRANOLA

FREEZE IT

Multigrain Waffles

These multigrain waffles are crispy, airy and lower in fat, calories and cholesterol than traditional waffles. But they still have all the great taste of the original.

—BETTY BLAIR BARTLETT, TN

PREP: 15 MIN. • **COOK:** 5 MIN./BATCH
MAKES: 28 WAFFLES

- 1 cup all-purpose flour
- 1 cup whole wheat flour
- 1 cup cornmeal
- 1 tablespoon sugar
- 1 tablespoon baking powder
- ¾ teaspoon baking soda
- ½ teaspoon salt
- 3 large eggs
- 4 large egg whites
- 3 cups buttermilk
- ½ cup unsweetened applesauce
- 3 tablespoons canola oil
- 2 tablespoons butter, melted
  Butter and maple syrup, optional

1. In a large bowl, combine the first seven ingredients. In another bowl, whisk the eggs, egg whites, buttermilk, applesauce, oil and butter; whisk into dry ingredients just until blended.
2. Bake in a preheated waffle iron according to manufacturer's directions until golden brown. Serve with butter and syrup if desired.

FREEZE OPTION *Cool waffles on wire racks. Freeze between layers of waxed paper in a resealable plastic freezer bag. To use, reheat waffles in a toaster on medium setting. Or, microwave each waffle on high for 30-60 seconds or until heated through.*

PER SERVING *2 waffles (calculated without butter and syrup) equals 187 cal., 7 g fat (2 g sat. fat), 52 mg chol., 336 mg sodium, 25 g carb., 2 g fiber, 7 g pro.* **Diabetic Exchanges:** *1½ starch, 1 fat.*

Turkey Sausage Patties

I developed this recipe as a way to deter my husband from eating pork sausage. The mixture also works well for making meatballs and burgers.

—YVONNE WOODRUFF SACRAMENTO, CA

PREP: 20 MIN. • **COOK:** 20 MIN.
MAKES: 2½ DOZEN

- 2 large eggs
- ⅔ cup seasoned bread crumbs
- 1 small onion, finely chopped
- 2 tablespoons Worcestershire sauce
- 3 garlic cloves, minced
- 2 teaspoons garlic salt
- 2 teaspoons dried thyme
- 2 teaspoons ground cumin
- ½ teaspoon crushed red pepper flakes
- ½ teaspoon pepper
- ⅛ teaspoon ground nutmeg
- 2 pounds lean ground turkey
- 5 teaspoons canola oil, divided

1. In a large bowl, combine the first 11 ingredients. Crumble turkey over mixture and mix well. Shape into thirty 2½-in. patties.
2. Heat 1 teaspoon oil in a large skillet over medium heat. Cook the sausage patties in batches over medium heat for 2-3 minutes on each side or until meat is no longer pink, using the remaining oil as needed.

PER SERVING *1 patty equals 70 cal., 4 g fat (1 g sat. fat), 38 mg chol., 204 mg sodium, 3 g carb., trace fiber, 6 g pro.* **Diabetic Exchange:** *1 lean meat.*

MULTIGRAIN WAFFLES

RAISIN NUT OATMEAL

Raisin Nut Oatmeal

There's no better feeling than waking up to a hot ready-to-eat breakfast. The oats, fruit and spices in this homey meal cook together while you sleep!

—**VALERIE SAUBER** ADELANTO, CA

PREP: 10 MIN. • **COOK:** 7 HOURS
MAKES: 6 SERVINGS

- 3½ **cups fat-free milk**
- 1 **large apple, peeled and chopped**
- ¾ **cup steel-cut oats**
- ¾ **cup raisins**
- 3 **tablespoons brown sugar**
- 4½ **teaspoons butter, melted**
- ¾ **teaspoon ground cinnamon**
- ½ **teaspoon salt**
- ¼ **cup chopped pecans**

In a 3-qt. slow cooker coated with cooking spray, combine the first eight ingredients. Cover and cook on low for 7-8 hours or until liquid is absorbed. Spoon oatmeal into bowls; sprinkle with pecans.

NOTE *You may substitute 1½ cups quick-cooking oats for the steel-cut oats and increase the fat-free milk to 4½ cups.*

PER SERVING *¾ cup with 2 teaspoons pecans equals 289 cal., 9 g fat (3 g sat. fat), 10 mg chol., 282 mg sodium, 47 g carb., 4 g fiber, 9 g pro.*

Blueberry Coffee Cake

Every time I have company for brunch or go to a potluck event, I'm asked to make this versatile coffee cake.

—**LESLIE PALMER** SWAMPSCOTT, MA

PREP: 20 MIN. • **BAKE:** 40 MIN. + COOLING
MAKES: 14 SERVINGS

- ⅓ **cup butter, softened**
- ¾ **cup plus 3 tablespoons sugar, divided**
- 1 **large egg**
- ¼ **cup egg substitute**
- 1 **teaspoon vanilla extract**
- 2 **cups all-purpose flour**
- 1 **teaspoon baking powder**
- 1 **teaspoon baking soda**
- ¼ **teaspoon salt**
- 1 **cup (8 ounces) reduced-fat sour cream**
- 1 **cup fresh or frozen blueberries**
- 2 **teaspoons ground cinnamon**
- 2 **teaspoons confectioners' sugar**

1. In a large bowl, beat the butter and ¾ cup sugar until crumbly, about 2 minutes. Beat in the egg, egg substitute and vanilla. Combine the flour, baking powder, baking soda and salt; add to egg mixture alternately with the sour cream. Gently fold in the blueberries.

2. Coat a 10-in. fluted tube pan with cooking spray and dust with flour. Spoon half of batter into prepared pan. Combine cinnamon and remaining sugar; sprinkle half over batter. Repeat layers.

3. Bake at 350° for 40-50 minutes or until a toothpick inserted near the center comes out clean. Cool coffee cake for 10 minutes before removing from pan to a wire rack to cool completely. Dust with confectioners' sugar before serving.

NOTE *If using frozen blueberries, use without thawing to avoid discoloring the batter.*

PER SERVING *1 piece equals 191 cal., 7 g fat (4 g sat. fat), 32 mg chol., 218 mg sodium, 30 g carb., 1 g fiber, 4 g pro. Diabetic Exchanges: 2 starch, 1½ fat.*

BACON-MAPLE
COFFEE CAKE

PER SERVING *1 piece equals 160 cal.,
5 g fat (2 g sat. fat), 27 mg chol., 183 mg
sodium, 25 g carb., 1 g fiber, 3 g pro.
Diabetic Exchanges: 1½ starch, 1 fat.*

⑤INGREDIENTS

Sweet Onion Pie

Chock-full of sweet onions, this creamy
pie makes a scrumptious addition to the
brunch buffet. By using less butter to
cook the onions and substituting lighter
ingredients, I cut calories and fat from this
tasty dish.

—**BARBARA REESE** CATAWISSA, PA

PREP: 35 MIN. • **BAKE:** 20 MIN.
MAKES: 8 SERVINGS

- 2 **sweet onions, halved and sliced**
- 1 **tablespoon butter**
- 1 **unbaked pastry shell (9 inches)**
- 1 **cup egg substitute**
- 1 **cup fat-free evaporated milk**
- 1 **teaspoon salt**
- ¼ **teaspoon pepper**

1. In a large nonstick skillet, cook
onions in butter over medium-low
heat for 30 minutes or until very
tender. Meanwhile, line unpricked
pastry shell with a double thickness
of heavy-duty foil.
2. Bake pastry shell at 450° for
6 minutes. Remove foil; cool on
a wire rack. Reduce heat to 425°.
3. Spoon onions into pastry shell. In a
small bowl, whisk the egg substitute,
milk, salt and pepper; pour over
onions. Bake for 20-25 minutes or
until a knife inserted near the center
comes out clean. Let stand for 5-10
minutes before cutting.

PER SERVING *1 piece equals 187 cal.,
9 g fat (4 g sat. fat), 10 mg chol., 510 mg
sodium, 20 g carb., 1 g fiber, 7 g pro.
Diabetic Exchanges: 1 starch, 1 lean
meat, 1 fat.*

Bacon-Maple Coffee Cake

The sleepyheads will roll out of bed when
they smell this sweet and savory coffee
cake baking. Nuts and bacon in the
crumbly topping blend with maple,
nutmeg and cinnamon.

—**ANGELA SPENGLER** TAMPA, FL

PREP: 25 MIN. • **BAKE:** 35 MIN. + COOLING
MAKES: 24 SERVINGS

- 2½ **cups all-purpose flour**
- 1 **cup packed brown sugar**
- ½ **teaspoon salt**
- ⅓ **cup cold butter**
- 2 **teaspoons baking powder**
- ½ **teaspoon baking soda**
- ½ **teaspoon ground cinnamon**
- ¼ **teaspoon ground nutmeg**
- 2 **large eggs**
- 1½ **cups buttermilk**
- ½ **cup maple syrup**
- ⅓ **cup unsweetened applesauce**
- 5 **bacon strips, cooked and crumbled**
- ½ **cup chopped walnuts**

1. In a large bowl, combine the flour,
brown sugar and salt. Cut in butter
until crumbly. Set aside ½ cup for
topping. Combine the baking powder,
baking soda, cinnamon and nutmeg;
stir into remaining flour mixture.
2. In a small bowl, whisk the eggs,
buttermilk, syrup and applesauce
until well blended. Gradually stir into
flour mixture until combined.
3. Spread into a 13x9-in. baking pan
coated with cooking spray. Sprinkle
with reserved topping, then bacon
and walnuts. Bake at 350° for 35-40
minutes or until a toothpick inserted
near the center comes out clean. Cool
on a wire rack.

Cocoa Pancakes

We love these chocolaty whole wheat pancakes that feel like a treat. The yogurt and raspberries are a delicious and good-for-you accent. Use one egg if you don't have egg substitute on hand.

—LISA DEMARSH MOUNT SOLON, VA

START TO FINISH: 25 MIN.
MAKES: 8 PANCAKES

- ¾ cup whole wheat flour
- ¼ cup sugar
- 2 tablespoons baking cocoa
- 1 teaspoon baking powder
- ⅛ teaspoon salt
- ⅛ teaspoon ground nutmeg
- ¾ cup fat-free milk
- ¼ cup egg substitute
- 1 tablespoon reduced-fat butter, melted
- 1 cup fresh raspberries
- ½ cup fat-free vanilla yogurt

1. In a small bowl, combine the first six ingredients. Combine the milk, egg substitute and butter; add to dry ingredients just until moistened.
2. Pour batter by scant ¼ cupfuls onto a hot griddle coated with cooking spray; turn when bubbles form on top. Cook until the second side is lightly browned. Serve with raspberries and yogurt.
NOTE *This recipe was tested with Land O'Lakes light stick butter.*
PER SERVING *2 pancakes with ¼ cup raspberries and 2 tablespoons yogurt equals 201 cal., 2 g fat (1 g sat. fat), 6 mg chol., 249 mg sodium, 40 g carb., 5 g fiber, 8 g pro.* **Diabetic Exchanges:** *2 starch, ½ fruit.*

Pineapple Oatmeal

Oatmeal for breakfast is a standard item, but I like to mix it up a bit. This version gets some natural sweetness from pineapple and pineapple juice. It is definitely worth the extra bit of effort!

—MARIA REGAKIS SAUGUS, MA

START TO FINISH: 15 MIN.
MAKES: 3 SERVINGS

- 1¼ cups water
- ½ cup unsweetened pineapple juice
- ¼ teaspoon salt
- 1 cup quick-cooking oats
- ¾ cup unsweetened pineapple tidbits
- ½ cup raisins
- 2 tablespoons brown sugar
- ¼ teaspoon ground cinnamon
- ¼ teaspoon vanilla extract
- ¼ cup chopped walnuts
  Fat-free milk, optional

1. In a large saucepan, bring water, pineapple juice and salt to a boil over medium heat. Add oats; cook and stir for 1-2 minutes or until thickened.
2. Remove from the heat. Stir in pineapple, raisins, brown sugar, cinnamon and vanilla. Cover and let stand for 2-3 minutes. Sprinkle with walnuts. Serve with milk if desired.
PER SERVING *¾ cup (calculated without milk) equals 323 cal., 8 g fat (1 g sat. fat), 0 chol., 210 mg sodium, 61 g carb., 5 g fiber, 6 g pro.*

PINEAPPLE OATMEAL

Applesauce Oatmeal Pancakes

This recipe makes light, fluffy pancakes that will have the entire family asking for seconds. They're wonderful for those on low-calorie diets. Try them topped with homemade sugarless applesauce.

—MARTHA CAGE WHEELING, WV

START TO FINISH: 30 MIN.
MAKES: 10 PANCAKES

- 1 cup quick-cooking oats
- ¼ cup whole wheat flour
- ¼ cup all-purpose flour
- 1 tablespoon baking powder
- 1 cup fat-free milk
- 2 tablespoons unsweetened applesauce
- 4 large egg whites

1. In a bowl, combine the oats, flours and baking powder. In another bowl, combine milk, applesauce and egg whites; add to dry ingredients and mix well.

2. Pour batter by ¼ cupfuls onto a heated griddle coated with cooking spray. Cook until bubbles appear on the top; turn and cook until lightly browned.

PER SERVING *2 pancakes equals 91 cal., 1 g fat (0 sat. fat), 1 mg chol., 323 mg sodium, 15 g carb., 0 fiber, 5 g pro.* **Diabetic Exchange: 1 starch.**

Makeover Hash and Eggs

Loaded with red potatoes and corned beef, our lightened-up version of the diner classic delivers fresh flavors with a healthy dose of fiber.

—TASTE OF HOME TEST KITCHEN

START TO FINISH: 30 MIN.
MAKES: 4 SERVINGS

ORIGINAL	MAKEOVER
450 Calories	**301** Calories
30g Fat	**12**g Fat
12g Sat. Fat	**3**g Sat. Fat

MAKEOVER HASH AND EGGS

- 1 large onion, chopped
- 1 tablespoon canola oil
- 6 medium red potatoes (about 1½ pounds), cut into ½-inch cubes
- ¼ cup water
- 3 packages (2 ounces each) thinly sliced deli corned beef, coarsely chopped
- ¼ teaspoon pepper
- 4 large eggs

1. In a large nonstick skillet, saute onion in oil until tender. Stir in potatoes and water. Bring to a boil. Reduce heat; cover and simmer for 15-20 minutes or until potatoes are tender. Stir in corned beef and pepper; heat through.

2. Meanwhile, in a large nonstick skillet coated with cooking spray, fry eggs as desired. Serve with corned beef hash.

PER SERVING *1 cup corned beef hash with 1 egg equals 301 cal., 12 g fat (3 g sat. fat), 239 mg chol., 652 mg sodium, 31 g carb., 4 g fiber, 18 g pro.*

TOP TIP

I added a splash of Worcestershire sauce, more black pepper and a bit of herbes de Provence for a little more flavor. I thought that it made closer to eight servings than four.

—EMPROPER TASTEOFHOME.COM

FAST FIX **Microwave Egg Sandwich**

If you're looking for a grab-and-go breakfast for busy mornings, this sandwich is high in protein, low in fat and keeps me full all morning. Plus, it's only about 200 calories!

—**BRENDA OTTO** REEDSBURG, WI

START TO FINISH: 15 MIN.
MAKES: 1 SERVING

- 1 piece Canadian bacon
- ¼ cup egg substitute
- 1 tablespoon salsa
- 1 tablespoon shredded reduced-fat cheddar cheese
- 1 whole wheat English muffin, split, toasted
- 3 spinach leaves

1. Place Canadian bacon on bottom of a 6-oz. ramekin or custard cup coated with cooking spray. Pour egg substitute over top. Microwave, uncovered, on high for 30 seconds; stir. Microwave 15-30 seconds or until egg is almost set. Top with salsa; sprinkle with cheese. Microwave just until cheese is melted, about 10 seconds.

2. Line bottom of English muffin with spinach. Place egg and Canadian bacon over spinach; replace English muffin top.
NOTE *This recipe was tested in a 1,100-watt microwave.*
PER SERVING *1 sandwich equals 218 cal., 4 g fat (2 g sat. fat), 12 mg chol., 751 mg sodium, 30 g carb., 5 g fiber, 17 g pro.* **Diabetic Exchanges:** *2 starch, 2 lean meat.*

Overnight French Toast

I tried this slimmed-down French toast recently, and the family really loved it! It's now in heavy rotation at the breakfast table.

—**SONYA LABBE** WEST HOLLYWOOD, CA

PREP: 15 MIN. + CHILLING • **BAKE:** 25 MIN.
MAKES: 8 SERVINGS

- 4 large eggs
- 1 cup egg substitute
- 3 cups fat-free milk
- ¼ cup sugar
- 2 teaspoons vanilla extract
- ¼ teaspoon salt
- 16 slices French bread (1 inch thick)

BERRY SAUCE
- 2 packages (12 ounces each) frozen unsweetened mixed berries, thawed
- ¼ cup sugar

1. In a large bowl, combine the eggs, egg substitute, milk, sugar, vanilla and salt. Place bread slices in two ungreased 13x9-in. baking dishes; pour egg mixture over top. Cover and refrigerate overnight.
2. Coat two 15x10x1-in. baking pans with butter-flavored cooking spray. Carefully transfer bread to prepared pans. Bake, uncovered, at 400° for 15 minutes. Carefully turn slices over. Bake 10-15 minutes longer or until bread is golden brown and slightly puffed.
3. Meanwhile, combine berries and sugar. Serve with French toast.
PER SERVING *2 slices French toast with ⅓ cup sauce equals 294 cal., 4 g fat (1 g sat. fat), 108 mg chol., 486 mg sodium, 50 g carb., 3 g fiber, 13 g pro.*

OVERNIGHT FRENCH TOAST

CALICO PEPPER FRITTATA

FAST FIX

Calico Pepper Frittata

My garden-fresh frittata has all-day appeal. I serve it for breakfast, brunch, lunch and even dinner. It's made on the stovetop so there's no need to heat up the oven.

—**LORETTA KELCINSKI** KUNKLETOWN, PA

START TO FINISH: 30 MIN.
MAKES: 4 SERVINGS

5	**large eggs**
1¼	**cups egg substitute**
1	**tablespoon grated Romano cheese**
½	**teaspoon salt**
⅛	**teaspoon pepper**

1 **tablespoon olive oil**
1 **medium sweet red pepper, chopped**
1 **medium green pepper, chopped**
1 **jalapeno pepper, seeded and chopped**
1 **medium onion, chopped**
1 **garlic clove, minced**

1. In a large bowl, whisk the first five ingredients until blended.

2. In a large nonstick skillet, heat oil over medium-high heat. Add peppers and onion; cook and stir until tender. Add garlic; cook 1 minute longer. Pour in egg mixture. Mixture should set immediately at the edges. Cook, uncovered, 8-10 minutes or until eggs are completely set, pushing cooked portions toward the center and letting uncooked eggs flow underneath. Cut into wedges.

NOTE *Wear disposable gloves when cutting hot peppers; the oils can burn skin. Avoid touching your face.*

PER SERVING *1 wedge equals 201 cal., 10 g fat (3 g sat. fat), 268 mg chol., 559 mg sodium, 10 g carb., 2 g fiber, 17 g pro.* **Diabetic Exchanges:** *2 lean meat, 2 vegetable, 1 fat.*

Crispy French Toast

Cornflakes add irresistible crunch to this easy baked French toast recipe. My light version uses egg substitute and skim milk, but still gets plenty of flavor from vanilla, spice and a kiss of orange.

—**FLO BURTNETT** GAGE, OK

PREP: 20 MIN. • **BAKE:** 15 MIN.
MAKES: 6 SERVINGS

- ½ **cup egg substitute**
- ½ **cup fat-free milk**
- ¼ **cup orange juice**
- 1 **teaspoon vanilla extract**
  Dash ground nutmeg
- 12 **slices day-old French bread**
  (¾ inch thick)
- 1½ **cups crushed cornflakes**

1. In a shallow dish, combine the egg substitute, milk, orange juice, vanilla and nutmeg. Add bread; soak for 5 minutes, turning once. Coat both sides of each bread slice with the cornflake crumbs.

2. Place in a 15x10x1-in. baking pan coated with cooking spray. Bake at 425° for 10 minutes; turn. Bake 5-8 minutes longer or until golden brown.
FREEZE OPTION *Remove baked French toast from pan to wire racks to cool. Freeze between layers of waxed paper in a resealable plastic freezer bag. To use, place frozen French toast on a greased baking sheet. Bake in a preheated 425° oven for 5-7 minutes or until heated through. Or, microwave each slice on high for 30-60 seconds or until heated through.*
PER SERVING *2 slices equals 200 cal., 1 g fat (trace sat. fat), trace chol., 421 mg sodium, 40 g carb., 1 g fiber, 7 g pro.* **Diabetic Exchange:** *3 starch.*

Banana Pancake Snowmen

You'll be saying "let it snow" when you see these adorable pancakes shaped like snowmen. Let little ones help decorate their own with pretzels for arms and chocolate chips, raisins or cranberries for faces and buttons.

—**PHYLLIS SCHMALZ** KANSAS CITY, KS

PREP: 15 MIN. • **COOK:** 5 MIN./BATCH
MAKES: 7 SNOWMEN

- 1 **cup complete buttermilk pancake mix**
- ¾ **cup water**
- ⅓ **cup mashed ripe banana**
- 1 **teaspoon confectioners' sugar**
  Pretzel sticks, chocolate chips, dried cranberries and/or halved banana slices

1. In a small bowl, stir the pancake mix, water and banana just until moistened.

2. Pour ¼ cup batter onto a greased hot griddle, making three circles to form a snowman. Turn when bubbles form on top. Cook until the second side is golden brown. Transfer to a serving plate. Repeat with the remaining batter.
3. Sprinkle with confectioners' sugar. Decorate snowmen with pretzels, chocolate chips, cranberries and/or banana if desired.
PER SERVING *1 snowman (calculated without decorations) equals 76 cal., 1 g fat (trace sat. fat), 0 chol., 277 mg sodium, 17 g carb., 1 g fiber, 1 g pro.* **Diabetic Exchange:** *1 starch.*

Chewy Granola Bars

These bars manage to be both soft and crispy at the same time. They make a nutritious portable treat.

—VIRGINIA KRITES CRIDERSVILLE, OH

PREP: 10 MIN. • **BAKE:** 25 MIN. + COOLING
MAKES: 2 DOZEN

- ½ cup butter, softened
- 1 cup packed brown sugar
- ¼ cup sugar
- 2 tablespoons honey
- ½ teaspoon vanilla extract
- 1 large egg
- 1 cup all-purpose flour
- 1 teaspoon ground cinnamon
- ½ teaspoon baking powder
- ¼ teaspoon salt
- 1½ cups quick-cooking oats
- 1¼ cups Rice Krispies
- 1 cup chopped nuts
- 1 cup raisins or semisweet chocolate chips, optional

1. In a large bowl, cream butter and sugars until light and fluffy. Add the honey, vanilla and egg; mix well. Combine the flour, cinnamon, baking powder and salt; gradually add to creamed mixture. Stir in oats, cereal and nuts. Add raisins or chocolate chips if desired.

2. Press into a greased 13x9-in. baking pan. Bake at 350° for 25-30 minutes or until the top is lightly browned. Cool on a wire rack. Cut into bars.

PER SERVING *1 bar equals 160 cal., 7 g fat (3 g sat. fat), 19 mg chol., 91 mg sodium, 22 g carb., 1 g fiber, 3 g pro. Diabetic Exchanges: 1½ starch, 1½ fat.*

Blue Cheese Souffle

Lightened up to fewer than 100 calories per serving and packed with protein, this rich and flavorful souffle will be the star of the breakfast table. It's also a nice side dish for beef.

—SARAH VASQUES MILFORD, NH

PREP: 25 MIN. • **BAKE:** 25 MIN.
MAKES: 8 SERVINGS

- 5 large egg whites
- 6 tablespoons grated Parmesan cheese, divided
- 3 tablespoons all-purpose flour
- ½ teaspoon salt
- ¼ teaspoon pepper
  Dash ground nutmeg
  Dash cayenne pepper
- 1 cup fat-free milk
- ⅓ cup crumbled blue cheese
- 4 large egg yolks
- ⅛ teaspoon cream of tartar

1. Let egg whites stand at room temperature for 30 minutes. Coat a 2-qt. souffle dish with cooking spray and lightly sprinkle with 2 tablespoons Parmesan cheese; set aside.

2. In a small saucepan, combine flour and seasonings. Gradually whisk in milk. Bring to a boil, stirring constantly. Cook and stir 1 minute longer or until thickened. Reduce heat. Stir in the blue cheese and remaining Parmesan cheese. Remove from the heat; transfer to a large bowl.

3. Stir a small amount of hot mixture into egg yolks; return all to the bowl, stirring constantly. Cool slightly.

4. In another large bowl with clean beaters, beat egg whites and cream of tartar until stiff peaks form. With a spatula, stir a fourth of the egg whites into cheese mixture until no white streaks remain. Fold in remaining egg whites until combined.

5. Transfer to prepared dish. Bake at 350° for 25-30 minutes or until the top is puffed and center appears set. Serve immediately.

PER SERVING *1 serving equals 95 cal., 5 g fat (3 g sat. fat), 111 mg chol., 335 mg sodium, 5 g carb., trace fiber, 8 g pro. Diabetic Exchanges: 1 medium-fat meat, ½ fat.*

CHEWY GRANOLA BARS

BLUE CHEESE SOUFFLE

Blackberry Whole Wheat Coffee Cake

This low-guilt coffee cake is high in luscious blackberry flavor. Wonderfully moist and tender, it's also good made with fresh or frozen blueberries or raspberries.

—CAROL FORCUM MARION, IL

PREP: 20 MIN. • **BAKE:** 35 MIN. + COOLING
MAKES: 20 SERVINGS

- 1½ cups all-purpose flour
- 1⅓ cups packed brown sugar
- 1 cup whole wheat flour
- 2 teaspoons baking powder
- ½ teaspoon baking soda
  - Dash salt
- 1 large egg
- 1 cup buttermilk
- ⅓ cup canola oil
- ⅓ cup unsweetened applesauce
- 2 teaspoons vanilla extract
- 2 cups fresh or frozen blackberries

1. In a large bowl, combine the first six ingredients. In a small bowl, combine the egg, buttermilk, oil, applesauce and vanilla. Stir into dry ingredients just until moistened. Fold in blackberries.

2. Transfer to a 13x9-in. baking pan coated with cooking spray. Bake at

375° for 35-40 minutes or until a toothpick inserted near the center comes out clean. Cool on a wire rack.

PER SERVING *1 piece equals 160 cal., 4 g fat (trace sat. fat), 11 mg chol., 102 mg sodium, 28 g carb., 2 g fiber, 3 g pro.* **Diabetic Exchanges:** *2 starch, 1 fat.*

⑤ INGREDIENTS

Cinnamon Fruit Biscuits

Because these sweet treats are so easy, I'm almost embarrassed when people ask me for the recipe. They're a snap to make with refrigerated buttermilk biscuits, sugar, cinnamon and your favorite fruit preserves.

—IONE BURHAM WASHINGTON, IA

PREP: 15 MIN. • **BAKE:** 15 MIN. + COOLING
MAKES: 10 SERVINGS

- ½ cup sugar
- ½ teaspoon ground cinnamon
- 1 tube (12 ounces) refrigerated buttermilk biscuits, separated into 10 biscuits
- ¼ cup butter, melted
- 10 teaspoons strawberry preserves

1. In a small bowl, combine sugar and cinnamon. Dip top and sides of biscuits in butter, then in cinnamon-sugar mixture.

2. Place on ungreased baking sheets. With the end of a wooden spoon handle, make a deep indentation in the center of each biscuit; fill with 1 teaspoon preserves.

3. Bake at 375° for 15-18 minutes or until golden brown. Cool for 15 minutes before serving (preserves will be hot).

PER SERVING *1 biscuit equals 178 cal., 5 g fat (3 g sat. fat), 12 mg chol., 323 mg sodium, 31 g carb., trace fiber, 3 g pro.* **Diabetic Exchanges:** *2 starch, 1 fat.*

⑤ INGREDIENTS FAST FIX

Lean Green Smoothie

Kids love the unusual color of this frosty and flavorful smoothie. It's fine-tuned to their liking with bananas, creamy yogurt and shh...spinach.

—MADISON MAYBERRY AMES, IA

START TO FINISH: 10 MIN.
MAKES: 4 SERVINGS

- ¾ cup fat-free milk
- 1½ cups (12 ounces) fat-free vanilla yogurt
- 1 cup ice cubes
- 1 cup fresh spinach
- 1 ripe medium banana
- 2 tablespoons lemon juice

In a blender, combine all ingredients; cover and process for 30 seconds or until smooth. Pour into chilled glasses; serve immediately.

PER SERVING *1 cup equals 99 cal., trace fat (trace sat. fat), 4 mg chol., 24 mg sodium, 19 g carb., 1 g fiber, 5 g pro.* **Diabetic Exchanges:** *1 fat-free milk, ½ fruit.*

Black Bean & White Cheddar Frittata

This is one of my favorite comfort foods for breakfast or even a quick dinner. I like to make it with lime salsa. But if you're looking for something with more kick, use hot salsa or add some chipotle pepper.

—AYSHA SCHURMAN AMMON, ID

PREP: 20 MIN. • **COOK:** 15 MIN.
MAKES: 6 SERVINGS

- 6   large eggs
- 3   large egg whites
- ¼   cup salsa
- 1   tablespoon minced fresh parsley
- ¼   teaspoon salt
- ¼   teaspoon pepper
- 1   tablespoon olive oil
- ⅓   cup finely chopped green pepper
- ⅓   cup finely chopped sweet red pepper
- 3   green onions, finely chopped
- 2   garlic cloves, minced
- 1   cup canned black beans, rinsed and drained
- ½   cup shredded white cheddar cheese
  Optional toppings: minced fresh cilantro, sliced ripe olives and additional salsa

1. Preheat broiler. In a large bowl, whisk the first six ingredients until blended.
2. In a 10-in. ovenproof skillet, heat oil over medium-high heat. Add peppers and green onions; cook and stir 3-4 minutes or until peppers are tender. Add garlic; cook 1 minute longer. Stir in beans. Reduce heat to medium; stir in egg mixture. Cook, uncovered, 4-6 minutes or until nearly set. Sprinkle with cheese.
3. Broil 3-4 in. from heat 3-4 minutes or until light golden brown and the eggs are completely set. Let stand 5 minutes. Cut into wedges. If desired, serve with toppings.

PER SERVING *1 wedge (calculated without toppings) equals 183 cal., 10 g fat (4 g sat. fat), 196 mg chol., 378 mg sodium, 9 g carb., 2 g fiber, 13 g pro.* **Diabetic Exchanges:** *2 medium-fat meat, ½ starch, ½ fat.*

BLACK BEAN & WHITE CHEDDAR FRITTATA

FAST FIX
Makeover Waffles

Dust off that waffle iron because these breakfast sensations are a fantastic way to start your day! A smart applesauce substitution cuts the fat in half.

—CAROL BURGER PHILLIPS, WI

START TO FINISH: 25 MIN.
MAKES: 10 WAFFLES

- 1¾ cups all-purpose flour
- 3 teaspoons baking powder
- ½ teaspoon salt
- 2 large egg yolks
- 1¾ cups fat-free milk
- ¼ cup canola oil
- ¼ cup unsweetened applesauce
- 2 large egg whites

1. In a large bowl, combine the flour, baking powder and salt. In a small bowl, whisk the egg yolks, milk, oil and applesauce. Stir into dry ingredients just until moistened.
2. In another small bowl, beat egg whites until stiff peaks form. Fold into batter. Bake in a preheated waffle iron according to manufacturer's directions until golden brown.
PER SERVING *2 waffles equals 321 cal., 13 g fat (2 g sat. fat), 84 mg chol., 538 mg sodium, 39 g carb., 1 g fiber, 10 g pro.*

MAKEOVER WAFFLES

ORIGINAL	MAKEOVER
437 Calories	**321** Calories
28g Fat	**13**g Fat
4g Sat. Fat	**2**g Sat. Fat

Sausage Egg Puff

I stir up this flavorful brunch dish at night so it's ready to bake up light and fluffy the next morning. The recipe came from a beautiful bed-and-breakfast my husband and I stayed at several years ago.

—TAMMY LAMB CAMPBELLSVILLE, KY

PREP: 15 MIN. + CHILLING
BAKE: 50 MIN. + STANDING
MAKES: 6 SERVINGS

- 1 package (12 ounces) frozen turkey breakfast sausage links, thawed
- 1 cup reduced-fat biscuit/baking mix
- 1 cup (4 ounces) shredded reduced-fat cheddar cheese
- 1 teaspoon ground mustard
- 1 teaspoon Italian seasoning
- 1 cup egg substitute
- 2 large eggs
- 2 cups fat-free milk

1. Remove sausage from casings; crumble into a large skillet. Cook until no longer pink; drain. In a large bowl, combine the biscuit mix, cheese, mustard and Italian seasoning; add sausage.
2. In another bowl, whisk the egg substitute, eggs and milk; stir into the sausage mixture. Transfer to a shallow 2-qt. baking dish coated with cooking spray. Cover the baking dish and refrigerate overnight.
3. Remove from the refrigerator 30 minutes before baking. Bake, uncovered, at 350° for 50-55 minutes or until a knife inserted near the center comes out clean.
PER SERVING *1 serving equals 336 cal., 18 g fat (6 g sat. fat), 123 mg chol., 813 mg sodium, 19 g carb., trace fiber, 25 g pro.*

Slow Cooker Honey Granola

It's so simple to put this granola together, and it really helps with breakfast on busy mornings. Change up the fruits to fit your preferences or the seasons.

—**ARISA CUPP** WARREN, OR

PREP: 10 MIN. • **COOK:** 2 HOURS + COOLING
MAKES: ABOUT 8 CUPS

- 4 **cups old-fashioned oats**
- 1 **cup sunflower kernels**
- 1 **cup flaked coconut**
- ½ **teaspoon salt**
- ½ **cup canola oil**
- ½ **cup honey**
- 1 **cup chopped dried pineapple**
- 1 **cup chopped dried mangoes**

1. In a 3-qt. slow cooker, combine oats, sunflower kernels, coconut and salt. In a small bowl, whisk oil and honey until blended. Stir into oats mixture. Cook, covered, on high 2 hours, stirring well every 20 minutes.
2. Remove granola to baking sheets, spreading evenly; cool completely. Stir in pineapple and mangoes. Store in airtight containers.
PER SERVING *½ cup equals 295 cal., 15 g fat (3 g sat. fat), 0 chol., 167 mg sodium, 38 g carb., 4 g fiber, 5 g pro.*

MINI HAM 'N' CHEESE FRITTATAS

⑤ INGREDIENTS
Mini Ham 'n' Cheese Frittatas

I found this recipe a few years ago and made some little changes to it. I'm diabetic, and it fits into my low-carb and low-fat diet. Every time I serve a brunch, the frittatas are the first to disappear, and nobody knows they are low in fat!

—**SUSAN WATT** BASKING RIDGE, NJ

PREP: 15 MIN. • **BAKE:** 25 MIN.
MAKES: 8 FRITTATAS

- ¼ **pound cubed fully cooked ham**
- 1 **cup (4 ounces) shredded fat-free cheddar cheese**
- 6 **large eggs**
- 4 **large egg whites**
- 3 **tablespoons minced chives**
- 2 **tablespoons fat-free milk**
- ¼ **teaspoon salt**
- ¼ **teaspoon pepper**

1. Divide ham among eight muffin cups coated with cooking spray; top with cheese. In a large bowl, beat eggs and whites. Beat in the chives, milk, salt and pepper. Pour egg mixture over cheese, filling each muffin cup three-fourths full.
2. Bake at 375° for 22-25 minutes or until a knife inserted near the center comes out clean. Carefully run a knife around edges to loosen; remove from pan. Serve warm.
PER SERVING *1 frittata equals 106 cal., 4 g fat (1 g sat. fat), 167 mg chol., 428 mg sodium, 2 g carb., trace fiber, 14 g pro.* **Diabetic Exchange:** *2 medium-fat meat.*

MONTEREY QUICHE

Monterey Quiche

This cheesy, slightly spicy quiche is always a hit with my family. *Taste of Home* lightened up my recipe to replicate my original version's mouthwatering taste, but with less fat, calories and cholesterol.
—PAM PRESSLY BEACHWOOD, OH

PREP: 25 MIN. • **BAKE:** 45 MIN.
MAKES: 2 QUICHES (6 SERVINGS EACH)

- ½ cup chopped onion
- 1 tablespoon butter
- 2 garlic cloves, minced
- 8 large egg whites, divided
- 4 large eggs
- 2 cups (16 ounces) 1% small-curd cottage cheese
- 2 cups (8 ounces) shredded reduced-fat Mexican cheese blend or Monterey Jack cheese, divided
- 2 cans (4 ounces each) chopped green chilies
- ⅓ cup all-purpose flour
- ¾ teaspoon baking powder
- ¼ teaspoon salt
- 2 unbaked deep-dish pastry shells (9 inches)

1. In a small nonstick skillet, cook onion in butter over medium-low heat until tender, stirring occasionally. Add garlic; cook 1 minute longer.

2. In a large bowl, combine 6 egg whites, eggs, cottage cheese, 1½ cups shredded cheese, chilies, flour, baking powder, salt and onion mixture. In a large bowl, beat remaining egg whites until stiff peaks form. Fold into cheese mixture. Pour into pastry shells.

3. Bake at 400° for 10 minutes. Reduce heat to 350°; bake 30 minutes. Sprinkle with remaining cheese; bake 5 minutes longer or until a knife inserted near the center comes out clean and cheese is melted. Let stand for 10 minutes before cutting.

PER SERVING *1 piece equals 265 cal., 14 g fat (5 g sat. fat), 88 mg chol., 610 mg sodium, 21 g carb., 1 g fiber, 16 g pro.*

FAST FIX

Lemon Breakfast Parfaits

I serve these refreshing parfaits as a lively start to a day. You can make the couscous mixture ahead, then cover and chill it overnight.
—JANELLE LEE APPLETON, WI

PREP: 25 MIN. + COOLING
MAKES: 6 SERVINGS

- ¾ cup fat-free milk
  Dash salt
- ⅓ cup uncooked couscous
- ½ cup reduced-fat sour cream
- ½ cup lemon yogurt
- 1 tablespoon honey
- ¼ teaspoon grated lemon peel
- 1 cup sliced peeled kiwifruit
- 1 cup fresh blueberries
- 1 cup fresh raspberries
  Chopped crystallized ginger and minced fresh mint

1. In a small saucepan, bring milk and salt to a boil. Stir in couscous. Remove from the heat; cover and let stand for 5-10 minutes or until milk is absorbed. Fluff with a fork; cool.

2. In a small bowl, combine the sour cream, yogurt, honey and lemon peel. Stir in couscous.

3. Combine the kiwi, blueberries and raspberries; spoon ¼ cup into each of six parfait glasses. Layer with couscous mixture and remaining fruit. Garnish with ginger and mint.

PER SERVING *1 parfait equals 146 cal., 2 g fat (1 g sat. fat), 8 mg chol., 64 mg sodium, 27 g carb., 3 g fiber, 5 g pro.*
Diabetic Exchanges: *1 starch, ½ fruit.*

Baked Peach Pancake

This dish makes for a dramatic presentation. I usually take it right from the oven to the table, fill it with peaches and sour cream, and serve bacon or ham alongside. Whenever I go home, my mom (the best cook I know) asks me to make this.

—**NANCY WILKINSON** PRINCETON, NJ

PREP: 10 MIN. • **BAKE:** 25 MIN.
MAKES: 6 SERVINGS

- 2 **cups fresh or frozen sliced peeled peaches**
- 4 **teaspoons sugar**
- 1 **teaspoon lemon juice**
- 3 **large eggs**
- ½ **cup all-purpose flour**
- ½ **cup 2% milk**
- ½ **teaspoon salt**
- 2 **tablespoons butter**
  Ground nutmeg
  Sour cream, optional

1. In a small bowl, combine peaches, sugar and lemon juice; set aside. In a large bowl, beat eggs until fluffy. Add the flour, milk and salt; beat until smooth.
2. Place butter in a 10-in. ovenproof skillet in a 400° oven for 3-5 minutes or until melted. Immediately pour batter into hot skillet. Bake for 20-25 minutes or until pancake has risen and puffed all over.
3. Fill with peach slices and sprinkle with nutmeg. Serve immediately with sour cream if desired.

PER SERVING *1 piece (calculated without sour cream) equals 149 cal., 7 g fat (4 g sat. fat), 105 mg chol., 272 mg sodium, 17 g carb., 1 g fiber, 5 g pro.* **Diabetic Exchanges:** *1 medium-fat meat, 1 fat, ½ starch, ½ fruit.*

Sunday Brunch Casserole

My favorite brunch dish got a makeover with egg substitute and lower-fat cheese. The lightened-up version still tastes delicious, but it won't weigh you down!

—**ALICE HOFMANN** SUSSEX, WI

PREP: 20 MIN. • **BAKE:** 30 MIN.
MAKES: 8 SERVINGS

- 6 **bacon strips**
- 1 **small onion, chopped**
- 1 **small green pepper, chopped**
- 1 **teaspoon canola oil**
- 2 **cartons (8 ounces each) egg substitute**
- 4 **large eggs**
- 1 **cup fat-free milk**
- 4 **cups frozen shredded hash brown potatoes, thawed**
- 1 **cup (4 ounces) shredded reduced-fat cheddar cheese**
- ¾ **teaspoon salt**
- ½ **teaspoon pepper**
- ¼ **teaspoon dill weed**

1. In a large skillet, cook bacon over medium heat until crisp. Remove to paper towels; drain. Crumble bacon and set aside. In the same skillet, saute onion and green pepper in oil until tender; remove with a slotted spoon.
2. In a large bowl, whisk the egg substitute, eggs and milk. Stir in the hash browns, cheese, salt, pepper, dill, onion mixture and bacon.
3. Transfer to a 13x9-in. baking dish coated with cooking spray. Bake, uncovered, at 350° for 30-35 minutes or until a knife inserted near the center comes out clean.

PER SERVING *1 piece equals 181 cal., 8 g fat (3 g sat. fat), 122 mg chol., 591 mg sodium, 11 g carb., 1 g fiber, 16 g pro.* **Diabetic Exchanges:** *2 lean meat, 1 starch.*

SUNDAY BRUNCH CASSEROLE

LAURA STENBERG'S
ASIAN BEEF AND NOODLES
PAGE125

Beef Entrees

From old-fashioned **comfort foods** such as meat loaf and sloppy joes to **Greek, Mexican and Italian specialties,** this chapter offers all the mealtime variety you could ask for. When you can't decide how to cook up a **healthy beef dinner,** turn here for the mouthwatering answer.

**MARIE RIZZIO'S
TENDERLOIN WITH CREMINI-
APRICOT STUFFING** *PAGE131*

**AMY LENTS'
MEXICAN SHREDDED BEEF WRAPS**
PAGE 118

**MEGAN NIEBUHR'S
BEEF & VEGGIE SLOPPY JOES**
PAGE 132

BALSAMIC-GLAZED
BEEF SKEWERS

Berry Nice Brisket

Cranberry juice and cranberry sauce make this tender brisket so tasty. It's wonderful for a holiday buffet.

—**CAROL HUNIHAN** ALAMOSA, CO

PREP: 15 MIN.
BAKE: 3 HOURS + STANDING
MAKES: 10-12 SERVINGS

- ¼ cup all-purpose flour
- 1 can (14½ ounces) beef broth
- 1 can (14 ounces) whole-berry cranberry sauce
- 1 cup cranberry juice
- 3 garlic cloves, minced
- 1 tablespoon minced fresh rosemary or 1 teaspoon dried rosemary, crushed
- 1 large onion, thinly sliced
- 1 fresh beef brisket (3 to 4 pounds)
- ½ teaspoon salt
- ¼ teaspoon pepper

1. In a large bowl, combine flour and broth until smooth. Stir in the cranberry sauce, cranberry juice, garlic and rosemary. Pour into a large roasting pan. Top with onion slices.
2. Season the brisket with salt and pepper. Place fat side up in pan. Cover and bake at 350° for 3-3½ hours or until tender, basting occasionally.
3. Remove brisket to a serving platter and let stand for 15 minutes. Thinly slice meat across the grain; serve with onion and pan juices.
NOTE *This is a fresh beef brisket, not corned beef.*
PER SERVING *3 ounces equals 219 cal., 5 g fat (2 g sat. fat), 48 mg chol., 298 mg sodium, 18 g carb., 1 g fiber, 24 g pro. Diabetic Exchanges: 3 lean meat, 1 starch.*

⑤ INGREDIENTS FAST FIX

Balsamic-Glazed Beef Skewers

With only five simple ingredients, these mouthwatering kabobs are a summertime favorite. To prevent the skewers from burning, soak them in water 30 minutes before threading on the steak and cherry tomatoes.

—**CAROLE FRASER** TORONTO, ON

START TO FINISH: 25 MIN.
MAKES: 4 SERVINGS

- ¼ cup balsamic vinaigrette
- ¼ cup barbecue sauce
- 1 teaspoon Dijon mustard
- 1 pound beef top sirloin steak, cut into 1-inch cubes
- 2 cups cherry tomatoes

1. In a large bowl, whisk vinaigrette, barbecue sauce and mustard until blended. Reserve ¼ cup mixture for basting. Add beef to remaining mixture; toss to coat.
2. Alternately thread beef and tomatoes on four metal or soaked wooden skewers. Moisten a paper towel with cooking oil; using long-handled tongs, rub on grill rack to coat lightly.
3. Grill skewers, covered, over medium heat or broil 4 in. from heat 6-9 minutes or until beef reaches desired doneness, turning occasionally and basting frequently with reserved vinaigrette mixture during the last 3 minutes.
PER SERVING *1 skewer equals 194 cal., 7 g fat (2 g sat. fat), 46 mg chol., 288 mg sodium, 7 g carb., 1 g fiber, 25 g pro. Diabetic Exchanges: 3 lean meat, 1½ fat, ½ starch.*

Beef Macaroni Skillet

This stovetop favorite is tasty and stick-to-your-ribs. It's easy to prepare, perfect for after a long day at work.

—CARMEN EDWARDS MIDLAND, TX

PREP: 15 MIN. • **COOK:** 30 MIN.
MAKES: 2 SERVINGS

- ½ pound lean ground beef (90% lean)
- ⅓ cup chopped onion
- ¼ cup chopped green pepper
- 1½ cups spicy hot V8 juice
- ½ cup uncooked elbow macaroni
- 1 teaspoon Worcestershire sauce
- ¼ teaspoon pepper

In a large skillet, cook the beef, onion and green pepper over medium heat until meat is no longer pink; drain. Stir in the remaining ingredients. Bring to a boil. Reduce heat; cover and simmer for 18-20 minutes or until macaroni is tender.

PER SERVING *1¼ cups equals 291 cal., 9 g fat (4 g sat. fat), 56 mg chol., 689 mg sodium, 25 g carb., 2 g fiber, 26 g pro. Diabetic Exchanges: 3 lean meat, 2 vegetable, 1 starch.*

BEEF PITAS WITH YOGURT SAUCE

FAST FIX ▶ Beef Pitas with Yogurt Sauce

I've always wanted to tour the Mediterranean, but this is as close as I'll get...for now. Top these gyros with a yogurt sauce that doubles as a dip for pita chips.

—DANIEL ANDERSON PLEASANT PRAIRIE, WI

START TO FINISH: 30 MIN.
MAKES: 4 SERVINGS

- 1 cup (8 ounces) fat-free plain yogurt
- ¼ cup minced fresh parsley
- 1 garlic clove, minced
- ⅛ teaspoon plus ½ teaspoon salt, divided
- 1 pound beef top sirloin steak, cut into thin strips
- 1 teaspoon dried oregano
- 1 teaspoon minced fresh rosemary
- ¼ teaspoon pepper
- 4 teaspoons olive oil, divided
- 1 large sweet onion, sliced
- 4 whole pita breads, warmed

1. In a small bowl, mix yogurt, parsley, garlic and ⅛ teaspoon salt. Toss beef with herbs, pepper and remaining salt.

2. In a large nonstick skillet, heat 2 teaspoons oil over medium-high heat. Add the onion; cook and stir for 4-6 minutes or until tender. Remove from pan.

3. In same skillet, heat remaining oil over medium-high heat. Add beef; cook and stir 2-3 minutes or until no longer pink. Serve on pitas; top with onion and sauce.

PER SERVING *1 filled pita with ¼ cup sauce equals 405 cal., 10 g fat (2 g sat. fat), 47 mg chol., 784 mg sodium, 45 g carb., 2 g fiber, 33 g pro. Diabetic Exchanges: 3 starch, 3 lean meat, 1 fat.*

Stamp-of-Approval Spaghetti Sauce

My father is pretty opinionated... especially about food. This recipe received his nearly unattainable stamp of approval, and I have yet to hear any disagreement from anyone who has tried it!

—MELISSA TAYLOR HIGLEY, AZ

PREP: 30 MIN. • **COOK:** 8 HOURS
MAKES: 12 SERVINGS (3 QUARTS)

- 2 **pounds ground beef**
- ¾ **pound bulk Italian sausage**
- 4 **medium onions, finely chopped**
- 8 **garlic cloves, minced**
- 4 **cans (14½ ounces each) diced tomatoes, undrained**
- 4 **cans (6 ounces each) tomato paste**
- ½ **cup water**
- ¼ **cup sugar**
- ¼ **cup Worcestershire sauce**
- 1 **tablespoon canola oil**
- ¼ **cup minced fresh parsley**
- 2 **tablespoons minced fresh basil or 2 teaspoons dried basil**
- 1 **tablespoon minced fresh oregano or 1 teaspoon dried oregano**
- 4 **bay leaves**
- 1 **teaspoon rubbed sage**
- ½ **teaspoon salt**
- ½ **teaspoon dried marjoram**
- ½ **teaspoon pepper**
  Hot cooked spaghetti

1. In a Dutch oven, cook the beef, sausage, onions and garlic over medium heat until meat is no longer pink; drain.

2. Transfer to a 5-qt. slow cooker. Stir in the tomatoes, tomato paste, water, sugar, Worcestershire sauce, canola oil and seasonings.

3. Cover and cook on low for 8-10 hours. Discard bay leaves. Serve with spaghetti.

FREEZE OPTION *Cool before placing in a freezer container. Cover and freeze for up to 3 months. Thaw in the refrigerator overnight. Place in a large saucepan; heat through, stirring occasionally. Serve with spaghetti.*

PER SERVING *1 cup sauce (calculated without spaghetti) equals 298 cal., 12 g fat (4 g sat. fat), 48 mg chol., 557 mg sodium, 30 g carb., 7 g fiber, 20 g pro.* **Diabetic Exchanges:** *4 vegetable, 2 lean meat, 2 fat.*

Bacon-Cheddar Meat Loaves

It's easy to get your family eating healthier with these fun little meat loaves. No one will guess they're light—they're topped with bacon and melted cheese!

—TONYA VOWELS VINE GROVE, KY

PREP: 20 MIN. • **BAKE:** 40 MIN.
MAKES: 4 SERVINGS

- 4 **egg whites**
- ½ **cup crushed reduced-fat Ritz crackers (about 12 crackers)**
- ⅓ **cup plus 8 teaspoons shredded reduced-fat cheddar cheese, divided**
- ¼ **cup chopped onion**
- ½ **teaspoon salt**
- ¼ **teaspoon pepper**
- 1 **pound lean ground beef (90% lean)**
- 2 **turkey bacon strips, cut in half**

1. In a large bowl, combine the egg whites, crackers, ⅓ cup cheese, onion, salt and pepper. Crumble beef over mixture and mix well. Shape into four small loaves; place in an ungreased 11x7-in. baking dish. Top each with a half-strip of bacon.

2. Bake at 350° for 35-40 minutes or until no pink remains and a thermometer reads 160°. Sprinkle with remaining cheese; bake for 2-3 minutes longer or until cheese is melted.

PER SERVING *1 meat loaf equals 296 cal., 15 g fat (6 g sat. fat), 86 mg chol., 672 mg sodium, 9 g carb., trace fiber, 30 g pro.* **Diabetic Exchanges:** *4 lean meat, ½ starch, ½ fat.*

STAMP-OF-APPROVAL SPAGHETTI SAUCE

FAST FIX Juicy & Delicious Mixed Spice Burgers

Not your average burgers, these Middle Eastern patties are seasoned with fresh herbs and warm spices such as cinnamon, pepper and nutmeg. Serving them with tzatziki sauce is optional, but you won't regret it if you do.

—**ANNE HENRY** TORONTO, ON

START TO FINISH: 30 MIN.
MAKES: 6 SERVINGS

- 1 **medium onion, finely chopped**
- 3 **tablespoons minced fresh parsley**
- 2 **tablespoons minced fresh mint**
- 1 **garlic clove, minced**
- ¾ **teaspoon ground allspice**
- ¾ **teaspoon pepper**
- ½ **teaspoon ground cinnamon**
- ½ **teaspoon salt**
- ¼ **teaspoon ground nutmeg**
- 1½ **pounds lean ground beef (90% lean)**
  Refrigerated tzatziki sauce, optional

1. In a large bowl, combine the first nine ingredients. Add beef; mix lightly but thoroughly. Shape into six 4x2-in. oblong patties.

2. Grill patties, covered, over medium heat or broil 4 in. from the heat for 4-6 minutes on each side or until a thermometer reads 160°. If desired, serve with sauce.

PER SERVING *1 burger (calculated without tzatziki sauce) equals 192 cal., 9 g fat (4 g sat. fat), 71 mg chol., 259 mg sodium, 3 g carb., 1 g fiber, 22 g pro.* **Diabetic Exchange:** *3 lean meat.*

FAST FIX Open-Faced Roast Beef Sandwiches

Arugula brings the zing to this sandwich. I usually make extras because most people who taste them want seconds.

—**MARY PRICE** YOUNGSTOWN, OH

START TO FINISH: 15 MIN.
MAKES: 8 SERVINGS

- 1 **pound sliced deli roast beef**
- 8 **slices ciabatta bread (½ inch thick)**
- 2 **cups fresh arugula**
- 2 **cups torn romaine**
- 4 **teaspoons olive oil**
- 1 **tablespoon lemon juice**
- 1 **tablespoon white wine vinegar**
- 1½ **teaspoons prepared horseradish**

Place roast beef on ciabatta slices. In a large bowl, combine arugula and romaine. In a small bowl, whisk remaining ingredients until blended. Drizzle over greens; toss to coat. Arrange over beef; serve immediately.

PER SERVING *1 open-faced sandwich equals 150 cal., 5 g fat (1 g sat. fat), 32 mg chol., 422 mg sodium, 14 g carb., 1 g fiber, 14 g pro.* **Diabetic Exchanges:** *2 lean meat, 1 starch, ½ fat.*

JUICY & DELICIOUS
MIXED SPICE BURGERS

FREEZE IT
Mostaccioli

Years ago, a friend shared her cheesy baked pasta recipe with me. I love to serve it with a salad and garlic bread. It's great for entertaining.

—MARGARET MCNEIL GERMANTOWN, TN

PREP: 25 MIN. • **BAKE:** 25 MIN.
MAKES: 2 CASSEROLES (6 SERVINGS EACH)

- 1 **package (16 ounces) mostaccioli**
- 1½ **pounds ground beef**
- 1¼ **cups chopped green pepper**
- 1 **cup chopped onion**
- 1 **jar (26 ounces) spaghetti sauce**
- 1 **can (10¾ ounces) condensed cheddar cheese soup, undiluted**
- 1½ **teaspoons Italian seasoning**
- ¾ **teaspoon pepper**
- 2 **cups (8 ounces) shredded part-skim mozzarella cheese, divided**

1. Preheat oven to 350°. Cook mostaccioli according to package directions. Meanwhile, in a large skillet, cook beef, green pepper and onion over medium heat until meat is no longer pink; drain. Stir in spaghetti sauce, soup, Italian seasoning and pepper.

2. Drain mostaccioli. Add mostaccioli and 1½ cups cheese to beef mixture. Transfer to two greased 11x7-in. baking dishes. Sprinkle with the remaining cheese.

3. Cover and bake 20 minutes. Uncover; bake 5-10 minutes longer or until bubbly and cheese is melted.

FREEZE OPTION *Cover and freeze unbaked casseroles up to 3 months. To use, thaw in refrigerator overnight. Remove from refrigerator 30 minutes before baking. Preheat oven to 350°. Bake, covered, 50-60 minutes or until a thermometer reads 165° and cheese is melted.*

PER SERVING *1 cup equals 351 cal., 12 g fat (5 g sat. fat), 42 mg chol., 633 mg sodium, 39 g carb., 3 g fiber, 22 g pro.* **Diabetic Exchanges:** *2½ starch, 2 lean meat, 1 fat.*

FAST FIX
Chili Beef Pasta

Right after I got married, my aunt gave me her recipe for skillet spaghetti and told me it was ideal for a quick weeknight meal. Over the years, I've tinkered with the ingredients and played with seasonings to make it a healthier dish that my family truly loves.

—KRISTEN KILLIAN DEPEW, NY

START TO FINISH: 30 MIN.
MAKES: 6 SERVINGS

- 1 **pound lean ground beef (90% lean)**
- 2 **tablespoons dried minced onion**
- 2 **teaspoons dried oregano**
- 2 **teaspoons chili powder**
- ½ **teaspoon garlic powder**
- ⅛ **teaspoon salt**
- 3 **cups tomato juice**
- 2 **cups water**
- 1 **can (6 ounces) tomato paste**
- 1 **teaspoon sugar**
- 8 **ounces uncooked whole wheat spiral pasta**
  Chopped tomatoes and minced fresh oregano, optional

1. In a Dutch oven, cook beef over medium heat 6-8 minutes or until no longer pink, breaking into crumbles; drain. Stir in seasonings.

2. Add tomato juice, water, tomato paste and sugar to pan; bring to a boil. Stir in pasta. Reduce heat; simmer, covered, 20-22 minutes or until pasta is tender, stirring occasionally. If desired, top with chopped tomatoes and oregano.

PER SERVING *1⅓ cups equals 319 cal., 7 g fat (2 g sat. fat), 47 mg chol., 442 mg sodium, 41 g carb., 6 g fiber, 24 g pro.* **Diabetic Exchanges:** *3 lean meat, 2 starch, 1 vegetable.*

FAST FIX ▶ Mexi-Mac Skillet

My husband and I love this simple recipe!
Because you don't need to precook the
macaroni, it's a time-saving dish.
—**MAURANE RAMSEY** FORT WAYNE, IN

START TO FINISH: 30 MIN.
MAKES: 5 SERVINGS

- 1 **pound lean ground beef**
  (90% lean)
- 1 **large onion, chopped**
- 1 **can (14½ ounces) diced tomatoes,**
  undrained
- 1 **can (8 ounces) tomato sauce**
- 1 **cup fresh or frozen corn**
- ½ **cup water**
- 1¼ **teaspoons chili powder**
- 1 **teaspoon dried oregano**
- ½ **teaspoon salt**
- ⅔ **cup uncooked elbow macaroni**
- ⅔ **cup shredded reduced-fat cheddar**
  cheese

1. In a large nonstick skillet, cook beef
and onion over medium-high heat 5-7
minutes or until beef is no longer pink,
breaking up beef into crumbles. Drain.
2. Stir in tomatoes, tomato sauce,
corn, water and seasonings; bring to a
boil. Stir in macaroni. Reduce heat;
simmer, covered, 15-20 minutes or
until macaroni is tender. Sprinkle
with cheese.
PER SERVING *1 cup equals 283 cal.,*
11 g fat (5 g sat. fat), 55 mg chol.,
716 mg sodium, 23 g carb., 4 g fiber,
25 g pro. **Diabetic Exchanges:** *3 lean*
meat, 1 starch, 1 vegetable.

TOP TIP

Mexi-Mac Skillet is easy. Changed it
up a little. Used Velveeta, cut back on
the oregano. This is a go-to when I
want fast comfort food.
—**SUBARD** TASTEOFHOME.COM

MOROCCAN BEEF KABOBS

Moroccan Beef Kabobs

My grandmother's homemade marinade
adds tang and tenderness to beef kabobs.
Her blend of herbs and spices punches up
the flavor without adding lots of calories.
—**JENNIFER SHAW** DORCHESTER, MA

PREP: 25 MIN. + MARINATING • **GRILL:** 10 MIN.
MAKES: 8 SERVINGS

- 1 **cup chopped fresh parsley**
- 1 **cup chopped fresh cilantro**
- ¼ **cup grated onion**
- 3 **tablespoons lemon juice**
- 2 **tablespoons olive oil**
- 1 **tablespoon ground cumin**
- 1 **tablespoon ground coriander**
- 1 **tablespoon paprika**
- 1 **tablespoon cider vinegar**
- 1 **tablespoon ketchup**
- 2 **garlic cloves, minced**
- 1 **teaspoon minced fresh gingerroot**
- 1 **teaspoon Thai red chili paste**
  Dash salt and pepper
- 2 **pounds beef top sirloin steak,**
  cut into 1-inch pieces

1. In a large resealable plastic bag,
combine the parsley, cilantro, onion,
lemon juice, oil, cumin, coriander,
paprika, vinegar, ketchup, garlic,
ginger, chili paste, salt and pepper;
add beef. Seal bag and turn to coat;
refrigerate for 8 hours or overnight.
2. Drain and discard marinade. On
eight metal or soaked wooden
skewers, thread beef cubes. Moisten
a paper towel with cooking oil; using
long-handled tongs, lightly coat the
grill rack.
3. Grill beef, covered, over medium-
high heat or broil 4 in. from the heat
for 8-12 minutes or until meat
reaches desired doneness, turning
occasionally.
PER SERVING *1 kabob equals 185 cal.,*
9 g fat (3 g sat. fat), 63 mg chol., 91 mg
sodium, 3 g carb., 1 g fiber, 22 g pro.
Diabetic Exchanges: *3 lean meat,*
½ fat.

MEXICAN SHREDDED BEEF WRAPS

SLOW COOKER
Mexican Shredded Beef Wraps

I first served this go-to slow cooker dish following my son's baptism. I made a double batch and fed a crowd of 20!

—**AMY LENTS** GRAND FORKS, ND

PREP: 20 MIN. • **COOK:** 6 HOURS
MAKES: 6 SERVINGS

- 1 small onion, finely chopped
- 1 jalapeno pepper, seeded and minced
- 3 garlic cloves, minced
- 1 boneless beef chuck roast (2 to 3 pounds)
- ½ teaspoon salt
- ½ teaspoon pepper
- 1 can (8 ounces) tomato sauce
- ¼ cup lime juice
- 1 tablespoon chili powder
- 1 teaspoon ground cumin
- ¼ teaspoon cayenne pepper
- 6 flour or whole wheat tortillas (8 inches)
  Optional toppings: torn romaine, chopped tomatoes and sliced avocado

1. Place onion, jalapeno and garlic in a 4-qt. slow cooker. Sprinkle roast with salt and pepper; place over vegetables. In a small bowl, mix tomato sauce, lime juice, chili powder, cumin and cayenne; pour over roast.
2. Cook, covered, on low 6-8 hours or until meat is tender. Remove roast; cool slightly. Shred meat with two forks; return to slow cooker. Serve beef on tortillas with toppings of your choice.
NOTE *Wear disposable gloves when cutting hot peppers; the oils can burn skin. Avoid touching your face.*

PER SERVING *1 wrap (calculated without optional toppings) equals 428 cal., 18 g fat (6 g sat. fat), 98 mg chol., 696 mg sodium, 31 g carb., 1 g fiber, 35 g pro.* **Diabetic Exchanges:** *5 lean meat, 2 starch.*

⑤ INGREDIENTS
Hamburger Casserole

This recipe has traveled all around the country! My mother started making it in Pennsylvania, then I brought it to Texas when I got married. I'm still making it in California, and my daughter treats her friends to the dish in Colorado.

—**HELEN CARMICHALL** SANTEE, CA

PREP: 20 MIN. • **COOK:** 45 MIN.
MAKES: 10 SERVINGS

- 2 pounds lean ground beef (90% lean)
- 4 pounds potatoes, peeled and sliced ¼ inch thick
- 1 large onion, sliced
- 1 teaspoon salt
- ½ teaspoon pepper
- 1 teaspoon beef bouillon granules
- 1 cup boiling water
- 1 can (28 ounces) diced tomatoes, undrained
  Minced fresh parsley, optional

In a Dutch oven, layer half of the meat, potatoes and onion. Sprinkle with half the salt and pepper. Repeat layers. Dissolve bouillon in water; pour over all. Top with tomatoes. Cover and cook over medium heat for 45-50 minutes or until potatoes are tender. Garnish with parsley if desired.
PER SERVING *1 cup equals 270 cal., 8 g fat (3 g sat. fat), 57 mg chol., 493 mg sodium, 30 g carb., 3 g fiber, 21 g pro.* **Diabetic Exchanges:** *3 lean meat, 2 starch.*

FAST FIX **Saucy Beef with Broccoli**

When I'm looking for a fast entree, I turn to my favorite beef and broccoli stir-fry. It features a tantalizing sauce made with garlic and ginger.
—**ROSA EVANS** ODESSA, MO

START TO FINISH: 30 MIN.
MAKES: 2 SERVINGS

- 1 tablespoon cornstarch
- ½ cup reduced-sodium beef broth
- ¼ cup sherry or additional beef broth
- 2 tablespoons reduced-sodium soy sauce
- 1 tablespoon brown sugar
- 1 garlic clove, minced
- 1 teaspoon minced fresh gingerroot
- 2 teaspoons canola oil, divided
- ½ pound beef top sirloin steak, cut into ¼-inch strips
- 2 cups fresh broccoli florets
- 8 green onions, cut into 1-inch pieces

1. In a small bowl, mix the first seven ingredients. In a large nonstick skillet, heat 1 teaspoon oil over medium-high heat. Add beef; stir-fry 1-2 minutes or until no longer pink. Remove from the pan.

2. Stir-fry broccoli in remaining oil 4-5 minutes or until crisp-tender. Add green onions; cook 1-2 minutes longer or just until tender.

3. Stir cornstarch mixture and add to pan. Bring to a boil; cook and stir for 2-3 minutes or until thickened. Return beef to the pan and heat mixture through.
PER SERVING *1¼ cups equals 313 cal., 11 g fat (3 g sat. fat), 68 mg chol., 816 mg sodium, 20 g carb., 4 g fiber, 29 g pro.*

FREEZE IT FAST FIX
Sirloin in Wine Sauce

This recipe is both a family favorite and one I enjoy making for company. The tender sirloin is delicious over pasta.
—**BARBARA KAMM** WILMINGTON, DE

START TO FINISH: 30 MIN.
MAKES: 4 SERVINGS

- 2 tablespoons all-purpose flour
- ⅛ teaspoon ground mustard
- 1 pound beef top sirloin steak, thinly sliced
- 2 tablespoons butter
- 1 can (10½ ounces) condensed beef consomme, undiluted
- ½ cup dry red wine or beef broth
- 1 jar (4½ ounces) sliced mushrooms, drained
- ¼ cup chopped green onions
- 1 teaspoon Worcestershire sauce
  Hot cooked linguine

1. In a large resealable plastic bag, combine flour and mustard. Add beef, a few pieces at a time, and shake to coat.

2. In a large skillet, brown beef in butter. Add consomme and wine. Stir in the mushrooms, onions and Worcestershire sauce. Bring to a boil. Reduce heat; simmer, uncovered, for 10-15 minutes or until sauce is thickened. Serve with linguine.

FREEZE OPTION *Cool beef mixture. Freeze in freezer containers. To use, partially thaw in refrigerator overnight. Heat through slowly in a covered skillet until a thermometer inserted into beef reads 165°, stirring occasionally and adding a little broth or water if necessary. Serve as directed.*
PER SERVING *¾ cup (calculated without linguine) equals 258 cal., 10 g fat (5 g sat. fat), 61 mg chol., 748 mg sodium, 7 g carb., 1 g fiber, 28 g pro.* **Diabetic Exchanges:** *3 lean meat, 1½ fat, ½ starch.*

SIRLOIN IN WINE SAUCE

Beef & Spinach Lo Mein

If you like good Chinese food, this dish will definitely satisfy. I discovered the recipe at an international luncheon, and now it's in regular rotation.

—**DENISE PATTERSON** BAINBRIDGE, OH

START TO FINISH: 30 MIN.
MAKES: 5 SERVINGS

- ¼ **cup hoisin sauce**
- 2 **tablespoons soy sauce**
- 1 **tablespoon water**
- 2 **teaspoons sesame oil**
- 2 **garlic cloves, minced**
- ¼ **teaspoon crushed red pepper flakes**
- 1 **pound beef top round steak, thinly sliced**
- 6 **ounces uncooked spaghetti**
- 4 **teaspoons canola oil, divided**
- 1 **can (8 ounces) sliced water chestnuts, drained**
- 2 **green onions, sliced**
- 1 **package (10 ounces) fresh spinach, coarsely chopped**
- 1 **red chili pepper, seeded and thinly sliced**

1. In a small bowl, mix the first six ingredients. Remove ¼ cup mixture to a large bowl; add beef and toss to coat. Marinate at room temperature 10 minutes.

2. Cook spaghetti according to package directions. Meanwhile, in a large skillet, heat 1½ teaspoons canola oil. Add half of the beef mixture; stir-fry 1-2 minutes or until no longer pink. Remove from pan. Repeat with an additional 1½ teaspoons oil and remaining beef mixture.

3. Stir-fry water chestnuts and green onions in remaining canola oil for 30 seconds. Stir in the spinach and remaining hoisin mixture; cook until spinach is wilted. Return beef to pan; heat through.

4. Drain the spaghetti; add to beef mixture and toss to combine. Sprinkle with chili pepper.

NOTE *Wear disposable gloves when cutting hot peppers; the oils can burn skin. Avoid touching your face.*

PER SERVING *1⅓ cups equals 363 cal., 10 g fat (2 g sat. fat), 51 mg chol., 652 mg sodium, 40 g carb., 4 g fiber, 28 g pro.* **Diabetic Exchanges:** *3 lean meat, 2 vegetable, 1½ starch, 1 fat.*

Sassy Pot Roast

We lost this recipe for several years, so it's even more special to us now that we found it again. I love walking into my house after a long day at the office and smelling this lovely pot roast.

—**SUSAN BURKETT** MONROEVILLE, PA

PREP: 15 MIN. • **COOK:** 8 HOURS
MAKES: 8 SERVINGS

- 1 **boneless beef chuck roast (2 pounds)**
- ½ **teaspoon salt**
- ½ **teaspoon pepper**
- 2 **teaspoons olive oil**
- 1 **large onion, chopped**
- 1 **can (8 ounces) tomato sauce**
- ¼ **cup water**
- ¼ **cup lemon juice**
- ¼ **cup cider vinegar**
- ¼ **cup ketchup**
- 2 **tablespoons brown sugar**
- 1 **tablespoon Worcestershire sauce**
- ½ **teaspoon ground mustard**
- ½ **teaspoon paprika**

1. Sprinkle beef with salt and pepper. In a large skillet, brown beef in oil on all sides; drain.

2. Transfer to a 4-qt. slow cooker. Sprinkle with onion. Combine the remaining ingredients and pour over the meat. Cover and cook on low for 8-10 hours or until meat is tender. Skim fat. If desired, thicken the cooking liquid.

PER SERVING *3 ounces cooked beef equals 243 cal., 12 g fat (4 g sat. fat), 74 mg chol., 443 mg sodium, 10 g carb., 1 g fiber, 23 g pro.* **Diabetic Exchange:** *3 lean meat.*

BEEF & SPINACH LO MEIN

SASSY POT ROAST

MAKEOVER LASAGNA

ORIGINAL	MAKEOVER
513 Calories	**298** Calories
35g Fat	**15**g Fat
17g Sat. Fat	**7**g Sat. Fat

Makeover Lasagna

The *Taste of Home* Test Kitchen cut the fat in my classic meat-lover's lasagna. We enjoy this healthier version, and now I can serve lasagna more often.

—JACOB KITZMAN SEATTLE, WA

PREP: 45 MIN. • **BAKE:** 45 MIN. + STANDING
MAKES: 12 SERVINGS

- ¾ **pound lean ground beef (90% lean)**
- ¾ **pound Italian turkey sausage links, casings removed**
- 1 **medium onion, chopped**
- 1 **medium green pepper, chopped**
- 1 **jar (26 ounces) spaghetti sauce**
- 1 **package (8 ounces) reduced-fat cream cheese, cubed**
- 1 **cup (8 ounces) 1% cottage cheese**
- 1 **large egg, lightly beaten**
- 1 **tablespoon minced fresh parsley**
- 6 **whole wheat lasagna noodles, cooked and drained**
- 1 **cup (4 ounces) shredded reduced-fat Italian cheese blend**
- 3 **teaspoons Italian seasoning, divided**
- 1 **cup (4 ounces) shredded part-skim mozzarella cheese**

1. In a large skillet, cook the beef, sausage, onion and green pepper over medium heat until meat is no longer pink; drain. Set aside 1 cup spaghetti sauce; stir remaining sauce into meat mixture. Bring to a boil. Reduce heat; simmer, uncovered, for 8-10 minutes or until thickened.

2. In a small saucepan, melt cream cheese over medium heat. Remove from the heat. Stir in the cottage cheese, egg and parsley.

3. Spread meat sauce into a 13x9-in. baking dish coated with cooking spray. Top with three noodles, Italian cheese blend, 1½ teaspoons Italian seasoning and cream cheese mixture. Layer with remaining noodles and reserved spaghetti sauce; sprinkle with the mozzarella and remaining Italian seasoning.

4. Cover and bake at 350° for 35 minutes. Bake, uncovered, for 10-15 minutes or until bubbly. Let stand for 15 minutes before cutting.

PER SERVING *1 piece equals 298 cal., 15 g fat (7 g sat. fat), 78 mg chol., 772 mg sodium, 17 g carb., 3 g fiber, 23 g pro.* **Diabetic Exchanges:** *3 lean meat, 1½ fat, 1 starch.*

THE SKINNY

The original recipe used a pound each of regular ground beef (80% lean) and Italian pork sausage. Changing to lighter ingredients and decreasing them by 25% cut the fat from 9 grams to 3 grams and saturated fat from 3 grams to 1 gram per serving. That's a savings of 67%!

So-Easy Swiss Steak

Let your slow cooker simmer up this fuss-free and flavorful Swiss steak. It's perfect for busy days...the longer it cooks, the better it tastes!

—**SARAH BURKS** WATHENA, KS

PREP: 10 MIN. • **COOK:** 6 HOURS
MAKES: 2 SERVINGS

- 1 tablespoon all-purpose flour
- ¼ teaspoon salt
- ⅛ teaspoon pepper
- ¾ pound beef top round steak
- ½ medium onion, cut into ¼-inch slices
- ⅓ cup chopped celery
- 1 can (8 ounces) tomato sauce

1. In a large resealable plastic bag, combine the flour, salt and pepper. Cut beef into two portions; add to bag and shake to coat.

2. Place onion in a 3-qt. slow cooker coated with cooking spray. Layer with the beef, celery and tomato sauce. Cover and cook on low for 6-8 hours or until meat is tender.

PER SERVING *1 serving equals 272 cal., 5 g fat (2 g sat. fat), 96 mg chol., 882 mg sodium, 13 g carb., 2 g fiber, 41 g pro.*

SLOW COOKER

Mediterranean Pot Roast Dinner

I first made this recipe one cold winter day. My family (adults, kids and dogs) were having a blast sledding and playing in the snow all day, and when we came inside supper was ready! The pot roast is perfect served with mashed potatoes, rice or crusty dinner rolls.

—**HOLLY BATTISTE** BARRINGTON, NJ

PREP: 30 MIN. • **COOK:** 8 HOURS
MAKES: 8 SERVINGS

- 2 pounds potatoes (about 6 medium), peeled and cut into 2-inch pieces
- 5 medium carrots (about ¾ pound), cut into 1-inch pieces
- 2 tablespoons all-purpose flour
- 1 boneless beef chuck roast (3 to 4 pounds)
- 1 tablespoon olive oil
- 8 large fresh mushrooms, quartered
- 2 celery ribs, chopped
- 1 medium onion, thinly sliced
- ¼ cup sliced Greek olives
- ½ cup minced fresh parsley, divided
- 1 can (14½ ounces) fire-roasted diced tomatoes, undrained
- 1 tablespoon minced fresh oregano or 1 teaspoon dried oregano
- 1 tablespoon lemon juice
- 2 teaspoons minced fresh rosemary or ½ teaspoon dried rosemary, crushed
- 2 garlic cloves, minced
- ¾ teaspoon salt
- ¼ teaspoon pepper
- ¼ teaspoon crushed red pepper flakes, optional

1. Place potatoes and carrots in a 6-qt. slow cooker. Sprinkle flour over all surfaces of roast. In a large skillet, heat oil over medium-high heat. Brown roast on all sides. Place over vegetables.

2. Add mushrooms, celery, onion, olives and ¼ cup parsley to slow cooker. In a small bowl, mix remaining ingredients; pour over top.

3. Cook, covered, on low 8-10 hours or until meat and vegetables are tender. Remove beef. Stir remaining parsley into vegetables. Serve beef with vegetables.

PER SERVING *3 ounces cooked beef with 1 cup vegetables equals 422 cal., 18 g fat (6 g sat. fat), 111 mg chol., 538 mg sodium, 28 g carb., 4 g fiber, 37 g pro.* **Diabetic Exchanges:** *5 lean meat, 1½ starch, 1 vegetable, ½ fat.*

MEDITERRANEAN POT ROAST DINNER

PEPPER STEAK WITH POTATOES

PER SERVING *1 cup equals 277 cal., 10 g fat (2 g sat. fat), 55 mg chol., 179 mg sodium, 27 g carb., 3 g fiber, 23 g pro.* **Diabetic Exchanges:** *2 meat, 2 vegetable, 1 starch.*

⑤ INGREDIENTS

Spud-Stuffed Peppers

We don't care for rice, so I created a stuffed pepper recipe that uses fresh potatoes from my garden.

—**JOYCE JANDERA** HANOVER, KS

PREP: 25 MIN. • **BAKE:** 40 MIN.
MAKES: 2 SERVINGS

- 2 **medium green peppers**
- ½ **pound lean ground beef (90% lean)**
- 1 **medium potato, peeled and grated**
- 1½ **teaspoons chili powder**
- ¼ **teaspoon salt**
  Dash coarsely ground pepper
- ¼ **cup shredded reduced-fat cheddar cheese**

1. Cut tops off peppers and remove seeds. In large saucepan, cook peppers in boiling water for 4-5 minutes. Drain and rinse in cold water; invert on paper towels.
2. In a nonstick skillet, cook beef and potato over medium heat until meat is no longer pink; drain. Stir in the chili powder, salt and pepper. Spoon mixture into peppers.
3. Place in a small baking pan coated with cooking spray. Cover and bake at 350° for 35 minutes. Sprinkle with cheese. Bake, uncovered, 5-10 minutes longer or until cheese is melted.
PER SERVING *1 stuffed pepper equals 332 cal., 12 g fat (6 g sat. fat), 66 mg chol., 487 mg sodium, 28 g carb., 5 g fiber, 29 g pro.* **Diabetic Exchanges:** *3 lean meat, 2 vegetable, 1 starch, 1 fat.*

FAST FIX ▶ **Pepper Steak with Potatoes**

I added potatoes to a favorite Asian pepper steak recipe. Now this meaty skillet dish satisfies everyone in my house full of hungry guys.

—**KRISTINE MARRA** CLIFTON PARK, NY

START TO FINISH: 30 MIN.
MAKES: 6 SERVINGS

- 1½ **pounds red potatoes (about 5 medium), sliced**
- ½ **cup water**
- 1 **cup beef broth**
- 4 **teaspoons cornstarch**
- ⅛ **teaspoon pepper**
- 2 **tablespoons olive oil, divided**
- 1 **beef top sirloin steak (1 pound), thinly sliced**
- 1 **garlic clove, minced**
- 1 **medium green pepper, julienned**
- 1 **small onion, chopped**

1. Place potatoes and water in a large microwave-safe dish. Microwave, covered, on high for 5-7 minutes or until tender.
2. Meanwhile, in a small bowl, mix broth, cornstarch and pepper until smooth. In a large skillet, heat 1 tablespoon oil over medium-high heat. Add beef; cook and stir for 2-3 minutes or until no longer pink. Add garlic; cook 1 minute longer. Remove from pan.
3. In the same pan, heat remaining oil. Add green pepper and onion; cook and stir until vegetables are crisp-tender. Stir cornstarch mixture and add to pan. Bring to a boil; cook and stir 1-2 minutes or until sauce is thickened. Add potatoes and beef to pan; heat through.
NOTE *This recipe was tested in a 1,100-watt microwave.*

Asian Beef and Noodles

This delicious, economical dish takes only five ingredients—all of which are easy to keep on hand. Serve with a dash of soy sauce and a side of fresh pineapple slices. You can also try it with ground turkey instead of beef.

—LAURA STENBERG WYOMING, MN

START TO FINISH: 20 MIN.
MAKES: 4 SERVINGS

- 1 **pound lean ground beef (90% lean)**
- 2 **packages (3 ounces each) Oriental ramen noodles, crumbled**
- 2½ **cups water**
- 2 **cups frozen broccoli stir-fry vegetable blend**
- ¼ **teaspoon ground ginger**
- 2 **tablespoons thinly sliced green onion**

1. In a large skillet, cook beef over medium heat until no longer pink; drain. Add the contents of one ramen noodle flavoring packet; stir until dissolved. Remove beef and set aside.

2. In the same skillet, combine the water, vegetables, ginger, noodles and contents of remaining flavoring packet. Bring to a boil. Reduce heat; cover and simmer for 3-4 minutes or until noodles are tender, stirring occasionally. Return beef to the pan and heat through. Stir in onion.

PER SERVING *1½ cups equals 377 cal., 15 g fat (7 g sat. fat), 56 mg chol., 624 mg sodium, 31 g carb., 3 g fiber, 27 g pro.* **Diabetic Exchanges:** *3 lean meat, 2 starch, 1 fat.*

FREEZE IT SLOW COOKER 🍲

Meat Loaf with Chili Sauce

I used to serve this meat loaf recipe in my cafe. Everyone asked for it. I adapted it for home with my slow cooker, where it's quite popular, too.

—ROBERT COX LAS CRUCES, NM

PREP: 20 MIN.
COOK: 3 HOURS + STANDING
MAKES: 8 SERVINGS

- 1 **large onion, finely chopped**
- ½ **cup seasoned bread crumbs**
- 1 **small green pepper, chopped**
- 2 **large eggs, lightly beaten**
- ½ **cup chili sauce**
- 2 **tablespoons spicy brown mustard**
- 3 **to 4 garlic cloves, minced**
- ¾ **teaspoon salt**
- ¼ **teaspoon dried oregano**
- ¼ **teaspoon dried basil**
- 2 **pounds lean ground beef (90% lean)**
  Additional chili sauce, optional

1. Cut four 20x3-in. strips of heavy-duty foil; crisscross so they resemble spokes of a wheel. Place strips on bottom and up sides of a 5-qt. slow cooker. Coat strips with cooking spray.
2. In a large bowl, combine the first 10 ingredients. Add beef; mix lightly

but thoroughly. Shape into a 9-in. round loaf. Place loaf in center of strips in slow cooker.
3. Cook, covered, on low 3-4 hours or until a thermometer reads at least 160°. If desired, spoon additional chili sauce over meat loaf. Let stand for 10 minutes. Using foil strips as handles, remove meat loaf to a platter.

FREEZE OPTION *Securely wrap and freeze cooled meat loaf in plastic wrap and foil. To use, partially thaw in refrigerator overnight. Unwrap meat loaf; reheat on a greased shallow baking pan in a preheated 350° oven until heated through and a thermometer inserted into center reads 165°.*

PER SERVING *1 slice equals 253 cal., 11 g fat (4 g sat. fat), 123 mg chol., 686 mg sodium, 12 g carb., 1 g fiber, 25 g pro.* **Diabetic Exchanges:** *3 lean meat, 1 starch.*

Cabbage Roll Casserole

I layer cabbage with tomato sauce and beef to create a hearty casserole that tastes like cabbage rolls, but without all the work.

—DOREEN MARTIN KITIMAT, BC

PREP: 20 MIN. • **BAKE:** 55 MIN.
MAKES: 12 SERVINGS

- 2 **pounds ground beef**
- 1 **large onion, chopped**
- 3 **garlic cloves, minced**
- 2 **cans (15 ounces each) tomato sauce, divided**
- 1 **teaspoon dried thyme**
- ½ **teaspoon dill weed**
- ½ **teaspoon rubbed sage**
- ¼ **teaspoon salt**
- ¼ **teaspoon pepper**
- ¼ **teaspoon cayenne pepper**
- 2 **cups cooked rice**
- 4 **bacon strips, cooked and crumbled**
- 1 **medium head cabbage (2 pounds), shredded**
- 1 **cup (4 ounces) shredded part-skim mozzarella cheese**

1. Preheat oven to 375°. In a large skillet, cook beef and onion over medium heat until meat is no longer pink. Add garlic; cook 1 minute longer. Drain. Stir in one can of tomato sauce and seasonings. Bring to a boil. Reduce heat; cover and simmer 5 minutes. Stir in rice and bacon; heat through. Remove from heat.

2. Layer a third of the cabbage in a greased 13x9-in. baking dish. Top with half of the meat mixture. Repeat layers; top with remaining cabbage. Pour remaining tomato sauce over top.

3. Cover and bake for 45 minutes. Uncover; sprinkle with cheese. Bake 10 minutes longer or until cheese is melted. Let stand 5 minutes before serving.

PER SERVING *1 serving equals 230 cal., 8 g fat (4 g sat. fat), 44 mg chol., 620 mg sodium, 18 g carb., 3 g fiber, 20 g pro.* **Diabetic Exchanges:** *3 vegetable, 2½ lean meat, ½ fat.*

Gingered Beef Stir-Fry

A friend who owns a bed-and-breakfast in Maryland shared this recipe with me. It's a deliciously different way to prepare asparagus. The zesty Asian flavors come through but aren't at all overpowering.

—SONJA BLOW NIXA, MO

PREP: 20 MIN. + MARINATING
COOK: 20 MIN.
MAKES: 4 SERVINGS

- 3 **tablespoons reduced-sodium soy sauce, divided**
- 1 **tablespoon sherry**
- ¼ **teaspoon minced fresh gingerroot or dash ground ginger**
- ½ **pound beef flank steak, cut into thin strips**
- 1 **teaspoon cornstarch**
- ½ **cup beef broth**
- 1½ **teaspoons hoisin sauce**
- ⅛ **teaspoon sugar**

- 2 **tablespoons canola oil, divided**
- 2 **pounds fresh asparagus, cut into 1-inch lengths**
- 1 **garlic clove, minced**
- 3 **cups hot cooked rice**

1. In a large resealable plastic bag, combine 2 tablespoons soy sauce, sherry and ginger; add beef. Seal the bag and turn to coat; refrigerate for 30 minutes.

2. In a small bowl, combine the cornstarch, broth, hoisin sauce, sugar and remaining soy sauce until smooth; set aside.

3. In a large skillet or wok, stir-fry beef in 1 tablespoon oil until no longer pink. Remove and set aside. Stir-fry asparagus in remaining oil until crisp-tender. Add the garlic; cook 1 minute longer.

4. Stir cornstarch mixture and add to the pan. Bring to a boil; cook and stir 2 minutes or until thickened. Return beef to the pan; heat through. Serve with rice.

PER SERVING *1¼ cups stir-fry with ¾ cup rice equals 347 cal., 12 g fat (2 g sat. fat), 27 mg chol., 645 mg sodium, 41 g carb., 2 g fiber, 18 g pro.* **Diabetic Exchanges:** *2 starch, 2 fat, 1 lean meat, 1 vegetable.*

FAST FIX Cheeseburger Macaroni Skillet

This is the ultimate simple, satisfying supper that uses items I typically have right in my own cupboard. Plus, cleanup's a snap since I cook it all in one skillet.

—**JULI MEYERS** HINESVILLE, GA

START TO FINISH: 30 MIN.
MAKES: 6 SERVINGS

- 1 **pound lean ground beef (90% lean)**
- 8 **ounces uncooked whole wheat elbow macaroni**
- 3 **cups reduced-sodium beef broth**
- ¾ **cup fat-free milk**
- 3 **tablespoons ketchup**
- 2 **teaspoons Montreal steak seasoning**
- 1 **teaspoon prepared mustard**
- ¼ **teaspoon onion powder**
- 1 **cup (4 ounces) shredded reduced-fat cheddar cheese**
  Minced chives

1. In a large skillet, cook the ground beef over medium heat 6-8 minutes or until no longer pink, breaking into crumbles; drain.

2. Stir in macaroni, broth, milk, ketchup, steak seasoning, mustard and onion powder; bring to a boil. Reduce heat; simmer, uncovered, 10-15 minutes or until macaroni is tender. Stir in cheese until melted. Sprinkle with chives.

PER SERVING *1 cup equals 338 cal., 11 g fat (5 g sat. fat), 64 mg chol., 611 mg sodium, 32 g carb., 4 g fiber, 27 g pro.*

Braised Hanukkah Brisket

My mother always used the most marbled cut of brisket she could find to make this recipe so she'd get the most flavor. When she added carrots to the pan, she threw in some potatoes, too. The best thing about this dish is that it's even tastier the next day.

—**ELLEN RUZINSKY** YORKTOWN HEIGHTS, NY

PREP: 25 MIN. • **COOK:** 2¾ HOURS
MAKES: 12 SERVINGS (4 CUPS VEGETABLES)

- 2 **tablespoons canola oil**
- 1 **fresh beef brisket (4 to 5 pounds)**
- 3 **celery ribs, cut into 1-inch pieces**
- 3 **large carrots, cut into ¼-inch slices**
- 2 **large onions, sliced**
- 1 **pound medium fresh mushrooms**
- ¾ **cup cold water**
- ¾ **cup tomato sauce**
- 3 **tablespoons Worcestershire sauce**
- 1 **tablespoon prepared horseradish**

1. In a Dutch oven, heat oil over medium heat. Brown brisket on both sides. Remove from pan.

2. Add celery, carrots and onions to same pan; cook and stir 4-6 minutes or until crisp-tender. Stir in remaining ingredients.

3. Return brisket to pan, fat side up. Bring mixture to a boil. Reduce heat; simmer, covered, 2½-3 hours or until meat is tender. Remove beef and vegetables; keep warm. Skim fat from pan juices. If desired, thicken juices.

4. Cut brisket diagonally across the grain into thin slices. Serve with vegetables and pan juices.

NOTE *This is a fresh beef brisket, not corned beef.*

PER SERVING *4 ounces cooked meat with ⅓ cup vegetables and ½ cup juices equals 247 cal., 9 g fat (3 g sat. fat), 64 mg chol., 189 mg sodium, 8 g carb., 2 g fiber, 33 g pro.* ***Diabetic Exchanges:*** *4 lean meat, 1 vegetable, ½ fat.*

BRAISED HANUKKAH BRISKET

TEXAS TACOS

Texas Tacos

I created this recipe by combining a bunch of ingredients that my kids like. I often keep the beef mixture warm in a slow cooker so the kids can quickly stuff it into taco shells after an afternoon of rigorous soccer practice.

—**SUSAN SCULLY** MASON, OH

START TO FINISH: 30 MIN.
MAKES: 10 SERVINGS

- 1½ **pounds lean ground beef (90% lean)**
- 1 **medium sweet red pepper, chopped**
- 1 **small onion, chopped**
- 1 **can (14½ ounces) diced tomatoes, drained**
- 1⅓ **cups frozen corn, thawed**
- 1 **can (8 ounces) tomato sauce**
- 2 **tablespoons chili powder**
- ½ **teaspoon salt**
- 1 **package (8.8 ounces) ready-to-serve brown rice**
- 20 **taco shells**
  Optional toppings: shredded lettuce, chopped fresh tomatoes and reduced-fat sour cream

1. In a Dutch oven, cook beef, red pepper and onion over medium heat 8-10 minutes or until beef is no longer pink and vegetables are tender, breaking up beef into crumbles. Drain.
2. Stir in tomatoes, corn, tomato sauce, chili powder and salt; bring to a boil. Add the rice and heat through. Serve in taco shells with toppings of your choice.
PER SERVING *2 tacos (calculated without optional toppings) equals 294 cal., 11 g fat (4 g sat. fat), 42 mg chol., 420 mg sodium, 30 g carb., 3 g fiber, 17 g pro.* **Diabetic Exchanges:** *2 starch, 2 lean meat.*

STEAK FRIED RICE

Steak Fried Rice

Perfect for an end-of-the-week meal, this sensational dish comes together quickly with leftover rice. I learned a great tip for the steak recently: Partially freeze it, and it will be easy to cut into thin slices.

—**SIMONE GARZA** EVANSVILLE, IN

START TO FINISH: 30 MIN.
MAKES: 4 SERVINGS

- 2 **eggs, lightly beaten**
- 2 **teaspoons olive oil**
- 1 **beef top sirloin steak (¾ pound), cut into thin strips**
- 4 **tablespoons reduced-sodium soy sauce, divided**
- 1 **package (12 ounces) broccoli coleslaw mix**
- 1 **cup frozen peas**
- 2 **tablespoons grated fresh gingerroot**
- 3 **garlic cloves, minced**
- 2 **cups cooked brown rice**
- 4 **green onions, sliced**

1. In a large nonstick skillet coated with cooking spray, cook and stir eggs over medium heat until no liquid egg remains, breaking up eggs into small pieces. Remove from pan; wipe skillet clean if necessary.
2. In the same pan, heat oil over medium-high heat. Add beef; stir-fry 1-2 minutes or until no longer pink. Stir in 1 tablespoon soy sauce; remove meat from pan.
3. Add coleslaw mix, peas, ginger and garlic to the pan; cook and stir until coleslaw mix is crisp-tender. Add rice and remaining soy sauce, tossing to combine rice with vegetable mixture and heat through. Stir in cooked eggs, beef and green onions; heat through.
PER SERVING *1½ cups equals 346 cal., 9 g fat (3 g sat. fat), 140 mg chol., 732 mg sodium, 36 g carb., 6 g fiber, 29 g pro.* **Diabetic Exchanges:** *3 lean meat, 2 starch, 1 vegetable, ½ fat.*

FREEZER BURRITOS

taco seasoning. Bring to a boil. Reduce the heat; simmer mixture, uncovered, for 2-3 minutes. Transfer to a large bowl; set aside.

2. In a food processor, combine pinto beans and water. Cover and process until almost smooth. Add to beef mixture. Stir in cheese.

3. Spoon ½ cup beef mixture down the center of each tortilla. Fold ends and sides over filling; roll up. Wrap each burrito in waxed paper and foil. Freeze for up to 1 month.

TO USE FROZEN BURRITOS *Remove foil and waxed paper. Place one burrito on a microwave-safe plate. Microwave on high for 2½-2¾ minutes or until a thermometer reads 165°, turning burrito over once. Let stand for 20 seconds.*

NOTE *This recipe was tested in a 1,100-watt microwave.*

PER SERVING *1 burrito equals 345 cal., 11 g fat (4 g sat. fat), 36 mg chol., 677 mg sodium, 40 g carb., 3 g fiber, 22 g pro.* **Diabetic Exchanges:** *2½ starch, 2 lean meat, ½ fat.*

DID YOU KNOW?

Beans pack a nutritional one-two punch of protein and fiber, which helps you feel fuller longer. They're a green source of protein that can help you economically stretch the meat in a recipe. Dried beans roughly double in volume when cooked. If you'd like to cook your own beans for a recipe, you'll need to cook ¾ to 1 cup of dried beans for each can called for in the recipe.

Freezer Burritos

I love burritos, but the frozen ones are so high in salt and chemicals. So I created these. They're great to have on hand for quick dinners or late-night snacks—I've even had them for breakfast!

—LAURA WINEMILLER DELTA, PA

PREP: 35 MIN. • **COOK:** 15 MIN.
MAKES: 12 SERVINGS

- 1¼ **pounds lean ground beef (90% lean)**
- ¼ **cup finely chopped onion**
- 1¼ **cups salsa**
- 2 **tablespoons reduced-sodium taco seasoning**
- 2 **cans (15 ounces each) pinto beans, rinsed and drained**
- ½ **cup water**
- 2 **cups (8 ounces) shredded reduced-fat cheddar cheese**
- 12 **flour tortillas (8 inches), warmed**

1. In a large skillet, cook beef and onion over medium heat until meat is no longer pink; drain. Stir in salsa and

Tenderloin with Cremini-Apricot Stuffing

The sweet and savory stuffing complements the beef tenderloin well. Your guests will be giving you kudos for serving such a unique entree.

—MARIE RIZZIO INTERLOCHEN, MI

PREP: 35 MIN. • **BAKE:** 35 MIN. + STANDING
MAKES: 10 SERVINGS

- 1 **cup sliced baby portobello (cremini) mushrooms**
- ⅓ **cup chopped onion**
- ⅓ **cup chopped celery**
- 2 **tablespoons butter**
- ½ **cup chopped dried apricots**
- 1 **tablespoon minced fresh rosemary**
- 1 **beef tenderloin roast (2½ pounds)**
- 1 **tablespoon olive oil**
- 3 **garlic cloves, minced**
- ½ **teaspoon salt**
- ¼ **teaspoon pepper**

1. In a large skillet, saute the mushrooms, onion and celery in butter until tender. Transfer to a small bowl; stir in the apricots and rosemary. Cool slightly.

2. Cut a lengthwise slit down the center of the tenderloin to within ½ in. of bottom. Open tenderloin so it lies flat. On each half, make another lengthwise slit down the center to within ½ in. of bottom; open roast and cover with plastic wrap. Flatten to ½-in. thickness. Remove plastic.

3. Spread mushroom mixture over meat. Roll up jelly-roll style, starting with a long side. Tie at 1½-in. to 2-in. intervals with kitchen string.

4. Combine the oil, garlic, salt and pepper; rub over roast. In a large ovenproof skillet, brown roast on all sides.

5. Bake at 425° for 35-50 minutes or until meat reaches desired doneness (for medium-rare, a thermometer should read 145°; medium, 160°; well-done, 170°). Let stand 10 minutes before slicing. Place slices on a platter and spoon pan juices over the top.

PER SERVING *1 serving equals 219 cal., 10 g fat (4 g sat. fat), 56 mg chol., 143 mg sodium, 6 g carb., 1 g fiber, 25 g pro.* **Diabetic Exchanges:** *3 lean meat, 1 fat, ½ starch.*

TENDERLOIN WITH CREMINI-APRICOT STUFFING

SLOW COOKER 🍲 Beef & Veggie Sloppy Joes

I'm always looking for ways to serve my family healthy and delicious food, so I started experimenting with my favorite veggies and ground beef. I came up with this favorite that my three kids actually request! This healthy take on sloppy joes reminds me of my own childhood.

—**MEGAN NIEBUHR** YAKIMA, WA

PREP: 35 MIN. • **COOK:** 5 HOURS
MAKES: 12 SERVINGS

- 4 **medium carrots, shredded (about 3½ cups)**
- 1 **medium yellow summer squash, shredded (about 2 cups)**
- 1 **medium zucchini, shredded (about 2 cups)**
- 1 **medium sweet red pepper, finely chopped**
- 2 **medium tomatoes, seeded and chopped**
- 1 **small red onion, finely chopped**
- ½ **cup ketchup**
- 3 **tablespoons minced fresh basil or 3 teaspoons dried basil**
- 3 **tablespoons molasses**
- 2 **tablespoons cider vinegar**
- 2 **garlic cloves, minced**
- ½ **teaspoon salt**
- ½ **teaspoon pepper**
- 2 **pounds lean ground beef (90% lean)**
- 12 **whole wheat hamburger buns, split**

1. In a 5- or 6-qt. slow cooker, combine the first 13 ingredients. In a large skillet, cook the beef over medium heat for 8-10 minutes or until no longer pink, breaking into crumbles. Drain; transfer beef to slow cooker. Stir to combine.

2. Cook, covered, on low 5-6 hours or until heated through and vegetables are tender. Using a slotted spoon, serve beef mixture on buns.

PER SERVING *1 sandwich equals 282 cal., 8 g fat (3 g sat. fat), 47 mg chol., 490 mg sodium, 34 g carb., 5 g fiber, 19 g pro.* **Diabetic Exchanges: 2 starch, 2 lean meat, 1 vegetable.**

Maple-Orange Pot Roast

This tender roast is a wonderful reminder of New England's autumn flavors. It always brings back memories of a friend's maple sap house in New Hampshire, where we're originally from.

—**CHRISTINA MARQUIS** ORLANDO, FL

PREP: 25 MIN. • **BAKE:** 3 HOURS
MAKES: 8 SERVINGS

- 1 **beef rump roast or bottom round roast (3 pounds)**
- ½ **cup orange juice**
- ¼ **cup sugar-free maple-flavored syrup**
- ¼ **cup white wine or chicken broth**
- 2 **tablespoons balsamic vinegar**
- 1 **tablespoon Worcestershire sauce**
- 1 **teaspoon grated orange peel**
- 1 **bay leaf**
- ½ **teaspoon salt**
- ¼ **teaspoon pepper**
- 1½ **pounds red potatoes, cut into large chunks**
- 5 **medium carrots, cut into 2-inch pieces**
- 2 **celery ribs, cut into 2-inch pieces**

- 2 **medium onions, cut into wedges**
- 4 **teaspoons cornstarch**
- ¼ **cup cold water**

1. In a large nonstick skillet coated with cooking spray, brown roast on all sides. Place in a roasting pan coated with cooking spray.

2. In the same skillet, combine the orange juice, syrup, wine, vinegar, Worcestershire sauce, orange peel, bay leaf, salt and pepper. Bring to a boil, stirring frequently; pour over meat.

3. Place the potatoes, carrots, celery and onions around roast. Cover and bake at 325° for 3 hours or until meat is tender. Remove meat and vegetables and keep warm. Pour pan juices into a measuring cup. Discard bay leaf and skim fat. Return to roasting pan.

4. In a small bowl, combine the cornstarch and water until smooth. Gradually stir into juices. Bring to a boil; cook and stir for 2 minutes or until thickened. Serve with pot roast and vegetables.

PER SERVING *3 ounces cooked beef with ¾ cup vegetables and 2 tablespoons gravy equals 335 cal., 8 g fat (3 g sat. fat), 102 mg chol., 264 mg sodium, 27 g carb., 4 g fiber, 36 g pro.* **Diabetic Exchanges: 3 lean meat, 2 vegetable, 1 starch.**

FAST FIX ▸ Family-Favorite Cheeseburger Pasta

I created this recipe to satisfy a cheeseburger craving. What a delicious way to lighten up a classic!

—RAQUEL HAGGARD EDMOND, OK

START TO FINISH: 30 MIN.
MAKES: 4 SERVINGS

- 1½ cups uncooked whole wheat penne pasta
- ¾ pound lean ground beef (90% lean)
- 2 tablespoons finely chopped onion
- 1 can (14½ ounces) no-salt-added diced tomatoes
- 2 tablespoons dill pickle relish
- 2 tablespoons prepared mustard
- 2 tablespoons ketchup
- 1 teaspoon steak seasoning
- ¼ teaspoon seasoned salt
- ¾ cup shredded reduced-fat cheddar cheese
  Chopped green onions, optional

1. Cook pasta according to package directions. Meanwhile, in a large skillet, cook beef and onion over medium heat until meat is no longer pink; drain. Drain pasta; add to meat.
2. Stir in the tomatoes, relish, mustard, ketchup, steak seasoning and seasoned salt. Bring mixture to a boil. Reduce heat; simmer, uncovered, for 5 minutes.
3. Sprinkle with cheese. Remove from the heat; cover and let stand until cheese is melted. Garnish with green onions if desired.
NOTE *This recipe was tested with McCormick's Montreal Steak Seasoning. Look for it in the spice aisle.*
PER SERVING *1½ cups equals 391 cal., 12 g fat (6 g sat. fat), 57 mg chol., 759 mg sodium, 43 g carb., 4 g fiber, 28 g pro.* **Diabetic Exchanges:** *3 lean meat, 2 starch, 1 vegetable, ½ fat.*

FAST FIX ▸ Stir-Fried Steak & Veggies

Here's a stir-fry that's even faster than Chinese takeout. It's an easy dinnertime winner at my house.

—VICKY PRIESTLEY ALUM CREEK, WV

START TO FINISH: 25 MIN.
MAKES: 6 SERVINGS

- 1½ cups uncooked instant brown rice
- 1 tablespoon cornstarch
- ½ cup cold water
- ¼ cup reduced-sodium soy sauce
- 1 tablespoon brown sugar
- ¾ teaspoon ground ginger
- ½ teaspoon chili powder
- ¼ teaspoon garlic powder
- ¼ teaspoon pepper
- 2 tablespoons canola oil, divided
- 1 pound beef top sirloin steak, cut into ½-inch cubes
- 1 package (16 ounces) frozen stir-fry vegetable blend, thawed

1. Cook rice according to package directions. Meanwhile, in a small bowl, mix cornstarch, water, soy sauce, brown sugar and seasonings until smooth.
2. In a large nonstick skillet coated with cooking spray, heat 1 tablespoon oil over medium-high heat. Add beef; stir-fry until no longer pink. Remove from pan. Stir-fry vegetables in the remaining oil until crisp-tender.
3. Stir cornstarch mixture and add to pan. Bring to a boil; cook and stir 1-2 minutes or until the sauce is thickened. Return beef to pan; heat through. Serve with rice.
PER SERVING *¾ cup stir-fry with ½ cup rice equals 304 cal., 8 g fat (2 g sat. fat), 42 mg chol., 470 mg sodium, 37 g carb., 3 g fiber, 19 g pro.* **Diabetic Exchanges:** *2 lean meat, 2 vegetable, 1½ starch, 1 fat.*

STIR-FRIED STEAK & VEGGIES

St. Paddy's Irish Beef Dinner

A variation on shepherd's pie, this hearty dish brings together saucy beef with mashed potatoes, parsnips and other vegetables. It's always the star of our March 17 meal.

—LORRAINE CALAND SHUNIAH, ON

PREP: 25 MIN. • **COOK:** 35 MIN.
MAKES: 4 SERVINGS

- 2   medium Yukon Gold potatoes
- 2   small parsnips
- ¾   pound lean ground beef (90% lean)
- 1   medium onion, chopped
- 2   cups finely shredded cabbage
- 2   medium carrots, halved and sliced
- 1   teaspoon dried thyme
- 1   teaspoon Worcestershire sauce
- 1   tablespoon all-purpose flour
- ¼   cup tomato paste
- 1   can (14½ ounces) reduced-sodium chicken or beef broth
- ½   cup frozen peas
- ¾   teaspoon salt, divided
- ½   teaspoon pepper, divided
- ¼   cup 2% milk
- 1   tablespoon butter

1. Peel potatoes and parsnips and cut into large pieces; place in a large saucepan and cover with water. Bring to a boil. Reduce heat; cover and cook for 10-15 minutes or until vegetables are tender. Drain.

2. Meanwhile, in a large skillet, cook beef and onion over medium heat until meat is no longer pink; drain. Stir in the cabbage, carrots, thyme and Worcestershire sauce.

3. In a small bowl, combine the flour, tomato paste and broth until smooth. Gradually stir into meat mixture. Bring to a boil. Reduce heat; cover and simmer for 15-20 minutes or until vegetables are tender. Stir in the peas, ¼ teaspoon salt and ¼ teaspoon of pepper.

4. Drain the potatoes and parsnips; mash with milk, butter and remaining salt and pepper. Serve with the meat mixture.

PER SERVING *1 cup meat mixture with ¾ cup potato mixture equals 369 cal., 11 g fat (5 g sat. fat), 62 mg chol., 849 mg sodium, 46 g carb., 8 g fiber, 24 g pro.* **Diabetic Exchanges:** *3 lean meat, 2 starch, 2 vegetable.*

FAST FIX

Spinach Beef Salad

This main-dish salad is as satisfying as it gets. It's crunchy, meaty and a little bit spicy. Best of all, you get a big portion because this dish is so good for you.

—JANET DINGLER CEDARTOWN, GA

START TO FINISH: 25 MIN.
MAKES: 4 SERVINGS

- 1   pound beef top sirloin steak, cut into thin strips
- 1   jalapeno pepper, seeded and chopped
- 1   garlic clove, minced
- ¼   cup lime juice
- 2   tablespoons brown sugar
- 2   tablespoons reduced-sodium soy sauce
- 1   teaspoon dried basil
- 1   teaspoon minced fresh mint or ½ teaspoon dried mint
- 1   teaspoon minced fresh gingerroot
- 6   cups torn fresh spinach
- 1   large sweet red pepper, julienned
- ½   medium cucumber, peeled and julienned

1. In a large nonstick skillet coated with cooking spray, cook beef and jalapeno over medium heat until beef is no longer pink. Add garlic; cook 1 minute longer.

2. In a small bowl, whisk lime juice, brown sugar, soy sauce, basil, mint and ginger. Place spinach, red pepper and cucumber in a large bowl; add beef mixture. Drizzle dressing over salad; toss to coat.

NOTE *Wear disposable gloves when cutting hot peppers; the oils can burn skin. Avoid touching your face.*

PER SERVING *2 cups equals 207 cal., 5 g fat (2 g sat. fat), 46 mg chol., 383 mg sodium, 14 g carb., 2 g fiber, 27 g pro.* **Diabetic Exchanges:** *3 lean meat, 2 vegetable.*

Beef & Rice Stuffed Cabbage Rolls

My family is quick to the table when I serve cabbage rolls. They are simple to make and really satisfy without being fattening.

—**LYNN BOWEN** GERALDINE, AL

PREP: 20 MIN. • **COOK:** 6 HOURS
MAKES: 6 SERVINGS

- 12 **cabbage leaves**
- 1 **cup cooked brown rice**
- ¼ **cup finely chopped onion**
- 1 **egg, lightly beaten**
- ¼ **cup fat-free milk**
- ½ **teaspoon salt**
- ¼ **teaspoon pepper**
- 1 **pound lean ground beef (90% lean)**

SAUCE

- 1 **can (8 ounces) tomato sauce**
- 1 **tablespoon brown sugar**
- 1 **tablespoon lemon juice**
- 1 **teaspoon Worcestershire sauce**

1. In batches, cook cabbage in boiling water 3-5 minutes or until crisp-tender. Drain; cool slightly. Trim the thick vein from the bottom of each cabbage leaf, making a V-shaped cut.
2. In a large bowl, combine rice, onion, egg, milk, salt and pepper. Add beef; mix lightly but thoroughly. Place about ¼ cup mixture on each cabbage leaf. Pull together cut edges of leaf to overlap; fold over filling. Fold in sides and roll up.
3. Place six rolls in a 4- or 5-qt. slow cooker, seam side down. In a bowl, mix sauce ingredients; pour half of the sauce over cabbage rolls. Top with remaining rolls and sauce. Cook, covered, on low 6-8 hours or until a thermometer inserted in beef reads 160° and cabbage is tender.
PER SERVING *2 cabbage rolls equals 204 cal., 7 g fat (3 g sat. fat), 83 mg chol., 446 mg sodium, 16 g carb., 2 g fiber, 18 g pro.* **Diabetic Exchanges:** *2 lean meat, 1 starch.*

SIRLOIN WITH MUSHROOM SAUCE

⑤ INGREDIENTS | FAST FIX ▶ Sirloin with Mushroom Sauce

A mouthwatering combination of rich mushroom sauce and peppery steak is a welcome way to finish off a busy day. Whenever visitors drop in around dinnertime, I pull out this recipe and it's ready before we know it.

—**JOE ELLIOTT** WEST BEND, WI

START TO FINISH: 30 MIN.
MAKES: 4 SERVINGS

- 1 **boneless beef sirloin steak (1 pound and ¾ inch thick)**
- 1 **teaspoon coarsely ground pepper**
- 2 **teaspoons canola oil**
- 1½ **cups sliced fresh mushrooms**
- ½ **cup beef broth**
- ½ **cup dry red wine or additional beef broth**

1. Preheat oven to 450°. Rub steak with pepper. In a heavy ovenproof skillet, heat oil over medium-high heat. Brown steak on both sides. Transfer to oven; roast 4 minutes or until meat reaches desired doneness (for medium-rare, a thermometer should read 145°; medium, 160°; well-done, 170°).
2. Remove steak from pan; tent with foil. Let meat stand for 10 minutes before slicing.
3. Add mushrooms to same pan; cook and stir over medium-high heat until golden brown. Add broth and wine, stirring to loosen browned bits from pan. Bring to a boil; cook until liquid is reduced by half. Thinly slice steak; serve with mushroom sauce.

PER SERVING *3 ounces cooked beef with ¼ cup mushroom sauce equals 214 cal., 9 g fat (3 g sat. fat), 77 mg chol., 161 mg sodium, 1 g carb., trace fiber, 27 g pro.* **Diabetic Exchanges:** *3 lean meat, ½ fat.*

**AGGIE ARNOLD-NORMAN'S
SLOW COOKER CHICKEN CACCIATORE**
PAGE 142

Chicken Favorites

Few dishes provide as much **down-home flavor** as those made with chicken. For **good-for-you fajitas, meatballs, Buffalo chicken, stir-fries** and even Southern-style Country Chicken with Gravy, look no further than the **tempting dishes** in this popular chapter.

HOLLY GOMEZ'S SAUSAGE & PEPPERS WITH CHEESE POLENTA *PAGE 154*

SARA RICHARDSON'S ROSEMARY CHICKEN WITH SPINACH & BEANS *PAGE 144*

DIANE NEMITZ'S CHICKEN FLORENTINE MEATBALLS *PAGE 160*

BLACKENED CHICKEN AND BEANS

Blackened Chicken and Beans

My husband loves any spicy food, and this is one quick-fix recipe we can both agree on. As the chicken cooks, whip up salads of lettuce, tomato, avocado and shredded cheddar cheese. Dinner's done!

—CHRISTINE ZONGKER SPRING HILL, KS

START TO FINISH: 20 MIN.
MAKES: 4 SERVINGS

- 2 teaspoons chili powder
- ¼ teaspoon salt
- ¼ teaspoon pepper
- 4 boneless skinless chicken breast halves (4 ounces each)
- 1 tablespoon canola oil
- 1 can (15 ounces) black beans, rinsed and drained
- 1 cup frozen corn
- 1 cup chunky salsa

1. Combine the chili powder, salt and pepper; rub over both sides of chicken. In a large nonstick skillet, cook the chicken in oil over medium heat for 4-5 minutes on each side or until a thermometer reads 170°. Remove and keep warm.

2. Add the beans, corn and salsa to the pan; heat through. Serve with chicken.

PER SERVING *1 chicken breast half with ¾ cup bean mixture equals 297 cal., 7 g fat (1 g sat. fat), 63 mg chol., 697 mg sodium, 30 g carb., 10 g fiber, 33 g pro.* **Diabetic Exchanges:** *3 lean meat, 2 starch, 1 fat.*

FAST FIX Lemon-Olive Chicken with Orzo

A fantastic combo of lemon and Greek olives really brightens up a weeknight dinner. Cooking the orzo in the same pan saves so much time.

—NANCY BROWN DAHINDA, IL

START TO FINISH: 30 MIN.
MAKES: 4 SERVINGS

- 1 tablespoon olive oil
- 4 boneless skinless chicken thighs (about 1 pound)
- 1 can (14½ ounces) reduced-sodium chicken broth
- ⅔ cup uncooked whole wheat orzo pasta
- ½ medium lemon, cut into 4 wedges
- ½ cup pitted Greek olives, sliced
- 1 tablespoon lemon juice
- 1 teaspoon dried oregano
- ¼ teaspoon pepper

1. In a large nonstick skillet, heat oil over medium heat. Brown chicken on both sides; remove from pan.

2. Add broth to skillet; increase heat to medium-high. Cook 1-2 minutes, stirring to loosen browned bits from pan. Stir in remaining ingredients; bring to a boil. Reduce heat; simmer, uncovered, 5 minutes, stirring occasionally.

3. Return chicken to pan. Cook, covered, 5-8 minutes or until pasta is tender and a thermometer inserted in chicken reads 170°.

PER SERVING *1 serving equals 345 cal., 17 g fat (3 g sat. fat), 76 mg chol., 636 mg sodium, 22 g carb., 5 g fiber, 26 g pro.* **Diabetic Exchanges:** *3 lean meat, 2 fat, 1 starch.*

SLOW COOKER

Lime Chicken Tacos

Lime juice adds bright taste to an easy taco filling that's surprisingly healthy. This fun recipe is great for a casual dinner with friends and family.

—**TRACY GUNTER** BOISE, ID

PREP: 10 MIN. • **COOK:** 5½ HOURS
MAKES: 12 TACOS

- 1½ **pounds boneless skinless chicken breasts**
- 3 **tablespoons lime juice**
- 1 **tablespoon chili powder**
- 1 **cup frozen corn, thawed**
- 1 **cup chunky salsa**
- 12 **fat-free flour tortillas (6 inches), warmed**
  Sour cream, shredded cheddar cheese and shredded lettuce, optional

1. Place the chicken in a 3-qt. slow cooker. Combine lime juice and chili powder; pour over chicken. Cover and cook on low for 5-6 hours or until chicken is tender.
2. Remove chicken; cool slightly. Shred meat with two forks and return to the slow cooker. Stir in corn and salsa.
3. Cover and cook mixture on low for 30 minutes or until heated through. Serve in tortillas, with sour cream, cheese and lettuce if desired.

PER SERVING *1 taco (calculated without sour cream and cheese) equals 148 cal., 2 g fat (trace sat. fat), 31 mg chol., 338 mg sodium, 18 g carb., 1 g fiber, 14 g pro.* **Diabetic Exchanges:** *2 lean meat, 1 starch.*

FAST FIX # Chicken & Fruit Spinach Salads

It takes only 10 minutes to prepare this substantial salad. Serve with whole grain rolls to round out the meal.

—**JESSE KLAUSMEIER** BURBANK, CA

START TO FINISH: 10 MIN.
MAKES: 4 SERVINGS

- 1 **package (6 ounces) fresh baby spinach**
- 1 **package (10 ounces) ready-to-use grilled chicken breast strips**
- 1 **can (11 ounces) mandarin oranges, drained**
- 1 **cup sliced fresh strawberries**
- 2 **slices red onion, separated into rings**
- ½ **cup reduced-fat raspberry vinaigrette**
- ¼ **cup honey-roasted sliced almonds**

Divide spinach among four serving plates. Top with chicken, oranges, strawberries and onion. Drizzle with vinaigrette and sprinkle with almonds.

PER SERVING *1 serving equals 223 cal., 10 g fat (1 g sat. fat), 42 mg chol., 835 mg sodium, 17 g carb., 2 g fiber, 21 g pro.* **Diabetic Exchanges:** *2 lean meat, 2 fat, 1 starch.*

CHICKEN & FRUIT SPINACH SALADS

SLOW COOKER 🍲 Herbed Slow Cooker Chicken

My daughter, who has two young sons to keep up with, shared this simple recipe with me several years ago. I've made it repeatedly over the years. The seasoning blend is just the thing for bone-in chicken breasts.

—SUNDRA HAUCK BOGALUSA, LA

PREP: 5 MIN. • **COOK:** 4 HOURS
MAKES: 4 SERVINGS

- 1 tablespoon olive oil
- 1 teaspoon paprika
- ½ teaspoon garlic powder
- ½ teaspoon seasoned salt
- ½ teaspoon dried thyme
- ½ teaspoon dried basil
- ½ teaspoon pepper
- ½ teaspoon browning sauce, optional
- 4 bone-in chicken breast halves (8 ounces each)
- ½ cup chicken broth

In a small bowl, combine the first eight ingredients; rub over chicken. Place in a 5-qt. slow cooker; add broth. Cover and cook on low for 4-5 hours or until chicken is tender.

PER SERVING *1 chicken breast half equals 211 cal., 7 g fat (2 g sat. fat), 91 mg chol., 392 mg sodium, 1 g carb., trace fiber, 33 g pro.* **Diabetic Exchanges:** *5 lean meat, 1 fat.*

FAST FIX ▶ Spicy Chicken Tomato Pitas

I'm not sure if this is a Mediterranean dish with a Southwestern flair or the other way around. All I know is that it's ideal for a summer dinner. The tomato relish is yummy as an appetizer with tortilla chips, so you may want to double it.

—CORI COOPER BOISE, ID

START TO FINISH: 30 MIN.
MAKES: 4 SERVINGS

SPICY CHICKEN TOMATO PITAS

TOMATO RELISH
- ¼ cup lemon juice
- 1 tablespoon olive oil
- 1 teaspoon ground coriander
- 1 teaspoon ground cumin
- ¼ teaspoon crushed red pepper flakes
- 4 medium tomatoes, seeded and chopped
- 1 small onion, chopped
- ¼ cup minced fresh parsley

CHICKEN PITAS
- 1 tablespoon ground cumin
- 1 tablespoon paprika
- 1½ teaspoons dried oregano
- 1½ teaspoons ground coriander
- ½ teaspoon crushed red pepper flakes
- ¼ teaspoon salt
- 4 boneless skinless chicken breast halves (4 ounces each)
- 8 whole wheat pita pocket halves

1. In a bowl, whisk the first five ingredients. Add tomatoes, onion and parsley; toss to coat. Refrigerate until serving.

2. Moisten a paper towel with cooking oil; using long-handled tongs, rub on grill rack to coat lightly. Combine cumin, paprika, oregano, coriander, pepper flakes and salt; rub onto both sides of chicken. Grill chicken, covered, over medium heat or broil 4 in. from heat 4-7 minutes on each side or until a thermometer reads 165°.

3. Cut chicken into slices. Serve in pita halves with relish.

PER SERVING *2 filled pita halves equals 383 cal., 9 g fat (2 g sat. fat), 63 mg chol., 558 mg sodium, 47 g carb., 9 g fiber, 32 g pro.*

FAST FIX ▶ Blueberry Chicken Salad

On weekday mornings, I whip up this fresh combo to take for lunch. It also works as a light summer supper, and it's a cinch to double for a shower or potluck.

—**KARI KELLEY** PLAINS, MT

START TO FINISH: 15 MIN.
MAKES: 4 SERVINGS

- 2 **cups fresh blueberries**
- 2 **cups cubed cooked chicken breast**
- ¾ **cup chopped celery**
- ½ **cup diced sweet red pepper**
- ½ **cup thinly sliced green onions**
- ¾ **cup (6 ounces) lemon yogurt**
- 3 **tablespoons mayonnaise**
- ½ **teaspoon salt**
  Bibb lettuce leaves, optional

1. Set aside a few blueberries for topping salad. In a large bowl, combine chicken, celery, red pepper, green onions and remaining blueberries. In a small bowl, mix yogurt, mayonnaise and salt. Add to chicken mixture; gently toss to coat.
2. Refrigerate until serving. If desired, serve over lettuce. Top with reserved blueberries.
PER SERVING *1 cup equals 277 cal., 11 g fat (2 g sat. fat), 60 mg chol., 441 mg sodium, 21 g carb., 3 g fiber, 23 g pro.* **Diabetic Exchanges:** *3 lean meat, 1 starch, 1 fat, ½ fruit.*

CHICKEN THIGHS WITH SAUSAGE

SLOW COOKER
Chicken Thighs with Sausage

Whether you're serving your family or special guests, here's a delicious entree that hits the spot. Smoked turkey sausage adds an enormous amount of flavor to the chicken and veggies.

—**JOANNE IOVINO** KINGS PARK, NY

PREP: 25 MIN. • **COOK:** 6 HOURS
MAKES: 8 SERVINGS

- 2 **medium carrots, chopped**
- 2 **celery ribs, chopped**
- 1 **large onion, finely chopped**
- 8 **bone-in chicken thighs (about 3 pounds), skin removed**
- 1 **package (14 ounces) smoked turkey sausage, cut into ½-inch slices**
- ¼ **cup ketchup**
- 6 **garlic cloves, minced**
- 1 **tablespoon Louisiana-style hot sauce**
- 1 **teaspoon dried basil**
- 1 **teaspoon paprika**
- 1 **teaspoon dried thyme**
- ½ **teaspoon dried oregano**
- ½ **teaspoon pepper**
- ¼ **teaspoon ground allspice**
- 1 **teaspoon browning sauce, optional**

1. In a 4- or 5-qt. slow cooker, combine the carrots, celery and onion. Top with chicken and sausage.
2. In a small bowl, combine the ketchup, garlic, hot sauce, seasonings and, if desired, browning sauce. Spoon over meats. Cover and cook on low for 6-8 hours or until chicken is tender.
PER SERVING *1 chicken thigh with ⅓ cup sausage mixture equals 280 cal., 12 g fat (4 g sat. fat), 118 mg chol., 675 mg sodium, 8 g carb., 1 g fiber, 33 g pro.* **Diabetic Exchanges:** *5 lean meat, ½ starch.*

Mango-Pineapple Chicken Tacos

I lived in the Caribbean as a child, and the tropical fruits in this slow-cooked taco filling bring me back to my childhood.

—**LISSA NELSON** PROVO, UT

PREP: 25 MIN. • **COOK:** 5 HOURS
MAKES: 16 SERVINGS

- 2 **medium mangoes, peeled and chopped**
- 1½ **cups cubed fresh pineapple or canned pineapple chunks, drained**
- 2 **medium tomatoes, chopped**
- 1 **medium red onion, finely chopped**
- 2 **small Anaheim peppers, seeded and chopped**
- 2 **green onions, finely chopped**
- 1 **tablespoon lime juice**
- 1 **teaspoon sugar**
- 4 **pounds bone-in chicken breast halves, skin removed**
- 3 **teaspoons salt**
- ¼ **cup packed brown sugar**
- 32 **taco shells, warmed**
- ¼ **cup minced fresh cilantro**

1. In a large bowl, combine the first eight ingredients. Place chicken in a 6-qt. slow cooker; sprinkle with salt and brown sugar. Top with mango mixture. Cover and cook on low for 5-6 hours or until chicken is tender.
2. Remove chicken; cool slightly. Strain cooking juices, reserving mango mixture and ½ cup juices. Discard remaining juices. When cool enough to handle, remove chicken from bones; discard bones.
3. Shred chicken with two forks. Return chicken and reserved mango mixture and cooking juices to slow cooker; heat through. Serve in taco shells; sprinkle with cilantro.

FREEZE OPTION *Freeze cooled meat mixture in freezer containers. To use, partially thaw in the refrigerator overnight. Heat through in a saucepan, stirring occasionally and adding a little broth if necessary.*

PER SERVING *2 tacos equals 246 cal., 7 g fat (2 g sat. fat), 51 mg chol., 582 mg sodium, 25 g carb., 2 g fiber, 21 g pro. Diabetic Exchanges: 3 lean meat, 1½ starch.*

Slow Cooker Chicken Cacciatore

My husband and I milk 125 cows. There are days when there's just no time left for cooking! It's really nice to be able to come into the house at night and smell this wonderful dinner simmering.

—**AGGIE ARNOLD-NORMAN** LIBERTY, PA

PREP: 15 MIN. • **COOK:** 6 HOURS
MAKES: 6 SERVINGS

- 2 **medium onions, thinly sliced**
- 1 **broiler/fryer chicken (3 to 4 pounds), cut up and skin removed**
- 2 **garlic cloves, minced**
- 1 **to 2 teaspoons dried oregano**
- 1 **teaspoon salt**
- ½ **teaspoon dried basil**
- ¼ **teaspoon pepper**
- 1 **bay leaf**
- 1 **can (14½ ounces) diced tomatoes, undrained**
- 1 **can (8 ounces) tomato sauce**
- 1 **can (4 ounces) mushroom stems and pieces, drained, or 1 cup sliced fresh mushrooms**
- ¼ **cup white wine or water**
  Hot cooked pasta

1. Place onions in a 5-qt. slow cooker. Add chicken, seasonings, tomatoes, tomato sauce, mushrooms and wine.
2. Cover and cook on low for 6-8 hours or until chicken is tender. Discard bay leaf. Serve chicken with sauce over pasta.

PER SERVING *1 serving (calculated without pasta) equals 207 cal., 6 g fat (2 g sat. fat), 73 mg chol., 787 mg sodium, 11 g carb., 3 g fiber, 27 g pro. Diabetic Exchanges: 4 lean meat, 2 vegetable.*

Warm Apricot Chicken Salad

This summer-fresh salad is topped with quickly marinated chicken. It's hearty, flavorful and nutritious. Even our kids like the sweet and tangy flavor.

—CAROLYN JOHNS LACEY, WA

START TO FINISH: 30 MIN.
MAKES: 4 SERVINGS

- 1 **pound boneless skinless chicken breasts, cut into strips**
- 2 **tablespoons orange marmalade**
- 1 **tablespoon reduced-sodium soy sauce**
- 6 **fresh apricots, sliced**
- 2 **teaspoons grated orange peel**
- ½ **pound fresh spinach, stems removed**
- 1 **medium sweet red pepper, julienned**
- 1 **tablespoon canola oil**
- ¼ **cup ranch salad dressing**
- ¼ **cup slivered almonds, toasted**

1. In a large bowl, combine the chicken, marmalade and soy sauce. Refrigerate for 20 minutes.
2. Meanwhile, toss apricots and orange peel. Place spinach on a serving platter or four salad plates; top with apricots. In a skillet, saute red pepper and chicken mixture in oil until chicken is no longer pink. Remove from heat; stir in salad dressing. Spoon over spinach and apricots; sprinkle with almonds.
PER SERVING *1 serving equals 343 cal., 18 g fat (3 g sat. fat), 65 mg chol., 529 mg sodium, 19 g carb., 4 g fiber, 27 g pro.* **Diabetic Exchanges:** *3 lean meat, 2 fat, 1 vegetable, 1 fruit.*

Greek-Style Chicken Burgers

The original recipe for these burgers called for lamb or beef, but I decided to try ground chicken to decrease the fat. The sauce doubles as a tasty dip for fresh veggie sticks and toasted pita chips.

—JUDY PUSKAS WALLACEBURG, ON

PREP: 25 MIN. • **GRILL:** 10 MIN.
MAKES: 4 SERVINGS

SAUCE
- ⅓ **cup fat-free plain Greek yogurt**
- ¼ **cup chopped peeled cucumber**
- ¼ **cup crumbled reduced-fat feta cheese**
- 1½ **teaspoons snipped fresh dill**
- 1½ **teaspoons lemon juice**
- 1 **small garlic clove, minced**

BURGERS
- 1 **medium onion, finely chopped**
- ¼ **cup dry bread crumbs**
- 1 **tablespoon dried oregano**
- 1 **tablespoon lemon juice**
- 2 **garlic cloves, minced**
- ½ **teaspoon salt**
- ¼ **teaspoon pepper**
- 1 **pound ground chicken**
- 4 **hamburger buns, split**
- 4 **lettuce leaves**
- 4 **tomato slices**

1. In a small bowl, mix the sauce ingredients; refrigerate until serving.
2. In a large bowl, combine the first seven burger ingredients. Add the chicken; mix lightly but thoroughly. Shape into four ½-in.-thick patties.
3. Moisten a paper towel with cooking oil; using long-handled tongs, rub on grill rack to coat lightly. Grill burgers, covered, over medium heat or broil 4 in. from heat 5-7 minutes on each side or until a thermometer reads 165°. Serve on buns with lettuce, tomato and sauce.
PER SERVING *1 burger equals 350 cal., 12 g fat (4 g sat. fat), 78 mg chol., 732 mg sodium, 35 g carb., 3 g fiber, 27 g pro.* **Diabetic Exchanges:** *3 lean meat, 2 starch, 1 vegetable.*

GREEK-STYLE CHICKEN BURGERS

Rosemary Chicken with Spinach & Beans

With two young boys constantly on the go, finding tricks to simplify meals is key. Since this recipe uses just one skillet, it's a cinch to prepare when I only have a half-hour to make dinner for my hungry family.

—SARA RICHARDSON LITTLETON, CO

START TO FINISH: 30 MIN.
MAKES: 4 SERVINGS

- 1 can (14½ ounces) stewed tomatoes
- 4 boneless skinless chicken breast halves (6 ounces each)
- 2 teaspoons dried rosemary, crushed
- ½ teaspoon salt
- ½ teaspoon pepper
- 4 teaspoons olive oil, divided
- 1 package (6 ounces) fresh baby spinach
- 2 garlic cloves, minced
- 1 can (15 ounces) white kidney or cannellini beans, rinsed and drained

1. Drain tomatoes, reserving juice; coarsely chop tomatoes. Pound chicken with a meat mallet to ¼-in. thickness. Rub with rosemary, salt and pepper. In a large skillet, heat 2 teaspoons oil over medium heat. Add chicken; cook 5-6 minutes on each side or until no longer pink. Remove and keep warm.

2. In same pan, heat remaining oil over medium-high heat. Add spinach and garlic; cook and stir 2-3 minutes or until spinach is wilted. Stir in beans, tomatoes and reserved juice; heat through. Serve with chicken.

PER SERVING *1 chicken breast half with ¾ cup sauce equals 348 cal., 9 g fat (2 g sat. fat), 94 mg chol., 729 mg sodium, 25 g carb., 6 g fiber, 41 g pro.* **Diabetic Exchanges:** *5 lean meat, 2 vegetable, 1 starch, 1 fat.*

ROSEMARY CHICKEN WITH SPINACH & BEANS

Greek Chicken Dinner

Feta cheese takes this chicken and potato dinner over the top. Serve alongside a lettuce salad tossed with pepperoncinis, black olives and low-fat vinaigrette for a fresh and healthy meal.

—*TASTE OF HOME* TEST KITCHEN

PREP: 15 MIN. • **BAKE:** 50 MIN.
MAKES: 6 SERVINGS

- 7 medium red potatoes, cut into 1-inch cubes
- 6 boneless skinless chicken thighs (about 1½ pounds)
- ½ cup reduced-fat sun-dried tomato salad dressing
- 2 teaspoons Greek seasoning
- 1 teaspoon dried basil
- ½ cup crumbled reduced-fat feta cheese

1. In a large bowl, combine first five ingredients. Transfer to a 13x9-in. baking dish coated with cooking spray.

2. Cover and bake at 400° for 40 minutes. Sprinkle with cheese. Bake, uncovered, for 10-15 minutes longer or until chicken juices run clear and potatoes are tender.

PER SERVING *1 serving equals 316 cal., 12 g fat (3 g sat. fat), 79 mg chol., 767 mg sodium, 25 g carb., 2 g fiber, 26 g pro.* **Diabetic Exchanges:** *3 lean meat, 1½ starch, 1 fat.*

Chicken 'n' Summer Squash Packets

These meal-in-one packets are an ideal way to use up your garden bounty. Tender chicken and seasoned veggies are tucked inside each foil-wrapped pack.

—SHARON SALVADOR LAKEPORT, CA

PREP: 20 MIN. • **BAKE:** 25 MIN.
MAKES: 4 SERVINGS

- 4 boneless skinless chicken breast halves (4 ounces each)
- ¼ teaspoon salt, divided
- ¼ teaspoon pepper, divided
- 1 medium onion, sliced
- 2 tablespoons Dijon mustard
- 1 small zucchini, sliced
- 1 small yellow summer squash, sliced
- 2 cups sliced fresh mushrooms
- ¾ teaspoon dried basil
- ⅛ teaspoon garlic powder
- ⅛ teaspoon paprika
- 1 tablespoon butter
- 1 tablespoon grated Parmesan cheese

1. Flatten chicken to ¼-in. thickness; sprinkle with ⅛ teaspoon each salt and pepper. Cut eight 15x12-in. rectangles of heavy-duty foil; place one rectangle on top of another to make four. Divide onion slices among the four rectangles; top with chicken, mustard, zucchini, yellow squash and mushrooms.

2. Combine basil, garlic powder, paprika and remaining salt and pepper; sprinkle over tops. Dot with butter. Fold foil around mixture and seal tightly. Place on a baking sheet.

3. Bake at 425° for 25-30 minutes or until a thermometer reads 165°. Open foil carefully to allow steam to escape. Sprinkle with Parmesan cheese.

PER SERVING *1 packet equals 206 cal., 7 g fat (3 g sat. fat), 71 mg chol., 449 mg sodium, 10 g carb., 3 g fiber, 27 g pro.* **Diabetic Exchanges:** *3 lean meat, 2 vegetable, 1 fat.*

CHICKEN A LA KING

SLOW COOKER
Chicken a la King

When I know I'll be having a busy day with little time to prepare a meal, I use my slow cooker to make Chicken a la King. It smells so good while it's cooking.

—ELEANOR MIELKE SNOHOMISH, WA

PREP: 10 MIN. • **COOK:** 7½ HOURS
MAKES: 6 SERVINGS

- 1 can (10¾ ounces) reduced-fat reduced-sodium condensed cream of chicken soup, undiluted
- 3 tablespoons all-purpose flour
- ¼ teaspoon pepper
  Dash cayenne pepper
- 1 pound boneless skinless chicken breasts, cubed
- 1 celery rib, chopped
- ½ cup chopped green pepper
- ¼ cup chopped onion
- 1 package (10 ounces) frozen peas, thawed
- 2 tablespoons diced pimientos, drained
  Hot cooked rice

In a 3-qt. slow cooker, combine soup, flour, pepper and cayenne until smooth. Stir in chicken, celery, green pepper and onion. Cover and cook on low for 7-8 hours or until meat juices run clear. Stir in peas and pimientos. Cook 30 minutes longer or until heated through. Serve with rice.

PER SERVING *1 cup equals 183 cal., 3 g fat (0 sat. fat), 52 mg chol., 284 mg sodium, 16 g carb., 0 fiber, 22 g pro.* **Diabetic Exchanges:** *2 lean meat, 1 starch.*

ORIGINAL	MAKEOVER
849 Calories	443 Calories
50g Fat	15g Fat
29g Sat. Fat	6g Sat. Fat

MAKEOVER CHICKEN POTPIES

Makeover Chicken Potpies

Cut through the flaky homemade crust to reveal a rich gravy brimming with hearty vegetables and juicy chicken. Chicken potpie delivers classic comfort-food flavors on days when it's icy cold outside.

—**JOHN SLIVON** MILTON, FL

PREP: 30 MIN. + CHILLING • **BAKE:** 20 MIN.
MAKES: 4 SERVINGS

- ¾ **cup plus 6 tablespoons all-purpose flour, divided**
- ¼ **teaspoon baking powder**
- ¼ **teaspoon salt**
- 3 **tablespoons cold butter, divided**
- 2 **tablespoons buttermilk**
- 1 **tablespoon canola oil**
- 1 **to 2 tablespoons cold water**
- 4 **medium carrots, sliced**
- 3 **celery ribs, sliced**
- 1 **large onion, chopped**
- 2½ **cups reduced-sodium chicken broth**
- ⅔ **cup fat-free milk**
- 2 **cups cubed cooked chicken breast**
- 1 **cup frozen peas**
- ⅛ **teaspoon pepper**
- 1 **egg white, lightly beaten**

1. In a small bowl, combine ¾ cup flour, baking powder and salt. Cut in 2 tablespoons butter until crumbly. Add buttermilk and oil; toss with a fork. Gradually add water, tossing with a fork until dough forms a ball. Cover and refrigerate for 1 hour.

2. For filling, in a large skillet, melt remaining butter. Add the carrots, celery and onion; saute until crisp-tender. In a small bowl, combine remaining flour with the broth and milk until smooth. Gradually stir into vegetable mixture. Bring to a boil; cook and stir for 2 minutes or until thickened. Stir in the chicken, peas and pepper. Transfer to four 16-oz. ramekins; set aside.

3. Divide dough into four portions. On a lightly floured surface, roll out dough to fit ramekins. Place dough over filling; trim and seal edges. Cut out a decorative center or cut slits in pastry. Brush with egg white.

4. Place ramekins on a baking sheet. Bake at 425° for 20-25 minutes or until crusts are golden brown.

PER SERVING *1 potpie equals 443 cal., 15 g fat (6 g sat. fat), 78 mg chol., 781 mg sodium, 45 g carb., 5 g fiber, 31 g pro.*

THE SKINNY

The original potpie's gravy was made with a roux of ⅔ cup butter and 5 tablespoons flour. The makeover combines 6 tablespoons flour with liquid instead. This mixture is stirred into the butter and vegetables to cook until thickened. The new technique saves 266 calories and 31 grams of fat per serving. And because the makeover doubles up on veggies, the filling is still hearty and rich.

Lime-Ginger Chicken Tenders

We cook chicken breasts often because they're low in fat, high in protein and almost always a good price at the grocery store. To keep things exciting, I add favorites like jalapenos, lime and ginger.

—SAMANTHA ANDERSON FORT WORTH, TX

START TO FINISH: 30 MIN.
MAKES: 4 SERVINGS

- ⅓ cup minced fresh cilantro
- 1 jalapeno pepper, seeded and minced
- 2 tablespoons lime juice
- 2 tablespoons olive oil
- 3 garlic cloves, minced
- 1½ teaspoons minced fresh gingerroot
- 1½ teaspoons grated lime peel
- ½ teaspoon salt
- ½ teaspoon ground cumin
- 1½ pounds chicken tenderloins

Preheat oven to 375°. In a large bowl, mix the first nine ingredients. Add chicken; toss to coat. Transfer to a greased 15x10x1-in. baking pan. Bake, uncovered, 20-25 minutes or until chicken is no longer pink.

NOTE *Wear disposable gloves when cutting hot peppers; the oils can burn skin. Avoid touching your face.*

PER SERVING *5 ounces cooked chicken equals 226 cal., 8 g fat (1 g sat. fat), 100 mg chol., 368 mg sodium, 2 g carb., trace fiber, 39 g pro.* **Diabetic Exchanges:** *5 lean meat, 1 fat.*

Spinach and Mushroom Smothered Chicken

Here's a healthier take on smothered chicken. It's extra-special to serve but not tricky to make. Melted provolone and a sprinkling of crunchy pecans make it feel decadent without breaking the calorie bank.

—KATRINA WAGNER GRAIN VALLEY, MO

START TO FINISH: 30 MIN.
MAKES: 4 SERVINGS

- 3 cups fresh baby spinach
- 1¾ cups sliced fresh mushrooms
- 3 green onions, sliced
- 2 tablespoons chopped pecans
- 1½ teaspoons olive oil
- 4 boneless skinless chicken breast halves (4 ounces each)
- ½ teaspoon rotisserie chicken seasoning
- 2 slices reduced-fat provolone cheese, halved

1. In a large skillet, saute the spinach, mushrooms, onions and pecans in oil until mushrooms are tender. Set aside and keep warm. Sprinkle chicken with seasoning.

2. Moisten a paper towel with cooking oil; using long-handled tongs, lightly coat the grill rack. Grill chicken, covered, over medium heat or broil 4 in. from the heat for 4-5 minutes on each side or until a thermometer reads 170°.

3. Top with cheese. Cover and grill 2-3 minutes longer or until cheese is melted. Top chicken breasts with spinach mixture.

PER SERVING *1 chicken breast half equals 203 cal., 9 g fat (2 g sat. fat), 68 mg chol., 210 mg sodium, 3 g carb., 2 g fiber, 27 g pro.* **Diabetic Exchanges:** *3 lean meat, 1 vegetable, 1 fat.*

SPINACH AND MUSHROOM SMOTHERED CHICKEN

OVEN-FRIED
CHICKEN DRUMSTICKS

Oven-Fried Chicken Drumsticks

This fabulous chicken uses Greek yogurt to create an amazing marinade that makes the chicken incredibly moist. No one will guess that it's been lightened up and not even fried!

—**KIMBERLY WALLACE** DENNISON, OH

PREP: 20 MIN. + MARINATING
BAKE: 40 MIN.
MAKES: 4 SERVINGS

- 1 **cup fat-free plain Greek yogurt**
- 1 **tablespoon Dijon mustard**
- 2 **garlic cloves, minced**
- 8 **chicken drumsticks (4 ounces each), skin removed**
- ½ **cup whole wheat flour**
- 1½ **teaspoons paprika**
- 1 **teaspoon baking powder**
- 1 **teaspoon salt**
- 1 **teaspoon pepper**
  Olive oil-flavored cooking spray

1. In a large resealable plastic bag, combine yogurt, mustard and garlic. Add chicken; seal bag and turn to coat. Refrigerate 8 hours or overnight.
2. Preheat oven to 425°. In another plastic bag, mix flour, paprika, baking powder, salt and pepper. Remove chicken from marinade and add, one piece at a time, to flour mixture; close bag and shake to coat. Place on a wire rack over a baking sheet; spritz with cooking spray. Bake 40-45 minutes or until a thermometer reads 180°.
PER SERVING *2 chicken drumsticks equals 227 cal., 7 g fat (1 g sat. fat), 81 mg chol., 498 mg sodium, 9 g carb., 1 g fiber, 31 g pro.* **Diabetic Exchanges:** *4 lean meat, ½ starch.*

CAROLINA-STYLE VINEGAR BBQ CHICKEN

---

(5) INGREDIENTS SLOW COOKER

Carolina-Style Vinegar BBQ Chicken

I live in Georgia, but I appreciate the tangy, sweet and slightly spicy taste of Carolina barbecue. I make my version in the slow cooker and when you walk in the door after being gone all day, the aroma will knock you off your feet!

—**RAMONA PARRIS** MARIETTA, GA

PREP: 10 MIN. • **COOK:** 4 HOURS
MAKES: 6 SERVINGS

- 2 **cups water**
- 1 **cup white vinegar**
- ¼ **cup sugar**
- 1 **tablespoon reduced-sodium chicken base**
- 1 **teaspoon crushed red pepper flakes**
- ¾ **teaspoon salt**
- 1½ **pounds boneless skinless chicken breasts**
- 6 **whole wheat hamburger buns, split, optional**

1. In a small bowl, mix the first six ingredients. Place chicken in a 3-qt. slow cooker; add vinegar mixture. Cook, covered, on low 4-5 hours or until chicken is tender.
2. Remove chicken; cool slightly. Reserve 1 cup cooking juices; discard remaining juices. Shred chicken with two forks. Return meat and reserved cooking juices to slow cooker; heat through. If desired, serve chicken mixture on buns.
NOTE *Look for chicken base near the broth and bouillon.*
PER SERVING *½ cup (calculated without buns) equals 134 cal., 3 g fat (1 g sat. fat), 63 mg chol., 228 mg sodium, 3 g carb., trace fiber, 23 g pro.* **Diabetic Exchange:** *3 lean meat.*

CITRUS-MARINATED CHICKEN

Citrus-Marinated Chicken

This juicy, zesty chicken stars in many of my family's summer meals. While there are a million ways to dress up poultry, you'll find yourself turning to this recipe again and again. It's that quick and easy.

—DEBORAH GRETZINGER GREEN BAY, WI

PREP: 10 MIN. + MARINATING • **GRILL:** 10 MIN.
MAKES: 6 SERVINGS

- ½ **cup lemon juice**
- ½ **cup orange juice**
- 6 **garlic cloves, minced**
- 2 **tablespoons canola oil**
- 1 **teaspoon salt**
- 1 **teaspoon ground ginger**
- 1 **teaspoon dried tarragon**
- ¼ **teaspoon pepper**
- 6 **boneless skinless chicken breast halves (6 ounces each)**

1. Combine the first eight ingredients in a large resealable plastic bag. Add the chicken; seal bag and turn to coat. Refrigerate for at least 4 hours.

2. Drain and discard marinade. Grill chicken, covered, over medium heat or broil 4 in. from the heat for 5-7 minutes on each side or until a thermometer reads 170°.
PER SERVING *1 chicken breast half equals 195 cal., 5 g fat (1 g sat. fat), 94 mg chol., 161 mg sodium, 1 g carb., trace fiber, 34 g pro.* **Diabetic Exchange:** *5 lean meat.*

FAST FIX
Summertime Orzo & Chicken

For lunch or dinner, this easy-as-can-be dish is likely to become a summertime staple in your house. If you prefer, grill the chicken breasts rather than cooking them in a skillet.

—FRAN MACMILLAN WEST MELBOURNE, FL

START TO FINISH: 30 MIN.
MAKES: 4 SERVINGS

- ¾ **cup uncooked orzo pasta**
- 1 **pound boneless skinless chicken breasts, cut into 1-inch pieces**
- 1 **medium cucumber, chopped**
- 1 **small red onion, chopped**
- ¼ **cup minced fresh parsley**
- 2 **tablespoons lemon juice**
- 1 **tablespoon olive oil**
- 1 **teaspoon salt**
- ¼ **teaspoon pepper**
- ¼ **cup crumbled reduced-fat feta cheese**

1. Cook pasta according to package directions. Meanwhile, in a large skillet coated with cooking spray, cook chicken over medium heat for 6-8 minutes or until no longer pink.
2. In a large bowl, combine the cucumber, onion, parsley and chicken. Drain pasta; stir into chicken mixture. In a small bowl, whisk the lemon juice, oil, salt and pepper. Pour over chicken mixture; toss to coat. Serve warm or cold. Just before serving, sprinkle with cheese.
PER SERVING *1¼ cups orzo mixture with 1 tablespoon cheese equals 323 cal., 7 g fat (2 g sat. fat), 65 mg chol., 742 mg sodium, 33 g carb., 2 g fiber, 30 g pro.* **Diabetic Exchanges:** *3 lean meat, 2 starch, 1 vegetable, 1 fat.*

Makeover Sour Cream Chicken Enchiladas

My husband knows he's in for a treat when I begin rolling these enchiladas. This is his favorite dish, and the makeover version is yummy! We think it's a home run.

—**RYNNETTA GARNER** DALLAS, TX

PREP: 30 MIN. • **BAKE:** 15 MIN.
MAKES: 12 SERVINGS

- **4 cups cubed cooked chicken breast**
- **1 tablespoon chili powder**
- **1 teaspoon garlic salt**
- **1 teaspoon ground cumin**
- **12 flour tortillas (8 inches), warmed**

SAUCE

- **2 tablespoons all-purpose flour**
- **1½ cups reduced-sodium chicken broth**
- **1½ cups (12 ounces) reduced-fat sour cream**
- **1 cup (4 ounces) shredded Monterey Jack cheese**
- **1 cup (4 ounces) shredded Mexican cheese blend**
- **Chopped tomatoes, optional**

1. In a large bowl, combine the chicken, chili powder, garlic salt and cumin. Place ⅓ cup chicken mixture down the center of each tortilla. Roll up and place seam side down in two 13x9-in. baking dishes coated with cooking spray.

2. In a large saucepan, whisk flour and broth until smooth. Bring to a boil; cook and stir for 2 minutes. Reduce heat; stir in sour cream and Monterey Jack cheese until melted. Pour sauce over enchiladas; sprinkle with Mexican cheese blend.

3. Bake, uncovered, at 350° for 15-20 minutes or until bubbly. Top with tomatoes if desired.

PER SERVING *1 enchilada (calculated without tomatoes) equals 338 cal., 13 g fat (6 g sat. fat), 63 mg chol., 645 mg sodium, 29 g carb., trace fiber, 25 g pro.* **Diabetic Exchanges:** *3 lean meat, 2 starch, 1 fat.*

THE SKINNY

The original enchiladas used canned chicken and full-sodium chicken broth. Switching to lower-salt ingredients and decreasing the abundant sauce by a fourth led to a sodium decrease of 45%.

MAKEOVER SOUR CREAM CHICKEN ENCHILADAS

	ORIGINAL	MAKEOVER
Calories	475	338
Fat	26g	13g
Sodium	1,176mg	645mg

FAST FIX ▶ Pecan-Crusted Chicken Nuggets

I loved chicken nuggets as a child. This baked version is healthier than the original, and it's a great meal for kids.

—**HAILI CARROLL** VALENCIA, CA

START TO FINISH: 30 MIN.
MAKES: 6 SERVINGS

- 1½ cups cornflakes
- 1 tablespoon dried parsley flakes
- 1 teaspoon salt
- ½ teaspoon garlic powder
- ½ teaspoon pepper
- ½ cup panko (Japanese) bread crumbs
- ½ cup finely chopped pecans
- 3 tablespoons 2% milk
- 1½ pounds boneless skinless chicken breasts, cut into 1-inch pieces
  Cooking spray

1. Preheat oven to 400°. Place the cornflakes, parsley, salt, garlic powder and pepper in a blender; cover and pulse until finely ground. Transfer to a shallow bowl; stir in bread crumbs and pecans. Place milk in another shallow bowl. Dip chicken in milk, then roll in crumb mixture to coat.

2. Place on a greased baking sheet; spritz chicken with cooking spray. Bake 12-16 minutes or until chicken is no longer pink, turning once halfway through cooking.

PER SERVING *3 ounces cooked chicken equals 206 cal., 9 g fat (1 g sat. fat), 63 mg chol., 290 mg sodium, 6 g carb., 1 g fiber, 24 g pro.* **Diabetic Exchanges:** *3 lean meat, 1 fat, ½ starch.*

FAST FIX ▶ Blueberry-Dijon Chicken

Blueberries and chicken may seem like a strange combination, but prepare to be dazzled. I add a sprinkling of minced fresh basil as the finishing touch.

—**SUSAN MARSHALL** COLORADO SPRINGS, CO

START TO FINISH: 30 MIN.
MAKES: 4 SERVINGS

- 4 boneless skinless chicken breast halves (6 ounces each)
- ¼ teaspoon salt
- ¼ teaspoon pepper
- 1 tablespoon butter
- ½ cup blueberry preserves
- ⅓ cup raspberry vinegar
- ¼ cup fresh or frozen blueberries
- 3 tablespoons Dijon mustard
  Minced fresh basil or tarragon, optional

1. Sprinkle chicken with salt and pepper. In a large skillet, cook the chicken in butter over medium heat for 6-8 minutes on each side or until a thermometer reads 170°. Remove and keep warm.

2. In the same skillet, combine the preserves, vinegar, blueberries and mustard, stirring to loosen browned bits from pan. Bring to a boil; cook and stir until thickened. Serve with chicken. Sprinkle with basil if desired.

PER SERVING *1 chicken breast half with 2 tablespoons sauce equals 331 cal., 7 g fat (3 g sat. fat), 102 mg chol., 520 mg sodium, 31 g carb., trace fiber, 34 g pro.* **Diabetic Exchanges:** *5 lean meat, 1½ starch, ½ fat.*

PECAN-CRUSTED CHICKEN NUGGETS

Bruschetta Chicken

We enjoy serving this tasty chicken to both family and to company. It just might become your new favorite way to use up summer tomatoes and basil.

—**CAROLIN CATTOI-DEMKIW** LETHBRIDGE, AB

PREP: 10 MIN. • **BAKE:** 30 MIN.
MAKES: 4 SERVINGS

- ½ **cup all-purpose flour**
- ½ **cup egg substitute**
- 4 **boneless skinless chicken breast halves (4 ounces each)**
- ¼ **cup grated Parmesan cheese**
- ¼ **cup dry bread crumbs**
- 1 **tablespoon butter, melted**
- 2 **large tomatoes, seeded and chopped**
- 3 **tablespoons minced fresh basil**
- 1 **tablespoon olive oil**
- 2 **garlic cloves, minced**
- ½ **teaspoon salt**
- ¼ **teaspoon pepper**

1. Preheat oven to 375°. Place flour and egg substitute in separate shallow bowls. Dip chicken in flour, then in egg substitute; place in a greased 13x9-in. baking dish. In a small bowl, mix cheese, bread crumbs and butter; sprinkle over chicken.

2. Loosely cover baking dish with foil. Bake for 20 minutes. Uncover; bake 5-10 minutes longer or until a thermometer reads 165°.

3. Meanwhile, in a small bowl, toss the tomatoes with the remaining ingredients. Spoon over chicken; bake 3-5 minutes or until tomato mixture is heated through.

PER SERVING *1 serving equals 316 cal., 11 g fat (4 g sat. fat), 75 mg chol., 563 mg sodium, 22 g carb., 2 g fiber, 31 g pro.* **Diabetic Exchanges:** *3 lean meat, 1½ fat, 1 starch, 1 vegetable.*

---

⑤INGREDIENTS
Crispy Buffalo Chicken Roll-Ups for Two

These winning chicken rolls with a crispy crust are both impressive and easy to make. My family and friends absolutely love them!

—**WILLIAM KEYS** KENNETT SQUARE, PA

PREP: 15 MIN. • **BAKE:** 30 MIN.
MAKES: 2 SERVINGS

- 2 **boneless skinless chicken breast halves (6 ounces each)**
- ¼ **teaspoon salt**
- ¼ **teaspoon pepper**
- 2 **tablespoons crumbled blue cheese**
- 2 **tablespoons hot pepper sauce**
- 1 **tablespoon mayonnaise**
- ½ **cup crushed cornflakes**

1. Preheat oven to 400°. Flatten chicken breasts to ¼-in. thickness. Season with salt and pepper; sprinkle with blue cheese. Roll up each from a short side and secure with toothpicks.

2. In a shallow bowl, combine pepper sauce and mayonnaise. Place the cornflakes in a separate shallow bowl. Dip chicken in pepper sauce mixture, then coat with the cornflakes. Place seam side down in a greased 11x7-in. baking dish.

3. Bake, uncovered, 30-35 minutes or until chicken is no longer pink. Discard toothpicks.

PER SERVING *1 serving equals 270 cal., 8 g fat (3 g sat. fat), 101 mg chol., 617 mg sodium, 10 g carb., trace fiber, 37 g pro.* **Diabetic Exchanges:** *5 lean meat, ½ starch, ½ fat.*

> **TOP TIP**
>
> I used Cholula for my hot sauce and used Rice Chex instead of cornflakes because that's what I had on hand. This will be put in my regular rotation. I'm a runner, and the taste and protein can't be beat!
> —QTPI3480 TASTEOFHOME.COM

SAUSAGE & PEPPERS WITH CHEESE POLENTA

Sausage & Peppers with Cheese Polenta

Who'd have thought that sausage and peppers could be healthy and light? Creamy Asiago polenta is the perfect backdrop for the sauteed meat mixture.

—HOLLY GOMEZ SEABROOK, NH

PREP: 20 MIN. • **COOK:** 20 MIN.
MAKES: 6 SERVINGS

- 3 **cups reduced-sodium chicken broth, divided**
- 1½ **cups water**
- 1 **cup cornmeal**
- 2 **teaspoons olive oil**
- 1 **package (12 ounces) fully cooked Italian chicken sausage links, cut into ½-inch slices**
- 1 **medium green pepper, sliced**
- 1 **medium sweet red pepper, sliced**
- 1 **medium onion, sliced**
- 1 **garlic clove, minced**
- ½ **cup shredded Asiago cheese**
- ½ **cup fat-free milk**
- 1 **teaspoon butter**

1. In a large heavy saucepan, bring 2½ cups broth and water to a boil. Reduce heat to a gentle boil; slowly whisk in cornmeal. Cook and stir with a wooden spoon 15-20 minutes or until polenta is thickened and pulls away cleanly from sides of pan.
2. Meanwhile, in a large skillet, heat oil over medium heat. Add sausage, peppers and onion; cook and stir 5-7 minutes or until vegetables are tender. Add garlic; cook 1 minute longer. Add remaining broth, stirring to loosen browned bits from pan; heat through.
3. Remove polenta from heat; stir in cheese, milk and butter until cheese is melted. Serve with sausage mixture.
PER SERVING *1 serving equals 269 cal., 10 g fat (4 g sat. fat), 54 mg chol., 647 mg sodium, 27 g carb., 2 g fiber, 17 g pro.* **Diabetic Exchanges:** *2 lean meat, 1½ starch, 1 vegetable, 1 fat.*

FAST FIX ▸ BLT Bow Tie Pasta Salad

I first had this summery salad at a family reunion, and it's become one of my husband's favorite dinners. Sometimes, we leave out the chicken and serve it as a side dish instead.

—JENNIFER MADSEN REXBURG, ID

START TO FINISH: 25 MIN.
MAKES: 6 SERVINGS

- 2½ **cups uncooked bow tie pasta**
- 6 **cups torn romaine**
- 1½ **cups cubed cooked chicken breast**
- 1 **medium tomato, diced**
- 4 **bacon strips, cooked and crumbled**
- ⅓ **cup reduced-fat mayonnaise**
- ¼ **cup water**
- 1 **tablespoon barbecue sauce**
- 1½ **teaspoons white vinegar**
- ¼ **teaspoon pepper**

1. Cook pasta according to package directions. Drain and rinse under cold water. In a large bowl, combine romaine, chicken, tomato, bacon and pasta.
2. In a small bowl, whisk the remaining ingredients. Pour over salad; toss to coat. Serve immediately.
PER SERVING *1¾ cups equals 253 cal., 8 g fat (2 g sat. fat), 37 mg chol., 239 mg sodium, 27 g carb., 2 g fiber, 17 g pro.* **Diabetic Exchanges:** *2 lean meat, 1½ starch, 1 vegetable, 1 fat.*

Makeover Spinach-Stuffed Chicken

For an easy, upscale chicken dish, you'll love these spinach-stuffed chicken breasts. You can also double the recipe without much effort.

—TASTE OF HOME TEST KITCHEN

START TO FINISH: 30 MIN.
MAKES: 4 SERVINGS

- 3 teaspoons olive oil, divided
- 4 cups fresh baby spinach
- 1 garlic clove, minced
- ½ cup reduced-fat garlic-herb spreadable cheese
- 1 teaspoon Italian seasoning, divided
- ⅓ cup plus ½ cup panko (Japanese) bread crumbs, divided
- 4 boneless skinless chicken breast halves (6 ounces each)
- ¼ teaspoon salt
- ¼ teaspoon pepper
- 1 egg white
- 1 tablespoon water

1. Preheat oven to 400°. In a large skillet, heat 1 teaspoon oil over medium-high heat. Add spinach; cook and stir 1-2 minutes or until wilted. Add garlic; cook 1 minute longer. Remove from heat. Stir in spreadable cheese, ¼ teaspoon Italian seasoning and ⅓ cup bread crumbs.

2. Cut a pocket horizontally in the thickest part of each chicken breast. Fill with spinach mixture and secure with toothpicks.

3. In a shallow bowl, toss remaining bread crumbs with salt, pepper and remaining Italian seasoning. In a separate shallow bowl, whisk egg white and water. Dip both sides of chicken in egg white mixture, then in crumb mixture, patting to help coating adhere.

4. In a large ovenproof skillet, heat remaining oil over medium heat. Brown chicken on each side. Place in oven; bake 15-18 minutes or until a thermometer inserted into chicken reads 165°. Discard toothpicks before serving.

PER SERVING *1 stuffed chicken breast half equals 332 cal., 12 g fat (5 g sat. fat), 112 mg chol., 459 mg sodium, 11 g carb., 1 g fiber, 41 g pro.* **Diabetic Exchanges:** *5 lean meat, 1 starch, 1 fat.*

THE SKINNY

The original recipe called for pan-frying the chicken in ¼ cup of olive oil. The fat in this dish was easily cut by browning the chicken on the stovetop, then baking it to finish. Instead of the original recipe's regular seasoned bread crumbs, a coating of panko bread crumbs is used to create a more crisp and airy texture that mimics fried food.

ORIGINAL	MAKEOVER
539 Calories	**332** Calories
35g Fat	**12**g Fat
13g Sat. Fat	**5**g Sat. Fat

MAKEOVER SPINACH-STUFFED CHICKEN

Applesauce Barbecue Chicken

You only need a few ingredients to create sweet and peppery chicken. The subtle flavor of apple sets this dish apart from the rest.

—DARLA ANDREWS LEWISVILLE, TX

START TO FINISH: 20 MIN.
MAKES: 4 SERVINGS

- 4 **boneless skinless chicken breast halves (6 ounces each)**
- ½ **teaspoon pepper**
- 1 **tablespoon olive oil**
- ⅔ **cup chunky applesauce**
- ⅔ **cup spicy barbecue sauce**
- 2 **tablespoons brown sugar**
- 1 **teaspoon chili powder**

Sprinkle chicken with pepper. In a large skillet, brown the chicken in oil on both sides. In a small bowl, combine the remaining ingredients; pour over the chicken. Cover and cook 7-10 minutes longer or until a thermometer reads 170°.

FREEZE OPTION *Cool chicken; transfer to a freezer container and freeze for up to 3 months. Thaw in the refrigerator overnight. Cover and microwave on high for 8-10 minutes or until heated through, stirring once.*

PER SERVING *1 chicken breast half with ⅓ cup sauce equals 308 cal., 8 g fat (2 g sat. fat), 94 mg chol., 473 mg sodium, 22 g carb., 1 g fiber, 35 g pro.* **Diabetic Exchanges:** *5 lean meat, 1½ starch, ½ fat.*

Chicken Fajitas

This is the best fajita recipe I've ever tried. It sounds complicated, but it really isn't. The servings are hearty, and it tastes so good that my husband and I never have a problem finishing it!

—KATHLEEN SMITH PITTSBURGH, PA

PREP: 15 MIN. + MARINATING
COOK: 15 MIN.
MAKES: 2 SERVINGS

- ¼ **cup lime juice**
- 1 **tablespoon reduced-sodium soy sauce**
- 2 **teaspoons canola oil**
- 1 **garlic clove, minced**
- ½ **teaspoon salt**
- ½ **teaspoon chili powder**
- ½ **teaspoon cayenne pepper**
- ¼ **teaspoon pepper**
- ½ **teaspoon liquid smoke, optional**
- 2 **boneless skinless chicken breast halves (4 ounces each)**

FILLING

- 2 **teaspoons canola oil**
- 1 **medium onion, julienned**
- ½ **small sweet red or green pepper, julienned**
- 1 **teaspoon reduced-sodium soy sauce**
- ½ **teaspoon lime juice**
- 4 **fat-free tortillas (6 inches), warmed**
  Salsa and sour cream, optional

1. In a large resealable plastic bag, combine the first eight ingredients; if desired, add liquid smoke. Add chicken; seal bag and turn to coat. Refrigerate at least 2 hours.

2. Drain the chicken, discarding marinade. Moisten a paper towel with cooking oil; using long-handled tongs, rub on grill rack to coat lightly. Grill chicken, covered, over medium heat or broil 4 in. from heat 4-6 minutes on each side or until a thermometer reads 170°.

3. In a large nonstick skillet, heat oil over medium-high heat. Add onion and pepper; cook and stir 5-7 minutes or until tender. Stir in soy sauce and lime juice.

4. Cut chicken into thin slices; add to vegetables. Serve with tortillas and, if desired, salsa and sour cream.

PER SERVING *1 serving (calculated without salsa and sour cream) equals 246 cal., 8 g fat (1 g sat. fat), 66 mg chol., 628 mg sodium, 15 g carb., 3 g fiber, 29 g pro.* **Diabetic Exchanges:** *3 lean meat, 1 starch, 1 fat.*

APPLESAUCE BARBECUE CHICKEN

CHICKEN FAJITAS

COUNTRY CHICKEN WITH GRAVY

3. Meanwhile, in a small saucepan, melt butter. Stir in the flour, pepper and salt until smooth. Gradually stir in the milk, broth and sherry. Bring to a boil; cook and stir for 1-2 minutes or until thickened. Stir in chives. Serve with chicken.

PER SERVING *1 chicken breast half with 2 tablespoons gravy equals 274 cal., 8 g fat (3 g sat. fat), 72 mg chol., 569 mg sodium, 20 g carb., trace fiber, 28 g pro.* **Diabetic Exchanges:** *3 lean meat, 1 starch, ½ fat.*

FAST FIX
Spicy Chicken Tenders

Here's a simple yet well-seasoned dish with the traditional flavors of Indian cuisine. Serve it with rice and a fresh veggie for a great meal. Curry lovers, take note!

—**CAROL DODDS** AURORA, ON

START TO FINISH: 30 MIN.
MAKES: 2 SERVINGS

- 1 tablespoon water
- ¼ teaspoon salt
- ¼ teaspoon crushed red pepper flakes
- ¼ teaspoon curry powder
- ⅛ teaspoon each ground turmeric, ginger and cinnamon
- ⅛ teaspoon paprika
- ½ pound chicken tenderloins

1. In a small bowl, combine water and seasonings; brush over all sides of chicken tenders. Place in a bowl and toss to coat; refrigerate for 15 minutes.
2. Place chicken on a broiler pan coated with cooking spray. Broil 3-4 in. from the heat for 3 minutes on each side or until meat is no longer pink.

PER SERVING *3 ounces cooked chicken equals 108 cal., 1 g fat (trace sat. fat), 67 mg chol., 343 mg sodium, 1 g carb., trace fiber, 26 g pro.* **Diabetic Exchange:** *3 lean meat.*

FAST FIX
Country Chicken with Gravy

This lightened-up take on classic Southern comfort food has been a hit at our house since the first time we tried it!

—**RUTH HELMUTH** ABBEVILLE, SC

START TO FINISH: 30 MIN.
MAKES: 4 SERVINGS

- ¾ cup crushed cornflakes
- ½ teaspoon poultry seasoning
- ½ teaspoon paprika
- ¼ teaspoon salt
- ¼ teaspoon dried thyme
- ¼ teaspoon pepper
- 2 tablespoons fat-free evaporated milk
- 4 boneless skinless chicken breast halves (4 ounces each)
- 2 teaspoons canola oil

GRAVY
- 1 tablespoon butter
- 1 tablespoon all-purpose flour
- ¼ teaspoon pepper
- ⅛ teaspoon salt
- ½ cup fat-free evaporated milk
- ¼ cup condensed chicken broth, undiluted
- 1 teaspoon sherry or additional condensed chicken broth
- 2 tablespoons minced chives

1. In a shallow bowl, combine the first six ingredients. Place milk in another shallow bowl. Dip chicken in milk, then roll in cornflake mixture.
2. In a large nonstick skillet coated with cooking spray, cook chicken in oil over medium heat for 6-8 minutes on each side or until a thermometer reads 170°.

Chicken Athena

With olives, sun-dried tomatoes, lemon juice and garlic, Greek flavors abound in my easy chicken dish that's prepared in the slow cooker. Serve it with orzo or couscous for a tasty accompaniment.

—RADELLE KNAPPENBERGER OVIEDO, FL

PREP: 15 MIN. • **COOK:** 4 HOURS
MAKES: 6 SERVINGS

- 6 **boneless skinless chicken breast halves (6 ounces each)**
- 2 **medium onions, chopped**
- ⅓ **cup sun-dried tomatoes (not packed in oil), chopped**
- ⅓ **cup pitted Greek olives, chopped**
- 2 **tablespoons lemon juice**
- 1 **tablespoon balsamic vinegar**
- 3 **garlic cloves, minced**
- ½ **teaspoon salt**

Place chicken in a 3-qt. slow cooker. Add the remaining ingredients. Cover and cook on low for 4 hours or until a thermometer reads 170°.

PER SERVING *1 chicken breast half equals 237 cal., 6 g fat (1 g sat. fat), 94 mg chol., 467 mg sodium, 8 g carb., 1 g fiber, 36 g pro.* **Diabetic Exchanges:** *4 lean meat, 1 vegetable, 1 fat.*

Grilled Chicken with Black Bean Salsa

Black bean salsa with mango gives this dish a Mexican taste without too much heat. I like to slice the chicken and serve it over a long grain and wild rice mix.

—TERRI CLOUSE CONNOQUENESSING, PA

PREP: 15 MIN. + MARINATING • **GRILL:** 10 MIN.
MAKES: 5 SERVINGS

- 1 **cup lime juice**
- 2 **tablespoons olive oil**
- 2 **teaspoons ground cumin**
- 1 **teaspoon salt**
- 1 **teaspoon dried oregano**
- ½ **teaspoon pepper**
- 5 **boneless skinless chicken breast halves (4 ounces each)**

BLACK BEAN SALSA

- 1 **can (15 ounces) black beans, rinsed and drained**
- 1 **mango, peeled and cubed**
- ¼ **cup minced fresh cilantro**
- 3 **tablespoons lime juice**
- 1 **tablespoon olive oil**
- 2 **teaspoons brown sugar**
- 1 **teaspoon minced jalapeno pepper**

1. In a small bowl, whisk the first six ingredients. Pour ⅔ cup marinade into a large resealable plastic bag. Add chicken; seal bag and turn to coat. Refrigerate 1-2 hours. Reserve remaining marinade for basting. In a small bowl, combine salsa ingredients; toss to combine.

2. Drain the chicken, discarding marinade. Grill chicken, covered, over medium heat or broil 4 in. from heat 5-6 minutes on each side or until a thermometer reads 170°, basting occasionally with reserved marinade during the last 4 minutes. Serve with salsa.

NOTE *Wear disposable gloves when cutting hot peppers; the oils can burn skin. Avoid touching your face.*

PER SERVING *1 chicken breast half with ½ cup salsa equals 266 cal., 7 g fat (1 g sat. fat), 63 mg chol., 339 mg sodium, 23 g carb., 4 g fiber, 27 g pro.* **Diabetic Exchanges:** *3 lean meat, 1½ starch, 1 fat.*

GRILLED CHICKEN WITH BLACK BEAN SALSA

FREEZE IT Chicken Florentine Meatballs

Served over squash in a chunky mushroom-tomato sauce, these tender meatballs are tops when it comes to great flavor.

—**DIANE NEMITZ** LUDINGTON, MI

PREP: 40 MIN. • **COOK:** 20 MIN.
MAKES: 6 SERVINGS

- 2 large eggs, lightly beaten
- 1 package (10 ounces) frozen chopped spinach, thawed and squeezed dry
- ½ cup dry bread crumbs
- ¼ cup grated Parmesan cheese
- 1 tablespoon dried minced onion
- 1 garlic clove, minced
- ¼ teaspoon salt
- ⅛ teaspoon pepper
- 1 pound ground chicken
- 1 medium spaghetti squash

SAUCE

- ½ pound sliced fresh mushrooms
- 2 teaspoons olive oil
- 1 can (14½ ounces) diced tomatoes, undrained
- 1 can (8 ounces) tomato sauce
- 2 tablespoons minced fresh parsley
- 1 garlic clove, minced
- 1 teaspoon dried oregano
- 1 teaspoon dried basil

1. Combine first eight ingredients. Crumble chicken over mixture and mix well. Shape into 1½-in. balls.

2. Place meatballs on a rack in a shallow baking pan. Bake, uncovered, at 400° for 20-25 minutes or until no longer pink. Meanwhile, cut squash in half lengthwise; discard seeds. Place squash cut side down on a microwave-safe plate. Microwave, uncovered, on high for 15-18 minutes or until tender.

3. For sauce, in a large nonstick skillet, saute mushrooms in oil until tender. Stir in the remaining ingredients. Bring to a boil. Reduce heat; simmer, uncovered, for 8-10 minutes or until slightly thickened. Add meatballs and heat through.

4. When squash is cool enough to handle, use a fork to separate strands. Serve with meatballs and sauce.

FREEZE OPTION *Place individual portions of cooled meatballs and squash in freezer containers. To use, partially thaw in refrigerator overnight. Microwave, covered, on high in a microwave-safe dish until heated through, gently stirring and adding a little water if necessary.*

NOTE *This recipe was tested in a 1,100-watt microwave.*

PER SERVING *1 serving equals 303 cal., 12 g fat (3 g sat. fat), 123 mg chol., 617 mg sodium, 31 g carb., 7 g fiber, 22 g pro.* **Diabetic Exchanges:** *3 lean meat, 2 starch, ½ fat.*

DID YOU KNOW?

Very lean ground meat works fine for crumbled meat dishes, such as tacos and sloppy joes. Meat with a higher fat content works better for burgers, meatballs and meat loaf, creating a mixture that holds together well.

CHICKEN FLORENTINE MEATBALLS

FAST FIX ▶ Orange Chicken Pasta Salad

Refreshing fruit teams up with chicken, pasta and veggies for the perfect single-serving salad. It makes an ideal hot-weather lunch.

—MARY LEWIS NORMAN, OK

START TO FINISH: 20 MIN.
MAKES: 1 SERVING

- ½ cup uncooked spiral pasta
- ½ cup cubed cooked chicken breast
- ¼ cup mandarin oranges
- ¼ cup chopped cucumber
- ¼ cup halved seedless red grapes
- 1 green onion, sliced

ORANGE VINAIGRETTE

- 3 tablespoons orange juice concentrate
- 1 tablespoon white vinegar
- 1 tablespoon olive oil

1. Cook pasta according to package directions; drain and rinse in cold water. In a small bowl, combine the pasta, chicken, oranges, cucumber, grapes and onion.

2. In another bowl, whisk the vinaigrette ingredients. Drizzle over salad and toss to coat. Refrigerate until serving.

PER SERVING *1¾ cups equals 529 cal., 17 g fat (3 g sat. fat), 54 mg chol., 52 mg sodium, 67 g carb., 2 g fiber, 28 g pro.*

FREEZE IT
Asian Chicken Thighs

A thick, tangy sauce coats golden brown chicken in my simple skillet recipe. I like to serve the chicken over long grain rice or with a helping of ramen noodle slaw.

—DAVE FARRINGTON MIDWEST CITY, OK

PREP: 15 MIN. • **COOK:** 50 MIN.
MAKES: 5 SERVINGS

- 5 teaspoons olive oil
- 5 bone-in chicken thighs (about 1¾ pounds), skin removed
- ⅓ cup water
- ¼ cup packed brown sugar
- 2 tablespoons orange juice
- 2 tablespoons reduced-sodium soy sauce
- 2 tablespoons ketchup
- 1 tablespoon white vinegar
- 4 garlic cloves, minced
- ½ teaspoon crushed red pepper flakes
- ¼ teaspoon Chinese five-spice powder
- 2 teaspoons cornstarch
- 2 tablespoons cold water
   Sliced green onions
   Hot cooked rice, optional

1. In a large skillet, heat oil over medium heat. Add chicken; cook 8-10 minutes on each side or until no longer pink. In a small bowl, whisk water, brown sugar, orange juice, soy sauce, ketchup, vinegar, garlic, pepper flakes and five-spice powder. Pour over chicken. Bring to a boil. Reduce

heat; simmer, uncovered, for 30-35 minutes or until chicken is tender, turning chicken occasionally.

2. In a small bowl, mix cornstarch and cold water until smooth; stir into pan. Bring to a boil; cook and stir 1 minute or until sauce is thickened. Sprinkle with green onions. If desired, serve with rice.

FREEZE OPTION *Cool chicken. Freeze in freezer containers. To use, partially thaw in refrigerator overnight. Heat slowly in a covered skillet until a thermometer inserted in chicken reads 165°, stirring occasionally and adding a little water if necessary.*

PER SERVING *1 chicken thigh (calculated without rice) equals 292 cal., 14 g fat (3 g sat. fat), 87 mg chol., 396 mg sodium, 15 g carb., trace fiber, 25 g pro.* **Diabetic Exchanges:** *3 lean meat, 1 starch, 1 fat.*

MARGARET BRACHER'S
SLOW-COOKED TURKEY WITH BERRY COMPOTE
PAGE 174

Turkey Specialties

Whether you're planning a **weeknight dinner** or a **Thanksgiving feast,** turkey is always a **tasty option** for the main event. With healthy makeovers of **classic grilled burgers, turkey and biscuits, stuffed peppers** and more, this chapter is brimming with **healthy new favorites** waiting for you to discover!

**CATHY DOBBINS'
GARLIC ROSEMARY TURKEY**

PAGE 171

**BARBARA KEMPEN'S
SAUSAGE PENNE BAKE**

PAGE 178

**DIANA RIOS'
ASIAN TURKEY LETTUCE CUPS**

PAGE 166

FREEZE IT **FAST FIX**

Buffalo Turkey Burgers

Celery and blue cheese dressing help tame the hot sauce on these juicy burgers. For an even lighter version, skip the buns and serve with lettuce leaves, sliced onion and chopped tomato.

—MARY PAX-SHIPLEY BEND, OR

START TO FINISH: 25 MIN.
MAKES: 4 SERVINGS

- 2 **tablespoons Louisiana-style hot sauce, divided**
- 2 **teaspoons ground cumin**
- 2 **teaspoons chili powder**
- 2 **garlic cloves, minced**
- ½ **teaspoon salt**
- ⅛ **teaspoon pepper**
- 1 **pound lean ground turkey**
- 4 **whole wheat hamburger buns, split**
- 1 **cup shredded lettuce**
- 2 **celery ribs, chopped**
- 2 **tablespoons fat-free blue cheese salad dressing**

1. In a bowl, combine 1 tablespoon hot sauce, cumin, chili powder, garlic, salt and pepper. Add turkey; mix lightly but thoroughly. Shape into four ½-in.-thick patties.

2. In a large nonstick skillet coated with cooking spray, cook burgers over medium heat 4-6 minutes on each side or until a thermometer reads 165°.

3. Serve burgers on buns with lettuce, celery, salad dressing and remaining hot sauce.

FREEZE OPTION *Place patties on a plastic wrap-lined baking sheet; wrap and freeze until firm. Remove from pan and transfer to a large resealable plastic bag; return to freezer. To use, grill frozen patties as directed, increasing time as necessary for a thermometer to read 165°.*

PER SERVING *1 burger equals 312 cal., 12 g fat (3 g sat. fat), 90 mg chol., 734 mg sodium, 28 g carb., 5 g fiber, 24 g pro.* **Diabetic Exchanges:** *3 lean meat, 2 starch, ½ fat.*

FAST FIX

Sausage Zucchini Skillet

I began serving a version of this easy recipe as a side dish with my grilled salmon. I later added sausage and rice to make it a complete meal on its own.

—DEBBY ABEL FLAT ROCK, NC

START TO FINISH: 25 MIN.
MAKES: 4 SERVINGS

- 1 **pound Italian turkey sausage links, casings removed**
- 2 **large zucchini, chopped**
- 1 **large sweet onion, chopped**
- 2 **garlic cloves, minced**
- 1 **can (14½ ounces) no-salt-added diced tomatoes, undrained**
- ¼ **teaspoon pepper**
- 2 **cups hot cooked rice**

1. Crumble sausage into a large nonstick skillet coated with cooking spray. Add zucchini and onion; cook and stir over medium heat until meat is no longer pink. Add the garlic; cook 1 minute longer. Drain.

2. Stir in tomatoes and pepper; bring to a boil. Reduce heat; simmer, uncovered, for 4-5 minutes or until liquid is evaporated. Serve with rice.

PER SERVING *1¼ cups sausage mixture with ½ cup rice equals 329 cal., 11 g fat (2 g sat. fat), 68 mg chol., 724 mg sodium, 36 g carb., 5 g fiber, 23 g pro.* **Diabetic Exchanges:** *3 lean meat, 2 vegetable, 1½ starch.*

BUFFALO TURKEY BURGERS

Makeover Sloppy Joe Mac and Cheese

This amazing dish combines two mealtime classics into one casserole! My grandchildren love it. The lightened-up version offers all the heartwarming comfort of the original, without the unnecessary fat!

—DOROTHY LEONE MEREDITH, NH

PREP: 1 HOUR • **BAKE:** 30 MIN.
MAKES: 10 SERVINGS

ORIGINAL	MAKEOVER
503 Calories	**390** Calories
26g Fat	**14**g Fat
16g Sat. Fat	**7**g Sat. Fat

MAKEOVER SLOPPY JOE MAC AND CHEESE

- 1 **package (16 ounces) elbow macaroni**
- ¾ **pound lean ground turkey**
- ½ **cup finely chopped celery**
- ½ **cup shredded carrot**
- 1 **can (14½ ounces) diced tomatoes, undrained**
- 1 **can (6 ounces) tomato paste**
- ½ **cup water**
- 1 **envelope sloppy joe mix**
- 1 **small onion, finely chopped**
- 1 **tablespoon butter**
- ⅓ **cup all-purpose flour**
- 1 **teaspoon ground mustard**
- ¾ **teaspoon salt**
- ¼ **teaspoon pepper**
- 4 **cups 2% milk**
- 1 **tablespoon Worcestershire sauce**
- 8 **ounces reduced-fat process cheese (Velveeta), cubed**
- 2 **cups (8 ounces) shredded cheddar cheese, divided**

1. Cook macaroni according to package directions. Meanwhile, in a large nonstick skillet, cook the turkey, celery and carrot over medium heat until meat is no longer pink and vegetables are tender; drain. Add the tomatoes, tomato paste, water and sloppy joe mix. Bring to a boil. Reduce heat; cover and simmer for 10 minutes, stirring occasionally.
2. Drain macaroni; set aside. In a large saucepan, saute onion in butter until tender. Stir in flour, mustard, salt and pepper until smooth. Gradually add milk and Worcestershire sauce. Bring to a boil; cook and stir for 1-2 minutes or until thickened. Remove from the heat. Stir in the process cheese until melted. Add macaroni and 1 cup cheddar cheese; mix well.
3. Spread two-thirds of the macaroni mixture into a 3-qt. or 13x9-in. baking dish coated with cooking spray. Spread with turkey mixture to within 2 in. of edges. Spoon the remaining macaroni mixture around edges of pan. Cover casserole and bake at 375° for 30-35 minutes or until bubbly. Sprinkle with remaining cheddar cheese; cover and let stand until cheese is melted.

PER SERVING *1 cup equals 390 cal., 14 g fat (7 g sat. fat), 55 mg chol., 923 mg sodium, 45 g carb., 3 g fiber, 23 g pro.*

THE SKINNY

The original recipe used half-and-half cream and 1 pound of cheddar in the macaroni. The makeover achieves the same creaminess with low-fat milk and a combo of reduced-fat Velveeta and shredded cheddar. Velveeta is an excellent melting cheese, making the macaroni saucy and rich.

ASIAN TURKEY LETTUCE CUPS

FAST FIX Asian Turkey Lettuce Cups

Here's a cool, crisp idea for a light lunch or even as appetizers for a summer party. When I want to make it easier for my kids to eat, I mix it all up with shredded lettuce and serve it as a salad.

—DIANA RIOS LYTLE, TX

START TO FINISH: 30 MIN.
MAKES: 4 SERVINGS

- 3 tablespoons reduced-sodium soy sauce
- 2 teaspoons sugar
- 2 teaspoons sesame oil
- 1 teaspoon Thai chili sauce, optional
- 1 pound lean ground turkey
- 1 celery rib, chopped
- 1 tablespoon minced fresh gingerroot
- 1 garlic clove, minced
- 1 can (8 ounces) water chestnuts, drained and chopped
- 1 medium carrot, shredded
- 2 cups cooked brown rice
- 8 Bibb or Boston lettuce leaves

1. In a small bowl, whisk soy sauce, sugar, sesame oil and, if desired, chili sauce until blended. In a large skillet, cook turkey and celery 6-9 minutes or until meat is no longer pink, breaking up turkey into crumbles; drain.

2. Add ginger and garlic to turkey; cook 2 minutes. Stir in soy sauce mixture, water chestnuts and carrot; cook 2 minutes longer. Stir in rice; heat through. Serve in lettuce leaves.

PER SERVING *2 lettuce cups equals 353 cal., 13 g fat (3 g sat. fat), 90 mg chol., 589 mg sodium, 35 g carb., 4 g fiber, 24 g pro.* **Diabetic Exchanges:** *3 lean meat, 2 starch, 1 vegetable, 1/2 fat.*

FAST FIX Italian Turkey Skillet

I try to find imaginative ways to use leftovers, especially turkey. This pasta toss is lightly coated with tomato sauce and accented with fresh mushrooms.

—PATRICIA KILE ELIZABETHTOWN, PA

START TO FINISH: 20 MIN.
MAKES: 8 SERVINGS

- 1 package (16 ounces) linguine
- 2 tablespoons canola oil
- 3/4 cup sliced fresh mushrooms
- 1 medium onion, chopped
- 1 celery rib, chopped
- 1 small green pepper, chopped
- 2 cups cubed cooked turkey
- 1 can (14½ ounces) diced tomatoes, drained
- 1 can (10¾ ounces) condensed tomato soup, undiluted
- 1 tablespoon Italian seasoning
- 1 tablespoon minced fresh parsley
- ¼ teaspoon pepper
- ⅛ teaspoon salt
- 1 cup (4 ounces) shredded cheddar cheese

1. Cook linguine according to package directions. Meanwhile, in a large skillet, heat oil over medium-high heat. Add mushrooms, onion, celery and green pepper; cook and stir until tender. Stir in turkey, tomatoes, soup and seasonings; heat through.

2. Drain linguine; add to the turkey mixture and toss to combine. If desired, sprinkle with cheese and let stand, covered, until cheese is melted.

PER SERVING *1 cup equals 338 cal., 7 g fat (1 g sat. fat), 27 mg chol., 362 mg sodium, 51 g carb., 4 g fiber, 19 g pro.*

Waldorf Turkey Salad

Crisp apples, celery and walnuts teamed up with turkey make any meal feel like a picnic. The combination of tastes and textures makes this salad a cool classic.

—**MITZI SENTIFF** ANNAPOLIS, MD

START TO FINISH: 25 MIN.
MAKES: 4 SERVINGS

- 1 cup (8 ounces) plain yogurt
- 2 tablespoons honey
- ⅛ to ¼ teaspoon ground ginger
- ¼ teaspoon salt
- 2 cups cubed cooked turkey breast
- 1 cup cubed apple
- 1 cup seedless red grapes, halved
- ½ cup thinly sliced celery
- ½ cup raisins
- 4 lettuce leaves
- 2 tablespoons chopped walnuts

In a small bowl, whisk the yogurt, honey, ginger and salt. In a large bowl, combine the turkey, apple, grapes, celery and raisins; add yogurt mixture and toss to coat. Serve on lettuce; sprinkle with walnuts.

PER SERVING *1¼ cups equals 294 cal., 5 g fat (2 g sat. fat), 68 mg chol., 233 mg sodium, 39 g carb., 2 g fiber, 25 g pro.* **Diabetic Exchanges:** *3 lean meat, 1½ fruit, 1 starch, ½ fat.*

Sausage Spinach Pizza

My husband loves pizza, and this is the best way for him to get his fix while staying within his carb range.

—**ELENA FALK** VERSAILLES, OH

PREP: 35 MIN. + RISING • **BAKE:** 10 MIN.
MAKES: 2 PIZZAS (8 SLICES EACH)

- 1 package (¼ ounce) active dry yeast
- 1 cup warm water (110° to 115°)
- 2¼ cups all-purpose flour
- 2 tablespoons olive oil
- 1 tablespoon sugar
- 2 teaspoons Italian seasoning
- ½ teaspoon salt
- ½ cup shredded Asiago cheese
- ¾ pound Italian turkey sausage links, thinly sliced
- 1 can (14½ ounces) Italian diced tomatoes, undrained
- 2 cups fresh baby spinach
- 6 slices reduced-fat provolone cheese, halved

1. In a large bowl, dissolve yeast in water. Add flour, oil, sugar, Italian seasoning and salt; beat on medium speed for 3 minutes or until smooth. Stir in Asiago cheese.

2. Turn onto a lightly floured surface; knead until smooth and elastic, about 5-6 minutes. Place in a bowl coated with cooking spray, turning once to coat the top. Cover and let rise in a warm place until doubled, about 1 hour.

3. Preheat oven to 425°. Punch dough down; divide in half. On a floured surface, roll each portion into a 13-in. circle. Transfer to two 12-in. pizza pans coated with cooking spray. Build up edges slightly. Prick thoroughly with a fork. Bake 5-8 minutes or until edges are lightly browned.

4. Meanwhile, in a large nonstick skillet, cook sausage over medium heat until no longer pink; drain. Place tomatoes in a food processor; cover and pulse until finely chopped.

5. Spread tomatoes over crusts; layer with spinach, sausage and provolone cheese. Bake 8-12 minutes or until crusts and cheese are lightly browned.

PER SERVING *2 slices equals 314 cal., 12 g fat (4 g sat. fat), 39 mg chol., 729 mg sodium, 34 g carb., 2 g fiber, 17 g pro.* **Diabetic Exchanges:** *2 starch, 2 lean meat, 1 vegetable, ½ fat.*

SAUSAGE SPINACH PIZZA

Italian Turkey Meat Loaf

It's easy to whip up this nutritious, high-fiber meat loaf on weeknights, and it makes fantastic sandwiches the next day. It's a little softer than most loaves, but it still slices perfectly and holds its shape while serving.

—LAURIE BOCK LYNDEN, WA

PREP: 15 MIN. • **BAKE:** 40 MIN.
MAKES: 6 SERVINGS

- 6 garlic cloves, halved
- 2 medium carrots, cut into chunks
- 1 small onion, cut into wedges
- 1 can (15 ounces) black beans, rinsed and drained
- 1 cup quick-cooking oats
- ½ cup fat-free milk
- 1 can (6 ounces) tomato paste, divided
- 3 teaspoons Italian seasoning, divided
- 1 teaspoon seasoned salt
- 1 package (20 ounces) lean ground turkey
- 1 tablespoon water

1. Preheat oven to 350°. Place the garlic, carrots and onion in a food processor; pulse until finely chopped. Add beans; process until blended. In a large bowl, combine oats, milk, half of the tomato paste, 1½ teaspoons Italian seasoning, seasoned salt and black bean mixture. Add turkey; mix lightly but thoroughly.
2. Shape into a loaf and place in an 11x7-in. baking dish coated with cooking spray. Bake, uncovered, for 30 minutes.
3. Combine water with the remaining tomato paste and Italian seasoning; spread over meat loaf. Bake meat loaf 10-15 minutes longer or until a thermometer reads 165°. Let stand 10 minutes before slicing.
PER SERVING *1 serving equals 298 cal., 9 g fat (2 g sat. fat), 75 mg chol., 517 mg sodium, 30 g carb., 6 g fiber, 25 g pro.* **Diabetic Exchanges:** *3 lean meat, 2 starch.*

FAST FIX # Quick & Easy Turkey Sloppy Joes

When we were first married and poor college students, I found this simple recipe and adjusted it to suit our tastes. The fresh bell pepper and red onion give it a wonderful flavor.

—KALLEE TWINER MARYVILLE, TN

START TO FINISH: 30 MIN.
MAKES: 8 SERVINGS

- 1 pound lean ground turkey
- 1 large red onion, chopped
- 1 large green pepper, chopped

- 1 can (8 ounces) tomato sauce
- ½ cup barbecue sauce
- 1 teaspoon dried oregano
- 1 teaspoon ground cumin
- 1 teaspoon chili powder
- ¼ teaspoon salt
- 8 hamburger buns, split

1. In a large skillet, cook turkey, onion and green pepper over medium heat for 6-8 minutes or until turkey is no longer pink and vegetables are tender, breaking up turkey into crumbles.
2. Stir in tomato sauce, barbecue sauce and seasonings. Bring to a boil. Reduce heat; simmer, uncovered, 10 minutes to allow flavors to blend, stirring occasionally. Serve in buns.
PER SERVING *1 sandwich equals 251 cal., 6 g fat (2 g sat. fat), 39 mg chol., 629 mg sodium, 32 g carb., 2 g fiber, 16 g pro.* **Diabetic Exchanges:** *2 lean meat, 1½ starch, 1 vegetable.*

FAST FIX ▶ Turkey a la King with Rice

Whenever I have leftover turkey, I go right to this quick and versatile recipe. It's a nice change from casseroles and so simple to prepare. Serve it over rice, noodles, biscuits or toast.

—PAT LEMKE BRANDON, WI

START TO FINISH: 30 MIN.
MAKES: 4 SERVINGS

- 2 tablespoons butter
- 1¾ cups sliced fresh mushrooms
- 1 celery rib, chopped
- ¼ cup chopped onion
- ¼ cup chopped green pepper
- ¼ cup all-purpose flour
- 1 cup reduced-sodium chicken broth
- 1 cup fat-free milk
- 2 cups cubed cooked turkey breast
- 1 cup frozen peas
- ½ teaspoon salt
- 2 cups hot cooked rice

1. In a large nonstick skillet, heat the butter over medium-high heat. Add the mushrooms, celery, onion and pepper; cook and stir until vegetables are tender.

2. In a small bowl, mix the flour and broth until smooth; stir into vegetable mixture. Stir in milk. Bring mixture to a boil; cook and stir for 1-2 minutes or until thickened.

3. Add the turkey, peas and salt; heat through. Serve with rice.

PER SERVING *1¼ cups turkey mixture with ½ cup rice equals 350 cal., 7 g fat (4 g sat. fat), 76 mg chol., 594 mg sodium, 40 g carb., 3 g fiber, 30 g pro.* **Diabetic Exchanges:** *3 lean meat, 2 starch, 1½ fat, 1 vegetable.*

Mediterranean One-Dish Meal

I came up with this recipe one night when I was improvising with what I had on hand. I love to make simple, healthy one-dish dinners with lots of vegetables. I prepare this recipe in a big pot so I can pile on as much spinach as will fit.

—DONNA JESSER EVERETT, WA

PREP: 15 MIN. • **COOK:** 25 MIN.
MAKES: 4 SERVINGS

- ¾ pound Italian turkey sausage links, cut into 1-inch pieces
- 1 medium onion, chopped
- 2 garlic cloves, minced
- 1 can (14½ ounces) no-salt-added diced tomatoes, undrained
- ¼ cup Greek olives
- 1 teaspoon dried oregano
- ½ cup quinoa, rinsed
- 3 cups fresh baby spinach
- ½ cup crumbled feta cheese

1. In a large nonstick saucepan coated with cooking spray, cook sausage and onion over medium heat until sausage is browned and onion is tender. Add garlic; cook 1 minute longer. Stir in the tomatoes, olives and oregano; bring to a boil.

2. Stir in quinoa. Top with spinach. Reduce heat; cover and simmer for 12-15 minutes or until liquid is absorbed. Remove from the heat; fluff with a fork. Sprinkle with cheese.

NOTE *Look for quinoa in the cereal, rice or organic food aisle.*

PER SERVING *1 cup equals 307 cal., 14 g fat (3 g sat. fat), 58 mg chol., 845 mg sodium, 26 g carb., 5 g fiber, 21 g pro.*

MEDITERRANEAN ONE-DISH MEAL

Turkey Burritos with Fresh Fruit Salsa

This lighter, produce-packed twist on traditional burritos is sure to be a hit with your family. Even our pickiest eater loves to munch on these with the sweet-spicy fruit salsa. Yum!

—**LISA EATON** KENNEBUNK, ME

PREP: 30 MIN. • **COOK:** 20 MIN.
MAKES: 10 SERVINGS

- 1 pint grape tomatoes, quartered
- 1 medium mango, peeled and chopped
- 2 medium kiwifruit, peeled and chopped
- 3 green onions, thinly sliced
- 3 tablespoons finely chopped red onion
- 1 jalapeno pepper, seeded and chopped
- 1 tablespoon lime juice

BURRITOS

- 1 pound lean ground turkey
- ½ teaspoon ground turmeric
- ¼ teaspoon ground cumin
- 1 tablespoon olive oil
- 2 garlic cloves, minced
- ½ cup Burgundy wine or reduced-sodium beef broth
- 1 jar (16 ounces) salsa
- 2 cups frozen corn, thawed
- 1 can (15 ounces) black beans, rinsed and drained
- 10 whole wheat tortillas (8 inches), warmed
- 1 cup (4 ounces) shredded reduced-fat cheddar cheese

1. For salsa, combine the first seven ingredients. Chill until serving.

2. In a large nonstick skillet over medium heat, cook turkey and spices in oil until meat is no longer pink. Add garlic; cook 1 minute longer. Drain. Stir in wine; simmer, uncovered, 3 minutes.

3. Stir in the salsa, corn and black beans. Bring to a boil. Reduce heat; simmer, uncovered, for 10-15 minutes or until much of the liquid has evaporated. Remove from the heat.

4. Spoon about ½ cup turkey mixture off center on each tortilla. Sprinkle with cheese. Fold sides and ends over filling and roll up. Serve with salsa.

NOTE *Wear disposable gloves when cutting hot peppers; the oils can burn skin. Avoid touching your face.*
PER SERVING *1 burrito with ⅓ cup salsa equals 371 cal., 11 g fat (3 g sat. fat), 44 mg chol., 553 mg sodium, 47 g carb., 6 g fiber, 18 g pro.* **Diabetic Exchanges:** *3 starch, 2 lean meat.*

FAST FIX ▶ Smoked Turkey and Apple Salad

An eye-catching dish, this refreshing salad is a great main course for summer. Dijon dressing pairs nicely with the turkey, while apples and walnuts add crunch.

—**CAROLYN JOHNS** LACEY, WA

START TO FINISH: 20 MIN.
MAKES: 4 SERVINGS

DRESSING

- 5 tablespoons olive oil
- 2 tablespoons cider vinegar
- 1 tablespoon Dijon mustard
- 1 teaspoon lemon-pepper seasoning
- ½ teaspoon salt, optional

SALAD

- 6 to 8 cups torn watercress or romaine
- 1 medium carrot, julienned
- 10 cherry tomatoes, halved
- 8 ounces smoked turkey, julienned
- 4 medium apples, sliced
- ⅓ cup chopped walnuts, toasted

1. Whisk together the dressing ingredients; set aside.

2. Just before serving, arrange salad greens on a platter or individual plates. Top with carrot, tomatoes, turkey and apples. Drizzle dressing over salad and toss to coat. Sprinkle with walnuts.

PER SERVING *1 serving equals 382 cal., 25 g fat (3 g sat. fat), 20 mg chol., 536 mg sodium, 29 g carb., 7 g fiber, 15 g pro.*

TURKEY BURRITOS WITH FRESH FRUIT SALSA

(5) INGREDIENTS

Garlic Rosemary Turkey

Garlic, herbs and lemon are such simple additions, but they're all you really need to make this holiday turkey shine. Our house smells incredible while the bird is roasting, and my family can hardly wait to eat.

—**CATHY DOBBINS** RIO RANCHO, NM

PREP: 10 MIN. • **BAKE:** 3 HOURS + STANDING
MAKES: 10 SERVINGS

- 1 turkey (10 to 12 pounds)
- 6 to 8 garlic cloves, peeled
- 2 large lemons, halved
- 2 tablespoons olive oil
- 2 teaspoons dried rosemary, crushed
- 1 teaspoon rubbed sage

1. Preheat oven to 325°. Cut six to eight small slits in turkey skin; insert garlic under the skin. Squeeze two lemon halves inside the turkey; squeeze remaining halves over outside of turkey. Place lemons in the cavity.

2. Tuck wings under turkey; tie drumsticks together. Place on a rack in a shallow roasting pan, breast side up. Brush with oil; sprinkle with rosemary and sage. Roast 1 hour.

3. Cover turkey with foil; roast for 2-2½ hours longer or until a thermometer inserted in thickest part of thigh reads 170°-175°. Baste occasionally with pan drippings.

4. Remove turkey from oven. Let stand 20 minutes before carving. If desired, skim fat and thicken pan drippings for gravy. Serve with turkey.

PER SERVING *9 ounces cooked turkey (calculated without gravy) equals 414 cal., 14 g fat (4 g sat. fat), 171 mg chol., 159 mg sodium, 2 g carb., trace fiber, 66 g pro.*

GARLIC ROSEMARY TURKEY

CARVE A TURKEY

1 Cut through skin between leg and body, using a carving knife. Pull leg outward with a fork and cut through the joint to remove the leg quarter.

2 Cut through the joint that connects the drumstick and thigh. Thinly slice the thigh meat and remove from the bone. Small drumsticks may be served whole. Or, to remove the meat, hold the drumstick upright and slice off the meat, working parallel to the bone.

3 Slice down one side of the breastbone until knife meets the base of the turkey. Cut horizontally into the turkey near the base to remove the breast half. Repeat on other side. Slice breast meat.

4 Cut through the joints to separate the wings from the carcass. Serve wings whole.

ORIGINAL	MAKEOVER
664 Calories	**359** Calories
36g Fat	**11**g Fat
16g Sat. Fat	**4**g Sat. Fat

MAKEOVER SAUSAGE-STUFFED PEPPERS

1. Cook rice according to package directions. Meanwhile, cut tops from peppers; chop tops, discarding stems, and set aside. Remove the seeds from peppers.

2. In a Dutch oven, cook peppers in boiling water for 3-5 minutes. Drain and rinse in cold water; set aside.

3. In a large skillet, cook the sausage, onion, celery, shallot and chopped green pepper over medium heat until meat is no longer pink and vegetables are tender; drain. Stir in the rice, soy sauce, chili powder, garlic powder and cayenne. Spoon into peppers. Place in an 8-in.-square baking dish coated with cooking spray.

4. Cover and bake at 350° for 35-40 minutes or until peppers are tender. Sprinkle with cheese; bake 5 minutes longer or until cheese is melted.

PER SERVING *1 stuffed pepper equals 359 cal., 11 g fat (4 g sat. fat), 46 mg chol., 621 mg sodium, 47 g carb., 5 g fiber, 18 g pro.* **Diabetic Exchanges:** *2 starch, 2 medium-fat meat, 2 vegetable.*

THE SKINNY

The original recipe started with a jambalaya mix. Substituting almost-as-convenient instant rice and spices from the cabinet helped the makeover version cut more than 1,300 mg of sodium per serving.

Other nutritional improvements include:

- Decreasing the amount of sausage from 1 pound and using turkey sausage instead of pork
- Decreasing the amount of cheddar cheese from ⅔ cup
- Bulking up the filling by adding flavorful vegetables

Makeover Sausage-Stuffed Peppers

I started preparing stuffed peppers only because my husband loves them so much. I was surprised to discover how much I enjoyed them, too. I prefer yellow or red bell peppers for mine, since they have a sweeter, more mild flavor than green.

—**TAMI KUEHL** LOUP CITY, NE

PREP: 45 MIN. • **BAKE:** 40 MIN.
MAKES: 4 SERVINGS

- 2 **cups instant brown rice**
- 4 **medium green peppers**
- ¾ **pound Italian turkey sausage links, casings removed**
- 1 **medium onion, chopped**
- 1 **celery rib, chopped**
- 1 **shallot, chopped**
- 1 **tablespoon reduced-sodium soy sauce**
- 1½ **teaspoons chili powder**
- ½ **teaspoon garlic powder**
- ½ **teaspoon cayenne pepper**
- ½ **cup shredded cheddar cheese**

Baked Mostaccioli

I often serve my signature baked pasta for dinner parties. It always gets tons of compliments.

—**DONNA EBERT** RICHFIELD, WI

PREP: 35 MIN. • **BAKE:** 30 MIN.
MAKES: 6 SERVINGS

- 8 **ounces uncooked mostaccioli**
- ½ **pound lean ground turkey**
- 1 **small onion, chopped**
- 1 **can (14½ ounces) diced tomatoes, undrained**
- 1 **can (6 ounces) tomato paste**
- ⅓ **cup water**
- 1 **teaspoon dried oregano**
- ½ **teaspoon salt**
- ⅛ **teaspoon pepper**
- 2 **cups (16 ounces) fat-free cottage cheese**
- 1 **teaspoon dried marjoram**
- 1½ **cups (6 ounces) shredded part-skim mozzarella cheese**
- ¼ **cup grated Parmesan cheese**

1. Cook mostaccioli according to package directions. Meanwhile, in a large saucepan, cook turkey and onion over medium heat until meat is no longer pink; drain if necessary.

2. Stir in the tomatoes, tomato paste, water, oregano, salt and pepper. Bring to a boil. Reduce heat; cover and simmer for 15 minutes.

3. In a small bowl, combine cottage cheese and marjoram; set aside. Drain the mostaccioli.

4. Spread ½ cup meat sauce into an 11x7-in. baking dish coated with cooking spray. Layer with half of the mostaccioli, meat sauce and mozzarella cheese. Top with cottage cheese mixture. Layer with remaining mostaccioli, meat sauce and mozzarella cheese. Sprinkle with Parmesan cheese (dish will be full).

5. Bake, uncovered, at 350° for 30-40 minutes or until bubbly and heated through.

PER SERVING *1⅓ cups equals 278 cal., 7 g fat (3 g sat. fat), 39 mg chol., 607 mg sodium, 32 g carb., 3 g fiber, 23 g pro.* **Diabetic Exchanges:** *3 medium-fat meat, 2 vegetable, 1½ starch.*

Vermont Turkey Loaf

The maple glaze on this turkey loaf makes it deliciously different from other meat loaves. I can easily double it for company, or make an extra loaf and freeze it for a hectic night.

—**KARI KELLEY** PLAINS, MT

PREP: 20 MIN. • **BAKE:** 20 MIN.
MAKES: 2 SERVINGS

- ⅓ **cup coarsely chopped onion**
- ⅓ **cup chopped fresh mushrooms**
- ⅓ **cup chopped carrot**
- ⅓ **cup dry bread crumbs**
- ¼ **teaspoon salt**
- ¼ **teaspoon pepper**
- ½ **pound lean ground turkey**
- 1 **tablespoon maple syrup**
- 1 **teaspoon Dijon mustard**

1. In a small skillet coated with cooking spray, saute the onion, mushrooms and carrot until tender; cool slightly.

2. In a small bowl, combine vegetables, bread crumbs, salt and pepper. Crumble turkey over mixture and mix well. Shape into a 6x3-in. loaf.

3. Place in an 8-in.-square baking dish coated with cooking spray. Bake, uncovered, at 375° for 15 minutes.

4. In a small bowl, combine syrup and mustard; pour half over the turkey loaf. Bake 5-10 minutes longer or until no pink remains and a thermometer reads 165°. Serve with remaining syrup mixture.

PER SERVING *½ meat loaf equals 292 cal., 11 g fat (3 g sat. fat), 90 mg chol., 629 mg sodium, 25 g carb., 2 g fiber, 23 g pro.* **Diabetic Exchanges:** *3 lean meat, 1 starch, 1 vegetable.*

VERMONT TURKEY LOAF

SLOW-COOKED TURKEY WITH BERRY COMPOTE

SLOW COOKER

Slow-Cooked Turkey with Berry Compote

We love to eat turkey, and this delicious dish is a great way to get all that yummy flavor without heating up the house. The berries make the perfect summery accompaniment.

—MARGARET BRACHER ROBERTSDALE, AL

PREP: 35 MIN. • **COOK:** 3 HOURS
MAKES: 12 SERVINGS (3¼ CUP COMPOTE)

- 1 teaspoon salt
- ½ teaspoon garlic powder
- ½ teaspoon dried thyme
- ½ teaspoon pepper
- 2 boneless turkey breast halves (2 pounds each)
- ⅓ cup water

COMPOTE

- 2 medium apples, peeled and finely chopped
- 2 cups fresh raspberries
- 2 cups fresh blueberries
- 1 cup white grape juice
- ¼ teaspoon crushed red pepper flakes
- ¼ teaspoon ground ginger

1. Mix salt, garlic powder, thyme and pepper; rub over turkey breasts. Place in a 5- or 6-qt. slow cooker. Pour water around turkey. Cook, covered, on low 3-4 hours (a thermometer inserted in turkey should read at least 165°).
2. Remove turkey from slow cooker; tent with foil. Let stand 10 minutes before slicing.
3. Meanwhile, in a large saucepan, combine compote ingredients. Bring to a boil. Reduce heat to medium; cook, uncovered, 15-20 minutes or until slightly thickened and apples are tender, stirring occasionally. Serve turkey with compote.
PER SERVING *5 ounces cooked turkey with ¼ cup compote equals 215 cal., 1 g fat (trace sat. fat), 94 mg chol., 272 mg sodium, 12 g carb., 2 g fiber, 38 g pro.* **Diabetic Exchanges:** *5 lean meat, 1 starch.*

FAST FIX
Fruited Turkey Wraps

These colorful wraps taste great and are great for you, too. Each is packed with lean protein, fresh fruit and crisp veggies, all wrapped up in whole-grain goodness.

—LISA RENSHAW KANSAS CITY, MO

START TO FINISH: 15 MIN.
MAKES: 4 SERVINGS

- ½ cup fat-free mayonnaise
- 1 tablespoon orange juice
- 1 teaspoon grated orange peel
- ¾ teaspoon curry powder
- 4 whole wheat tortillas (8 inches), room temperature
- 2 cups finely shredded Chinese or napa cabbage
- 1 small red onion, thinly sliced
- 1 can (11 ounces) mandarin oranges, drained
- ⅔ cup dried cranberries
- ½ pound thinly sliced deli smoked turkey

Combine mayonnaise, orange juice, peel and curry; spread over tortillas. Top with cabbage, onion, oranges, cranberries and turkey. Roll up.
PER SERVING *1 wrap equals 332 cal., 5 g fat (trace sat. fat), 23 mg chol., 845 mg sodium, 54 g carb., 5 g fiber, 17 g pro.*

Makeover Turkey Biscuit Bake

This creamy casserole delivers true comfort-food flavor. It's one of my favorites to prepare for the family. Even better, the test cooks at *Taste of Home* created a healthy version.

—**DIANE HYATT** OREGONIA, OH

PREP: 30 MIN. • **BAKE:** 15 MIN.
MAKES: 9 SERVINGS

- 1 **cup baby carrots, halved lengthwise**
- 1 **cup julienned parsnips**
- 1 **tablespoon water**
- 2 **cups sliced fresh mushrooms**
- 2 **tablespoons butter**
- ½ **cup all-purpose flour**
- ½ **teaspoon salt**
- ⅛ **teaspoon white pepper**
- 4 **cups fat-free milk**
- 3 **cups diced cooked turkey breast**
- ½ **cup frozen peas, thawed**

BISCUITS
- 1 **cup all-purpose flour**
- ½ **cup cake flour**
- ¾ **teaspoon baking powder**
- ½ **teaspoon salt**
- ⅛ **teaspoon baking soda**
- 1 **large egg**
- ½ **cup buttermilk**
- 2 **tablespoons butter, melted**

1. In a microwave-safe bowl, combine the carrots, parsnips and water; cover and microwave on high for 4-5 minutes or until tender. Drain and set aside.

2. In a large nonstick skillet, saute mushrooms in butter until tender. Combine the flour, salt, white pepper and milk until smooth; stir into mushrooms. Bring to a boil; cook and stir for 1-2 minutes or until thickened. Stir in the carrots, parsnips, turkey and peas. Transfer to a 13x9-in. baking dish coated with cooking spray.

3. For biscuits, in a bowl, combine the flours, baking powder, salt and baking soda. Combine the egg, buttermilk and butter; stir into dry ingredients until a soft dough forms. Drop biscuit dough into nine mounds over the turkey mixture.

4. Bake at 425° for 15-18 minutes or until a toothpick inserted into biscuits comes out clean and biscuits are golden brown.

PER SERVING ⅔ *cup turkey mixture with 1 biscuit equals 290 cal., 7 g fat (4 g sat. fat), 82 mg chol., 494 mg sodium, 32 g carb., 2 g fiber, 24 g pro.*

Diabetic Exchanges: 2 starch, 2 lean meat, 1 vegetable, 1 fat.

THE SKINNY

The makeover adds carrots, parsnips and peas to the filling, increases turkey from 2 cups, and uses lots of fresh mushrooms instead of a 6-ounce jar. It decreases the biscuit topping by 50% and uses a much leaner dough. Cake flour helps to keep the biscuits fluffy and light, even though they are lower in fat.

ORIGINAL	MAKEOVER
624 Calories	290 Calories
40g Fat	7g Fat
25g Sat. Fat	4g Sat. Fat

MAKEOVER TURKEY BISCUIT BAKE

RED BEANS AND SAUSAGE

Red Beans and Sausage

Turkey sausage makes this traditional dish more health-conscious, while a zesty blend of seasonings adds some spark.

—**CATHY WEBSTER** MORRIS, IL

START TO FINISH: 20 MIN.
MAKES: 6 SERVINGS

- 1 **medium green pepper, diced**
- 1 **medium onion, chopped**
- 1 **tablespoon canola oil**
- 2 **garlic cloves, minced**
- 2 **cans (16 ounces each) kidney beans, rinsed and drained**
- ½ **pound smoked turkey sausage, sliced**
- ¾ **cup water**
- 1 **teaspoon Cajun seasoning**
- ⅛ **teaspoon hot pepper sauce**
   Hot cooked rice, optional

1. In a large saucepan, saute green pepper and onion in oil until tender. Add garlic; cook 1 minute longer.
2. Add the next five ingredients and bring to a boil. Reduce heat; cook for 5-7 minutes or until sausage is heated through. Serve with rice if desired.
PER SERVING ⅔ cup (calculated without rice) equals 212 cal., 4 g fat (1 g sat. fat), 24 mg chol., 706 mg sodium, 27 g carb., 8 g fiber, 16 g pro. *Diabetic Exchanges: 2 lean meat, 1½ starch, ½ fat.*

Turkey Marsala

This recipe originally called for beef, but I substituted turkey to make it healthier. It's easy to prepare, but the rich sauce makes it seem like you spent all day in the kitchen. I serve this with a baked sweet potato and a green vegetable.

—**DEBORAH WILLIAMS** PEORIA, AZ

PREP: 10 MIN. • **COOK:** 30 MIN.
MAKES: 4 SERVINGS

TURKEY MARSALA

- 1 **package (20 ounces) turkey breast tenderloins**
- ¼ **cup all-purpose flour**
- ½ **teaspoon salt, divided**
- ½ **teaspoon pepper, divided**
- 1 **tablespoon olive oil**
- 1 **tablespoon butter**
- ½ **pound sliced fresh mushrooms**
- ½ **cup reduced-sodium chicken broth**
- ½ **cup Marsala wine**
- 1 **teaspoon lemon juice**

1. Cut tenderloins crosswise in half; pound with a meat mallet to ¾-in. thickness. In a shallow bowl, mix flour and ¼ teaspoon each salt and pepper. Dip turkey in flour mixture to coat both sides; shake off excess.
2. In a large nonstick skillet, heat oil over medium heat. Add turkey; cook 6-8 minutes on each side or until a thermometer reads 165°. Remove from pan; keep warm.
3. In same skillet, heat butter over medium-high heat. Add mushrooms; cook and stir 3-4 minutes or until tender. Stir in broth and wine. Bring to a boil; cook until liquid is reduced by half, about 12 minutes. Stir in lemon juice and the remaining salt and pepper. Serve with turkey.
PER SERVING 1 serving equals 295 cal., 8 g fat (3 g sat. fat), 77 mg chol., 482 mg sodium, 12 g carb., 1 g fiber, 36 g pro. *Diabetic Exchanges: 4 lean meat, 1½ fat, 1 starch.*

DID YOU KNOW?

Marsala is a fortified (higher alcohol) wine from Sicily that's popular in Italian cooking. It's made in dry and sweet styles. Use dry Marsala or cooking Marsala for the Turkey Marsala recipe. You can substitute sherry if you don't have Marsala.

Sausage Penne Bake

No one would guess a dish this cheesy and satisfying could be healthy, but this magnificent casserole is also chock-full of eggplant, tomatoes and whole wheat pasta. Win!

—BARBARA KEMPEN CAMBRIDGE, MN

PREP: 35 MIN. • **BAKE:** 20 MIN.
MAKES: 8 SERVINGS

- 2 **cups uncooked whole wheat penne pasta**
- ¾ **pound Italian turkey sausage links, casings removed**
- 1 **small eggplant, peeled and cut into ½-inch cubes**
- 1 **medium onion, chopped**
- ½ **cup dry red wine or chicken broth**
- 3 **garlic cloves, minced**
- 1 **can (28 ounces) crushed tomatoes**
- 2 **cups (8 ounces) shredded part-skim mozzarella cheese, divided**
- 3 **tablespoons chopped ripe olives**
- 2 **teaspoons dried basil**
- ¼ **teaspoon pepper**
- ½ **cup grated Parmesan cheese**

1. Cook pasta according to package directions. Meanwhile, in a large skillet, cook the sausage, eggplant and onion over medium heat until meat is no longer pink; drain.

2. Add wine and garlic, stirring to loosen browned bits from pan. Stir in tomatoes. Bring to a boil. Reduce heat; simmer, uncovered, for 10 minutes or until slightly thickened. Drain pasta. Add pasta, 1½ cups mozzarella cheese, olives, basil and pepper to skillet.

3. Transfer to a 3-qt. baking dish coated with cooking spray. Sprinkle with Parmesan cheese and remaining mozzarella cheese. Bake, uncovered, at 350° for 20-25 minutes or until heated through.

PER SERVING *1 cup equals 325 cal., 11 g fat (5 g sat. fat), 46 mg chol., 623 mg sodium, 35 g carb., 7 g fiber, 23 g pro.* **Diabetic Exchanges:** *3 lean meat, 1½ starch, 1 vegetable, 1 fat.*

Italian-Style Cabbage Rolls

Here's a great way to get your family to eat their veggies. Not only is this one of my gang's favorite dinners, but my son loves to help me roll the turkey filling into the cabbage leaves.

—ERIKA NIEHOFF EVELETH, MN

PREP: 45 MIN. • **BAKE:** 50 MIN.
MAKES: 5 SERVINGS

- ⅓ **cup uncooked brown rice**
- 1 **medium head cabbage**
- ½ **cup shredded carrot**
- ¼ **cup finely chopped onion**
- ¼ **cup egg substitute**
- 1 **can (10¾ ounces) reduced-sodium condensed tomato soup, undiluted, divided**
- 1 **can (10¾ ounces) reduced-fat reduced-sodium condensed vegetable beef soup, undiluted, divided**
- 2 **tablespoons Italian seasoning, divided**
- ¼ **teaspoon cayenne pepper**
- ¼ **teaspoon pepper**
- 1 **pound lean ground turkey**

1. Cook rice according to package directions. Meanwhile, cook cabbage in boiling water just until leaves fall off head. Set aside 10 large leaves for rolls. (Refrigerate remaining cabbage for another use.) Cut out the thick vein from the bottom of each reserved leaf, making a V-shaped cut.

2. In a large bowl, combine the carrot, onion, egg substitute, 2 tablespoons tomato soup, 2 tablespoons vegetable soup, 1 tablespoon Italian seasoning, cayenne, pepper and rice. Crumble turkey over mixture and mix well. Place about ⅓ cupful on each cabbage leaf. Overlap cut ends of leaf; fold in sides, beginning from the cut end. Roll up completely to enclose filling.

3. Place the rolls seam side down in an 11x7-in. baking dish coated with cooking spray. Combine remaining soups; pour over the cabbage rolls. Sprinkle with remaining Italian seasoning. Cover and bake at 350° for 50-60 minutes or until cabbage is tender and a thermometer reads 165°.

PER SERVING *2 cabbage rolls equals 293 cal., 10 g fat (3 g sat. fat), 74 mg chol., 582 mg sodium, 29 g carb., 4 g fiber, 22 g pro.* **Diabetic Exchanges:** *3 lean meat, 1½ starch, 1 vegetable.*

Hazelnut & Lemon-Crusted Turkey Breast

Here is proof that simple recipes can still be special. Placing the turkey breast over sliced lemon results in a sensational main course.

—LORRAINE CALAND SHUNIAH, ON

PREP: 15 MIN.
BAKE: 1¼ HOURS + STANDING
MAKES: 6 SERVINGS

- ½ cup hazelnuts, toasted
- ¼ cup olive oil
- 3 tablespoons minced fresh rosemary or 1 tablespoon dried rosemary, crushed
- 3 tablespoons lemon juice
- 2 tablespoons butter, softened
- 2 garlic cloves, minced
- 2 teaspoons grated lemon peel
- ¼ teaspoon salt
- ¼ teaspoon pepper
- 1 boneless skinless turkey breast half (2 pounds)
- 1 medium lemon, thinly sliced

1. Place the first nine ingredients in a food processor; cover and process until finely chopped. Rub mixture over turkey.
2. Arrange lemon slices in a foil-lined 13x9-in. baking pan; top with the turkey breast.
3. Bake, uncovered, at 325° for 1¼-1½ hours or until a thermometer reads 170°. Let stand for 10 minutes before slicing.
PER SERVING *4 ounces cooked turkey equals 346 cal., 19 g fat (2 g sat. fat), 94 mg chol., 174 mg sodium, 5 g carb., 2 g fiber, 39 g pro.* **Diabetic Exchanges:** *5 lean meat, 2½ fat.*

TURKEY GYROS

FAST FIX▶ Turkey Gyros

Greek seasoning, feta cheese and cucumber sauce give my lightened-up gyros an authentic taste. Instead of feta cheese, we sometimes use cheddar or Monterey Jack.

—DONNA GARVIN GLENS FALLS, NY

START TO FINISH: 25 MIN.
MAKES: 4 SERVINGS

- 1 medium cucumber, peeled
- ⅔ cup reduced-fat sour cream
- ¼ cup finely chopped onion
- 2 teaspoons dill weed
- 2 teaspoons lemon juice
- 1 teaspoon olive oil
- ½ pound turkey breast tenderloin, cut into ¼-inch slices
- 1½ teaspoons salt-free Greek seasoning
- 8 thin tomato slices
- 4 pita breads (6 inches), warmed
- 1½ cups shredded lettuce
- 2 tablespoons crumbled feta cheese

1. Finely chop one-third of the cucumber; place in a small bowl. Toss with sour cream, onion, dill and lemon juice. Thinly slice the remaining cucumber.
2. In a nonstick skillet, heat oil over medium-high heat. Add turkey; cook and stir 5-7 minutes or until no longer pink. Sprinkle with Greek seasoning.
3. Serve turkey, tomato and sliced cucumber on pita breads. Top with lettuce, cheese and sauce.
PER SERVING *1 gyro equals 328 cal., 7 g fat (4 g sat. fat), 53 mg chol., 446 mg sodium, 42 g carb., 3 g fiber, 24 g pro.* **Diabetic Exchanges:** *2½ starch, 2 lean meat, 1 vegetable, 1 fat.*

FAST FIX ▶ Makeover Turkey Burgers

The unique combination of fruit and mayonnaise puts this grilled burger over the top. You can easily substitute nectarines for the peaches. Both fruits are delicious!

—CHARLENE CHAMBERS

ORMOND BEACH, FL

START TO FINISH: 25 MIN.
MAKES: 6 SERVINGS

- 1½ teaspoons canola oil
- 2 small peaches, peeled and chopped
- ½ teaspoon minced fresh gingerroot
- 4 teaspoons reduced-sodium teriyaki sauce, divided
- ¼ cup chopped red onion
- ½ teaspoon pepper
- ¼ teaspoon salt
- 1½ pounds lean ground turkey
- ⅓ cup fat-free mayonnaise
- 6 multigrain hamburger buns, split and toasted
  Optional toppings: lettuce leaves and slices of peaches, red onion and tomatoes

1. In a skillet, heat oil over medium-high heat. Add peaches and ginger; cook and stir until peaches are tender. Stir in 1 teaspoon teriyaki sauce; cook 1 minute longer. Transfer to a small bowl; cool slightly.

2. In a large bowl, combine onion, pepper, salt and remaining teriyaki sauce. Add the turkey; mix lightly but thoroughly. Shape mixture into six ½-in.-thick patties.

3. Moisten a paper towel with cooking oil; using long-handled tongs, rub on grill rack to coat lightly. Grill burgers, covered, over medium heat or broil 4 in. from heat 5-6 minutes on each side or until a thermometer reads 165°.

4. Stir mayonnaise into peach mixture. Serve burgers on buns with peach mayo and toppings as desired.

PER SERVING *1 burger (calculated without optional toppings) equals 319 cal., 14 g fat (3 g sat. fat), 91 mg chol., 580 mg sodium, 25 g carb., 2 g fiber, 25 g pro.* ***Diabetic Exchanges:*** *3 lean meat, 2 starch, 1 fat.*

ORIGINAL	*MAKEOVER*
461 Calories	319 Calories
24g Fat	14g Fat
7g Sat. Fat	3g Sat. Fat

MAKEOVER TURKEY BURGERS

THE SKINNY

This makeover's only changes from the original were to use lean ground turkey instead of ground beef and fat-free mayo instead of full-fat. The fat savings are impressive, including a cut to saturated fat of more than 50%.

Pear & Turkey Sausage Rigatoni

FAST FIX

The sweet pear, salty sausage and creamy blue cheese are a wonderful combination in this one-pot supper. Now we don't have to go to an expensive restaurant to get an elegant meal.

—**DEBBY HARDEN** LANSING, MI

START TO FINISH: 30 MIN.
MAKES: 6 SERVINGS

- 8 **ounces uncooked rigatoni or large tube pasta**
- 2 **Italian turkey sausage links (4 ounces each), casings removed**
- 2 **medium pears, sliced**
- 2 **cups fresh baby spinach**
- ½ **cup half-and-half cream**
- ½ **cup crumbled blue cheese, divided**
  Toasted sliced almonds, optional

1. Cook rigatoni according to package directions. Meanwhile, in a Dutch oven, cook sausage over medium heat 6-8 minutes or until no longer pink, breaking into large crumbles. Add the pears; cook and stir 3-5 minutes or until lightly browned.

2. Drain rigatoni; add to sausage mixture. Add spinach, cream and ¼ cup cheese; cook 3-4 minutes or until spinach is wilted, stirring occasionally. Top with remaining cheese. If desired, sprinkle with almonds.

NOTE *To toast nuts, bake in a shallow pan in a 350° oven for 5-10 minutes or cook in a skillet over low heat until lightly browned, stirring occasionally.*

PER SERVING *1⅓ cups (calculated without almonds) equals 273 cal., 9 g fat (4 g sat. fat), 32 mg chol., 333 mg sodium, 37 g carb., 3 g fiber, 13 g pro.* **Diabetic Exchanges:** *2½ starch, 2 medium-fat meat.*

---

(5)INGREDIENTS SLOW COOKER

Slow Cooker Turkey Breast

Here's an easy recipe to try when you're craving turkey. It uses pantry ingredients, which is handy.

—**MARIA JUCO** MILWAUKEE, WI

PREP: 10 MIN. • **COOK:** 5 HOURS
MAKES: 14 SERVINGS

- 1 **bone-in turkey breast (6 to 7 pounds), skin removed**
- 1 **tablespoon olive oil**
- 1 **teaspoon dried minced garlic**
- 1 **teaspoon seasoned salt**
- 1 **teaspoon paprika**
- 1 **teaspoon Italian seasoning**
- 1 **teaspoon pepper**
- ½ **cup water**

Brush turkey with oil. Combine the garlic, seasoned salt, paprika, Italian seasoning and pepper; rub over turkey. Transfer to a 6-qt. slow cooker; add water. Cover and cook on low for 5-6 hours or until tender.

PER SERVING *4 ounces cooked turkey equals 174 cal., 2 g fat (trace sat. fat), 101 mg chol., 172 mg sodium, trace carb., trace fiber, 37 g pro.* **Diabetic Exchange:** *4 lean meat.*

PEAR & TURKEY SAUSAGE RIGATONI

Pepperoni Baked Ziti

I took a favorite family recipe and put my own nutritious spin on it to create this casserole. The pepperoni and cheeses add traditional Italian flair.

—ANDREA ABRAHAMSEN BRENTWOOD, CA

PREP: 20 MIN. • **BAKE:** 30 MIN.
MAKES: 10 SERVINGS

- 1 package (1 pound) uncooked ziti or small tube pasta
- ½ pound lean ground turkey
- 2 cans (one 29 ounces, one 8 ounces) tomato sauce, divided
- 1½ cups (6 ounces) shredded part-skim mozzarella cheese, divided
- 1 can (8 ounces) mushroom stems and pieces, drained
- 5 ounces frozen chopped spinach, thawed and squeezed dry
- ½ cup reduced-fat ricotta cheese
- 4 teaspoons Italian seasoning
- 2 garlic cloves, minced
- ½ teaspoon garlic powder
- ½ teaspoon crushed red pepper flakes
- ¼ teaspoon pepper
- ½ cup water
- 1 tablespoon grated Parmesan cheese
- 1½ ounces sliced turkey pepperoni

1. Cook pasta according to package directions.
2. Meanwhile, in a large nonstick skillet, cook turkey over medium heat until no longer pink; drain. Transfer to a large bowl. Add the 29-oz. can of tomato sauce, 1 cup mozzarella cheese, mushrooms, spinach, ricotta cheese, Italian seasoning, garlic, garlic powder, pepper flakes and pepper. Drain pasta; fold into turkey mixture.

3. Transfer to a 13x9-in. baking dish coated with cooking spray. Combine the water and remaining tomato sauce; pour over the pasta mixture. Sprinkle with Parmesan cheese and remaining mozzarella cheese. Top with pepperoni.
4. Cover casserole and bake at 350° for 25-30 minutes or until bubbly. Uncover; bake 5 minutes longer or until cheese is melted.

PER SERVING *1 cup equals 306 cal., 7 g fat (3 g sat. fat), 37 mg chol., 795 mg sodium, 42 g carb., 4 g fiber, 20 g pro.* **Diabetic Exchanges:** *2½ starch, 2 lean meat, 1 vegetable.*

FAST FIX ▸ Turkey Reubens

Even diehard fans of the diner favorite will enjoy this lighter take. My sandwich is lower in fat and calories, yet still has all the classic Reuben ingredients people crave.

—ELIZABETH MYERS WILLIAMSPORT, PA

START TO FINISH: 25 MIN.
MAKES: 4 SERVINGS

- 8 slices rye bread
- ½ pound thinly sliced deli turkey
- ½ cup sauerkraut, rinsed and well drained
- 4 slices reduced-fat Swiss cheese
- ¼ cup fat-free Thousand Island salad dressing

1. On four slices of bread, layer the turkey, sauerkraut, cheese and salad dressing. Top with remaining bread. Spritz both sides of sandwiches with butter-flavored cooking spray.
2. In a large nonstick skillet over medium heat, toast sandwiches on both sides until cheese is melted.

PER SERVING *1 sandwich equals 310 cal., 8 g fat (3 g sat. fat), 35 mg chol., 1,398 mg sodium, 39 g carb., 5 g fiber, 22 g pro.*

PEPPERONI BAKED ZITI

TURKEY TACO SALAD

(5) INGREDIENTS

Golden Apricot-Glazed Turkey Breast

Basted with a simple glaze, this turkey bakes to a beautiful golden brown. Make it the centerpiece of your holiday table; you'll be glad you did.

—**GREG FONTENOT** THE WOODLANDS, TX

PREP: 10 MIN. • **BAKE:** 1½ HOURS + STANDING
MAKES: 15 SERVINGS

- ½ **cup apricot preserves**
- ¼ **cup balsamic vinegar**
- ¼ **teaspoon pepper**
  Dash salt
- 1 **bone-in turkey breast (5 pounds)**

1. Preheat oven to 325°. Combine preserves, vinegar, pepper and salt. Place turkey breast on a rack in a large shallow roasting pan.

2. Bake, uncovered, 1½-2 hours or until a thermometer reads 170°, basting every 30 minutes with apricot mixture. (Cover loosely with foil if turkey browns too quickly.) Cover and let stand 15 minutes before slicing.

PER SERVING *4 ounces cooked turkey equals 236 cal., 8 g fat (2 g sat. fat), 81 mg chol., 84 mg sodium, 8 g carb., trace fiber, 32 g pro.* **Diabetic Exchanges:** *4 lean meat, ½ starch.*

FAST FIX

Turkey Taco Salad

I discovered this taco salad while I was on a health kick. My husband and I love it now. When I served it at a family birthday party, everyone eagerly asked for the recipe.

—**ANGELA MATSON** AMBOY, WA

START TO FINISH: 30 MIN.
MAKES: 4 SERVINGS

- 12 **ounces ground turkey**
- 1 **medium sweet red pepper, chopped**
- 1 **small sweet yellow pepper, chopped**
- ⅓ **cup chopped onion**
- 3 **garlic cloves, minced**
- 1½ **cups salsa**
- ½ **cup canned kidney beans, rinsed and drained**
- 2 **teaspoons chili powder**
- 1 **teaspoon ground cumin**
- 8 **cups torn romaine**
- 2 **tablespoons fresh cilantro leaves**
  Optional toppings: chopped tomatoes, shredded cheddar cheese and crushed tortilla chips

1. In a large skillet, cook the turkey, peppers, onion and garlic over medium heat 6-8 minutes or until turkey is no longer pink and the vegetables are tender, breaking up turkey into crumbles. Drain.

2. Stir in salsa, beans, chili powder and cumin; heat through. Divide the romaine among four plates. Top with turkey mixture; sprinkle with cilantro and toppings of your choice. Serve immediately.

PER SERVING *1 cup turkey mixture with 2 cups romaine (calculated without optional toppings) equals 275 cal., 13 g fat (4 g sat. fat), 58 mg chol., 525 mg sodium, 21 g carb., 6 g fiber, 18 g pro.* **Diabetic Exchanges:** *2 medium-fat meat, 1½ starch.*

BARBARA GERRIETS'
BARBECUED COUNTRY RIBS
PAGE 193

Pork, Ham & More

There's **no need to give up your favorite foods** just because you're **eating right.** Here you'll find lip-smacking barbecued **ribs,** holiday **hams,** satisfying **stews,** and even irresistible **pizzas** and **pastas,** all of which **slash calories and fat.**

RACHEL SCHULTZ'S APPLE-CINNAMON PORK LOIN

PAGE 192

BRIGITTE SCHALLER'S JIFFY GROUND PORK SKILLET

PAGE 194

KERRY DINGWALL'S CHERRY-GLAZED LAMB CHOPS

PAGE 204

FAST FIX ▶ Light Linguine Carbonara

When we have to rush off at night, I make this speedy pasta with veggies and bacon. Pass with breadsticks or garlic toast and dinner's done.

—MARY JO MILLER MANSFIELD, OH

START TO FINISH: 25 MIN.
MAKES: 4 SERVINGS

- 8 **ounces uncooked linguine**
- ½ **cup frozen peas**
- 1 **egg**
- 1 **cup fat-free evaporated milk**
- ¼ **cup finely chopped sweet red pepper**
- ⅛ **teaspoon crushed red pepper flakes**
- ⅛ **teaspoon pepper**
- ½ **cup grated Parmesan cheese, divided**
- 2 **bacon strips, cooked and crumbled**

1. In a 6-qt. stockpot, cook the linguine according to package directions, adding peas during the last 2 minutes of cooking.

1. Meanwhile, in a small saucepan, whisk egg, milk, red pepper, pepper flakes and pepper until blended; cook and stir over medium-low heat until mixture is just thick enough to coat a spoon and a thermometer reads at least 160°. Stir in ¼ cup cheese and bacon; remove from heat.

2. Drain linguine; return to pot. Add sauce and toss to coat. Serve with remaining cheese.

PER SERVING *1 cup equals 352 cal., 7 g fat (3 g sat. fat), 66 mg chol., 349 mg sodium, 52 g carb., 3 g fiber, 20 g pro.*

SLOW COOKER Chinese Pork Chops

These delicious pork chops are so saucy and tender. I got the recipe years ago and it's been a family favorite ever since.

—SHARON CRIDER JUNCTION CITY, KS

PREP: 15 MIN. • **COOK:** 3 HOURS
MAKES: 6 SERVINGS

- 6 **boneless pork loin chops (4 ounces each)**
- 1 **small onion, finely chopped**
- ⅓ **cup ketchup**
- 3 **tablespoons brown sugar**
- 3 **tablespoons water**
- 3 **tablespoons reduced-sodium soy sauce**
- 1 **garlic clove, minced**
- 1 **teaspoon ground ginger**
- 3 **cups hot cooked rice**

Place pork chops in a 3-qt. slow cooker coated with cooking spray. In a small bowl, combine the onion, ketchup, brown sugar, water, soy sauce, garlic and ginger. Pour over chops. Cover and cook on low for 3-4 hours or until meat is tender. Serve with rice and cooking juices.

PER SERVING *1 pork chop with ½ cup rice and 3 tablespoons juices equals 305 cal., 7 g fat (2 g sat. fat), 55 mg chol., 496 mg sodium, 34 g carb., 1 g fiber, 25 g pro.* **Diabetic Exchanges:** *3 lean meat, 2 starch.*

LIGHT LINGUINE CARBONARA

Italian Pork Stew

Don't skip the anchovy paste in this stew! It gives a savory, salty flavor, but doesn't taste fishy at all. Add a salad and artisan bread for an absolutely incredible meal.

—**LYNNE GERMAN** WOODLAND HILLS, CA

PREP: 30 MIN. • **COOK:** 2¼ HOURS
MAKES: 8 SERVINGS (2 QUARTS)

- ⅔ cup all-purpose flour
- 2 pounds boneless pork loin, cut into 1-inch pieces
- 4 tablespoons olive oil, divided
- 1 large onion, chopped
- 5 garlic cloves, crushed
- 1 can (28 ounces) diced tomatoes, undrained
- 1 cup dry red wine or beef broth
- 3 bay leaves
- 1 cinnamon stick (3 inches)
- 1 tablespoon tomato paste
- 1 tablespoon red wine vinegar
- 1 teaspoon anchovy paste
- 1 teaspoon each dried oregano, basil and sage leaves
- ½ teaspoon salt
- ½ teaspoon crushed red pepper flakes
- ¼ teaspoon pepper
- ¼ cup minced fresh parsley
  Hot cooked bow tie pasta
  Grated Parmesan cheese

1. Place flour in a large resealable plastic bag. Add pork, a few pieces at a time, and shake to coat. In a Dutch oven, brown pork in 3 tablespoons oil in batches. Remove and keep warm.
2. In the same pan, saute onion in remaining oil until crisp-tender. Add garlic; cook 1 minute longer. Stir in the tomatoes, wine, bay leaves, cinnamon, tomato paste, vinegar, anchovy paste, herbs, salt, pepper flakes, pepper and pork; bring to a boil.
3. Reduce the heat; cover and simmer for 1½ hours, stirring occasionally. Stir in parsley. Cover and cook for 30-40 minutes or until meat is tender. Skim fat; discard the bay leaves and cinnamon stick.
4. Serve with pasta; sprinkle with grated cheese.
FREEZE OPTION *Place individual portions of cooled stew in freezer containers and freeze. To use, partially thaw in refrigerator overnight. Heat through in a saucepan, stirring occasionally and adding a little water if necessary.*
PER SERVING *1 cup (calculated without pasta and cheese) equals 256 cal., 12 g fat (3 g sat. fat), 59 mg chol., 349 mg sodium, 12 g carb., 2 g fiber, 24 g pro.* ***Diabetic Exchanges:*** *3 lean meat, 1 vegetable, 1 fat.*

ITALIAN PORK STEW

FAST FIX ▶
Skillet Cassoulet

This quick skillet version of a French classic is chock-full of flavor. Kielbasa, ham and cannellini beans make the stew a hearty meal-in-one dinner.

—**BARBARA BRITTAIN** SANTEE, CA

START TO FINISH: 30 MIN.
MAKES: 3 SERVINGS

- 2 teaspoons canola oil
- ¼ pound smoked turkey kielbasa, cut into ½-inch slices
- ¼ pound fully cooked boneless ham, cubed
- 2 medium carrots, sliced
- 1 celery rib, sliced
- ½ medium red onion, sliced
- 2 garlic cloves, minced
- 1 can (15 ounces) no-salt-added white kidney or cannellini beans, rinsed and drained
- 1 can (14½ ounces) no-salt-added diced tomatoes, undrained
- ¾ teaspoon dried thyme
- ⅛ teaspoon pepper

1. In a large skillet, heat oil over medium-high heat. Add kielbasa, ham, carrots, celery and onion; cook and stir until sausage is browned and vegetables are tender. Add garlic; cook 1 minute longer.

2. Stir in remaining ingredients. Bring to a boil. Reduce heat; simmer, uncovered, 4-5 minutes or until heated through.

PER SERVING *1⅓ cups equals 282 cal., 8 g fat (1 g sat. fat), 43 mg chol., 901 mg sodium, 33 g carb., 10 g fiber, 22 g pro.*

SLOW COOKER 🍲
Hoisin Pork Wraps

This flavorful pork with its tasty slaw is great for get-togethers because guests can make their own wraps. Even my grandchildren find the combo irresistible.

—**LINDA WOO** DERBY, KS

PREP: 25 MIN. • **COOK:** 7 HOURS
MAKES: 15 SERVINGS

- 1 boneless pork loin roast (3 pounds)
- 1 cup hoisin sauce, divided
- 1 tablespoon minced fresh gingerroot
- 6 cups shredded red cabbage
- 1½ cups shredded carrots
- ¼ cup thinly sliced green onions
- 3 tablespoons rice vinegar
- 4½ teaspoons sugar
- 15 flour tortillas (8 inches), warmed

1. Cut roast in half. Combine ⅓ cup hoisin sauce and ginger; rub over pork. Transfer to a 3-qt. slow cooker. Cover and cook on low for 7-8 hours or until pork is tender.

2. Meanwhile, in a large bowl, combine the cabbage, carrots, onions, vinegar and sugar. Chill until serving.

3. Shred meat with two forks and return to the slow cooker; heat through. Place 2 teaspoons remaining hoisin sauce down the center of each tortilla; top with ⅓ cup shredded pork and ⅓ cup coleslaw. Roll up.

PER SERVING *1 serving equals 314 cal., 8 g fat (2 g sat. fat), 46 mg chol., 564 mg sodium, 37 g carb., 1 g fiber, 23 g pro.* *Diabetic Exchanges: 2½ starch, 2 lean meat.*

SKILLET CASSOULET

FAST FIX ▶ Cinnamon-Apple Pork Chops

When I found this recipe online years ago, it quickly became a favorite. The ingredients are easy to keep on hand, and the one-pan cleanup is a bonus.

—**CHRISTINA PRICE** PITTSBURGH, PA

START TO FINISH: 25 MIN.
MAKES: 4 SERVINGS

- 2 **tablespoons reduced-fat butter, divided**
- 4 **boneless pork loin chops (4 ounces each)**
- 3 **tablespoons brown sugar**
- 1 **teaspoon ground cinnamon**
- ½ **teaspoon ground nutmeg**
- ¼ **teaspoon salt**
- 4 **medium tart apples, thinly sliced**
- 2 **tablespoons chopped pecans**

1. In a large skillet, heat 1 tablespoon butter over medium heat. Add pork chops; cook 4-5 minutes on each side or until a thermometer reads 145°. Meanwhile, in a small bowl, mix brown sugar, cinnamon, nutmeg and salt.

2. Remove chops; keep warm. Add apples, pecans, brown sugar mixture and remaining butter to pan; cook and stir until apples are tender. Serve with pork chops.

NOTE *This recipe was tested with Land O'Lakes light stick butter.*

PER SERVING *1 pork chop with ⅔ cup apple mixture equals 316 cal., 12 g fat (4 g sat. fat), 62 mg chol., 232 mg sodium, 31 g carb., 4 g fiber, 22 g pro.*
***Diabetic Exchanges:** 3 lean meat, 1 starch, 1 fruit, 1 fat.*

CINNAMON-APPLE PORK CHOPS

ITALIAN PORK AND POTATO CASSEROLE

chol., 506 mg sodium, 38 g carb., 4 g fiber, 39 g pro. **Diabetic Exchanges:** 5 lean meat, 2½ starch.

FAST FIX
Pork Chops with Parmesan Sauce

Tender skillet chops make a speedy weeknight meal. These are finished with a creamy and flavorful Parmesan sauce. Here's a new family favorite!
—*TASTE OF HOME* TEST KITCHEN

START TO FINISH: 20 MIN.
MAKES: 4 SERVINGS

- 4 **boneless pork loin chops (4 ounces each)**
- ½ **teaspoon salt**
- ¼ **teaspoon pepper**
- 1 **tablespoon butter**
- 2 **tablespoons all-purpose flour**
- 1 **cup fat-free milk**
- ⅓ **cup grated Parmesan cheese**
- 2 **tablespoons grated onion**
- 3 **teaspoons minced fresh parsley**
- ¼ **teaspoon dried thyme**
- ¼ **teaspoon ground nutmeg**

1. Sprinkle pork chops with salt and pepper. In a large nonstick skillet coated with cooking spray, cook chops in butter over medium heat until meat juices run clear; remove and keep warm.
2. Combine flour and milk until smooth; stir into pan. Bring to a boil; cook and stir for 2 minutes or until thickened. Stir in the remaining ingredients; heat through. Serve with chops.
PER SERVING *1 pork chop with 3 tablespoons sauce equals 244 cal., 11 g fat (5 g sat. fat), 69 mg chol., 475 mg sodium, 7 g carb., trace fiber, 27 g pro.* **Diabetic Exchanges:** 4 lean meat, ½ starch, ½ fat.

⑤ INGREDIENTS Italian Pork and Potato Casserole

The aroma of this hearty dish baking brings back fond memories of home. My mother created the recipe years ago, using the ingredients she had on hand.
—**THERESA KREYCHE** TUSTIN, CA

PREP: 10 MIN. • **BAKE:** 45 MIN.
MAKES: 6 SERVINGS

- 6 **cups sliced red potatoes**
- 3 **tablespoons water**
- 1 **garlic clove, minced**
- ½ **teaspoon salt**
- ⅛ **teaspoon pepper**
- 6 **boneless pork loin chops (6 ounces each)**
- 1 **jar (24 ounces) marinara sauce**
- ¼ **cup shredded Parmesan cheese**

1. Place the potatoes and water in a microwave-safe dish. Cover and microwave on high for 5 minutes or until almost tender; drain.
2. Place potatoes in a 13x9-in. baking dish coated with cooking spray. Sprinkle with garlic, salt and pepper. Top with pork chops and marinara sauce. Cover and bake at 350° for 40-45 minutes or until a thermometer inserted into pork reads 145° and potatoes are tender.
3. Sprinkle with cheese. Bake, uncovered, 3-5 minutes longer or until cheese is melted. Let stand for 5 minutes before serving.
PER SERVING *1 pork chop with 1 cup potatoes and ½ cup sauce equals 412 cal., 11 g fat (4 g sat. fat), 84 mg*

SLOW COOKER

Pork and Apple Curry

Here's a mild curry dish that's sure to please American palates. For fun, try varying the garnishes. Add some chopped peanuts or a spoonful of chutney.

—**NANCY RECK** MILL VALLEY, CA

PREP: 15 MIN. • **COOK:** 5½ HOURS
MAKES: 8 SERVINGS

- 2 **pounds boneless pork loin roast, cut into 1-inch cubes**
- 1 **medium apple, peeled and chopped**
- 1 **small onion, chopped**
- ½ **cup orange juice**
- 1 **tablespoon curry powder**
- 1 **teaspoon chicken bouillon granules**
- 1 **garlic clove, minced**
- ½ **teaspoon salt**
- ½ **teaspoon ground ginger**
- ¼ **teaspoon ground cinnamon**
- 2 **tablespoons cornstarch**
- 2 **tablespoons cold water**
  Hot cooked rice, optional
- ¼ **cup raisins**
- ¼ **cup flaked coconut, toasted**

1. In a 3-qt. slow cooker, combine the first 10 ingredients. Cover and cook on low for 5-6 hours or until meat is tender.
2. Increase heat to high. In a small bowl, combine cornstarch and water until smooth; stir into slow cooker. Cover and cook for 30 minutes or until thickened, stirring once.
3. Serve with rice if desired. Sprinkle with raisins and coconut.
PER SERVING *⅔ cup curry mixture with 1½ teaspoons each of raisins and coconut (calculated without rice) equals 235 cal., 9 g fat (4 g sat. fat), 68 mg chol., 341 mg sodium, 13 g carb., 1 g fiber, 25 g pro.* **Diabetic Exchanges: 3 lean meat, 1 fruit.**

Pizza Lover's Pie

Love pizza? Then you'll love the tasty spin this recipe puts on it. Plus, it's easy to tailor for picky eaters.

—**CAROL GILLESPIE** CHAMBERSBURG, PA

PREP: 20 MIN. • **BAKE:** 20 MIN.
MAKES: 8 SERVINGS

- ¼ **pound bulk pork sausage**
- ½ **cup chopped green pepper**
- ¼ **cup chopped onion**
- 1 **loaf (1 pound) frozen bread dough, thawed and halved**
- 2 **cups (8 ounces) shredded part-skim mozzarella cheese**
- ½ **cup grated Parmesan cheese**
- 1 **can (8 ounces) pizza sauce**
- 8 **slices pepperoni**
- 1 **can (4 ounces) mushroom stems and pieces, drained**
- ¼ **teaspoon dried oregano, divided**

1. In a large skillet, cook the sausage, pepper and onion over medium heat until meat is no longer pink; drain. Set aside.
2. Roll half of dough into a 12-in. circle. Transfer to a greased 9-in. deep-dish pie plate. Layer with half of the mozzarella cheese, Parmesan cheese and pizza sauce. Top with the sausage mixture, pepperoni slices, mushrooms and ⅛ teaspoon oregano.
3. Roll out remaining dough to fit top of pie. Place over filling; seal edges. Layer with remaining pizza sauce, cheeses and oregano. Bake at 400° for 18-22 minutes or until golden brown.
PER SERVING *1 piece equals 305 cal., 12 g fat (5 g sat. fat), 27 mg chol., 743 mg sodium, 32 g carb., 3 g fiber, 17 g pro.* **Diabetic Exchanges: 2 starch, 2 medium-fat meat.**

PIZZA LOVER'S PIE

Apple-Cinnamon Pork Loin

I love to make this slow-cooked dish for chilly fall dinners with my family—the delightful apple-cinnamon aroma fills our entire house. The pork roast tastes even better served with buttery homemade mashed potatoes.

—RACHEL SCHULTZ LANSING, MI

PREP: 20 MIN. • **COOK:** 6 HOURS
MAKES: 6 SERVINGS

- 1   boneless pork loin roast (2 to 3 pounds)
- ½   teaspoon salt
- ¼   teaspoon pepper
- 1   tablespoon canola oil
- 3   medium apples, peeled and sliced, divided
- ¼   cup honey
- 1   small red onion, halved and sliced
- 1   tablespoon ground cinnamon
     Minced fresh parsley, optional

1. Sprinkle roast with salt and pepper. In a large skillet, brown roast in oil on all sides; cool slightly. With a paring knife, cut about sixteen 3-in.-deep slits in sides of roast; insert one apple slice into each slit.

2. Place half of the remaining apples in a 4-qt. slow cooker. Place roast over apples. Drizzle with honey; top with onion and remaining apples. Sprinkle with cinnamon.

3. Cover and cook on low 6-8 hours or until meat is tender. Remove pork and apple mixture; keep warm.

4. Transfer cooking juices to a small saucepan. Bring to a boil; cook until liquid is reduced by half. Serve with pork and apple mixture. Sprinkle with parsley if desired.

PER SERVING *1 serving equals 290 cal., 10 g fat (3 g sat. fat), 75 mg chol., 241 mg sodium, 22 g carb., 2 g fiber, 29 g pro.* **Diabetic Exchanges:** *4 lean meat, 1 starch, ½ fruit, ½ fat.*

APPLE-CINNAMON PORK LOIN

Wild Rice Venison Stew

With three hunters in the family and plenty of wild rice on hand, this hearty stew is a regular must-make at our house.

—DARLA HASELTINE WYOMING, MN

PREP: 15 MIN. • **COOK:** 2 HOURS
MAKES: 6 SERVINGS

- ⅓   cup all-purpose flour
- ½   teaspoon pepper
- 1½ pounds venison, cut into 1-inch cubes
- 2   tablespoons canola oil
- 2¾ cups water
- 1   can (14½ ounces) beef broth
- ½   teaspoon beef bouillon granules
- 2   medium potatoes, peeled and cubed
- 1   medium onion, cut into wedges
- 2   medium carrots, cut into ¾-inch pieces
- ⅓   cup uncooked wild rice

1. In a large resealable plastic bag, combine flour and pepper. Add venison; shake to coat. In a Dutch oven, brown meat in oil in batches. Add the water, broth and bouillon; bring to a boil. Reduce heat; cover and simmer for 1¼ hours.

2. Add vegetables and rice. Reduce heat; cover and simmer for 30-40 minutes or until rice is tender.

PER SERVING *1 cup equals 301 cal., 8 g fat (2 g sat. fat), 103 mg chol., 362 mg sodium, 24 g carb., 2 g fiber, 32 g pro.* **Diabetic Exchanges:** *3½ lean meat, 1½ starch, 1 vegetable.*

DID YOU KNOW?

Venison is a lean choice low in saturated fat. Four ounces deer venison contains 215 calories, 4 grams fat and 2 grams saturated fat. Four ounces lean beef stew meat contains 265 calories, 12 grams fat and 5 grams saturated fat.

Molasses-Glazed Pork Chops

How can you go wrong with these savory chops that only call for a handful of ingredients? Best of all, they're impressive enough to serve guests!

—ANGELA SPENGLER TAMPA, FL

START TO FINISH: 30 MIN.
MAKES: 4 SERVINGS

- ¼ cup molasses
- 1 tablespoon Worcestershire sauce
- 1½ teaspoons brown sugar
- 4 boneless pork loin chops
  (¾ inch thick and 5 ounces each)

1. In a small bowl, combine molasses, Worcestershire sauce and brown sugar. Reserve 3 tablespoons sauce for serving.
2. Grill pork, covered, over medium heat or broil 4 in. from heat 4-5 minutes on each side or until a thermometer reads 145°, brushing with remaining sauce during the last 3 minutes of cooking. Let stand 5 minutes before serving. Serve with reserved sauce.
PER SERVING *1 pork chop with about 2 teaspoons sauce equals 256 cal., 8 g fat (3 g sat. fat), 68 mg chol., 89 mg sodium, 17 g carb., 0 fiber, 27 g pro.* **Diabetic Exchanges:** *4 lean meat, 1 starch.*

BARBECUED COUNTRY RIBS

Barbecued Country Ribs

I created this sauce many years ago when I adapted a recipe I saw in a magazine. The original called for much more oil. I usually triple the sauce and keep some in my freezer to use on chicken, beef or pork.

—BARBARA GERRIETS TOPEKA, KS

PREP: 25 MIN. • **BAKE:** 2 HOURS
MAKES: 8 SERVINGS

- 2½ pounds boneless country-style pork ribs
- 2 teaspoons liquid smoke, optional
- ½ teaspoon salt
- 1 cup water

BARBECUE SAUCE
- ⅔ cup chopped onion
- 1 tablespoon canola oil
- ¾ cup each water and ketchup
- ⅓ cup lemon juice
- 3 tablespoons sugar
- 3 tablespoons Worcestershire sauce
- 2 tablespoons prepared mustard
- ½ teaspoon salt
- ½ teaspoon pepper
- ¼ teaspoon liquid smoke, optional

1. Place ribs in an 11x7-in. baking dish coated with cooking spray. Sprinkle with liquid smoke if desired and salt. Add water to pan. Cover and bake at 350° for 1 hour.
2. Meanwhile, in a saucepan, saute onion in oil until tender. Add the remaining sauce ingredients; bring to a boil. Reduce heat; simmer, uncovered, for 15 minutes or until slightly thickened.
3. Drain ribs; top with half of the barbecue sauce. Cover and bake 1 hour longer or until meat is tender, basting every 20 minutes. Serve with the remaining sauce.
FREEZE OPTION *Place cooled meat mixture in freezer containers. To use, partially thaw in refrigerator overnight. Microwave, covered, on high in a microwave-safe dish until heated through, gently stirring and adding a little water if necessary.*
PER SERVING *4 ounces cooked pork with 2 tablespoons sauce equals 292 cal., 14 g fat (4 g sat. fat), 91 mg chol., 668 mg sodium, 14 g carb., 1 g fiber, 28 g pro.* **Diabetic Exchanges:** *4 lean meat, 1 starch, ½ fat.*

JIFFY GROUND PORK SKILLET

freezer containers. To use, partially thaw in refrigerator overnight. Heat through in a saucepan, stirring occasionally and adding a little tomato sauce if necessary.

PER SERVING *1⅓ cups equals 317 cal., 14 g fat (5 g sat. fat), 61 mg chol., 408 mg sodium, 27 g carb., 2 g fiber, 21 g pro.*

⑤INGREDIENTS FAST FIX

Just Peachy Pork Tenderloin

I had a pork tenderloin and ripe peaches and decided to put them together. The results couldn't have been more irresistible! Here's a fresh entree that tastes like summer.

—**JULIA GOSLIGA** ADDISON, VT

START TO FINISH: 20 MIN.
MAKES: 4 SERVINGS

- 1 **pound pork tenderloin, cut into 12 slices**
- ½ **teaspoon salt**
- ¼ **teaspoon pepper**
- 2 **teaspoons olive oil**
- 4 **medium peaches, peeled and sliced**
- 1 **tablespoon lemon juice**
- ¼ **cup peach preserves**

1. Flatten each tenderloin slice to ¼-in. thickness. Sprinkle with salt and pepper. In a large nonstick skillet over medium heat, cook pork in oil until tender. Remove and keep warm.
2. Add peaches and lemon juice to skillet, stirring to loosen browned bits. Cook and stir for 3-4 minutes or until peaches are tender. Stir in pork and preserves; heat through.
PER SERVING *1 serving equals 241 cal., 6 g fat (2 g sat. fat), 63 mg chol., 340 mg sodium, 23 g carb., 2 g fiber, 23 g pro.* **Diabetic Exchanges:** *3 lean meat, 1 fruit, ½ starch, ½ fat.*

FREEZE IT FAST FIX

Jiffy Ground Pork Skillet

Some people call it dinner hour, but many of us call it rush hour. Slow down with this super-easy meal. The only thing you'll have left over is time to share with your family at the table.

—**BRIGITTE SCHALLER** FLEMINGTON, MO

START TO FINISH: 30 MIN.
MAKES: 5 SERVINGS

- 1½ **cups uncooked penne pasta**
- 1 **pound ground pork**
- ½ **cup chopped onion**
- 1 **can (14½ ounces) stewed tomatoes, undrained**
- 1 **can (8 ounces) tomato sauce**
- 1 **teaspoon Italian seasoning**
- 1 **medium zucchini, cut into ¼-inch slices**

1. Cook pasta according to package directions. Meanwhile, in a large skillet, cook pork and onion over medium heat until meat is no longer pink; drain. Add the tomatoes, tomato sauce and Italian seasoning. Bring to a boil. Reduce heat; cover and cook for 5 minutes to allow flavors to blend.
2. Drain pasta; add to skillet. Stir in zucchini. Cover and cook 3-5 minutes or until zucchini is crisp-tender.
FREEZE OPTION *Transfer individual portions of cooled pasta mixture to*

FREEZE IT **SLOW COOKER**

Baja Pork Tacos

Here's my copycat version of the best Mexican food we've ever tasted. The original recipe used beef, but we love these succulent tacos with tender shredded pork.

—ARIELLA WINN MESQUITE, TX

PREP: 10 MIN. • **COOK:** 8 HOURS
MAKES: 12 SERVINGS

- 1 boneless pork sirloin roast (3 pounds)
- 5 cans (4 ounces each) chopped green chilies
- 2 tablespoons reduced-sodium taco seasoning
- 1 tablespoon ground cumin
- 24 corn tortillas (6 inches), warmed
- 3 cups shredded lettuce
- 1½ cups (6 ounces) shredded part-skim mozzarella cheese

1. Cut roast in half; place in a 3- or 4-qt. slow cooker. In a small bowl, combine the chilies, taco seasoning and cumin; pour over pork. Cover and cook on low for 8-10 hours or until meat is tender.
2. Remove pork; cool slightly. Skim fat from cooking juices. Shred meat with two forks; return to slow cooker and heat through. Spoon ¼ cup meat onto each tortilla; top each taco with 2 tablespoons lettuce and 1 tablespoon of cheese.

FREEZE OPTION *Cool pork mixture; freeze in freezer containers up to 3 months. Thaw in the refrigerator overnight. Place in a Dutch oven; heat through. Serve as directed.*

PER SERVING *2 tacos equals 326 cal., 10 g fat (4 g sat. fat), 76 mg chol., 469 mg sodium, 28 g carb., 4 g fiber, 30 g pro.* **Diabetic Exchanges:** *3 lean meat, 2 starch, 1 fat.*

Green Bean Ham Quiche

Here's a delicious, healthful way to use up leftover ham. Green beans make the dish fresh and snappy. Cheddar cheese works great in this, too, if you don't have Swiss on hand.

—SANDY FLICK TOLEDO, OH

PREP: 20 MIN. • **BAKE:** 35 MIN.
MAKES: 8 SERVINGS

- ½ pound fresh green beans, trimmed and cut into 1-inch pieces
- 1 cup cubed fully cooked ham
- 1 jar (6 ounces) sliced mushrooms, drained
- 1 cup (4 ounces) shredded Swiss cheese
- ½ cup finely chopped onion
- ⅛ teaspoon garlic powder
- 3 eggs, lightly beaten
- 1½ cups 2% milk
- ¾ cup biscuit/baking mix
- ½ teaspoon salt
- ¼ teaspoon pepper

1. Place beans in a large saucepan and cover with water. Bring to a boil; cook, uncovered, for 5 minutes or until crisp-tender.
2. Meanwhile, in a large bowl, combine ham, mushrooms, cheese, onion and garlic powder. Drain beans; stir into ham mixture. Transfer to a 9-in. deep-dish pie plate coated with cooking spray.
3. In a small bowl, combine the eggs, milk, biscuit mix, salt and pepper just until blended; pour over ham mixture.
4. Bake 400° for 35-40 minutes or until a knife inserted near the center comes out clean. Let quiche stand for 5 minutes before cutting.

PER SERVING *1 slice equals 198 cal., 10 g fat (5 g sat. fat), 108 mg chol., 686 mg sodium, 14 g carb., 2 g fiber, 13 g pro.* **Diabetic Exchanges:** *1½ lean meat, 1 starch, 1 fat.*

BAJA PORK TACOS

1. In a small bowl, combine the cornstarch and pineapple juice until smooth. Stir in cranberry and barbecue sauces; set aside.

2. In a large skillet, stir-fry pork in oil for 3 minutes or until meat is no longer pink. Sprinkle with salt and pepper. Remove from the pan and keep warm.

3. Add green pepper and pineapple to pan; stir-fry for 2 minutes. Stir cornstarch mixture and add to skillet. Bring to a boil. Cook and stir for 2 minutes or until thickened. Add pork; heat through. Serve with rice, noodles or wonton strips.

FREEZE OPTION *Place cooled meat mixture in freezer containers. To use, partially thaw in refrigerator overnight. Heat through slowly in a covered skillet, stirring occasionally and adding a little water if necessary.*

PER SERVING *1¼ cups (calculated without rice) equals 268 cal., 7 g fat (2 g sat. fat), 63 mg chol., 444 mg sodium, 28 g carb., 1 g fiber, 23 g pro.*

⑤INGREDIENTS | FAST FIX
Honey-Mustard Pork Tenderloin

Here's a dinner that's quick, easy and good. I usually have all the ingredients on hand to prepare it, and everyone enjoys the honey-mustard flavor.

—**JOYCE MOYNIHAN** LAKEVILLE, MN

START TO FINISH: 30 MIN.
MAKES: 4 SERVINGS

- 1 pork tenderloin (1 pound)
- **GLAZE**
- ¼ cup honey
- 2 tablespoons brown sugar
- 2 tablespoons cider vinegar
- 1 tablespoon prepared mustard
- ½ teaspoon salt
- ¼ teaspoon pepper

1. Place pork on a greased rack in a 15x10x 1-in. baking pan lined with foil. Combine glaze ingredients; set aside 3 tablespoons for basting. Spoon the remaining glaze over pork.

2. Bake the tenderloin, uncovered, at 400° for 24-28 minutes or until a thermometer reads 145°, basting occasionally with the reserved glaze. Let the pork stand for 5 minutes before slicing.

PER SERVING *3 ounces cooked pork equals 226 cal., 4 g fat (1 g sat. fat), 63 mg chol., 386 mg sodium, 25 g carb., trace fiber, 23 g pro.* **Diabetic Exchanges:** *3 lean meat, 1½ starch.*

FREEZE IT | FAST FIX
Cranberry Sweet-and-Sour Pork

This fresh take on the beloved Asian-style dish is guaranteed to cause a stir at the dinner table.

—**GERT SNYDER** WEST MONTROSE, ON

START TO FINISH: 20 MIN.
MAKES: 6 SERVINGS

- 1 tablespoon cornstarch
- ½ cup unsweetened pineapple juice
- 1 cup whole-berry cranberry sauce
- ½ cup barbecue sauce
- 1½ pounds pork tenderloin, cut into ½-inch cubes
- 1 tablespoon canola oil
- ½ teaspoon salt
- ¼ teaspoon pepper
- 1 medium green pepper, cut into strips
- ¾ cup pineapple tidbits
  Hot cooked rice, chow mein noodles or crispy wonton strips

BACON-SWISS PORK CHOPS

Bacon-Swiss Pork Chops

I'm always looking for quick and easy recipes that are special enough to serve company. These pork chops smothered in bacon and melted Swiss are one of those dishes.

—**KEITH MILLER** FORT GRATIOT, MI

START TO FINISH: 25 MIN.
MAKES: 4 SERVINGS

- 2 **bacon strips, chopped**
- 1 **medium onion, chopped**
- 4 **boneless pork loin chops (4 ounces each)**
- ½ **teaspoon garlic powder**
- ¼ **teaspoon salt**
- 2 **slices reduced-fat Swiss cheese, halved**

1. In a nonstick skillet coated with cooking spray, cook bacon and onion over medium heat until bacon is crisp, stirring occasionally. Drain on paper towels; discard drippings.

2. Sprinkle pork chops with garlic powder and salt. Add pork chops to same pan; cook over medium heat 3-4 minutes on each side or until a thermometer reads 145°. Top pork with bacon mixture and cheese. Cook, covered, on low heat for 1-2 minutes or until cheese is melted. Let stand 5 minutes before serving.

PER SERVING *1 pork chop equals 218 cal., 10 g fat (4 g sat. fat), 64 mg chol., 268 mg sodium, 4 g carb., 1 g fiber, 27 g pro.* **Diabetic Exchanges:** *4 lean meat, ½ fat.*

Mediterranean Pork and Orzo

On a really busy day, this meal-in-a-bowl is one of my top picks. It's quick to put together, leaving a lot more time to relax at the table.

—**MARY RELYEA** CANASTOTA, NY

START TO FINISH: 30 MIN.
MAKES: 6 SERVINGS

- 1½ **pounds pork tenderloin**
- 1 **teaspoon coarsely ground pepper**
- 2 **tablespoons olive oil**
- 3 **quarts water**
- 1¼ **cups uncooked orzo pasta**
- ¼ **teaspoon salt**
- 1 **package (6 ounces) fresh baby spinach**
- 1 **cup grape tomatoes, halved**
- ¾ **cup crumbled feta cheese**

1. Rub pork with pepper; cut into 1-in. cubes. In a large nonstick skillet, heat oil over medium heat. Add pork; cook and stir 8-10 minutes or until no longer pink.

2. Meanwhile, in a Dutch oven, bring water to a boil. Stir in orzo and salt; cook, uncovered, 8 minutes. Stir in spinach; cook 45-60 seconds longer or until orzo is tender and spinach is wilted. Drain.

3. Add tomatoes to the pork and heat through. Stir in orzo mixture and cheese.

PER SERVING *1⅓ cups equals 372 cal., 11 g fat (4 g sat. fat), 71 mg chol., 306 mg sodium, 34 g carb., 3 g fiber, 31 g pro.* **Diabetic Exchanges:** *3 lean meat, 2 starch, 1 vegetable, 1 fat.*

ORIGINAL	MAKEOVER
438 Calories	**345** Calories
24g Fat	**13**g Fat
11g Sat. Fat	**6**g Sat. Fat

MAKEOVER RIGATONI WITH BACON AND ASPARAGUS

Makeover Rigatoni with Bacon and Asparagus

Wouldn't it be great to find a company-worthy dish that not only impresses with its taste, but also delivers with healthy nutritional numbers? Look no further.

—JOANIE FUSON INDIANAPOLIS, IN

PREP: 25 MIN. • **COOK:** 20 MIN.
MAKES: 8 SERVINGS

- 1 pound fresh asparagus, trimmed and coarsely chopped
- 1 package (16 ounces) rigatoni
- 2 tablespoons butter
- 1 tablespoon olive oil
- 1 garlic clove, minced
- ⅔ cup half-and-half cream
- ½ cup shredded part-skim mozzarella cheese
- 8 bacon strips, cooked and crumbled
- ¼ cup minced fresh parsley
- ½ teaspoon salt
- ⅛ teaspoon coarsely ground pepper
- ¼ cup grated Parmigiano-Reggiano cheese

1. Fill a 6-qt. stockpot ¾ full with water; bring to a boil. Add asparagus; cook, uncovered, 3 minutes or until tender. Remove with a slotted spoon and immediately drop into ice water. Drain and pat dry.

2. Return water to a boil; cook the rigatoni according to package directions. Meanwhile, in a small saucepan, heat butter and oil over medium-high heat. Add garlic; cook and stir 1 minute. Stir in cream. Bring to a boil. Reduce heat; simmer, uncovered, 3-4 minutes or until slightly thickened. Stir in mozzarella cheese until melted.

3. Drain rigatoni; return to pan. Stir in asparagus, bacon, parsley, salt, pepper and cream sauce. Sprinkle with Parmigiano-Reggiano cheese.
PER SERVING *1¼ cups equals 345 cal., 13 g fat (6 g sat. fat), 32 mg chol., 428 mg sodium, 44 g carb., 2 g fiber, 15 g pro.*

THE SKINNY

In Europe, Parmigiano-Reggiano and Parmesan are considered the same cheese. But in the U.S., Parmesan is a generic term that may not come from Italy's Parmigiano-Reggiano region. Using the authentic Italian cheese in the makeover (in a lesser amount than the original's ½ cup) ensures a cheesy richness with less fat and calories.

SLOW COOKER Cranberry-Mustard Pork Loin

This dressed-up pork loin is so easy that you only have to spend a few minutes preparing it. The roast is a family favorite because it's tasty, and a favorite of mine because it's fast to get started!

—LAURA COOK WILDWOOD, MO

PREP: 15 MIN. • **COOK:** 4 HOURS
MAKES: 8 SERVINGS

- 1 boneless pork loin roast (2 pounds)
- 1 can (14 ounces) whole-berry cranberry sauce
- ¼ cup Dijon mustard
- 3 tablespoons brown sugar
- 3 tablespoons lemon juice
- 1 tablespoon cornstarch
- ¼ cup cold water

1. Place roast in a 3-qt. slow cooker. Combine the cranberry sauce, mustard, brown sugar and lemon juice; pour over roast. Cover and cook on low for 4-5 hours or until meat is tender. Remove roast and keep warm.

2. Strain cooking juices into a 2-cup measuring cup; add enough water to measure 2 cups. In a small saucepan, combine cornstarch and cold water until smooth; stir in cooking juices. Bring to a boil; cook and stir for 2 minutes or until thickened. Serve with pork.

PER SERVING *3 ounces cooked pork with ¼ cup gravy equals 255 cal., 6 g fat (2 g sat. fat), 56 mg chol., 236 mg sodium, 28 g carb., 1 g fiber, 22 g pro.*

SLOW COOKER Sunday Pot Roast

With the help of a slow cooker, you can prepare a down-home dinner any day of the week, not just on Sundays. The roast turns out tender and savory every time.

—BRANDY SCHAEFER GLEN CARBON, IL

PREP: 10 MIN. + CHILLING • **COOK:** 8 HOURS
MAKES: 14 SERVINGS

- 1 teaspoon dried oregano
- ½ teaspoon onion salt
- ½ teaspoon caraway seeds
- ½ teaspoon pepper
- ¼ teaspoon garlic salt
- 1 boneless pork loin roast (3½-4 pounds), trimmed
- 6 medium carrots, peeled and cut into 1½-inch pieces
- 3 large potatoes, peeled and quartered
- 3 small onions, quartered
- 1½ cups beef broth
- ⅓ cup all-purpose flour
- ⅓ cup cold water
- ¼ teaspoon browning sauce, optional

1. In a small bowl, combine the first five ingredients; rub over roast. Wrap roast in plastic wrap and refrigerate overnight.

2. Place carrots, potatoes and onions in a 6-qt. slow cooker; add broth.

Unwrap roast; place in slow cooker. Cook, covered, on low 8-10 hours or until meat and vegetables are tender.

3. Transfer roast and vegetables to a serving platter; tent with foil. Pour cooking juices into a small saucepan. In a small bowl, mix flour and water until smooth; stir into pan. Bring to a boil; cook and stir 2 minutes or until thickened. If desired, add browning sauce. Serve roast with gravy.

PER SERVING *1 serving equals 233 cal., 5 g fat (2 g sat. fat), 56 mg chol., 249 mg sodium, 21 g carb., 2 g fiber, 24 g pro.* **Diabetic Exchanges:** *3 lean meat, 1½ starch.*

Roasted Pork Tenderloin and Vegetables

There are no complicated steps to follow when preparing this medley of tender pork and veggies. Just season with herbs, then pop in the oven.

—DIANE MARTIN BROWN DEER, WI

PREP: 20 MIN. • **BAKE:** 25 MIN.
MAKES: 6 SERVINGS

- 2 **pork tenderloins (¾ pound each)**
- 2 **pounds red potatoes, quartered**
- 1 **pound carrots, halved and cut into 2-inch pieces**
- 1 **medium onion, cut into wedges**
- 1 **tablespoon olive oil**
- 2 **teaspoons dried rosemary, crushed**
- 1 **teaspoon rubbed sage**
- ½ **teaspoon salt**
- ¼ **teaspoon pepper**

1. Preheat oven to 450°. Place pork in a shallow roasting pan coated with cooking spray; arrange the potatoes, carrots and onion around the pork. Drizzle with oil. Combine seasonings; sprinkle over meat and vegetables.

2. Bake, uncovered, 25-35 minutes or until meat reaches desired doneness (for medium-rare, a thermometer should read 145°; medium, 160°) and vegetables are tender, stirring vegetables occasionally. Remove pork from oven; tent with foil. Let stand 5 minutes before slicing.

NOTE *If pork is done before the vegetables are tender, remove from oven and keep warm. Continue cooking vegetables until tender.*

PER SERVING *3 ounces cooked meat with 1 cup vegetables equals 331 cal., 7 g fat (2 g sat. fat), 67 mg chol., 299 mg sodium, 40 g carb., 5 g fiber, 28 g pro.* **Diabetic Exchanges:** *3 lean meat, 2 starch, 1 vegetable.*

Pork Medallions with Strawberry Sauce

Pork tenderloin paired with strawberries is a heavenly match, made even more special with a tangy feta garnish. Serve with roasted spring vegetables for the perfect company dinner.

—KATHERINE WOLLGAST FLORISSANT, MO

PREP: 15 MIN. • **COOK:** 20 MIN.
MAKES: 8 SERVINGS

- 1½ **cups reduced-sodium beef broth**
- 2 **cups chopped fresh strawberries, divided**
- ½ **cup white wine vinegar**
- ¼ **cup packed brown sugar**
- ¼ **cup reduced-sodium soy sauce**
- 3 **garlic cloves, minced**
- 2 **pounds pork tenderloin, cut into ½-inch slices**
- 1 **teaspoon garlic powder**
- ½ **teaspoon salt**
- ½ **teaspoon pepper**
- 2 **tablespoons canola oil**
- 2 **tablespoons cornstarch**
- 2 **tablespoons cold water**
- ½ **cup crumbled feta cheese**
- ½ **cup chopped green onions**

1. In a large saucepan, combine broth, 1 cup strawberries, vinegar, brown sugar, soy sauce and garlic; bring to a boil. Reduce heat; simmer, uncovered, 15 minutes or until slightly thickened. Strain mixture and set aside liquid, discarding solids.

2. Sprinkle pork with garlic powder, salt and pepper. In a large skillet, heat oil over medium heat. Brown pork in batches on both sides. Remove and keep warm.

3. Add broth mixture to the pan; bring to a boil. Combine cornstarch and water until smooth and gradually stir into skillet.

4. Return pork to the pan. Bring to a boil. Reduce heat; cook and stir 2 minutes or until sauce is thickened and pork is tender. Top each serving with cheese, onions and remaining chopped strawberries.

PER SERVING *1 serving equals 244 cal., 9 g fat (2 g sat. fat), 68 mg chol., 649 mg sodium, 15 g carb., 1 g fiber, 25 g pro.* **Diabetic Exchanges:** *3 lean meat, 1 starch, ½ fat.*

PORK MEDALLIONS WITH STRAWBERRY SAUCE

SPICED PORK WITH
BOURBON SAUCE

¼ cup Dijon mustard
¼ teaspoon ground ginger

1. Place ham on a rack in a shallow roasting pan. Score the surface of the ham, making diamond shapes ¼ in. deep. Add cider and orange juice to pan. Loosely cover ham with foil; bake at 325° for 1 hour. Combine remaining ingredients; brush some over ham.
2. Bake, uncovered, 45-60 minutes longer or until a thermometer reads 140°, brushing occasionally with glaze. Serve with remaining glaze.
PER SERVING *4 ounces ham equals 219 cal., 5 g fat (2 g sat. fat), 80 mg chol., 1,061 mg sodium, 17 g carb., trace fiber, 27 g pro.*

FAST FIX ▶ Spiced Pork with Bourbon Sauce

I don't remember where I found this recipe, but it's become one of my favorite entrees to serve company.
—**KATHY KANTRUD** FENTON, MI

START TO FINISH: 25 MIN.
MAKES: 4 SERVINGS

- ½ **cup bourbon**
- ¼ **cup packed dark brown sugar**
- 3 **tablespoons white vinegar**
- 3 **tablespoons reduced-sodium soy sauce**
- 2 **garlic cloves, minced**
- ½ **teaspoon pepper**
- ½ **teaspoon chili powder**
- ¼ **teaspoon ground cinnamon**
- ⅛ **teaspoon salt**
- ⅛ **teaspoon ground allspice**
- 1 **pork tenderloin (1 pound), cut into 12 slices**

1. In a small saucepan, combine the bourbon, brown sugar, vinegar, soy sauce, garlic and pepper. Bring to a boil; cook until liquid is reduced to about ½ cup, stirring occasionally.

2. Combine chili powder, cinnamon, salt and allspice; rub over pork.
3. In a large skillet coated with cooking spray, cook pork over medium heat for 2-4 minutes on each side or until tender. Serve with sauce.
PER SERVING *3 ounces cooked pork with 2 tablespoons sauce equals 221 cal., 4 g fat (1 g sat. fat), 63 mg chol., 581 mg sodium, 15 g carb., trace fiber, 23 g pro.* **Diabetic Exchanges: 3 lean meat, 1 starch.**

Baked Ham with Orange Glaze

This festive ham is brushed with a sweet-tangy mustard and marmalade glaze. It's worthy of any special occasion.
—***TASTE OF HOME*** TEST KITCHEN

PREP: 15 MIN. • **BAKE:** 1¾ HOURS
MAKES: 15 SERVINGS

- 1 **fully cooked bone-in ham (6 to 7 pounds)**
- 2 **cups apple cider**
- 2 **cups orange juice**
- ⅓ **cup orange marmalade**
- ¼ **cup packed brown sugar**

HOW TO

CARVE A BONE-IN HAM

❶ Place cut surface of ham on cutting board. Insert a skewer from top to bottom along the bone. With skewer as a guide, cut the largest piece from ham.

❷ Cut the piece across the grain into slices. Place slices on a serving platter and keep warm.

❸ Continue, using skewer as a guide to cut sections from ham while avoiding the bone. Slice.

Irish Stew

This satisfying stew is chock-full of potatoes, turnips, carrots and lamb. I like to serve it with Irish soda bread, which makes a hearty St. Patrick's Day meal.

—**LOIS GELZER** STANDISH, ME

PREP: 20 MIN. • **COOK:** 1¾ HOURS
MAKES: 6 SERVINGS

- 1½ **pounds lamb stew meat**
- 2 **teaspoons olive oil**
- 4 **cups water**
- 2 **cups sliced peeled potatoes**
- 1 **medium onion, sliced**
- ½ **cup sliced carrot**
- 1 **small turnip, peeled and chopped**
- 1 **teaspoon salt**
- ½ **teaspoon each dried marjoram, thyme and rosemary, crushed**
- ⅛ **teaspoon pepper**
- 2 **tablespoons all-purpose flour**
- 3 **tablespoons fat-free milk**
- ½ **teaspoon browning sauce, optional**
- 3 **tablespoons minced fresh parsley**

1. In a Dutch oven, brown lamb in oil over medium-high heat. Add water; bring to a boil. Reduce heat; cover and simmer for 1 hour.

2. Add the potatoes, onion, carrot, turnip and seasonings. Bring to a boil. Reduce heat; cover and simmer for 30 minutes or until the vegetables are tender.

3. In a small bowl, combine the flour, milk and, if desired, browning sauce until smooth; stir into stew. Add parsley. Bring to a boil; cook and stir for 2 minutes or until thickened.

PER SERVING *1½ cups equals 279 cal., 9 g fat (3 g sat. fat), 92 mg chol., 469 mg sodium, 17 g carb., 2 g fiber, 31 g pro.* **Diabetic Exchanges:** *3 lean meat, 1 starch, 1 vegetable.*

SLOW-COOKED JAMBALAYA

SLOW COOKER
Slow-Cooked Jambalaya

Sausage, chicken and shrimp keep this dish hearty and satisfying. Made easy with canned items and other kitchen staples, it's perfect for casual get-togethers.

—**SHERRY HUNTWORK** GRETNA, NE

PREP: 20 MIN. • **COOK:** 6¼ HOURS
MAKES: 12 SERVINGS

- 1 **pound smoked kielbasa or Polish sausage, sliced**
- ½ **pound boneless skinless chicken breasts, cut into 1-inch cubes**
- 1 **can (14½ ounces) beef broth**
- 1 **can (14½ ounces) diced tomatoes, undrained**
- 2 **celery ribs, chopped**
- ⅓ **cup tomato paste**
- 4 **garlic cloves, minced**
- 1 **tablespoon dried parsley flakes**
- 1½ **teaspoons dried basil**
- 1 **teaspoon cayenne pepper**
- ½ **teaspoon salt**
- ½ **teaspoon dried oregano**
- 1 **pound cooked medium shrimp, peeled and deveined**
- 2 **cups cooked rice**

1. In a 4-qt. slow cooker, combine the first 12 ingredients. Cover and cook on low for 6-7 hours or until chicken is no longer pink.

2. Stir in the shrimp and rice. Cover and cook 15 minutes longer or until heated through.

PER SERVING *1 cup equals 228 cal., 11 g fat (4 g sat. fat), 95 mg chol., 692 mg sodium, 12 g carb., 1 g fiber, 18 g pro.* **Diabetic Exchanges:** *2 lean meat, 1 starch, 1 fat.*

CHERRY-GLAZED LAMB CHOPS

FAST FIX Cherry-Glazed Lamb Chops

An elegant sauce studded with cherries is the ideal partner for classic rosemary lamb chops. Try my recipe for a quiet dinner in with that special someone.

—**KERRY DINGWALL** PONTE VEDRA, FL

START TO FINISH: 25 MIN.
MAKES: 2 SERVINGS

    1   teaspoon dried rosemary, crushed
    ¼   teaspoon salt
    ¼   teaspoon pepper, divided
    4   lamb loin chops (4 ounces each)
    1   garlic clove, minced
    ¼   cup beef broth
    ¼   cup cherry preserves
    ¼   cup balsamic vinegar

1. Combine rosemary, salt and ⅛ teaspoon pepper; rub over lamb chops. In a large skillet coated with cooking spray, cook chops over medium heat for 4-6 minutes on each side or until meat reaches desired doneness (for medium-rare, a thermometer should read 145°; medium, 160°; well-done, 170°). Remove and keep warm.
2. Add garlic to the pan; cook for 1 minute. Stir in broth, preserves, vinegar and remaining pepper; cook for 2-4 minutes or until thickened. Return chops to pan; turn to coat.
PER SERVING *2 lamb chops with 2 tablespoons sauce equals 331 cal., 9 g fat (3 g sat. fat), 90 mg chol., 495 mg sodium, 32 g carb., trace fiber, 29 g pro.*

Pork with Blueberry Herb Sauce

A different and delicious way to use blueberries, this delightful sauce would also be great over chicken. The blend of berries and balsamic makes an interesting flavor contrast.

—**LIBBY WALP** CHICAGO, IL

PREP: 15 MIN. • **COOK:** 20 MIN.
MAKES: 4 SERVINGS

    1   garlic clove, minced
    1   teaspoon pepper
    ½   teaspoon salt
    ⅛   teaspoon cayenne pepper
    4   boneless pork loin chops
        (6 ounces each)
    2   cups fresh blueberries
    ¼   cup packed brown sugar
    2   tablespoons minced fresh parsley
    1   tablespoon balsamic vinegar
    2   teaspoons butter
    1   teaspoon minced fresh thyme or
        ¼ teaspoon dried thyme
    1   teaspoon fresh sage or ¼ teaspoon
        dried sage leaves

1. In a small bowl, combine the garlic, pepper, salt and cayenne; sprinkle over pork.
2. In a large ovenproof skillet coated with cooking spray, brown pork chops. Bake, uncovered, at 350° for 10-15 minutes or until a thermometer reads 160°. Remove pork and keep warm.
3. Add remaining ingredients to the pan. Cook and stir over medium heat until thickened, about 8 minutes. Serve with pork.
PER SERVING *1 pork chop with ¼ cup sauce equals 343 cal., 12 g fat (5 g sat. fat), 87 mg chol., 364 mg sodium, 25 g carb., 2 g fiber, 33 g pro.* **Diabetic Exchanges:** *5 lean meat, 1 starch, ½ fruit.*

Christmas Carol Ham

Supper is so simple when you prepare this slow-cooked ham. My family loves it! Simmering in pineapple juice makes the ham so flavorful.

—JULIE WILLIQUETTE HARTSELLE, AL

PREP: 10 MIN. • **COOK:** 2 HOURS
MAKES: 8 SERVINGS

- 2 **pounds fully cooked boneless ham, cut into eight slices**
- ½ **cup packed brown sugar**
- ¼ **cup unsweetened pineapple juice**
- 1½ **teaspoons white vinegar**
- ¼ **teaspoon ground mustard**

Place ham slices in a 3-qt. slow cooker. In a small bowl, combine the brown sugar, pineapple juice, vinegar and mustard; pour over ham. Cover and cook on low for 2-3 hours or until heated through.

PER SERVING *1 slice equals 177 cal., 4 g fat (1 g sat. fat), 58 mg chol., 1,182 mg sodium, 15 g carb., trace fiber, 21 g pro.*

German Deli Pizza

Take the chill off with robust German flavors in an unexpected dish: pizza! Your gang will go crazy for the authentic taste, right down to the tender caraway-seasoned crust.

—CINDY REAMS PHILIPSBURG, PA

PREP: 40 MIN. + RISING • **BAKE:** 15 MIN.
MAKES: 6 SLICES

DOUGH
- ⅔ **cup water (70° to 80°)**
- 1 **tablespoon olive oil**
- 1 **teaspoon caraway seeds**
- ¼ **teaspoon salt**
- 1½ **cups bread flour**
- ½ **cup rye flour**
- 1 **teaspoon active dry yeast**

SAUCE
- ⅓ **cup chopped red onion**
- 1 **tablespoon butter**
- 1 **tablespoon all-purpose flour**
- 1 **cup fat-free evaporated milk**
- 1 **tablespoon spicy brown mustard**
- ¼ **cup shredded Swiss cheese**

TOPPINGS
- ⅓ **cup thinly sliced red onion**
- 1 **cup cubed fully cooked ham**
- 1 **cup (4 ounces) shredded Swiss cheese**

1. In bread machine pan, place dough ingredients in order suggested by manufacturer. Select dough setting (check the dough after 5 minutes of mixing; add 1 to 2 tablespoons of water or flour if needed).
2. When cycle is completed, turn dough onto a lightly floured surface. Punch dough down; roll into a 13-in. circle.

Transfer to a 12-in. pizza pan coated with cooking spray; build up edges slightly. Cover and let rest for 10 minutes.
3. Prick dough thoroughly with a fork. Bake at 400° for 6-8 minutes or until edges are lightly browned.
4. Meanwhile, for sauce, in a small saucepan, saute chopped onion in butter until tender. Stir in flour until blended; gradually add evaporated milk and mustard. Bring to a boil; cook and stir for 2 minutes or until thickened. Remove from the heat; stir in cheese. Spread over crust. Top with sliced onion, ham and cheese. Bake for 12-15 minutes or until crust and cheese are lightly browned.

PER SERVING *1 slice equals 330 cal., 12 g fat (6 g sat. fat), 36 mg chol., 546 mg sodium, 37 g carb., 3 g fiber, 19 g pro.* **Diabetic Exchanges:** *2½ starch, 2 lean meat, 1 fat.*

GERMAN DELI PIZZA

**MANDY RIVERS'
OVEN-BARBECUED SALMON**
PAGE 210

Fish & Seafood

These pages are **brimming with under-the-sea delights,** so there's no need to fish for a **savory seafood** option. Discover healthy meals that are a snap to make and are **sure to disappear** just as quickly!

**KRISTIN KOSSAK'S
HALIBUT SOFT TACOS**

PAGE 217

**MARVIN MEUSER JR.'S
SHRIMP AND SCALLOP COUSCOUS**

PAGE 223

**NANCY DAUGHERTY'S
COD DELIGHT**

PAGE 227

Mediterranean Cod

My friends and I agree that this is one of the best things we have ever eaten. We each take a bundle and eat it right out of the parchment paper—makes cleanup very easy!

—MELISSA CHILTON HARLOWTON, MT

PREP: 25 MIN. • **BAKE:** 15 MIN.
MAKES: 4 SERVINGS

- 4 **cups shredded cabbage**
- 1 **large sweet onion, thinly sliced**
- 4 **garlic cloves, minced**
- 4 **cod fillets (6 ounces each)**
- ¼ **cup pitted Greek olives, chopped**
- ½ **cup crumbled feta cheese**
- ¼ **teaspoon salt**
- ¼ **teaspoon pepper**
- 4 **teaspoons olive oil**

1. Cut parchment paper or heavy-duty foil into four 18x12-in. pieces; place 1 cup cabbage on each. Top with onion, garlic, cod, olives, cheese, salt and pepper; drizzle with oil.

2. Fold parchment paper over fish. Bring edges of paper together on all sides and crimp to seal, forming a packet. Repeat with remaining packets. Place on baking sheets.

3. Bake at 450° for 12-15 minutes or until fish flakes easily with a fork. Open the packets carefully to allow steam to escape.

PER SERVING *1 packet equals 270 cal., 10 g fat (3 g sat. fat), 72 mg chol., 532 mg sodium, 12 g carb., 3 g fiber, 31 g pro.* **Diabetic Exchanges:** *5 lean meat, 2 vegetable, 2 fat.*

FAST FIX
Herbed Tuna Sandwiches

Give tuna salad an upgrade in a flash. Herbs and cheese make this simple sandwich a standout, perfect for a no-fuss lunch or dinner.

—MARIE CONNOR VIRGINIA BEACH, VA

START TO FINISH: 20 MIN.
MAKES: 4 SERVINGS

- 1 **can (12 ounces) light tuna in water, drained and flaked**
- 2 **hard-cooked large eggs, chopped**
- ⅓ **cup fat-free mayonnaise**
- ¼ **cup minced chives**
- 2 **teaspoons minced fresh parsley**
- ½ **teaspoon dried basil**
- ¼ **teaspoon onion powder**
- 8 **slices whole wheat bread, toasted**
- ½ **cup shredded reduced-fat cheddar cheese**

1. In a small bowl, combine the first seven ingredients. Place four slices of toast on an ungreased baking sheet; top with tuna mixture and sprinkle with cheese.

2. Broil 3-4 in. from the heat for 1-2 minutes or until cheese is melted. Top with remaining toast.

PER SERVING *1 sandwich equals 332 cal., 9 g fat (4 g sat. fat), 144 mg chol., 864 mg sodium, 30 g carb., 4 g fiber, 34 g pro.* **Diabetic Exchanges:** *4 lean meat, 2 starch.*

MEDITERRANEAN COD

Simple Snapper Dinner

This recipe yields a complete dinner with fish, herbed rice and stir-fried veggies. And it takes only a few minutes of prep time.

—MARY ANN PALESTINO BROOKLYN, NY

PREP: 20 MIN. • **COOK:** 55 MIN.
MAKES: 4 SERVINGS

- 1½ cups water
- ¾ cup uncooked brown rice
- 1½ teaspoons reduced-sodium beef bouillon granules
- 1½ teaspoons dried parsley flakes
- 1½ teaspoons dried minced onion
- ¼ teaspoon garlic powder
- 1 medium red onion, thinly sliced
- 2 garlic cloves, minced
- 2 teaspoons canola oil
- ½ pound fresh snow peas
- 1½ cups shredded carrots
- 1 tablespoon balsamic vinegar
- 4 red snapper fillets (5 ounces each)
- 2 teaspoons blackening seasoning

1. In a small saucepan, combine the first six ingredients. Bring to a boil. Reduce heat; cover and simmer for 40-45 minutes or until rice is tender.
2. Meanwhile, in a large nonstick skillet coated with cooking spray, cook onion and garlic in oil over medium-high heat for 2 minutes. Add peas; cook 2 minutes. Add carrots; cook 2 minutes longer or until vegetables are tender. Stir in vinegar. Remove and keep warm.
3. Sprinkle both sides of fillets with blackening seasoning. In the same skillet, cook fillets over medium-high heat for 4 minutes on each side or until fish flakes easily with a fork. Serve with rice and vegetables.

PER SERVING *1 fish fillet with ¾ cup vegetable mixture and ½ cup rice equals 353 cal., 6 g fat (1 g sat. fat), 50 mg chol., 305 mg sodium, 41 g carb., 5 g fiber, 34 g pro.* **Diabetic Exchanges:** *4 lean meat, 2 starch, 2 vegetable, ½ fat.*

SHRIMP & CHICKEN SAUSAGE WITH GRITS

FAST FIX ▶ Shrimp & Chicken Sausage with Grits

I'm originally from Tennessee and I'd never had shrimp and grits until I moved to South Carolina. I think my version is just as tasty as the traditional ones I've sampled, but it's easier on the waistline.

—ATHENA RUSSELL FLORENCE, SC

START TO FINISH: 30 MIN.
MAKES: 5 SERVINGS

- 3 cups water
- 1 cup quick-cooking grits
- 4 ounces reduced-fat cream cheese, cubed
- 3 fully cooked spicy chicken sausage links (3 ounces each), cut into ½-inch slices
- 2 teaspoons canola oil, divided
- 2 garlic cloves, minced
- 2 green onions, chopped, divided
- 4 teaspoons whole wheat flour
- 1½ cups chicken broth
- ¼ cup fat-free evaporated milk
- 1 pound uncooked medium shrimp, peeled and deveined
- 1 medium tomato, chopped

1. In a large saucepan, bring water to a boil. Slowly stir in grits. Reduce the heat; cook and stir for 5-7 minutes or until thickened. Stir in cream cheese until melted.
2. Meanwhile, in a large skillet, brown sausage in 1 teaspoon oil. Remove and keep warm.
3. In the same pan, heat remaining oil over medium-high heat. Add garlic and half of the green onions; cook and stir for 1 minute. Stir in flour until blended; gradually whisk in broth and milk. Bring to a boil, stirring constantly; cook and stir 2 minutes or until thickened.
4. Stir in shrimp and sausage; cook for 3-5 minutes or until shrimp turn pink. Serve with grits; top with tomato and remaining green onion.

PER SERVING *¾ cup shrimp mixture with ¾ cup grits equals 367 cal., 13 g fat (5 g sat. fat), 161 mg chol., 810 mg sodium, 30 g carb., 2 g fiber, 31 g pro.* **Diabetic Exchanges:** *4 lean meat, 2 starch, ½ fat.*

SHRIMP WITH
TOMATOES & FETA

FAST FIX ▸ Oven-Barbecued Salmon

Late last summer, the South Carolina heat drove me indoors and away from my grill. So I changed my favorite over-the-coals recipe baked it in the oven. I'm happy to say it's just as tasty.

—MANDY RIVERS LEXINGTON, SC

START TO FINISH: 25 MIN.
MAKES: 5 SERVINGS

- 5 salmon fillets (6 ounces each)
- 3 tablespoons orange juice
- 2 tablespoons lemon juice
- 2 tablespoons brown sugar
- 1 tablespoon chili powder
- 1 tablespoon paprika
- ½ teaspoon salt
- ½ teaspoon garlic powder
- ½ teaspoon ground cumin

1. Preheat oven to 425°. Place salmon in a greased 15x10x1-in. baking pan; drizzle with orange and lemon juices.
2. In a small bowl, mix remaining ingredients; sprinkle over fillets. Bake 13-15 minutes or until fish flakes easily with a fork.
PER SERVING *1 fillet equals 301 cal., 16 g fat (3 g sat. fat), 85 mg chol., 340 mg sodium, 9 g carb., 1 g fiber, 29 g pro. Diabetic Exchanges: 4 lean meat, 1 fat, ½ starch.*

FAST FIX ▸ Shrimp with Tomatoes & Feta

Any recipe that's special enough for company but easy enough for a weeknight is a star in my book. All you need to finish off the meal is a side salad and some crusty French bread to soak up the delicious tomato broth.

—SUSAN SEYMOUR VALATIE, NY

START TO FINISH: 30 MIN.
MAKES: 6 SERVINGS

- 3 tablespoons olive oil
- 2 shallots, finely chopped
- 2 garlic cloves, minced
- 6 plum tomatoes, chopped
- ½ cup white wine or chicken broth
- 1 tablespoon dried oregano
- ½ teaspoon salt
- ½ teaspoon crushed red pepper flakes
- ¼ teaspoon sweet paprika
- 2 pounds uncooked large shrimp, peeled and deveined
- ⅔ cup crumbled feta cheese
- 2 teaspoons minced fresh mint
  Hot cooked rice

1. In a large skillet, heat oil over medium-high heat. Add shallots and garlic; cook and stir until tender. Add tomatoes, wine, oregano, salt, pepper flakes and paprika; bring to a boil. Reduce heat; simmer, uncovered, 5 minutes.
2. Stir in shrimp and cheese; cook 5-6 minutes or until shrimp turn pink. Stir in mint. Serve with rice.
PER SERVING *1 cup (calculated without rice) equals 261 cal., 11 g fat (3 g sat. fat), 191 mg chol., 502 mg sodium, 8 g carb., 2 g fiber, 28 g pro. Diabetic Exchanges: 4 lean meat, 1 vegetable, 1 fat.*

Makeover Fish and Chips

Enjoy moist, flavorful fish with a coating that's as crunchy and golden as deep-fried. And you can easily bake up crispy fries to serve alongside. This makeover is a must-try for the fish lover.

—**JANICE MITCHELL** AURORA, CO

PREP: 10 MIN. • **BAKE:** 35 MIN.
MAKES: 4 SERVINGS

- 1 **pound potatoes (about 2 medium)**
- 2 **tablespoons olive oil**
- ¼ **teaspoon pepper**

FISH

- ⅓ **cup all-purpose flour**
- ¼ **teaspoon pepper**
- 1 **large egg**
- 2 **tablespoons water**
- ⅔ **cup crushed cornflakes**
- 1 **tablespoon grated Parmesan cheese**
- ⅛ **teaspoon cayenne pepper**
- 1 **pound haddock or cod fillets**
  Tartar sauce, optional

1. Preheat oven to 425°. Peel and cut the potatoes lengthwise into ½-in.-thick slices; cut slices into ½-in.-thick sticks.

2. In a large bowl, toss potatoes with oil and pepper. Transfer to a 15x10x1-in. baking pan coated with cooking spray. Bake the potatoes, uncovered, 25-30 minutes or until golden brown and crisp, stirring once.

3. Meanwhile, in a shallow bowl, mix flour and pepper. In another shallow bowl, whisk egg with water. In a third bowl, toss crushed cornflakes with cheese and cayenne. Dip fish in flour mixture to coat both sides; shake off excess. Dip in egg mixture, then in cornflake mixture, patting to help coating adhere.

4. Place on a baking sheet coated with cooking spray. Bake 10-12 minutes or until fish just begins to flake easily with a fork. Serve with potatoes and, if desired, tartar sauce.

PER SERVING *1 serving equals 376 cal., 9 g fat (2 g sat. fat), 120 mg chol., 228 mg sodium, 44 g carb., 2 g fiber, 28 g pro.* **Diabetic Exchanges:** *3 starch, 3 lean meat, 1½ fat.*

THE SKINNY

Tossing the potatoes with a little oil and baking them along with the fish fillets instead of deep-frying the dinner saves an amazing 138 calories and 16 grams of fat per serving.

ORIGINAL	MAKEOVER
514 Calories	376 Calories
25 g Fat	9 g Fat
2 g Sat. Fat	2 g Sat. Fat

MAKEOVER FISH AND CHIPS

FAST FIX ▶ Baked Walleye

We live close to Lake Erie, which is nicknamed the Walleye Capital of the World. I came up with this recipe as an easy way to serve that succulent fish.

—**JOYCE SZYMANSKI** MONROE, MI

START TO FINISH: 30 MIN.
MAKES: 4 SERVINGS

- ¾ **cup chopped onion**
- ¾ **cup chopped green pepper**
- ¾ **cup chopped celery**
- 1 **tablespoon dried parsley flakes**
- ½ **teaspoon garlic powder**
- ½ **teaspoon pepper**
- ½ **teaspoon seasoned salt**
- 1 **cup reduced-sodium V8 juice**
- 1 **pound walleye fillets**

1. In a small saucepan, bring the first eight ingredients to a boil. Reduce heat; simmer, uncovered, until vegetables are crisp-tender, stirring occasionally.

2. Place fish in a greased 13x9-in. baking dish. Pour vegetable mixture over the fish. Cover and bake at 350° for 15-20 minutes or until fish flakes easily with a fork.

PER SERVING *1 serving equals 137 cal., 1 g fat (0 sat. fat), 82 mg chol., 314 mg sodium, 9 g carb., 0 fiber, 22 g pro. Diabetic Exchanges: 3 lean meat, 1½ vegetable.*

CRUSTED RED SNAPPER

Crusted Red Snapper

This dish is so easy yet so elegant. The veggies steam and flavor the fish from below, while the crunchy topping adds instant appeal.

—**KELLY REMINGTON** ARCATA, CA

PREP: 25 MIN. • **BAKE:** 20 MIN.
MAKES: 6 SERVINGS

- 2 **medium tomatoes, chopped**
- 1 **each medium green, sweet yellow and red peppers, chopped**
- 1 **cup chopped leeks (white portion only)**
- ½ **cup chopped celery leaves**
- 2 **garlic cloves, minced**
- 6 **red snapper fillets (4 ounces each)**

TOPPING

- ½ **cup panko (Japanese) bread crumbs**
- ½ **cup coarsely crushed baked Parmesan and Tuscan herb potato chips**
- ¼ **cup grated Parmesan cheese**
- ½ **teaspoon salt**
- ½ **teaspoon paprika**
- ¼ **teaspoon cayenne pepper**
- ¼ **teaspoon pepper**
- 2 **tablespoons butter, melted**

1. In a 15x10x1-in. baking pan coated with cooking spray, combine the tomatoes, peppers, leeks, celery leaves and garlic; arrange fillets over the vegetable mixture.

2. In a small bowl, combine the bread crumbs, chips, cheese, salt, paprika, cayenne and pepper; stir in butter. Sprinkle over fillets. Bake, uncovered, at 425° for 18-22 minutes or until fish flakes easily with a fork.

PER SERVING *1 fillet with ⅔ cup vegetable mixture equals 237 cal., 7 g fat (3 g sat. fat), 53 mg chol., 396 mg sodium, 16 g carb., 3 g fiber, 26 g pro. Diabetic Exchanges: 3 lean meat, 1 vegetable, 1 fat, ½ starch.*

Italian Tilapia

This dish is so simple, you might as well add it to your list of go-to recipes.

—KIMBERLY MCGEE MOSHEIM, TN

PREP: 10 MIN. • **BAKE:** 40 MIN.
MAKES: 4 SERVINGS

- 4 tilapia fillets (6 ounces each)
- ¼ teaspoon pepper
- 1 can (14½ ounces) diced tomatoes with basil, oregano and garlic, drained
- 1 large onion, halved and thinly sliced
- 1 medium green pepper, julienned
- ¼ cup shredded Parmesan cheese

1. Preheat oven to 350°. Place tilapia in a 13x9-in. baking dish coated with cooking spray; sprinkle with pepper. Spoon tomatoes over tilapia; top with onion and green pepper.
2. Cover and bake 30 minutes. Uncover; sprinkle with cheese. Bake 10-15 minutes longer or until fish flakes easily with a fork.
PER SERVING *1 serving equals 215 cal., 4 g fat (2 g sat. fat), 86 mg chol., 645 mg sodium, 12 g carb., 2 g fiber, 36 g pro.* **Diabetic Exchanges:** *4 lean meat, 2 vegetable.*

TILAPIA TOSTADAS

FAST FIX # Tilapia Tostadas

Even my non-fish-loving family enjoys this Southwest specialty. It's a real winner.

—JENNIFER KOLB OVERLAND PARK, KS

START TO FINISH: 30 MIN.
MAKES: 4 SERVINGS

- ¼ cup all-purpose flour
- 1 teaspoon chili powder
- ½ teaspoon salt
- ½ teaspoon pepper
- ¼ teaspoon garlic powder
- 4 tilapia fillets (6 ounces each)
- 1 tablespoon butter
- 8 corn tortillas (6 inches)
  Cooking spray
- 2 cups angel hair coleslaw mix
- 2 tablespoons reduced-fat mayonnaise
- 2 tablespoons reduced-fat sour cream
- 1 tablespoon lime juice
- 1 teaspoon grated lime peel
- 1 cup canned black beans, rinsed and drained
- ½ avocado, thinly sliced

1. In a large resealable plastic bag, combine the flour, chili powder, salt, pepper and garlic powder. Add tilapia fillets, one at a time, and shake to coat.
2. In a large nonstick skillet over medium heat, cook fillets in butter for 5-6 minutes on each side or until fish flakes easily with a fork. Meanwhile, place tortillas on a baking sheet and spritz with cooking spray. Broil 3-4 in. from the heat for 2-3 minutes on each side or until crisp.
3. In a small bowl, toss the coleslaw mix, mayonnaise, sour cream, lime juice and peel. Cut fish into large pieces. On each tortilla, layer coleslaw, black beans, fish and avocado.
PER SERVING *2 tostadas equals 437 cal., 12 g fat (4 g sat. fat), 95 mg chol., 659 mg sodium, 44 g carb., 7 g fiber, 40 g pro.* **Diabetic Exchanges:** *5 lean meat, 3 starch, 1½ fat.*

LEMONY PARSLEY BAKED COD

FAST FIX Lemony Parsley Baked Cod

If there's one thing I hate, it's overcooking a good piece of fish. The trick is to cook the fillets at a high temperature for a short amount of time. It'll keep the fish moist and tender.

—**SHERRY DAY** PINCKNEY, MI

START TO FINISH: 25 MIN.
MAKES: 4 SERVINGS

- 3 **tablespoons minced fresh parsley**
- 2 **tablespoons lemon juice**
- 1 **tablespoon grated lemon peel**
- 1 **tablespoon olive oil**
- 2 **garlic cloves, minced**
- ¼ **teaspoon salt**
- ⅛ **teaspoon pepper**
- 4 **cod fillets (6 ounces each)**
- 2 **green onions, chopped**

Preheat oven to 400°. In a small bowl, mix the first seven ingredients. Place cod in an ungreased 11x7-in. baking dish; top with parsley mixture. Sprinkle with green onions. Bake, covered, 10-15 minutes or until fish flakes easily with a fork.

PER SERVING *1 fillet equals 161 cal., 4 g fat (1 g sat. fat), 65 mg chol., 95 mg sodium, 2 g carb., 1 g fiber, 27 g pro. **Diabetic Exchanges:** 4 lean meat, ½ fat.*

TOP TIP

You can use a less expensive olive oil than virgin or extra-virgin for cooking and baking. The higher grades have a more delicate flavor that shines in salads and uncooked foods but is generally lost in recipes that require cooking. Pure olive oil works fine— and sometimes even better—for cooked recipes.

FAST FIX Shrimp Artichoke Pasta

This healthy pasta looks as if it came from an Italian restaurant. When I'm in a rush, I use jarred tomato sauce and omit the tomatoes and seasonings. You can also fix this ahead and reheat it for convenience.

—**NANCY DEANS** ACTON, ME

START TO FINISH: 30 MIN.
MAKES: 6 SERVINGS

- 9 **ounces uncooked linguine**
- 2 **tablespoons olive oil**
- 1 **cup sliced fresh mushrooms**
- 1 **pound uncooked medium shrimp, peeled and deveined**
- 3 **medium tomatoes, chopped**
- 1 **can (14 ounces) water-packed artichoke hearts, rinsed, drained and halved**
- 1 **can (6 ounces) pitted ripe olives, drained and halved**
- 2 **garlic cloves, minced**
- 1 **teaspoon dried oregano**
- ½ **teaspoon salt**
- ½ **teaspoon dried basil**
- ⅛ **teaspoon pepper**

1. Cook linguine according to package directions. Meanwhile, in a large skillet, heat oil over medium-high heat. Add mushrooms; cook and stir 4 minutes. Add remaining ingredients; cook and stir 5 minutes or until shrimp turn pink.

2. Drain the linguine; serve with the shrimp mixture.

PER SERVING *1 cup shrimp mixture with ¾ cup linguine equals 328 cal., 9 g fat (1 g sat. fat), 112 mg chol., 748 mg sodium, 41 g carb., 3 g fiber, 21 g pro. **Diabetic Exchanges:** 2 starch, 2 lean meat, 1½ fat, 1 vegetable.*

SHRIMP ARTICHOKE PASTA

FAST FIX ▶ Tuna with Citrus Ponzu Sauce

I like this Asian-inspired tuna because it's easy to prepare, delicious and good for you, too. It's a popular dish with my friends.

—DIANE HALFERTY CORPUS CHRISTI, TX

START TO FINISH: 20 MIN.
MAKES: 4 SERVINGS

- ½ teaspoon Chinese five-spice powder
- ¼ teaspoon salt
- ¼ teaspoon cayenne pepper
- 4 tuna steaks (6 ounces each)
- 1 tablespoon canola oil
- ¼ cup orange juice
- 2 green onions, thinly sliced
- 1 tablespoon lemon juice
- 1 tablespoon reduced-sodium soy sauce
- 2 teaspoons rice vinegar
- 1 teaspoon brown sugar
- ¼ teaspoon minced fresh gingerroot

1. Combine the five-spice powder, salt and cayenne; sprinkle over tuna steaks. In a large skillet, cook tuna in oil over medium heat for 2-3 minutes on each side for medium-rare or until slightly pink in the center; remove and keep warm.
2. Combine the orange juice, onions, lemon juice, soy sauce, vinegar, brown sugar and ginger; pour into skillet. Cook for 1-2 minutes or until slightly thickened. Serve with tuna.

PER SERVING *1 tuna steak with 1 tablespoon sauce equals 234 cal., 5 g fat (1 g sat. fat), 77 mg chol., 364 mg sodium, 5 g carb., trace fiber, 40 g pro. Diabetic Exchanges: 5 lean meat, ½ fat.*

FAST FIX ▶ Tilapia with Jasmine Rice

This zesty tilapia is to die for. Fragrant jasmine rice brings a special touch to the meal. And it gets even better—each serving has only 5 grams of fat!

—SHIRL PARSONS CAPE CARTERET, NC

START TO FINISH: 30 MIN.
MAKES: 2 SERVINGS

- ¾ cup water
- ½ cup uncooked jasmine rice
- 1½ teaspoons butter
- ¼ teaspoon ground cumin
- ¼ teaspoon seafood seasoning
- ¼ teaspoon pepper
- ⅛ teaspoon salt
- 2 tilapia fillets (6 ounces each)
- ¼ cup fat-free Italian salad dressing

1. In a large saucepan, bring the water, rice and butter to a boil. Reduce the heat; cover and simmer for 15-20 minutes or until liquid is absorbed and rice is tender.
2. Combine the seasonings; sprinkle over fillets. Place salad dressing in a large skillet; cook over medium heat until heated through. Add fish; cook for 3-4 minutes on each side or until fish flakes easily with a fork. Serve with rice.

PER SERVING *1 fillet with ¾ cup rice equals 356 cal., 5 g fat (3 g sat. fat), 91 mg chol., 743 mg sodium, 41 g carb., 1 g fiber, 35 g pro. Diabetic Exchanges: 4 lean meat, 3 starch, ½ fat.*

TUNA WITH CITRUS PONZU SAUCE

Halibut Soft Tacos

FAST FIX

I sometimes serve the fish wrapped in lettuce instead of tortillas. Either way, the mango salsa tastes amazing with grilled halibut. This warm-weather favorite is quick, colorful and full of nutrients.

—**KRISTIN KOSSAK** BOZEMAN, MT

START TO FINISH: 30 MIN.
MAKES: 4 SERVINGS

- 1 medium mango, peeled and cubed
- ½ cup cubed avocado
- ¼ cup chopped red onion
- 2 tablespoons chopped seeded jalapeno pepper
- 1 tablespoon minced fresh cilantro
- 3 teaspoons olive oil, divided
- 1 teaspoon lemon juice
- 1 teaspoon honey
- 1 pound halibut steaks (¾ inch thick)
- ½ teaspoon salt
- ¼ teaspoon pepper
- 4 Bibb lettuce leaves
- 4 flour tortillas (6 inches), warmed
- 4 teaspoons sweet Thai chili sauce

1. In a small bowl, combine the mango, avocado, onion, jalapeno, cilantro, 2 teaspoons oil, lemon juice and honey; set aside. Brush halibut with remaining oil; sprinkle with salt and pepper.

2. Moisten a paper towel with cooking oil; using long-handled tongs, lightly coat the grill rack. Grill halibut, covered, over high heat or broil 3-4 in. from the heat for 3-5 minutes on each side or until fish flakes easily with a fork.

3. Place lettuce leaves on tortillas; top with fish and mango mixture. Drizzle with chili sauce.

NOTE *Wear disposable gloves when cutting hot peppers; the oils can burn skin. Avoid touching your face.*

PER SERVING *1 taco with ⅓ cup mango salsa equals 330 cal., 12 g fat (1 g sat. fat), 36 mg chol., 648 mg sodium, 28 g carb., 2 g fiber, 28 g pro.* **Diabetic Exchanges:** *3 lean meat, 2 starch, 1 fat.*

Tangerine Cashew Snapper

FAST FIX

Sweet from the tangerines and crunchy from chopped cashews, these healthy snapper fillets are pleasing to the palate.

—**CRYSTAL JO BRUNS** ILIFF, CO

START TO FINISH: 30 MIN.
MAKES: 4 SERVINGS

- 4 tangerines
- 2 tablespoons lime juice
- 2 tablespoons reduced-sodium soy sauce
- 1 tablespoon brown sugar
- 2 teaspoons minced fresh gingerroot
- 1 teaspoon sesame oil
- ⅛ teaspoon crushed red pepper flakes
- 4 red snapper fillets (4 ounces each)
- ⅓ cup chopped unsalted cashews
- 2 green onions, thinly sliced

1. Peel, slice and remove seeds from two tangerines; chop the fruit and place in a small bowl. Squeeze juice from remaining tangerines; add to bowl. Stir in the lime juice, soy sauce, brown sugar, ginger, sesame oil and pepper flakes.

2. Place fillets in a 13x9-in. baking dish coated with cooking spray. Pour tangerine mixture over fillets; sprinkle with cashews and green onions. Bake, uncovered, at 425° for 15-20 minutes or until fish flakes easily with a fork.

PER SERVING *1 fillet with about 2 tablespoons sauce equals 260 cal., 8 g fat (2 g sat. fat), 40 mg chol., 358 mg sodium, 22 g carb., 2 g fiber, 26 g pro.* **Diabetic Exchanges:** *3 lean meat, 1 fruit, 1 fat.*

PEKING SHRIMP

3. Stir cornstarch mixture and add to the pan. Bring to a boil; cook and stir for 2 minutes or until thickened. Add tomato; heat through. Serve with rice if desired.

PER SERVING *¾ cup (calculated without rice) equals 237 cal., 8 g fat (1 g sat. fat), 168 mg chol., 532 mg sodium, 21 g carb., 1 g fiber, 19 g pro.* **Diabetic Exchanges:** *2 lean meat, 1½ fat, 1 starch, 1 vegetable.*

FAST FIX ▶ Broiled Parmesan Tilapia

Even picky eaters will find a way to love fish when you plate up this toasty Parmesan fish. I serve the fillets with mashed cauliflower and a green salad for a low-calorie meal everyone can enjoy.

—**TRISHA KRUSE** EAGLE, ID

START TO FINISH: 20 MIN.
MAKES: 6 SERVINGS

- 6 **tilapia fillets (6 ounces each)**
- ¼ **cup grated Parmesan cheese**
- ¼ **cup reduced-fat mayonnaise**
- 2 **tablespoons lemon juice**
- 1 **tablespoon butter, softened**
- 1 **garlic clove, minced**
- 1 **teaspoon minced fresh basil or ¼ teaspoon dried basil**
- ½ **teaspoon seafood seasoning**

1. Place fillets on a broiler pan coated with cooking spray. In a small bowl, combine remaining ingredients; spread over fillets.
2. Broil 3-4 in. from the heat for 10-12 minutes or until fish flakes easily with a fork.

PER SERVING *1 fillet equals 207 cal., 8 g fat (3 g sat. fat), 94 mg chol., 260 mg sodium, 2 g carb., trace fiber, 33 g pro.* **Diabetic Exchanges:** *5 lean meat, 1 fat.*

FAST FIX ▶ Peking Shrimp

In the summer, we spend as much time as possible at our vacation home in a beach town. I prepare lots of seafood because it's so fresh and readily available there, but this main dish is a year-round favorite.

—**JANET EDWARDS** BEAVERTON, OR

START TO FINISH: 25 MIN.
MAKES: 4 SERVINGS

- 1 **tablespoon cornstarch**
- ¼ **cup cold water**
- ¼ **cup corn syrup**
- 2 **tablespoons reduced-sodium soy sauce**
- 2 **tablespoons sherry or chicken broth**
- 1 **garlic clove, minced**
- ¼ **teaspoon ground ginger**
- 1 **small green pepper, cut into 1-inch pieces**
- 2 **tablespoons canola oil**
- 1 **pound uncooked medium shrimp, peeled and deveined**
- 1 **medium tomato, cut into wedges Hot cooked rice, optional**

1. In a small bowl, combine the cornstarch and water until smooth. Stir in the corn syrup, soy sauce, sherry, garlic and ginger; set aside.
2. In a nonstick skillet or wok, stir-fry green pepper in oil for 3 minutes. Add shrimp; cook 3 minutes longer or until shrimp turn pink.

FAST FIX ▶

Walnut-Crusted Salmon

Whenever I can get salmon for a good price, I always turn to this simple and delicious recipe. It's good served with mashed potatoes and fresh green beans.

—EDIE DESPAIN LOGAN, UT

START TO FINISH: 25 MIN.
MAKES: 4 SERVINGS

- 4 **salmon fillets (4 ounces each)**
- 4 **teaspoons Dijon mustard**
- 4 **teaspoons honey**
- 2 **slices whole wheat bread, torn into pieces**
- 3 **tablespoons finely chopped walnuts**
- 2 **teaspoons canola oil**
- ½ **teaspoon dried thyme**

1. Preheat oven to 400°. Place salmon on a baking sheet coated with cooking spray. Mix mustard and honey; brush over salmon. Place bread in a food processor; pulse until coarse crumbs form. Transfer to a small bowl. Stir in the walnuts, oil and thyme; press onto salmon.
2. Bake 12-15 minutes or until topping is lightly browned and fish just begins to flake easily with a fork.

PER SERVING *1 fillet equals 295 cal., 17 g fat (3 g sat. fat), 57 mg chol., 243 mg sodium, 13 g carb., 1 g fiber, 22 g pro.* **Diabetic Exchanges:** *3 lean meat, 1 starch, ½ fat.*

FAST FIX ▶ # Greek Fish Fillets

Olives, onion, dill and feta cheese combine in this tangy Greek-inspired topping to boost the flavor of tilapia or your favorite white fish. I usually serve it with a side of rice.

—JENNIFER MASLOWSKI NEW YORK, NY

START TO FINISH: 25 MIN.
MAKES: 4 SERVINGS

- 4 **tilapia fillets (4 ounces each)**
- ⅛ **teaspoon salt**
- ⅛ **teaspoon pepper**
- 2 **tablespoons plain yogurt**
- 1 **tablespoon butter, softened**
- 1½ **teaspoons lime juice**
- ½ **small red onion, finely chopped**
- ¼ **cup pitted Greek olives**
- ½ **teaspoon dill weed**
- ¼ **teaspoon paprika**
- ⅛ **teaspoon garlic powder**
- ¼ **cup crumbled feta cheese**

1. Sprinkle tilapia with salt and pepper. Place on a broiler pan coated with cooking spray.
2. Combine the yogurt, butter and lime juice. Stir in the onion, olives and seasonings. Spread down the middle of each fillet; sprinkle with feta cheese.
3. Broil 3-4 in. from the heat for 6-9 minutes or until fish flakes easily with a fork.

PER SERVING *1 fillet equals 170 cal., 7 g fat (3 g sat. fat), 67 mg chol., 344 mg sodium, 3 g carb., 1 g fiber, 23 g pro.* **Diabetic Exchanges:** *3 lean meat, 1½ fat.*

GREEK FISH FILLETS

FAST FIX

Homemade Fish Sticks

I'm a nutritionist and I needed a healthy fish fix. Moist inside and crunchy outside, these fish sticks are wonderful with oven fries or roasted veggies and a low-fat homemade tartar sauce.

—JENNIFER ROWLAND ELIZABETHTOWN, KY

START TO FINISH: 25 MIN.
MAKES: 2 SERVINGS

- ½ **cup dry bread crumbs**
- ½ **teaspoon salt**
- ½ **teaspoon paprika**
- ½ **teaspoon lemon-pepper seasoning**
- ½ **cup all-purpose flour**
- 1 **large egg, beaten**
- ¾ **pound cod fillets, cut into 1-inch strips**
  Butter-flavored cooking spray

1. Preheat oven to 400°. In a shallow bowl, mix bread crumbs and seasonings. Place flour and egg in separate shallow bowls. Dip fish in flour to coat both sides; shake off excess. Dip in the egg, then in the crumb mixture, patting to help coating adhere.

2. Place on a baking sheet coated with cooking spray; spritz with butter-flavored cooking spray. Bake for 10-12 minutes or until fish just begins to flake easily with a fork, turning once.

PER SERVING *1 serving equals 278 cal., 4 g fat (1 g sat. fat), 129 mg chol., 718 mg sodium, 25 g carb., 1 g fiber, 33 g pro.* **Diabetic Exchanges:** *4 lean meat, 1½ starch.*

Tasty Tuna Casserole

This is not your usual tuna casserole. The macaroni and tuna are coated in a rich and creamy sauce with a kiss of tomato.

—ELSIE EPP NEWTON, KS

PREP: 20 MIN. • **BAKE:** 20 MIN.
MAKES: 4 SERVINGS

- 2 **cups uncooked elbow macaroni**
- 1 **can (12 ounces) albacore white tuna in water**
- 1 **can (8 ounces) tomato sauce**
- 4 **ounces reduced-fat cream cheese, cubed**
- 1 **small onion, finely chopped**
- ¼ **teaspoon salt**
- ½ **teaspoon dried oregano**

1. Cook macaroni according to package directions. Meanwhile, in a large bowl, combine the remaining ingredients. Drain macaroni; stir into tuna mixture.

2. Transfer to a 2-qt. baking dish coated with cooking spray. Cover and bake at 350° for 20-25 minutes or until heated through.

PER SERVING *1½ cups equals 334 cal., 9 g fat (5 g sat. fat), 56 mg chol., 851 mg sodium, 33 g carb., 2 g fiber, 29 g pro.* **Diabetic Exchanges:** *3 lean meat, 2 starch, 1 fat.*

HOMEMADE FISH STICKS

Sweet-Chili Salmon with Blackberries

My garden is often my cooking inspiration. Because I tend a large berry patch, I have the joy of using just-picked berries to add natural sweetness and pop to savory dishes.

—ROXANNE CHAN ALBANY, CA

START TO FINISH: 25 MIN.
MAKES: 4 SERVINGS

- 1 **cup fresh or frozen blackberries, thawed**
- 1 **cup finely chopped English cucumber**
- 1 **green onion, finely chopped**
- 2 **tablespoons sweet chili sauce, divided**
- 4 **salmon fillets (6 ounces each)**
- ½ **teaspoon salt**
- ½ **teaspoon pepper**

1. In a small bowl, combine the blackberries, cucumber, green onion and 1 tablespoon chili sauce; toss to coat. Moisten a paper towel with cooking oil; using long-handled tongs, rub on grill rack to coat lightly. Sprinkle salmon with salt and pepper.
2. Place fillets on grill rack, skin side down. Grill fish, covered, over medium-high heat or broil 4 in. from heat 10-12 minutes or until fish flakes easily with a fork, brushing with remaining chili sauce during the last 2-3 minutes of cooking. Serve with blackberry mixture.
PER SERVING *1 fillet with ½ cup berry mixture equals 303 cal., 16 g fat (3 g sat. fat), 85 mg chol., 510 mg sodium, 9 g carb., 2 g fiber, 30 g pro. Diabetic Exchanges: 5 lean meat, ½ starch.*

SCALLOPS WITH CITRUS GLAZE

Scallops with Citrus Glaze

These scallops are especially good when served on steamed rice with a green salad on the side.

—PATRICIA NIEH PORTOLA VALLEY, CA

START TO FINISH: 20 MIN.
MAKES: 4 SERVINGS

- 12 **sea scallops (about 1½ pounds)**
- ½ **teaspoon pepper**
- ¼ **teaspoon salt**
- 2 **tablespoons olive oil, divided**
- 4 **garlic cloves, minced**
- ½ **cup orange juice**
- ¼ **cup lemon juice**
- 1 **tablespoon reduced-sodium soy sauce**
- ½ **teaspoon grated orange peel**

1. Sprinkle scallops with pepper and salt. In a large skillet, saute scallops in 1 tablespoon oil until firm and opaque. Remove and keep warm.
2. In the same skillet, cook garlic in remaining oil for 1 minute. Add the juices, soy sauce and orange peel. Bring to a boil; cook and stir for 5 minutes or until thickened. Serve with scallops.
PER SERVING *3 scallops with 2 teaspoons glaze equals 235 cal., 8 g fat (1 g sat. fat), 56 mg chol., 574 mg sodium, 10 g carb., trace fiber, 29 g pro. Diabetic Exchanges: 4 lean meat, 1½ fat.*

TILAPIA WITH TOMATO-ORANGE RELISH

Tilapia with Tomato-Orange Relish

The mild flavor and tender texture of tilapia go beautifully with fresh relish. This dish makes a big impression with just a little work.

—HELEN CONWELL PORTLAND, OR

START TO FINISH: 25 MIN.
MAKES: 6 SERVINGS

- 6 tilapia fillets (6 ounces each)
- 3 tablespoons butter, melted
- ½ teaspoon salt, divided
- ½ teaspoon lemon-pepper seasoning
- 1 medium tomato, seeded and chopped
- 1 medium orange, peeled, sectioned and chopped
- ⅓ cup finely chopped red onion
- 1 tablespoon capers, drained
- 1½ tablespoons brown sugar
- 1 tablespoon red wine vinegar

1. Place fish in a greased 15x10x1-in. baking pan. Drizzle with butter; sprinkle with ¼ teaspoon salt and the lemon pepper. Bake at 425° for 10 minutes or until fish flakes easily with a fork.

2. In a small bowl, combine the tomato, orange, onion, capers, brown sugar, vinegar and remaining salt. Serve with fish.

PER SERVING *1 fillet with 8 teaspoons relish equals 219 cal., 7 g fat (4 g sat. fat), 98 mg chol., 381 mg sodium, 7 g carb., 1 g fiber, 32 g pro.* ***Diabetic Exchanges:*** *5 lean meat, 1 fat, ½ starch.*

Open-Faced Salmon Sandwiches

My husband and I love fish of any kind, and this recipe is a healthy, delicious way for us to enjoy burgers. I keep several cans of salmon in my pantry so we can whip these up whenever we want. They're quick for unexpected company, too.

—KATNEE CABECEIRAS SOUTH PRAIRIE, WA

START TO FINISH: 25 MIN.
MAKES: 4 SERVINGS

- 1 large egg, lightly beaten
- 1 small onion, finely chopped
- 1 small green pepper, finely chopped
- ⅓ cup soft bread crumbs
- 1 tablespoon lemon juice
- 1 teaspoon reduced-sodium teriyaki sauce
- ¼ teaspoon dried parsley flakes
- ¼ teaspoon dried basil
- ¼ teaspoon pepper
- 1 can (14¾ ounces) salmon, drained, bones and skin removed
- 2 English muffins, split and toasted
  Lettuce leaves and tomato slices, optional

1. In a small bowl, combine the first nine ingredients. Fold in salmon. Shape into four patties.

2. In a large nonstick skillet coated with cooking spray, cook patties over medium heat for 4-5 minutes on each side or until lightly browned. Serve on English muffin halves with lettuce and tomato if desired.

PER SERVING *1 sandwich equals 270 cal., 10 g fat (2 g sat. fat), 99 mg chol., 757 mg sodium, 19 g carb., 2 g fiber, 26 g pro.* ***Diabetic Exchanges:*** *3 lean meat, 1 starch.*

FAST FIX ▸ Shrimp and Scallop Couscous

This quick and satisfying skillet dish is a favorite of mine. It uses summer veggies in a sensational blend of flavors.

—MARVIN MEUSER JR. PRINCETON, IN

START TO FINISH: 30 MIN.
MAKES: 4 SERVINGS

- 2 medium zucchini, julienned
- 1 medium green pepper, julienned
- 2 tablespoons olive oil
- 3 plum tomatoes, chopped
- 4 green onions, chopped
- 1 tablespoon minced fresh basil or 1 teaspoon dried basil
- 3 teaspoons chili powder
- 1 garlic clove, minced
- ½ teaspoon dried oregano
- ½ pound uncooked medium shrimp, peeled and deveined
- ½ pound bay scallops
- ¼ teaspoon salt
- ⅛ teaspoon pepper
  Hot cooked couscous or rice
  Thinly sliced fresh basil leaves, optional

1. In a large skillet, saute zucchini and green pepper in oil until tender. Add the tomatoes, green onions, basil, chili powder, garlic and oregano. Bring to a boil. Reduce heat; simmer, uncovered, for 5 minutes.

2. Stir in the shrimp, scallops, salt and pepper. Return to a boil. Reduce heat; simmer, uncovered, for 5 minutes or until shrimp turn pink and scallops are opaque. Serve with couscous. Garnish with sliced basil if desired.

PER SERVING *1 cup (calculated without couscous) equals 201 cal., 9 g fat (1 g sat. fat), 88 mg chol., 342 mg sodium, 11 g carb., 3 g fiber, 21 g pro.* **Diabetic Exchanges:** *3 lean meat, 1½ fat, 1 vegetable.*

SHRIMP AND SCALLOP COUSCOUS

Coconut Shrimp with Dipping Sauce

With crispy coconut breading and a sweet apricot sauce, these delicious shrimp would be ideal for any occasion, from an appetizer party to a weeknight dinner.

—TASTE OF HOME TEST KITCHEN

PREP: 1 HOUR + MARINATING
BAKE: 15 MIN. • **MAKES:** 5 SERVINGS

- 1 **can (13.66 ounces) light coconut milk, divided**
- 1 **jalapeno pepper, seeded and chopped**
- ¼ **cup minced fresh cilantro**
- 1¼ **pounds uncooked medium shrimp**
- ¾ **cup all-purpose flour**
- 4 **large egg whites**
- ¾ **cup panko (Japanese) bread crumbs**
- ¾ **cup flaked coconut, lightly toasted**
- ⅓ **cup reduced-sugar apricot preserves**
- 1 **teaspoon spicy brown mustard**

1. Place 2 tablespoons coconut milk in a small bowl; cover and refrigerate. In a large resealable plastic bag, combine the jalapeno, cilantro and remaining coconut milk. Peel and devein shrimp, leaving tails on. Add to bag; seal and turn to coat. Refrigerate for 1 hour.

2. Place flour in a shallow bowl. In another bowl, lightly beat the egg whites. In a third bowl, combine bread crumbs and coconut. Drain shrimp and discard marinade. Dip shrimp in flour and egg whites, then roll in crumb mixture.

3. Place shrimp on a baking sheet coated with cooking spray. Bake at 400° for 7-9 minutes on each side or until lightly browned. Meanwhile, for dipping sauce, add preserves and mustard to the reserved coconut milk. Serve with shrimp.

NOTE *Wear disposable gloves when cutting hot peppers; the oils can burn skin. Avoid touching your face.*

PER SERVING *About 10 shrimp with 5 teaspoons sauce equals 324 cal., 11 g fat (8 g sat. fat), 168 mg chol., 316 mg sodium, 30 g carb., 1 g fiber, 23 g pro.* **Diabetic Exchanges:** *3 lean meat, 2 starch, 2 fat.*

FAST FIX ▶ Egg Foo Yong

Forget ordering Chinese food—make it at home tonight! You can throw together this easy version of a classic in only about half an hour. The authentic flavors will have you hooked.

—SHERRI MELOTIK OAK CREEK, WI

START TO FINISH: 30 MIN.
MAKES: 4 SERVINGS

- 1 **can (14 ounces) chop suey vegetables, drained**
- ½ **pound peeled and deveined cooked small shrimp, coarsely chopped**
- 4 **green onions, thinly sliced**
- 4 **large eggs, beaten**
- 2 **tablespoons canola oil**

GREEN PEA SAUCE

- 2 **tablespoons cornstarch**
- 1 **teaspoon chicken bouillon granules**
- 2 **cups cold water**
- 1½ **teaspoons reduced-sodium soy sauce**
- ½ **cup frozen peas, thawed**

1. In a large bowl, combine the chop suey vegetables, shrimp and green onions. Stir in eggs. In a large nonstick skillet, heat 1 teaspoon oil. Drop the vegetable mixture by ¼ cupfuls into skillet. Cook in batches until browned on both sides, using the remaining oil as needed.

2. In a small saucepan, combine cornstarch and bouillon. Gradually stir in water and soy sauce until smooth. Bring to a boil; cook and stir for 2 minutes or until thickened. Add peas and heat through. Serve with egg foo yong.

PER SERVING *3 patties with ½ cup sauce equals 242 cal., 13 g fat (2 g sat. fat), 298 mg chol., 497 mg sodium, 10 g carb., 2 g fiber, 20 g pro.* **Diabetic Exchanges:** *3 lean meat, 1½ fat, ½ starch.*

FAST FIX ▶

Orange Tilapia in Parchment

Sweet orange juice and spicy cayenne pepper give tilapia fabulous flavor. A bonus? Cleanup is a breeze!

—TIFFANY DIEBOLD NASHVILLE, TN

START TO FINISH: 30 MIN.
MAKES: 4 SERVINGS

- ¼ **cup orange juice**
- 4 **teaspoons grated orange peel**
- ¼ **teaspoon salt**
- ¼ **teaspoon cayenne pepper**
- ¼ **teaspoon pepper**
- 4 **tilapia fillets (6 ounces each)**
- ½ **cup julienned carrot**
- ½ **cup julienned zucchini**

1. Preheat oven to 450°. In a small bowl, combine first five ingredients; set aside. Cut parchment paper or heavy-duty foil into four 18x12-in. lengths; place a fish fillet on each. Top with carrot and zucchini; drizzle with orange juice mixture.

2. Fold parchment paper over fish. Working from bottom inside corner, fold up about ¾ in. of the paper and crimp both layers to seal. Repeat, folding edges up and crimping, until a half-moon-shaped packet is formed. Repeat for remaining packets. Place on baking sheets.

3. Bake 12-15 minutes or until fish flakes easily with a fork. Open packets carefully to allow steam to escape.

PER SERVING *1 packet equals 158 cal., 2 g fat (1 g sat. fat), 83 mg chol., 220 mg sodium, 4 g carb., 1 g fiber, 32 g pro.* **Diabetic Exchange:** *5 lean meat.*

TERIYAKI MAHI MAHI

⑤ INGREDIENTS FAST FIX ▶

Teriyaki Mahi Mahi

My versatile recipe is tasty with salad, vegetables or rice, and it works well with cod or halibut fillets, too. Blot the fish thoroughly with paper towels before cooking so a nice brown crust can form.

—MICHELLE IBARRIENTOS TORRANCE, CA

START TO FINISH: 20 MIN.
MAKES: 4 SERVINGS

- 4 **mahi mahi fillets (6 ounces each)**
- ¼ **teaspoon garlic powder**
- ¼ **teaspoon pepper**
- 1 **tablespoon canola oil**
- 1 **teaspoon minced fresh gingerroot**
- ¼ **cup reduced-sodium teriyaki sauce**

1. Sprinkle mahi mahi with garlic powder and pepper. In a large skillet, cook mahi mahi in oil over medium-high heat for 4-5 minutes on each side or until fish flakes easily with a fork. Remove and keep warm.

2. In the same skillet, saute ginger for 30 seconds. Stir in teriyaki sauce; heat through. Serve over mahi mahi.

PER SERVING *1 fish fillet with 1 tablespoon sauce equals 192 cal., 5 g fat (1 g sat. fat), 124 mg chol., 470 mg sodium, 3 g carb., trace fiber, 33 g pro.* **Diabetic Exchanges:** *5 lean meat, ½ fat.*

⑤ INGREDIENTS
Crumb-Topped Haddock

My delightful fish with a creamy sauce and crisp cracker topping is a breeze to make.

—**DEBBIE SOLT** LEWISTOWN, PA

PREP: 5 MIN. • **BAKE:** 35 MIN.
MAKES: 6 SERVINGS

- 2 **pounds haddock or cod fillets**
- 1 **can (10¾ ounces) condensed cream of shrimp soup, undiluted**
- 1 **teaspoon grated onion**
- 1 **teaspoon Worcestershire sauce**
- 1 **cup crushed Ritz crackers (about 25 crackers)**

1. Preheat oven to 375°. Arrange fillets in a greased 13x9-in. baking dish. Combine the soup, onion and Worcestershire sauce; pour over fish.
2. Bake, uncovered, 20 minutes. Sprinkle with cracker crumbs. Bake 15 minutes longer or until fish flakes easily with a fork.

PER SERVING *1 serving equals 248 cal., 7 g fat (2 g sat. fat), 94 mg chol., 631 mg sodium, 14 g carb., trace fiber, 31 g pro.* **Diabetic Exchanges:** *lean meat, 1 starch, 1 fat.*

⑤ INGREDIENTS FAST FIX ▶
Honey Grilled Shrimp

My husband got this super-simple recipe from a man who sold shrimp at the fish market. It's now become our family's absolute favorite shrimp recipe. We've served it on many occasions, and always with great success. Enjoy!

—**LISA BLACKWELL** HENDERSON, NC

PREP: 20 MIN. + MARINATING
GRILL: 10 MIN. • **MAKES:** 8 SERVINGS

- 1 **bottle (8 ounces) Italian salad dressing**

- 1 **cup honey**
- ½ **teaspoon minced garlic**
- 2 **pounds uncooked medium shrimp, peeled and deveined**

1. In a small bowl, combine salad dressing, honey and garlic; set aside ½ cup. Pour remaining marinade into a large resealable plastic bag; add shrimp. Seal bag and turn to coat; refrigerate for 30 minutes. Cover and refrigerate reserved marinade.
2. Drain shrimp and discard marinade. Thread shrimp onto eight metal or soaked wooden skewers. Moisten a paper towel with cooking oil; using long-handled tongs, rub on grill rack to coat lightly.
3. Grill, uncovered, over medium heat or broil 4 in. from the heat for 1½-2 minutes on each side. Baste with reserved marinade. Grill or broil 2-3 minutes longer or until the shrimp are pink and firm, turning and basting frequently.

PER SERVING *1 serving equals 175 cal., 5 g fat (1 g sat. fat), 168 mg chol., 383 mg sodium, 14 g carb., trace fiber, 18 g pro.* **Diabetic Exchanges:** *3 lean meat, 1 starch, 1 fat.*

CRUMB-TOPPED HADDOCK

FAST FIX ▶ Scallops with Chipotle-Orange Sauce

We love this spicy seafood dish. It makes a special dinner for two, or you can double the recipe for dinner guests.

—**JAN JUSTICE** CATLETTSBURG, KY

START TO FINISH: 15 MIN.
MAKES: 2 SERVINGS

- ¾ **pound sea scallops**
- ¼ **teaspoon paprika**
- ¼ **teaspoon salt, divided**
- 2 **teaspoons butter**
- ¼ **cup orange juice**
- ¼ **teaspoon ground chipotle pepper**
  Hot cooked linguine, optional
- 2 **tablespoons thinly sliced green onion**

1. Sprinkle scallops with paprika and ⅛ teaspoon salt. In a nonstick skillet coated with cooking spray, melt butter over medium heat. Add scallops; cook for 3-4 minutes on each side or until firm and opaque.
2. Add orange juice and remaining salt to the pan; bring to a boil. Remove from the heat; stir in chipotle pepper.
3. Serve over linguine if desired. Garnish with green onion.
PER SERVING *1 serving (calculated without linguine) equals 200 cal., 5 g fat (3 g sat. fat), 66 mg chol., 608 mg sodium, 8 g carb., trace fiber, 29 g pro.* ***Diabetic Exchanges:*** *4 lean meat, 1 fat.*

COD DELIGHT

FAST FIX ▶ Cod Delight

I used to make this in the oven, but then I discovered that the microwave lets me enjoy it even faster. It's a pretty dish to serve to company. In fact, many friends and extended family now cook this at home.

—**NANCY DAUGHERTY** CORTLAND, OH

START TO FINISH: 15 MIN.
MAKES: 4 SERVINGS

- 1 **small tomato, chopped**
- ⅓ **cup finely chopped onion**
- 2 **tablespoons water**
- 2 **tablespoons canola oil**
- 4 **to 5 teaspoons lemon juice**
- 1 **teaspoon dried parsley flakes**
- ½ **teaspoon dried basil**
- 1 **small garlic clove, minced**
- ⅛ **teaspoon salt**
- 4 **cod fillets (4 ounces each)**
- 1 **teaspoon seafood seasoning**

In a small bowl, combine the first nine ingredients. Place cod in an 11x7-in. baking dish; top with tomato mixture. Sprinkle with seafood seasoning. Microwave, covered, on high 5-6 minutes or until fish just begins to flake easily with a fork.
NOTE *This recipe was tested in a 1,100-watt microwave.*
PER SERVING *1 serving equals 154 cal., 8 g fat (1 g sat. fat), 43 mg chol., 304 mg sodium, 3 g carb., 1 g fiber, 18 g pro.* ***Diabetic Exchanges:*** *3 lean meat, 1 fat.*

JENNIFER FISHER'S
TROPICAL FUSION SALAD WITH
SPICY TORTILLA RIBBONS *PAGE 235*

Meatless

Along with makeovers of favorites like **classic mac & cheese,** these pages are stocked with **heart-smart meatless dishes** for any occasion. Whether you need a **quick, healthy dinner** for Meatless Monday or a festive lasagna **worthy of a special occasion,** just turn here for **comfort-food specialties** that flavorfully shake up your dinner routine.

**VERONICA VICHIT-VADAKAN'S
PHILLY CHEESE FAKES FOR TWO**

PAGE 239

**KATHRYN CONRAD'S
HERB GARDEN LASAGNAS**

PAGE 241

**SHIRLEY KACMARIK'S
SPINACH-TOMATO PHYLLO BAKE**

PAGE 236

FAST FIX ▶ Gnocchi with White Beans

Here's one of those no-muss, no-fuss recipes you can toss together in a single pan. It's also good with crumbled Italian chicken sausage if you need to please any meat lovers in your house.

—JULI MEYERS HINESVILLE, GA

START TO FINISH: 30 MIN.
MAKES: 6 SERVINGS

- 1 tablespoon olive oil
- 1 medium onion, chopped
- 2 garlic cloves, minced
- 1 package (16 ounces) potato gnocchi
- 1 can (15 ounces) white kidney or cannellini beans, rinsed and drained
- 1 can (14½ ounces) Italian diced tomatoes, undrained
- 1 package (6 ounces) fresh baby spinach
- ¼ teaspoon pepper
- ½ cup shredded part-skim mozzarella cheese
- 3 tablespoons grated Parmesan cheese

1. In a large skillet, heat oil over medium-high heat. Add onion; cook and stir until tender. Add garlic and cook 1 minute longer. Add gnocchi; cook and stir 5-6 minutes or until golden brown. Stir in beans, tomatoes, spinach and pepper. Heat through.
2. Sprinkle with cheeses. Cover and remove from the heat. Let stand 3-4 minutes or until cheese is melted.
NOTE *Look for potato gnocchi in the pasta or frozen foods section.*
PER SERVING *1 cup equals 307 cal., 6 g fat (2 g sat. fat), 13 mg chol., 789 mg sodium, 50 g carb., 6 g fiber, 13 g pro.*

GNOCCHI WITH WHITE BEANS

FAST FIX ▶

Mushroom Burgers

Even the most stubborn meat-and-potatoes people have a change of heart when they bite into of one of these cheddar mushroom burgers.

—DENISE HOLLEBEKE PENHOLD, AB

START TO FINISH: 25 MIN.
MAKES: 4 SERVINGS

- 2 cups finely chopped fresh mushrooms
- 2 large eggs, lightly beaten
- ½ cup dry bread crumbs
- ½ cup shredded cheddar cheese
- ½ cup finely chopped onion
- ¼ cup all-purpose flour
- ½ teaspoon salt
- ¼ teaspoon dried thyme
- ¼ teaspoon pepper
- 1 tablespoon canola oil
- 4 whole wheat hamburger buns, split
- 4 lettuce leaves

1. In a large bowl, combine the first nine ingredients. Shape into four ¾-in.-thick patties.
2. In a large skillet, heat the oil over medium heat. Add burgers; cook 3-4 minutes on each side or until crisp and lightly browned. Serve on buns with lettuce.
PER SERVING *1 burger equals 330 cal., 13 g fat (5 g sat. fat), 121 mg chol., 736 mg sodium, 42 g carb., 5 g fiber, 14 g pro.* **Diabetic Exchanges:** *3 starch, 1 medium-fat meat, ½ fat.*

Margherita Pita Pizzas

My husband plants the garden, and I harvest and cook the fruits of his labor. My favorite way to use plum tomatoes is with this easy pizza. It is so good!

—**ROSEMARIE WELESKI** NATRONA HEIGHTS, PA

START TO FINISH: 20 MIN.
MAKES: 4 SERVINGS

- 4 **pita breads (6 inches)**
- 2 **teaspoons olive oil**
- 2 **garlic cloves, minced**
- 2 **cups (8 ounces) shredded part-skim mozzarella cheese**
- 3 **plum tomatoes, thinly sliced**
- ¼ **teaspoon garlic powder**
- 1 **teaspoon Italian seasoning**
  Thinly sliced fresh basil, optional

1. Place pita breads on an ungreased baking sheet; brush with oil. Top with garlic, 1 cup cheese, tomatoes, garlic powder and remaining cheese; sprinkle with Italian seasoning.

2. Bake at 425° for 10-12 minutes or until cheese is melted. Top with basil if desired.

PER SERVING *1 pizza equals 340 cal., 12 g fat (6 g sat. fat), 33 mg chol., 588 mg sodium, 38 g carb., 2 g fiber, 20 g pro.* **Diabetic Exchanges:** *2 starch, 2 medium-fat meat, ½ fat.*

SWEET POTATOES WITH CILANTRO BLACK BEANS

Sweet Potatoes with Cilantro Black Beans

As a vegan, I'm always looking for delicious, easy dishes to share. A touch of peanut butter (or almond butter) gives these loaded sweet potatoes a special flavor.

—**KAYLA CAPPER** OJAI, CA

START TO FINISH: 20 MIN.
MAKES: 4 SERVINGS

- 4 **medium sweet potatoes (about 8 ounces each)**
- 1 **tablespoon olive oil**
- 1 **small sweet red pepper, chopped**
- 2 **green onions, chopped**
- 1 **can (15 ounces) black beans, rinsed and drained**
- ½ **cup salsa**
- ¼ **cup frozen corn**
- 2 **tablespoons lime juice**
- 1 **tablespoon creamy peanut butter**
- 1 **teaspoon ground cumin**
- ¼ **teaspoon garlic salt**
- ¼ **cup minced fresh cilantro**
  Additional minced fresh cilantro, optional

1. Scrub sweet potatoes; pierce several times with a fork. Place on a microwave-safe plate. Microwave, uncovered, on high 6-8 minutes or until tender, turning once.

2. Meanwhile, in a large skillet, heat oil over medium-high heat. Add pepper and green onions; cook and stir 3-4 minutes or until tender. Stir in beans, salsa, corn, lime juice, peanut butter, cumin and garlic salt; heat through. Stir in cilantro.

3. With a sharp knife, cut an X in each sweet potato. Fluff pulp with a fork. Spoon bean mixture over potatoes. If desired, sprinkle with additional cilantro.

PER SERVING *1 potato with ½ cup black bean mixture equals 400 cal., 6 g fat (1 g sat. fat), 0 chol., 426 mg sodium, 77 g carb., 12 g fiber, 11 g pro.*

Spinach 'n' Broccoli Enchiladas

I like to top this wonderful meatless meal with lettuce and serve it with extra picante sauce. It's quick, easy, filled with fresh flavor and definitely satisfying!

—**LESLEY TRAGESSER** CHARLESTON, MO

PREP: 25 MIN. • **BAKE:** 25 MIN.
MAKES: 8 SERVINGS

- 1 medium onion, chopped
- 2 teaspoons olive oil
- 1 package (10 ounces) frozen chopped spinach, thawed and squeezed dry
- 1 cup finely chopped fresh broccoli
- 1 cup picante sauce, divided
- ½ teaspoon garlic powder
- ½ teaspoon ground cumin
- 1 cup (8 ounces) 1% cottage cheese
- 1 cup (4 ounces) shredded reduced-fat cheddar cheese, divided
- 8 flour tortillas (8 inches), warmed

1. Preheat oven to 350°. In a large nonstick skillet over medium heat, cook and stir onion in oil until tender. Add the spinach, broccoli, ⅓ cup picante sauce, garlic powder and cumin; heat through.

2. Remove from heat; stir in the cottage cheese and ½ cup cheddar cheese. Spoon about ⅓ cup spinach mixture down center of each tortilla. Roll up and place seam side down in a 13x9-in. baking dish coated with cooking spray. Spoon remaining picante sauce over top.

3. Cover and bake 20-25 minutes or until heated through. Uncover; sprinkle with remaining cheese. Bake 5 minutes or until cheese is melted.

PER SERVING *1 enchilada equals 246 cal., 8 g fat (3 g sat. fat), 11 mg chol., 614 mg sodium, 32 g carb., 2 g fiber, 13 g pro.* **Diabetic Exchanges:** *1½ starch, 1 lean meat, 1 vegetable, ½ fat.*

Rosemary Butternut Squash Lasagna

I came up with a flavorful fall lasagna recipe when our garden had an overabundance of butternut squash. This is now our favorite way to use it.

—**CHRISTINE WOOD** TIPTON, IA

PREP: 30 MIN. • **BAKE:** 50 MIN. + STANDING
MAKES: 8 SERVINGS

- 9 uncooked whole grain lasagna noodles
- 1 medium butternut squash (about 3 pounds), peeled and cut crosswise into ¼-inch slices
- 2 tablespoons olive oil
- 1 teaspoon salt, divided
- 6 tablespoons all-purpose flour
- 4 cups fat-free milk
- 6 garlic cloves, minced
- 1 tablespoon minced fresh rosemary
- 1⅓ cups shredded Parmesan cheese

1. Preheat oven to 425°. Cook noodles according to package directions; drain.
2. In a large bowl, combine squash, oil and ½ teaspoon salt; toss to coat.

Transfer to a 15x10x1-in. baking pan coated with cooking spray. Bake for 10-15 minutes or until tender; remove from oven. Reduce heat to 375°.

3. Place flour and remaining salt in a large saucepan; gradually whisk in the milk. Bring to a boil, stirring constantly. Cook and stir 1-2 minutes or until thickened. Stir in the garlic and rosemary.

4. Spread 1 cup sauce into a 13x9-in. baking dish coated with cooking spray. Layer with three noodles, ⅓ cup cheese, a third of the squash and 1 cup sauce. Repeat layers twice. Sprinkle with remaining cheese.

5. Cover and bake 40 minutes. Uncover; bake 10 minutes or until bubbly and top is lightly browned. Let stand 10 minutes before serving.

PER SERVING *1 piece equals 275 cal., 8 g fat (3 g sat. fat), 12 mg chol., 577 mg sodium, 40 g carb., 6 g fiber, 14 g pro.* **Diabetic Exchanges:** *2½ starch, ½ fat-free milk, ½ fat.*

Portobello Pizza Burgers

Portobello mushrooms are a tasty meatless option, especially tucked inside a bun with melted cheese.

—**SALLY LAUF** WEST DEPTFORD, NJ

START TO FINISH: 25 MIN.
MAKES: 4 SERVINGS

- 4 **large portobello mushrooms (4 to 4½ inches)**
- 4 **teaspoons plus 1 tablespoon olive oil, divided**
- 1½ **cups finely chopped plum tomatoes**
- ¾ **cup shredded part-skim mozzarella cheese**
- 1½ **teaspoons Italian seasoning**
- 4 **hamburger buns, split**

1. Preheat broiler. Remove and discard stems from mushrooms; with a spoon, scrape and remove gills. Brush caps with 4 teaspoons oil. Place in an ungreased 15x10x1-in. baking pan, stem side down. Broil 4 in. from heat 5 minutes.

2. In a small bowl, mix tomatoes, cheese and Italian seasoning with remaining oil. Remove mushrooms from broiler; turn over and fill caps with tomato mixture.

3. Broil 4-6 minutes longer or until mushrooms are tender and cheese is melted. Serve on buns.

NOTE *Mushrooms may also be grilled. Place mushroom caps on grill rack over medium heat, stem side down. Grill, covered, 5 minutes. Remove from grill; fill caps with tomato mixture. Grill, covered, 4-6 minutes longer or until mushrooms are tender and cheese is melted. Serve on buns.*

PER SERVING *1 burger equals 284 cal., 13 g fat (4 g sat. fat), 12 mg chol., 314 mg sodium, 29 g carb., 3 g fiber, 12 g pro.* **Diabetic Exchanges:** *2 starch, 1½ fat, 1 medium-fat meat, 1 vegetable.*

Stir-Fry Rice Bowl

My meatless version of Korean *bibimbap* is tasty, pretty and easy to tweak for different spice levels. Koreans usually eat this rice dish with some beef, but I top mine with a poached egg.

—**DEVON DELANEY** WESTPORT, CT

START TO FINISH: 30 MIN.
MAKES: 4 SERVINGS

- 1 **tablespoon canola oil**
- 2 **medium carrots, julienned**
- 1 **medium zucchini, julienned**
- ½ **cup sliced baby portobello mushrooms**
- 1 **cup bean sprouts**
- 1 **cup fresh baby spinach**
- 1 **tablespoon water**
- 1 **tablespoon reduced-sodium soy sauce**
- 1 **tablespoon chili garlic sauce**
- 4 **large eggs**
- 3 **cups hot cooked brown rice**
- 1 **teaspoon sesame oil**

1. In a large skillet, heat canola oil over medium-high heat. Add carrots, zucchini and mushrooms; cook and stir 3-5 minutes or until carrots are crisp-tender. Add the bean sprouts, spinach, water, soy sauce and chili garlic sauce; cook just until spinach is wilted. Remove from heat; keep warm.

2. Place 2-3 in. of water in a large skillet with high sides. Bring to a boil; adjust heat to maintain a gentle simmer. Break cold eggs, one at a time, into a small bowl; holding bowl close to surface of water, slip egg into water.

3. Cook, uncovered, 3-5 minutes or until whites are completely set and yolks begin to thicken but are not hard. Using a slotted spoon, lift eggs out of water.

4. Serve rice in bowls; top with vegetables. Drizzle with sesame oil. Top each serving with a poached egg.

PER SERVING *1 serving equals 305 cal., 11 g fat (2 g sat. fat), 186 mg chol., 364 mg sodium, 40 g carb., 4 g fiber, 12 g pro.* **Diabetic Exchanges:** *2 starch, 1 medium-fat meat, 1 vegetable, 1 fat.*

STIR-FRY RICE BOWL

ORIGINAL	MAKEOVER
438 Calories	**324** Calories
24g Fat	**11**g Fat
67mg Cholesterol	**27**mg Cholesterol

MAKEOVER PENNE ALLA VODKA

Makeover Penne alla Vodka

This makeover of my favorite dish is still as creamy and rich as the original, but it now has less than half the fat and cholesterol!

—**DEBRA TORRES** LYNCHBURG, VA

PREP: 15 MIN. • **COOK:** 40 MIN.
MAKES: 8 SERVINGS

- 1 **large onion, chopped**
- 1 **tablespoon olive oil**
- 4 **garlic cloves, minced**
- 2 **cans (one 28 ounces, one 14.5 ounces) diced tomatoes**
- ¼ **cup vodka**
- 1 **package (12 ounces) whole wheat penne pasta**
- 2 **teaspoons prepared pesto**
- ¼ **teaspoon salt**
- ¼ **teaspoon crushed red pepper flakes**
- 2 **tablespoons all-purpose flour**
- ½ **cup heavy whipping cream**
- 1 **cup whole milk**
- ½ **cup shredded Parmesan cheese**

1. In a large saucepan, saute onion in oil until tender. Add garlic; cook 1 minute longer. Stir in tomatoes and vodka. Bring to a boil. Reduce heat; simmer, uncovered, for 30-35 minutes or until slightly thickened, stirring occasionally.

2. Meanwhile, cook penne according to package directions.

3. Stir the pesto, salt and pepper flakes into tomato mixture. In a small bowl, combine flour and cream until smooth; stir into pan. Add milk. Bring to a boil; cook and stir for 2 minutes or until slightly thickened. Drain penne; serve with sauce. Sprinkle with Parmesan cheese.

PER SERVING *⅔ cup pasta with ⅔ cup sauce and 1 tablespoon cheese equals 324 cal., 11 g fat (5 g sat. fat), 27 mg chol., 379 mg sodium, 44 g carb., 7 g fiber, 12 g pro.* **Diabetic Exchanges:** *2 starch, 2 vegetable, 2 fat.*

THE SKINNY

The makeover replaces 1½ cups heavy cream with a mixture of cream and whole milk, thickened to the correct consistency with a little flour. This change slashed 76 calories and 38 mg cholesterol from each serving. Whole milk gives rich mouthfeel to light custards and cream fillings, too.

Veggie Lasagna

This is my daughter-in-law's recipe. It's tasty and a little different from typical lasagnas—even the meatless ones!

—ALYCE WYMAN PEMBINA, ND

PREP: 30 MIN. • **BAKE:** 40 MIN. + STANDING
MAKES: 2 LASAGNAS (9 SERVINGS EACH)

- 18 uncooked lasagna noodles
- 2 large eggs
- 2 large egg whites
- 2 cartons (15 ounces each) reduced-fat ricotta cheese
- 4 teaspoons dried parsley flakes
- 2 teaspoons dried basil
- 2 teaspoons dried oregano
- 1 teaspoon pepper
- 8 cups garden-style spaghetti sauce
- 4 cups (16 ounces) shredded part-skim mozzarella cheese
- 2 packages (16 ounces each) frozen cut green beans or 8 cups cut fresh green beans
- ⅔ cup grated Parmesan cheese

1. Cook noodles according to package directions. Meanwhile, in a small bowl, whisk the eggs, egg whites, ricotta cheese, parsley, basil, oregano and pepper; set aside.

2. In each of two 13x9-in. baking dishes coated with cooking spray, spread 1 cup spaghetti sauce. Drain noodles; place three noodles over spaghetti sauce in each dish.

3. Layer each with a quarter of the ricotta mixture, 1 cup spaghetti sauce, 1 cup mozzarella cheese, three lasagna noodles and half of green beans. Top each with remaining ricotta mixture and 1 cup spaghetti sauce. Layer with remaining lasagna noodles, spaghetti sauce and mozzarella cheese. Sprinkle Parmesan cheese over each.

4. Cover and freeze one lasagna up to 3 months. Bake the remaining lasagna, uncovered, at 375° for 40-45 minutes or until bubbly and edges are lightly browned. Let stand for 10 minutes before serving.

TO USE FROZEN LASAGNA *Thaw in the refrigerator overnight. Remove from the refrigerator 30 minutes before baking. Cover and bake at 375° for 1¼-1½ hours or until bubbly. Let stand for 10 minutes before serving.*
PER SERVING *1 piece equals 320 cal., 10 g fat (5 g sat. fat), 56 mg chol., 713 mg sodium, 38 g carb., 5 g fiber, 18 g pro.* **Diabetic Exchanges:** *2 starch, 2 lean meat, 2 vegetable.*

FAST FIX **Tropical Fusion Salad with Spicy Tortilla Ribbons**

The fresh taste of this colorful salad makes it a perfect choice for a spring or summer meal. Served with spicy tortilla strips, it's a unique offering with a variety of textures.

—JENNIFER FISHER AUSTIN, TX

START TO FINISH: 30 MIN.
MAKES: 4 SERVINGS

- 2 cups cubed peeled papaya
- 1 can (15 ounces) black beans, rinsed and drained
- 1 medium ripe avocado, peeled and cubed
- 1 cup frozen corn, thawed
- ½ cup golden raisins
- ¼ cup minced fresh cilantro
- ¼ cup orange juice
- 2 serrano peppers, seeded and chopped
- 2 tablespoons lime juice
- 1 tablespoon cider vinegar
- 2 garlic cloves, minced
- 2 teaspoons ground ancho chili pepper, divided
- ¼ teaspoon sugar
- ¼ teaspoon salt
- 2 corn tortillas (6 inches), cut into ¼-inch strips
  Cooking spray

1. Preheat oven to 350°. In a bowl, combine papaya, beans, avocado, corn, raisins, cilantro, orange juice, peppers, lime juice, vinegar, garlic, ½ teaspoon chili pepper, sugar and salt.

2. Place tortilla strips on a greased baking sheet; spritz with cooking spray. Sprinkle with remaining chili pepper. Bake 8-10 minutes or until crisp. Top salad with tortilla strips.
NOTE *Wear disposable gloves when cutting hot peppers; the oils can burn skin. Avoid touching your face.*
PER SERVING *1¼ cups salad with about 10 tortilla ribbons equals 321 cal., 8 g fat (1 g sat. fat), 0 chol., 380 mg sodium, 58 g carb., 11 g fiber, 9 g pro.*

SPINACH-TOMATO PHYLLO BAKE

Spinach-Tomato Phyllo Bake

My flaky phyllo pie is a lightened-up version of the beloved Greek classic, spanakopita. No one will miss the meat when this tasty vegetarian recipe is on the menu.

—SHIRLEY KACMARIK
GLASGOW, SCOTLAND

PREP: 25 MIN. • **BAKE:** 55 MIN. + STANDING
MAKES: 6 SERVINGS

- 4 eggs, lightly beaten
- 2 packages (10 ounces each) frozen chopped spinach, thawed and squeezed dry
- 1 cup (4 ounces) crumbled feta cheese
- ½ cup 1% cottage cheese
- 3 green onions, sliced
- 1 teaspoon dill weed
- ½ teaspoon salt
- ¼ teaspoon pepper
- ¼ teaspoon ground nutmeg
- 10 sheets phyllo dough (14x9-inch size)
  Butter-flavored cooking spray
- 3 large tomatoes, sliced

1. Preheat oven to 350°. In a large bowl, combine first nine ingredients; set aside.
2. Spritz one sheet of phyllo dough with butter-flavored cooking spray. Place in an 8-in.-square baking dish coated with cooking spray, allowing one end of dough to hang over edge of dish. Repeat with four more phyllo sheets, staggering the overhanging phyllo around edges of dish. (Keep remaining phyllo covered with plastic wrap and a damp towel to prevent it from drying out.)
3. Spoon a third of the spinach mixture into crust. Layer with half of the tomatoes, another third of the spinach mixture, remaining tomatoes and remaining spinach mixture. Spritz and layer remaining phyllo dough as before.
4. Gently fold ends of dough over filling and toward center of baking dish; spritz with butter-flavored spray. Cover edges with foil. Bake 55-60 minutes or until a thermometer reads 160°. Let stand 15 minutes before cutting.
PER SERVING *1 piece equals 216 cal., 9 g fat (3 g sat. fat), 153 mg chol., 652 mg sodium, 21 g carb., 5 g fiber, 15 g pro. Diabetic Exchanges: 2 medium-fat meat, 2 vegetable, 1 starch.*

Red Beans and Rice Salad

Mango lends a sweet tropical twist to our warm-weather version of red beans and rice. Green pepper and onion add the perfect bit of crunch.

—TASTE OF HOME TEST KITCHEN

PREP: 10 MIN. + CHILLING
MAKES: 4 SERVINGS

- 2 cups cooked brown rice
- 1 can (16 ounces) kidney beans, rinsed and drained
- ¾ cup finely chopped green pepper
- ½ cup cubed peeled mango or peaches (½-inch cubes)
- ½ cup finely chopped red onion
- ½ cup salsa, well drained
- ½ teaspoon salt
- ⅛ teaspoon pepper
- 2 tablespoons minced fresh cilantro

In a large bowl, combine the first eight ingredients. Cover and refrigerate for 1 hour or until chilled. Sprinkle with cilantro before serving.
PER SERVING *1¼ cups equals 245 cal., 1 g fat (trace sat. fat), 0 chol., 624 mg sodium, 48 g carb., 9 g fiber, 10 g pro. Diabetic Exchanges: 2 starch, 2 vegetable, 1 lean meat.*

Sweet Potato & Bean Quesadillas

This recipe is special to me because it's fun, easy, fast, healthy and delicious!

—BRITTANY HUBBARD

ST. PAUL, MN

START TO FINISH: 30 MIN.
MAKES: 4 SERVINGS

- 2 **medium sweet potatoes**
- 4 **whole wheat tortillas (8 inches)**
- ¾ **cup canned black beans, rinsed and drained**
- ½ **cup shredded pepper jack cheese**
- ¾ **cup salsa**

1. Scrub sweet potatoes; pierce several times with a fork. Place on a microwave-safe plate. Microwave, uncovered, on high 7-9 minutes or until very tender, turning once.
2. When cool enough to handle, cut each potato lengthwise in half. Scoop out pulp. Spread onto one half of each tortilla; top with beans and cheese.

Fold other half of tortilla over filling.
3. Heat a griddle or skillet over medium heat. Cook quesadillas 2-3 minutes on each side or until golden brown and cheese is melted. Serve with salsa.

PER SERVING *1 quesadilla with 3 tablespoons salsa equals 306 cal., 8 g fat (3 g sat. fat), 15 mg chol., 531 mg sodium, 46 g carb., 6 g fiber, 11 g pro.*

SWEET POTATO & BEAN QUESADILLAS

Roasted Butternut Linguine

Squash is one of our favorite vegetables, and this is my husband's preferred fall dish. He looks forward to it all year.

—KIM CAPUTO CANNON FALLS, MN

PREP: 20 MIN. • **BAKE:** 45 MIN.
MAKES: 4 SERVINGS

- 4 **cups cubed peeled butternut squash**
- 1 **medium red onion, chopped**
- 3 **tablespoons olive oil**
- ¼ **teaspoon crushed red pepper flakes**
- ½ **pound uncooked linguine**
- 2 **cups julienned Swiss chard**
- 1 **tablespoon minced fresh sage**
- ½ **teaspoon salt**
- ¼ **teaspoon pepper**

1. Preheat oven to 350°. Place the squash and onion in a 15x10x1-in. baking pan coated with cooking spray. Combine the oil and pepper flakes; drizzle over vegetables and toss to coat.
2. Bake, uncovered, 45-50 minutes or until tender, stirring occasionally.
3. Meanwhile, cook the linguine according to package directions; drain and place in a large bowl. Add squash mixture, Swiss chard, sage, salt and pepper; toss to combine.

PER SERVING *1½ cups equals 384 cal., 12 g fat (2 g sat. fat), 0 chol., 344 mg sodium, 64 g carb., 6 g fiber, 10 g pro.*

Vegetable Jambalaya

This rice dish is the answer when you crave Creole but don't have chicken or sausage on hand. And since it uses convenient canned beans in place of meat, the flavorful entree won't leave you hungry.

—**CRYSTAL JO BRUNS** ILIFF, CO

PREP: 10 MIN. • **COOK:** 30 MIN.
MAKES: 6 SERVINGS

- 1 tablespoon canola oil
- 1 medium green pepper, chopped
- 1 medium onion, chopped
- 1 celery rib, chopped
- 3 garlic cloves, minced
- 2 cups water
- 1 can (14½ ounces) diced tomatoes, undrained
- 1 can (8 ounces) tomato sauce
- ½ teaspoon Italian seasoning
- ¼ teaspoon salt
- ¼ teaspoon crushed red pepper flakes
- ⅛ teaspoon fennel seed, crushed
- 1 cup uncooked long grain rice
- 1 can (16 ounces) butter beans, rinsed and drained
- 1 can (16 ounces) red beans, rinsed and drained

1. In a Dutch oven, heat oil over medium-high heat. Add the green pepper, onion and celery; cook and stir until tender. Add garlic; cook 1 minute longer.

2. Add the water, tomatoes, tomato sauce and seasonings. Bring to a boil; stir in rice. Reduce heat; cover and simmer for 15-18 minutes or until liquid is absorbed and rice is tender. Stir in beans; heat through.

PER SERVING *1⅓ cups equals 281 cal., 3 g fat (trace sat. fat), 0 chol., 796 mg sodium, 56 g carb., 9 g fiber, 11 g pro.*

VEGETABLE JAMBALAYA

Snappy Baked Ziti

I decided one night that instead of waiting for water to boil, I'd throw pasta in the casserole dish and bake it. This satisfying meal doesn't take long to put together after work.

—VICKY PALMER ALBUQUERQUE, NM

PREP: 20 MIN. • **BAKE:** 65 MIN.
MAKES: 8 SERVINGS

- 1 medium onion, chopped
- 1 tablespoon olive oil
- 3 garlic cloves, minced
- 2 cans (28 ounces each) Italian crushed tomatoes
- 1½ cups water
- ½ cup dry red wine or reduced-sodium chicken broth
- 1 tablespoon sugar
- 1 teaspoon dried basil
- 1 package (16 ounces) ziti
- 8 slices provolone cheese

1. In a stockpot, saute onion in oil until tender. Add garlic; cook 1 minute longer. Stir in tomatoes, water, wine, sugar and basil. Bring to a boil; remove from heat. Stir in ziti.

2. Transfer to a greased 13x9-in. baking dish. Cover and bake at 350° for 1 hour. Top with cheese. Bake, uncovered, for 4-6 minutes or until cheese is melted.

PER SERVING *1½ cups equals 381 cal., 8 g fat (4 g sat. fat), 15 mg chol., 763 mg sodium, 60 g carb., 4 g fiber, 16 g pro.*

TOP TIP

I added sweet red pepper, chopped, and cooked sweet Italian sausage to one side of the dish (wife does not like meat). I used the wine. This was simple/easy and very good.
—JWFY TASTEOFHOME.COM

PHILLY CHEESE FAKES FOR TWO

Philly Cheese Fakes for Two

Savory mushrooms are the key to this twist on the popular Philly cheese steak sandwich—a toasty meatless meal option that's tasty, too.

—VERONICA VICHIT-VADAKAN
PORTLAND, OR

PREP: 30 MIN. • **BROIL:** 5 MIN.
MAKES: 2 SERVINGS

- 2 tablespoons lemon juice
- 2 garlic cloves, minced
- 1½ teaspoons olive oil
- ¼ teaspoon smoked paprika
- ⅛ teaspoon salt
- ⅛ teaspoon pepper
- ½ pound sliced fresh shiitake mushrooms
- 1 medium green pepper, sliced
- ¼ cup thinly sliced onion
- 2 hoagie buns, split
- 2 slices reduced-fat provolone cheese

1. In a small bowl, whisk the first six ingredients. In a large bowl, combine mushrooms, green pepper and onion. Pour dressing over vegetables; toss to coat.

2. Transfer to a 15x10x1-in. baking pan coated with cooking spray. Bake at 450° for 15-20 minutes or until crisp-tender, stirring once.

3. Divide mushroom mixture between bun bottoms and top with cheese. Broil bun halves 3-4 in. from the heat for 2-3 minutes or until cheese is melted.

PER SERVING *1 sandwich equals 344 cal., 12 g fat (4 g sat. fat), 10 mg chol., 681 mg sodium, 47 g carb., 4 g fiber, 17 g pro.*

RATATOUILLE WITH POLENTA

Ratatouille with Polenta

Created in the Provence region of France, ratatouille features the best of summer's vegetables. Hot polenta makes it more substantial for a meatless main dish.

—*TASTE OF HOME* TEST KITCHEN

PREP: 20 MIN. • **COOK:** 15 MIN.
MAKES: 4 SERVINGS

- ½ **pound small fresh mushrooms, halved**
- 1 **medium sweet red pepper, chopped**
- 1 **small onion, chopped**
- 4 **teaspoons olive oil, divided**
- 4 **cups cubed peeled eggplant**
- 1 **small zucchini, chopped**
- 1 **cup cherry tomatoes**
- 2 **garlic cloves, minced**
- 1½ **teaspoons Italian seasoning**
- ½ **teaspoon salt**
- 1 **tube (1 pound) polenta, cut into ½-inch slices**
  Grated Parmesan cheese, optional

1. In a large skillet, saute the mushrooms, pepper and onion in 2 teaspoons oil until almost tender. Add the eggplant, zucchini, tomatoes, garlic, Italian seasoning and salt.

Saute for 8-10 minutes or until the vegetables are tender.
2. In another skillet, cook polenta slices in remaining oil over medium-high heat for 3-4 minutes on each side or until lightly browned. Serve with ratatouille; sprinkle with cheese if desired.

PER SERVING *1½ cups ratatouille with 3 pieces of polenta equals 195 cal., 5 g fat (1 g sat. fat), 0 chol., 689 mg sodium, 34 g carb., 6 g fiber, 6 g pro.* **Diabetic Exchanges:** *3 vegetable, 1 starch, 1 fat.*

FAST FIX ▶ Indian Spiced Chickpea Wraps

Raita, an Indian condiment made with yogurt, elevates this vegetarian dish into a satisfying gourmet wrap. I sometimes substitute diced mango or cucumber for the pineapple and add fresh herbs like cilantro or mint.

—**JENNIFER BECKMAN** FALLS CHURCH, VA

START TO FINISH: 30 MIN.
MAKES: 4 SERVINGS (1⅓ CUPS SAUCE)

RAITA

- 1 **cup (8 ounces) reduced-fat plain yogurt**
- ½ **cup drained unsweetened pineapple tidbits**
- ¼ **teaspoon salt**
- ¼ **teaspoon ground cumin**

WRAPS

- 2 **teaspoons canola oil**
- 1 **small onion, chopped**
- 1 **tablespoon minced fresh gingerroot**
- 2 **garlic cloves, minced**
- ½ **teaspoon curry powder**
- ¼ **teaspoon each salt, ground cumin and ground coriander**
- ¼ **teaspoon cayenne pepper, optional**
- 1 **can (15 ounces) chickpeas or garbanzo beans, rinsed and drained**
- 1 **cup canned crushed tomatoes**
- 4 **whole wheat tortillas (8 inches), warmed**
- 3 **cups fresh baby spinach**

1. In a small bowl, mix raita ingredients; set aside.
2. For wraps, in a nonstick skillet coated with cooking spray, heat oil over medium-high heat. Add onion; cook and stir until tender. Add ginger, garlic and seasonings; cook and stir 1 minute longer.
3. Stir in chickpeas and tomatoes. Bring to a boil. Reduce heat; simmer, uncovered, for 5-8 minutes or until slightly thickened, stirring occasionally.
4. Near the center of each tortilla, arrange spinach and the chickpea mixture; top with raita. Roll up tightly; serve immediately.

PER SERVING *1 wrap equals 355 cal., 9 g fat (1 g sat. fat), 3 mg chol., 745 mg sodium, 56 g carb., 9 g fiber, 13 g pro.*

Herb Garden Lasagnas

I love the taste and texture of these homemade noodles and the beautiful lasagnas they make. A healthy dose of fresh herbs gives this dish its unique flavor.

—**KATHRYN CONRAD** MILWAUKEE, WI

PREP: 45 MIN. + STANDING • **BAKE:** 30 MIN.
MAKES: 6 SERVINGS

- 2 **large eggs**
- 1 **large egg yolk**
- ¼ **cup water**
- 1 **tablespoon olive oil**
- ½ **teaspoon coarsely ground pepper**
- ¼ **teaspoon salt**
- 1½ **cups all-purpose flour**
- ½ **cup semolina flour**

FILLING

- 1 **cup whole-milk ricotta cheese**
- 1 **large egg white, lightly beaten**
- 2 **tablespoons shredded carrot**
- 1 **tablespoon minced fresh basil**
- 1 **tablespoon thinly sliced green onion**
- 1 **teaspoon minced fresh mint**
- ¼ **teaspoon salt**
- 1 **cup crumbled queso fresco or feta cheese, divided**
- 4 **cups chopped tomatoes (about 6 medium), divided**
  - **Optional toppings: thinly sliced green onion, fresh basil and fresh mint**

1. In a small bowl, whisk the first six ingredients. On a clean work surface, mix all-purpose and semolina flours; form into a mound. Make a large well in the center. Pour egg mixture into well. Using a fork or fingers, gradually mix flour mixture into egg mixture, forming a soft dough (dough will be soft and slightly sticky).

2. Lightly dust work surface with flour; knead dough gently five times. Divide into six portions; cover with plastic wrap. Let rest 30 minutes.

3. In a small bowl, mix the first seven filling ingredients; stir in ½ cup queso fresco. Grease six individual 12-oz. au gratin dishes; place on baking sheets. Preheat oven to 350°.

4. Fill a Dutch oven three-fourths full with salted water; bring to a boil. On a floured surface, roll each portion of dough into a 20x4-in. rectangle, dusting dough with additional flour as needed.

5. For each lasagna, add one noodle to boiling water; cook 1-2 minutes or until al dente. Place one-fifth of the noodle in bottom of a prepared dish; top with 1 tablespoon ricotta mixture and 2 tablespoons tomato. Fold noodle back to cover filling; repeat three times, topping and folding the noodle each time.

6. Sprinkle lasagnas with remaining queso fresco and tomatoes. Bake, covered, 30-35 minutes or until heated through. If desired, sprinkle with additional herbs.

PER SERVING *1 individual lasagna equals 363 cal., 13 g fat (6 g sat. fat), 135 mg chol., 343 mg sodium, 44 g carb., 3 g fiber, 19 g pro.* **Diabetic Exchanges:** *2½ starch, 2 medium-fat meat, 1 vegetable, ½ fat.*

HERB GARDEN LASAGNAS

FAST FIX
Fresh Corn & Tomato Fettuccine

This recipe combines delicious whole wheat pasta with the best of fresh garden produce. It's tossed with heart-healthy olive oil, and a little feta cheese gives it bite.

—ANGELA SPENGLER TAMPA, FL

START TO FINISH: 30 MIN.
MAKES: 4 SERVINGS

- 8 ounces uncooked whole wheat fettuccine
- 2 medium ears sweet corn, husks removed
- 2 teaspoons plus 2 tablespoons olive oil, divided
- ½ cup chopped sweet red pepper
- 4 green onions, chopped
- 2 medium tomatoes, chopped
- ½ teaspoon salt
- ½ teaspoon pepper
- 1 cup crumbled feta cheese
- 2 tablespoons minced fresh parsley

1. In a Dutch oven, cook fettuccine according to package directions, adding corn during the last 8 minutes of cooking.
2. Meanwhile, in a small skillet, heat 2 teaspoons oil over medium-high heat. Add red pepper and green onions; cook and stir until tender.
3. Drain pasta and corn; transfer pasta to a large bowl. Cool corn slightly; cut corn from cob and add to pasta. Add tomatoes, salt, pepper, remaining oil and the pepper mixture; toss to combine. Top with cheese and parsley.
PER SERVING *2 cups equals 422 cal., 15 g fat (4 g sat. fat), 15 mg chol., 580 mg sodium, 56 g carb., 10 g fiber, 17 g pro.*

Zucchini Crust Pizza

My mother-in-law shared the recipe for this unique pizza with me. Its nutritious zucchini crust makes it just right for brunch, lunch or a light supper.

—RUTH DENOMME ENGLEHART, ON

PREP: 15 MIN. • **BAKE:** 25 MIN.
MAKES: 6 SLICES

- 3 cups shredded zucchini
- ¾ cup egg substitute
- ⅓ cup all-purpose flour
- ½ teaspoon salt
- 2 cups (8 ounces) shredded part-skim mozzarella cheese
- 2 small tomatoes, halved and thinly sliced
- ½ cup chopped onion
- ½ cup julienned green pepper
- 1 teaspoon dried oregano
- ½ teaspoon dried basil
- 3 tablespoons shredded Parmesan cheese

1. In a large bowl, combine zucchini and egg substitute. Stir in flour and salt. Spread onto a 12-in. pizza pan coated with cooking spray.
2. Bake at 450° for 8 minutes. Reduce the heat to 350°. Sprinkle with the mozzarella, tomatoes, onion, green pepper, oregano, basil and Parmesan cheese. Bake for 15-20 minutes or until onion is tender and the cheese is melted.
PER SERVING *1 slice equals 190 cal., 8 g fat (5 g sat. fat), 24 mg chol., 431 mg sodium, 13 g carb., 2 g fiber, 17 g pro.* **Diabetic Exchanges:** *2 lean meat, 2 vegetable, ½ fat.*

FRESH CORN & TOMATO FETTUCCINE

ZUCCHINI CRUST PIZZA

FAST FIX ▸ Orzo-White Bean Greek Salad

In just 30 minutes, I can put together this hearty salad of pasta, cannellini beans and veggies. It's healthy, delicious and perfect for a crowd.

—MYA ZERONIS PITTSBURGH, PA

START TO FINISH : 30 MIN.
MAKES: 8 SERVINGS

- 2½ cups uncooked whole wheat orzo pasta (about 1 pound)
- 1 can (15 ounces) white kidney or cannellini beans, rinsed and drained
- 3 medium tomatoes, finely chopped
- 1 English cucumber, finely chopped
- 2 cups (8 ounces) crumbled feta cheese
- 1¼ cups pitted Greek olives (about 6 ounces), chopped
- 1 medium sweet yellow pepper, finely chopped
- 1 medium green pepper, finely chopped
- 1 cup fresh mint leaves, chopped
- ½ medium red onion, finely chopped
- ¼ cup lemon juice
- 2 tablespoons olive oil
- 1 tablespoon grated lemon peel
- 3 garlic cloves, minced
- ½ teaspoon pepper

1. Cook orzo according to package directions. Drain orzo; rinse with cold water.

2. Meanwhile, in a large bowl, combine remaining ingredients. Stir in orzo. Refrigerate until serving.

PER SERVING *1¾ cups equals 411 cal., 17 g fat (4 g sat. fat), 15 mg chol., 740 mg sodium, 51 g carb., 13 g fiber, 14 g pro.*

Mimi's Lentil Medley

I made this one summer evening by putting together what I had on hand. My husband, Ken, gave it his top rating. "You can make this again soon," he said.

—MARY ANN HAZEN ROCHESTER HILLS, MI

PREP: 15 MIN. • **COOK:** 25 MIN.
MAKES: 8 SERVINGS

- 1 cup dried lentils, rinsed
- 2 cups water
- 2 cups sliced fresh mushrooms
- 1 medium cucumber, cubed
- 1 medium zucchini, cubed
- 1 small red onion, chopped
- ½ cup chopped soft sun-dried tomato halves (not packed in oil)
- ½ cup rice vinegar
- ¼ cup minced fresh mint
- 3 tablespoons olive oil
- 2 teaspoons honey
- 1 teaspoon dried basil
- 1 teaspoon dried oregano
- 4 cups fresh baby spinach, chopped
- 1 cup (4 ounces) crumbled feta cheese

1. Place lentils in a small saucepan. Add water; bring to a boil. Reduce heat; simmer, covered, 20-25 minutes or until tender. Drain and rinse in cold water.

2. Transfer to a large bowl. Add mushrooms, cucumber, zucchini, onion and tomatoes. In a small bowl, whisk vinegar, mint, oil, honey, basil and oregano. Drizzle over the lentil mixture; toss to coat. Add spinach and cheese; toss to combine.

PER SERVING *1¼ cups equals 225 cal., 8 g fat (2 g sat. fat), 8 mg chol., 404 mg sodium, 29 g carb., 5 g fiber, 10 g pro.* **Diabetic Exchanges:** *1½ fat, 1 starch, 1 vegetable.*

ORZO-WHITE BEAN GREEK SALAD

Special Egg Salad

This recipe proves you don't have to sacrifice flavor to eat lighter. These yummy, satisfying egg salad sandwiches are sure to be well-received whenever you serve them.

—**JUDY NISSEN** SIOUX FALLS, SD

PREP: 15 MIN. + CHILLING
MAKES: 6 SERVINGS

- 3 **ounces reduced-fat cream cheese**
- ¼ **cup fat-free mayonnaise**
- ½ **teaspoon sugar**
- ¼ **teaspoon onion powder**
- ¼ **teaspoon garlic powder**
- ⅛ **teaspoon salt**
- ⅛ **teaspoon pepper**
- 6 **hard-cooked large eggs, chopped**
- 12 **slices whole wheat bread, toasted**
- 6 **lettuce leaves**

In a small bowl, beat the cream cheese until smooth. Beat in the mayonnaise, sugar, onion powder, garlic powder, salt and pepper; fold in the eggs. Cover and refrigerate for 1 hour. Serve on toast with lettuce.

PER SERVING *1 sandwich equals 259 cal., 10 g fat (4 g sat. fat), 225 mg chol., 528 mg sodium, 30 g carb., 4 g fiber, 13 g pro.* ***Diabetic Exchanges:*** *2 starch, 1½ fat, 1 lean meat.*

PINTO BEAN TOSTADAS

FAST FIX

Pinto Bean Tostadas

Ready-to-go pinto beans and crispy corn tortillas prove how easy it is to make a healthy meal. Sometimes I add some chopped leftover meat to the tostadas, but they're equally satisfying just as they are.

—**LILY JULOW** LAWRENCEVILLE, GA

START TO FINISH: 30 MIN.
MAKES: 6 SERVINGS

- ¼ **cup sour cream**
- ¾ **teaspoon grated lime peel**
- ¼ **teaspoon ground cumin**
- ½ **teaspoon salt, divided**
- 2 **tablespoons canola oil, divided**
- 2 **garlic cloves, minced**
- 2 **cans (15 ounces each) pinto beans, rinsed and drained**
- 1 **to 2 teaspoons hot pepper sauce**
- 1 **teaspoon chili powder**
- 6 **corn tortillas (6 inches)**
- 2 **cups shredded lettuce**
- ½ **cup salsa**
- ¾ **cup crumbled queso fresco or feta cheese**
  Lime wedges

1. In a small bowl, mix sour cream, lime peel, cumin and ¼ teaspoon salt. In a large saucepan, heat 1 tablespoon oil over medium heat. Add garlic; cook and stir just until fragrant, about 45 seconds. Stir in beans, pepper sauce, chili powder and the remaining salt; heat through, stirring occasionally. Keep warm.

2. Brush both sides of tortillas with remaining oil. Place a large skillet over medium-high heat. Add tortillas in two batches; cook 2-3 minutes on each side or until lightly browned and crisp.

3. To serve, arrange beans and lettuce over tostada shells; top with salsa, sour cream mixture and cheese. Serve with lime wedges.

PER SERVING *1 tostada equals 291 cal., 10 g fat (3 g sat. fat), 14 mg chol., 658 mg sodium, 38 g carb., 8 g fiber, 11 g pro.* ***Diabetic Exchanges:*** *2½ starch, 1 lean meat, 1 fat.*

COCONUT-GINGER CHICKPEAS & TOMATOES

Spinach Burritos

I made up this recipe a couple of years ago after trying a similar dish in a restaurant. Our oldest son tells me these burritos are awesome! Plus, they're easy and inexpensive.

—**DOLORES ZORNOW** POYNETTE, WI

PREP: 20 MIN. • **BAKE:** 20 MIN.
MAKES: 6 SERVINGS

- ½ **cup chopped onion**
- 2 **garlic cloves, minced**
- 2 **teaspoons butter**
- 1 **package (10 ounces) frozen chopped spinach, thawed and squeezed dry**
- ⅛ **teaspoon pepper**
- 6 **fat-free flour tortillas (10 inches), warmed**
- ¾ **cup picante sauce, divided**
- 2 **cups (8 ounces) shredded reduced-fat cheddar cheese, divided**

1. In a large skillet, saute onion and garlic in butter until tender. Add spinach and pepper; cook for 2-3 minutes or until heated through.
2. Place about 3 tablespoonfuls off center on each tortilla; top with 1 tablespoon of picante sauce and 2 tablespoons of cheese. Fold sides and ends over filling and roll up.
3. Place seam side down in a 13x9-in. baking dish coated with cooking spray. Top with remaining picante sauce and cheese.
4. Bake, uncovered, at 350° for 20-25 minutes or until the sauce is bubbly and cheese is melted.
PER SERVING *1 burrito equals 262 cal., 9 g fat (0 sat. fat), 25 mg chol., 550 mg sodium, 31 g carb., 0 fiber, 17 g pro.* **Diabetic Exchanges:** *1½ starch, 1½ meat, 1 vegetable.*

FAST FIX
Coconut-Ginger Chickpeas & Tomatoes

This is my go-to quick dish. When you add the tomatoes, you can also toss in some chopped green peppers to make it even more colorful.

—**MALA UDAYAMURTHY** SAN JOSE, CA

START TO FINISH: 30 MIN.
MAKES: 6 SERVINGS

- 2 **tablespoons canola oil**
- 2 **medium onions, chopped (about 1⅓ cups)**
- 3 **large tomatoes, seeded and chopped (about 2 cups)**
- 1 **jalapeno pepper, seeded and chopped**
- 1 **tablespoon minced fresh gingerroot**
- 2 **cans (15 ounces each) chickpeas or garbanzo beans, rinsed and drained**
- ¼ **cup water**
- 1 **teaspoon salt**
- 1 **cup light coconut milk**
- 3 **tablespoons minced fresh cilantro**
- 4½ **cups hot cooked brown rice**
  Additional minced fresh cilantro, optional

1. In a large skillet, heat oil over medium-high heat. Add onions; cook and stir until crisp-tender. Add tomatoes, jalapeno and ginger; cook and stir 2-3 minutes longer or until vegetables are tender.
2. Stir in chickpeas, water and salt; bring to a boil. Reduce heat; simmer, uncovered, 4-5 minutes or until liquid is almost evaporated. Remove from heat; stir in coconut milk and cilantro.
3. Serve with rice; sprinkle with additional cilantro if desired.
NOTE *Wear disposable gloves when cutting hot peppers; the oils can burn skin. Avoid touching your face.*
PER SERVING *⅔ cup chickpea mixture with ¾ cup rice equals 402 cal., 12 g fat (3 g sat. fat), 0 chol., 590 mg sodium, 65 g carb., 10 g fiber, 11 g pro.*

Makeover Mac & Cheese

Macaroni and cheese is the king of comfort foods, and this sensational version doesn't leave anything out. It's bubbling with creamy, cheesy goodness. I got the original recipe from my sister-in-law and am so glad to have this lightened-up version!

—**APRIL TAYLOR** HOLCOMB, KS

PREP: 30 MIN. • **BAKE:** 25 MIN.
MAKES: 10 SERVINGS

- 1 **package (16 ounces) elbow macaroni**
- ⅓ **cup all-purpose flour**
- ½ **teaspoon garlic powder**
- ½ **teaspoon pepper**
- ¼ **teaspoon salt**
- 2 **cups fat-free half-and-half**
- 2 **tablespoons butter**
- 2 **cups fat-free milk**
- 3 **cups (12 ounces) shredded reduced-fat sharp cheddar cheese**

TOPPING
- 2 **tablespoons butter**
- 1 **medium onion, chopped**
- 5 **cups cubed bread**
- ½ **cup shredded reduced-fat cheddar cheese**

1. Preheat oven to 350°. Cook macaroni according to package directions; drain.
2. Meanwhile, in small bowl, whisk flour, seasonings and half-and-half until smooth. In a large saucepan, melt butter over medium heat. Stir in the half-and-half mixture. Add milk. Bring to a gentle boil, stirring constantly; remove from heat. Add cheese; stir until melted. Stir in macaroni. Transfer to a 13x9-in. baking dish coated with cooking spray.
3. For topping, in a large skillet, heat butter over medium-high heat. Add onion; cook and stir until tender. Add cubed bread; cook and stir 2 minutes longer. Sprinkle over the macaroni mixture; top with cheese.
4. Bake, uncovered, 25-30 minutes or until heated through.
PER SERVING *1 cup equals 432 cal., 15 g fat (9 g sat. fat), 41 mg chol., 526 mg sodium, 55 g carb., 2 g fiber, 21 g pro.*

THE SKINNY

If you prepare the mac & cheese without the bread crumb topping, you can save an additional 89 calories, 4 grams of fat, 3 grams saturated fat, 10 mg cholesterol, 172 mg sodium and 10 grams carbs per serving.

ORIGINAL	MAKEOVER
672 Calories	432 Calories
42g Fat	15g Fat
28g Sat. Fat	9g Sat. Fat

MAKEOVER MAC & CHEESE

Portobellos with Ratatouille

These veggie-stuffed mushrooms are so hearty, meat eaters in the house won't feel left out. An appealing entree, it's bursting with color, taste and texture.
—MARIE RIZZIO INTERLOCHEN, MI

PREP: 30 MIN. • **BAKE:** 25 MIN.
MAKES: 4 SERVINGS

- 1 large onion, chopped
- 1 tablespoon plus 1 teaspoon olive oil, divided
- 5 garlic cloves, minced, divided
- 1 small eggplant, peeled and cubed
- 2 medium zucchini, cubed
- 1 medium sweet red pepper, chopped
- ¼ cup tomato paste
- 2 teaspoons red wine vinegar
- 1 teaspoon minced fresh thyme or ¼ teaspoon dried thyme
- ½ teaspoon salt
- ⅛ teaspoon pepper
  Dash cayenne pepper
- 2 medium tomatoes, chopped
- 4 large portobello mushrooms (4 to 4½ inches)
- 2 packages (6 ounces each) fresh baby spinach
  Minced fresh parsley and shaved Parmesan cheese

1. In a large skillet, saute onion in 1 tablespoon oil until tender. Add 3 garlic cloves; cook 1 minute longer. Stir in the eggplant, zucchini, red pepper, tomato paste, vinegar and seasonings.
2. Transfer to a 15x10x1-in. baking pan coated with cooking spray. Bake at 400° for 10 minutes. Stir in tomatoes; bake 15-20 minutes longer or until vegetables are tender.
3. Meanwhile, remove and discard stems and gills from mushrooms. Place mushrooms, stem side up, on a baking sheet coated with cooking spray; drizzle with remaining oil and sprinkle with remaining garlic. Bake at 400° for 20-25 minutes or until tender, turning once.
4. Place spinach in a large nonstick skillet coated with cooking spray; cook and stir for 4-5 minutes or until wilted.
5. Divide spinach among four plates; top with mushrooms. Fill mushrooms with ratatouille; sprinkle with parsley and cheese.
PER SERVING *1 mushroom with ½ cup cooked spinach and 1 cup ratatouille (calculated without cheese) equals 184 cal., 6 g fat (1 g sat. fat), 0 chol., 397 mg sodium, 29 g carb., 9 g fiber, 9 g pro.* **Diabetic Exchanges: 2 starch, 1 fat.**

⑤ INGREDIENTS FAST FIX

Stovetop Macaroni and Cheese

Creamy, cheesy and just plain luscious, this lightened-up version of the classic comfort food will become a must-have at your house.
—NANCY LANGROCK SOUTHBURY, CT

START TO FINISH: 30 MIN.
MAKES: 8 SERVINGS

- 1 package (16 ounces) elbow macaroni
- 2 tablespoons all-purpose flour
- 2 cups fat-free milk
- 1 package (16 ounces) reduced-fat process cheese (Velveeta), cubed
- 1 cup (4 ounces) shredded sharp cheddar cheese, divided

1. Cook macaroni according to package directions. Meanwhile, in a large saucepan, combine flour and milk until smooth. Bring to a boil; cook and stir for 2 minutes or until thickened. Stir in process cheese and ½ cup cheddar cheese until smooth. Drain macaroni; stir into cheese sauce.
2. Remove from the heat; sprinkle with remaining cheese. Cover and let stand for 5 minutes or until cheese is melted.
PER SERVING *1 cup equals 403 cal., 11 g fat (6 g sat. fat), 36 mg chol., 944 mg sodium, 54 g carb., 2 g fiber, 23 g pro.*

PORTOBELLOS WITH RATATOUILLE

Veggie Nicoise Salad

More and more people in my workplace are becoming vegetarians. When we cook or eat together, the focus is on fresh produce. This salad combines some of our favorite ingredients in one dish—and with the hard-cooked eggs and kidney beans, it delivers enough protein to satisfy those who are skeptical of vegetarian fare.

—ELIZABETH KELLEY CHICAGO, IL

PREP: 40 MIN. • **COOK:** 25 MIN.
MAKES: 6 SERVINGS

- ⅓ cup olive oil
- ¼ cup lemon juice
- 2 teaspoons minced fresh oregano
- 2 teaspoons minced fresh thyme
- 1 teaspoon Dijon mustard
- 1 garlic clove, minced
- ¼ teaspoon coarsely ground pepper
- ⅛ teaspoon salt
- 1 pound small red potatoes, halved
- 1 pound fresh asparagus, trimmed
- ½ pound fresh green beans, trimmed
- 1 can (16 ounces) kidney beans, rinsed and drained
- 1 small red onion, halved and thinly sliced
- 2 bunches romaine, torn
- 6 hard-cooked large eggs, quartered
- 1 jar (6½ ounces) marinated quartered artichoke hearts, drained
- ½ cup Nicoise or kalamata olives

1. In a small bowl, whisk the first eight ingredients; set aside.

2. Place potatoes in a small saucepan and cover with water. Bring to a boil. Reduce the heat; cover and simmer for 10-15 minutes or until tender. Drain. Drizzle warm potatoes with 1 tablespoon vinaigrette; toss to coat and set aside.

VEGGIE NICOISE SALAD

3. In a large saucepan, bring 4 cups water to a boil. Add asparagus; cook for 2-4 minutes or until crisp-tender. With tongs, remove asparagus and immediately place in ice water. Drain and pat dry.

4. Return water to a boil. Add green beans; cook for 3-4 minutes or until crisp-tender. Remove beans and place in ice water. Drain and pat dry.

5. In a small bowl, combine the kidney beans, onion and 1 tablespoon vinaigrette; toss to coat. Set aside.

6. Just before serving, toss asparagus with 1 tablespoon vinaigrette; toss green beans with 2 teaspoons vinaigrette. Place romaine in a large bowl; drizzle with remaining vinaigrette and toss to coat. Transfer to a serving platter; arrange the vegetables, kidney bean mixture, eggs, artichoke hearts and olives over lettuce.

PER SERVING *1 serving equals 431 cal., 26 g fat (5 g sat. fat), 212 mg chol., 565 mg sodium, 37 g carb., 9 g fiber, 17 g pro.*

LOADED MEXICAN PIZZA

2 cups chopped fresh spinach
2 tablespoons minced fresh cilantro
   Hot pepper sauce to taste
½ cup shredded reduced-fat cheddar
   cheese
½ cup shredded pepper jack cheese

1. In a small bowl, mash black beans. Stir in the onion, yellow pepper, chili powder and cumin. In another small bowl, combine the tomatoes, jalapeno and garlic.

2. Place crust on an ungreased 12-in. pizza pan; spread with bean mixture. Top with tomato mixture and spinach. Sprinkle with cilantro, pepper sauce and cheeses.

3. Bake at 400° for 12-15 minutes or until cheese is melted.

NOTE *Wear disposable gloves when cutting hot peppers; the oils can burn skin. Avoid touching your face.*

PER SERVING *1 slice equals 297 cal., 9 g fat (4 g sat. fat), 17 mg chol., 566 mg sodium, 41 g carb., 6 g fiber, 15 g pro.* **Diabetic Exchanges:** *2½ starch, 1 lean meat, 1 vegetable.*

HOW TO

PEEL GARLIC

To quickly peel fresh garlic, gently crush the clove with the flat side of a large knife blade. If you don't have a large knife, you can crush the garlic with a small can. The peel is easy to remove after the garlic clove has been crushed.

FAST FIX
Loaded Mexican Pizza

My husband, Steve, is a picky eater, but this healthy pizza has so much flavor he actually looks forward to it. And leftovers are no problem, because this is one of those rare meals that taste even better the next day.

—**MARY BARKER** KNOXVILLE, TN

START TO FINISH: 30 MIN.
MAKES: 6 SLICES

1 can (15 ounces) black beans, rinsed and drained
1 medium red onion, chopped
1 small sweet yellow pepper, chopped
3 teaspoons chili powder
¾ teaspoon ground cumin
3 medium tomatoes, chopped
1 jalapeno pepper, seeded and finely chopped
1 garlic clove, minced
1 prebaked 12-inch thin pizza crust

Tofu-Stuffed Pasta Shells

Jazz up tofu with cheese, spinach and garlic, then accent with an easy tomato sauce to complete the entree. Your gang won't even miss the meat in this flavorful pasta dish.

—**JENNI DISE** PHOENIX, AZ

PREP: 25 MIN. • **BAKE:** 35 MIN.
MAKES: 5 SERVINGS

- 15 uncooked jumbo pasta shells
- 1½ cups silken firm tofu
- 3 tablespoons grated Romano cheese, divided
- 2 garlic cloves, peeled
- 1 package (10 ounces) frozen chopped spinach, thawed and squeezed dry
- 1 can (14½ ounces) Italian diced tomatoes, drained
- 1 can (8 ounces) tomato sauce
- ¼ cup dry red wine or vegetable broth
- ½ cup shredded part-skim mozzarella cheese

1. Cook pasta shells according to package directions. Meanwhile, in a blender, combine the tofu, 2 tablespoons Romano cheese and garlic; cover and process until smooth.

(Add 1 tablespoon water if mixture is too thick.) Add spinach; process until blended. Drain shells; stuff with tofu mixture.

2. In a small bowl, combine the tomatoes, tomato sauce and wine. Spread about ½ cup sauce in an 11x7-in. baking dish coated with cooking spray. Arrange stuffed shells over sauce. Top with remaining sauce.

3. Cover and bake at 350° for 25 minutes. Uncover; sprinkle with mozzarella and remaining Romano cheese. Bake 8-10 minutes longer or until shells are heated through and cheese is melted.

PER SERVING *3 stuffed shells equals 262 cal., 5 g fat (2 g sat. fat), 10 mg chol., 754 mg sodium, 39 g carb., 4 g fiber, 14 g pro.* **Diabetic Exchanges: 3 vegetable, 1½ starch, 1 lean meat.**

FAST FIX

Garden Quinoa Salad

Not only is this recipe delicious, but it is healthful as well. Serve it hot or cold, and pack up the leftovers for easy, portable lunches.

—**PATRICIA NIEH** PORTOLA VALLEY, CA

START TO FINISH: 30 MIN.
MAKES: 4 SERVINGS

- 1½ cups quinoa, rinsed and well drained
- 3 cups water
- 1 pound fresh asparagus, cut into 2-inch pieces
- ½ pound fresh sugar snap peas
- ½ pound fresh green beans, trimmed
- 2 tablespoons olive oil
- 2 tablespoons lemon juice
- 2 tablespoons minced fresh parsley
- 1 teaspoon grated lemon peel
- ¾ teaspoon salt
- 1 cup cherry tomatoes, halved
- 3 tablespoons salted pumpkin seeds or pepitas

1. In a large saucepan, cook and stir quinoa over medium-high heat for 3-5 minutes or until toasted. Add water; bring to a boil. Reduce heat; simmer, covered, 12-15 minutes or until liquid is absorbed. Transfer to a large bowl.

2. Meanwhile, in a large saucepan, bring 4 cups water to a boil. Add asparagus and snap peas; cook, uncovered, 2-4 minutes or just until crisp-tender. Remove vegetables and immediately drop into ice water.

3. Return water to a boil. Add green beans; cook 3-4 minutes or until crisp-tender. Remove beans and drop into ice water. Drain vegetables; pat dry.

4. In a small bowl, whisk oil, lemon juice, parsley, lemon peel and salt. Add tomatoes and blanched vegetables to quinoa; drizzle with dressing and toss to combine. Top with pumpkin seeds.

PER SERVING *2¼ cups with about 2 teaspoons pumpkin seeds equals 417 cal., 15 g fat (2 g sat. fat), 0 chol., 533 mg sodium, 58 g carb., 9 g fiber, 16 g pro.*

DIANE ROTH'S
LIGHT CHEESECAKE
PAGE 268

Desserts

Give your sweet tooth a workout while still sticking to your diet! These delectable **cookies, cakes, custards, crisps** and more will satisfy everybody's craving for something sweet. Best of all, no one will suspect you **cut the sugar and fat.**

SUE SCHMIDTKE'S FRUIT & GRANOLA CRISP WITH YOGURT *PAGE 267*

BARBARA WORREL'S ZUCCHINI CHOCOLATE CAKE WITH ORANGE GLAZE *PAGE 269*

JENNY LEIGHTY'S IRISH CREAM CUPCAKES *PAGE 254*

Irish Cream Cupcakes

If you're looking for a grown-up cupcake, give these a try. You'll have a hard time limiting yourself to one—good thing they're lighter!

—JENNY LEIGHTY WEST SALEM, OH

PREP: 25 MIN. • **BAKE:** 20 MIN. + COOLING
MAKES: 2 DOZEN

- ½ cup butter, softened
- 1½ cups sugar
- 2 large eggs
- ¾ cup unsweetened applesauce
- 2 teaspoons vanilla extract
- 2½ cups all-purpose flour
- 3 teaspoons baking powder
- ½ teaspoon salt
- ½ cup Irish cream liqueur

FROSTING

- ⅓ cup butter, softened
- 4 ounces reduced-fat cream cheese
- 6 tablespoons Irish cream liqueur
- 4 cups confectioners' sugar

1. In a large bowl, beat butter and sugar until crumbly, about 2 minutes. Add eggs, one at a time, beating well after each addition. Beat in applesauce and vanilla (mixture may appear curdled). Combine the flour, baking powder and salt; add to the creamed mixture alternately with liqueur, beating well after each addition.

2. Fill paper-lined muffin cups two-thirds full. Bake at 350° for 18-22 minutes or until a toothpick inserted near the center comes out clean. Cool for 10 minutes before removing from pans to wire racks to cool completely.

3. For frosting, in a large bowl, beat butter and cream cheese until fluffy. Beat in liqueur. Add confectioners' sugar; beat until smooth. Pipe over tops of cupcakes. Refrigerate leftovers.

PER SERVING *1 cupcake equals 273 cal., 9 g fat (5 g sat. fat), 38 mg chol., 170 mg sodium, 45 g carb., trace fiber, 2 g pro.*

IRISH CREAM CUPCAKES

SLOW COOKER

Slow Cooker Baked Apples

Coming home to this irresistible dessert on a dreary day is just wonderful; it's slow-cooker easy.

—EVANGELINE BRADFORD ERLANGER, KY

PREP: 25 MIN. • **COOK:** 4 HOURS
MAKES: 6 SERVINGS

- 6 medium tart apples
- ½ cup raisins
- ⅓ cup packed brown sugar
- 1 tablespoon grated orange peel
- 1 cup water
- 3 tablespoons thawed orange juice concentrate
- 2 tablespoons butter

1. Core apples and peel the top third of each if desired. Combine the raisins, brown sugar and orange peel; spoon into apples. Place the apples in a 5-qt. slow cooker.

2. Pour water around apples. Drizzle with orange juice concentrate. Dot with butter. Cover and cook on low for 4-5 hours or until apples are tender.

PER SERVING *1 stuffed apple equals 203 cal., 4 g fat (2 g sat. fat), 10 mg chol., 35 mg sodium, 44 g carb., 4 g fiber, 1 g pro.*

Maple Walnut Biscotti

Biscotti is the perfect complement to coffee or tea. For even more maple flavor, replace the melted chocolate with an icing of ½ cup confectioners' sugar mixed with 2 tablespoons maple syrup. Lightly drizzle over the cookies and allow to set.

—SUSAN ROGERS BRATTLEBORO, VT

PREP: 30 MIN. • **BAKE:** 35 MIN. + COOLING
MAKES: 28 BISCOTTI

- 2 **large eggs**
- 1 **large egg white**
- ⅓ **cup maple syrup**
- ¼ **cup sugar**
- 1 **teaspoon vanilla extract**
- 1¾ **cups all-purpose flour**
- ½ **cup oat flour**
- 1 **teaspoon baking soda**
- ½ **cup chopped walnuts**
- ½ **cup dried cranberries**
- ⅓ **cup dark chocolate chips or white baking chips**

1. In a small bowl, beat eggs, egg white, syrup, sugar and vanilla until blended. Combine flours and baking soda; gradually add to egg mixture and mix well (dough will be sticky). Stir in walnuts and cranberries.

2. With floured hands, shape dough into two 10x2½-in. rectangles on a parchment paper-lined baking sheet. Bake at 350° for 22-26 minutes or until set.

3. Reduce heat to 325°. Place pan on a wire rack. When cool enough to handle, transfer to a cutting board; cut diagonally with a serrated knife into ½-in. slices. Place cut side down on ungreased baking sheets. Bake for 9-11 minutes on each side or until golden brown. Remove to wire racks to cool.

4. In a microwave, melt chocolate chips; stir until smooth. Place biscotti on a waxed paper-lined baking sheet. Drizzle with chocolate; chill until set.

MAPLE WALNUT BISCOTTI

Store in an airtight container.
NOTE *As a substitute for ½ cup of oat flour, process ½ cup plus 2 tablespoons quick-cooking or old-fashioned oats until finely ground.*
PER SERVING *1 cookie equals 93 cal., 3 g fat (1 g sat. fat), 15 mg chol., 52 mg sodium, 15 g carb., 1 g fiber, 2 g pro.*
***Diabetic Exchange:** 1 starch.*

DID YOU KNOW?

Most vanilla comes from Madagascar and Reunion Island—formerly known as the Bourbon Islands—off the southeast coast of Africa. Bourbon vanilla is celebrated for its strong, clear vanilla flavor and creamy finish.

LEMON-BERRY SHORTCAKE

Ice Cream Cone Treats

I came up with this recipe as a way for my grandkids to enjoy Rice Krispies Treats without getting sticky hands. You can also pack the cereal mixture into paper cups and insert a freezer pop stick to create cute pops.

—**MABEL NOLAN** VANCOUVER, WA

START TO FINISH: 15 MIN.
MAKES: 12 SERVINGS

Colored sprinkles
4   **cups miniature marshmallows**
3   **tablespoons butter**
6   **cups crisp rice cereal**
12 **ice cream cones**

1. Place sprinkles in a shallow bowl. In a microwave or in a large saucepan over low heat, melt marshmallows and butter. Remove from heat; stir in cereal.

2. Using buttered hands, shape cereal mixture into 12 balls. Pack each ball into an ice cream cone. Dip tops in sprinkles.

PER SERVING *1 serving equals 146 cal., 3 g fat (2 g sat. fat), 8 mg chol., 170 mg sodium, 28 g carb., trace fiber, 1 g pro.*

Lemon-Berry Shortcake

Bake a simple cake using fresh strawberries, and enjoy this summertime classic with a generous layer of whipped topping and berries.

—**MERYL HERR** GRAND RAPIDS, MI

PREP: 30 MIN. • **BAKE:** 20 MIN. + COOLING
MAKES: 8 SERVINGS

1⅓ **cups all-purpose flour**
½   **cup sugar**
2   **teaspoons baking powder**
¼   **teaspoon salt**
1   **large egg**
⅔   **cup buttermilk**
¼   **cup butter, melted**
1   **tablespoon lemon juice**
1   **teaspoon grated lemon peel**
1   **teaspoon vanilla extract**
1   **cup sliced fresh strawberries**
TOPPING
1½ **cups sliced fresh strawberries**
1   **tablespoon lemon juice**
1   **teaspoon sugar**
2   **cups reduced-fat whipped topping**

1. In a large bowl, combine the flour, sugar, baking powder and salt. In another bowl, combine the egg, buttermilk, butter, lemon juice, lemon peel and vanilla. Stir into dry ingredients just until moistened. Fold in strawberries. Pour into a greased and floured 9-in. round baking pan.
2. Bake at 350° for 20-25 minutes or until a toothpick inserted near the center comes out clean. Cool for 10 minutes before removing from pan to a wire rack to cool completely.
3. For topping, in a large bowl, combine strawberries, lemon juice and sugar. Cover and refrigerate until serving. Spread whipped topping over cake. Drain strawberries; arrange over top.
PER SERVING *1 slice equals 252 cal., 9 g fat (6 g sat. fat), 42 mg chol., 245 mg sodium, 40 g carb., 2 g fiber, 4 g pro.*

Almond Pear Tart

I had never seen a "pie without a pan" until my daughter brought back this wonderful recipe from a Rotary Club exchange program in Belgium. It's still a family favorite after all these years.

—**SHERRY LAMAY** CAPITAN, NM

PREP: 15 MIN. • **BAKE:** 20 MIN. + COOLING
MAKES: 8 SERVINGS

> Pastry for single-crust pie (9 inches)
> ¾ cup plus 2 teaspoons sugar, divided
> 3 tablespoons all-purpose flour
> 4 cups sliced peeled fresh pears (about 4 medium)
> 3 tablespoons sliced almonds

1. On a lightly floured surface, roll dough into a 10-in. circle. Transfer to a parchment paper-lined baking sheet.
2. In a large bowl, combine ¾ cup sugar and flour; add pears and toss to coat. Spoon over the pastry to within 2 in. of edges. Fold up edges of pastry over filling, leaving center uncovered. Sprinkle with remaining sugar.
3. Bake at 450° for 15 minutes or until crust is golden and filling is bubbly. Sprinkle with almonds; bake 5 minutes longer. Using the parchment paper, slide tart onto a wire rack to cool.
PER SERVING *1 slice equals 269 cal., 8 g fat (3 g sat. fat), 5 mg chol., 100 mg sodium, 48 g carb., 2 g fiber, 2 g pro.*

Lemon Meringue Cupcakes

Classic lemon meringue pie was the inspiration for these gorgeous little cupcakes. The tangy treats hide a surprise lemon pie filling beneath the icing of fluffy toasted meringue. Make them for your next special gathering.

—**ANDREA QUIROZ** CHICAGO, IL

PREP: 30 MIN. • **BAKE:** 25 MIN. + COOLING
MAKES: 2 DOZEN

> 1 package lemon cake mix (regular size)
> 1⅓ cups water
> ⅓ cup canola oil
> 3 large eggs
> 1 tablespoon grated lemon peel
> 1 cup lemon creme pie filling
> **MERINGUE**
> 3 large egg whites
> ½ teaspoon cream of tartar
> ½ cup sugar

1. In a large bowl, combine the cake mix, water, oil, eggs and lemon peel; beat on low speed for 30 seconds. Beat on medium for 2 minutes.
2. Fill paper-lined muffin cups two-thirds full. Bake at 350° for 18-22 minutes or until a toothpick inserted near the center comes out clean.
3. Cut a small hole in the corner of a pastry or plastic bag; insert a very small tip. Fill with pie filling. Push the tip into the top of each cupcake to fill.
4. In a large bowl, beat egg whites and cream of tartar on medium speed until soft peaks form. Gradually beat in sugar, 1 tablespoon at a time, on high until stiff glossy peaks form and sugar is dissolved. Pipe over tops of cupcakes.
5. Bake at 400° for 5-8 minutes or until meringue is golden brown. Cool for 10 minutes before removing from pans to wire racks to cool completely. Store in an airtight container in the refrigerator.
PER SERVING *1 cupcake equals 153 cal., 5 g fat (1 g sat. fat), 28 mg chol., 176 mg sodium, 25 g carb., trace fiber, 2 g pro.* **Diabetic Exchanges:** *1½ starch, 1½ fat.*

LEMON MERINGUE CUPCAKES

Rhubarb Oat Bars

These soft rhubarb bars provide just the right amount of tartness and sweetness. They are simply unbeatable!

—RENETTE CRESSEY FORT MILL, SC

PREP: 20 MIN. • **BAKE:** 25 MIN. + COOLING
MAKES: 16 BARS

- 1½ cups chopped fresh or frozen rhubarb
- 1 cup packed brown sugar, divided
- 4 tablespoons water, divided
- 1 teaspoon lemon juice
- 4 teaspoons cornstarch
- 1 cup old-fashioned oats
- ¾ cup all-purpose flour
- ½ cup flaked coconut
- ½ teaspoon salt
- ⅓ cup butter, melted

1. In a large saucepan, combine the rhubarb, ½ cup brown sugar, 3 tablespoons water and lemon juice. Bring to a boil. Reduce heat to medium; cook and stir for 4-5 minutes or until rhubarb is tender.

2. Combine the cornstarch and remaining water until smooth; gradually stir into rhubarb mixture. Bring to a boil; cook and stir for 2 minutes or until thickened. Remove from the heat; set aside.

3. In a large bowl, combine the oats, flour, coconut, salt and remaining brown sugar. Stir in butter until mixture is crumbly.

4. Press half of the oats mixture into a greased 8-in-square baking dish. Spread with the rhubarb mixture. Sprinkle with remaining oat mixture and press down lightly.

5. Bake at 350° for 25-30 minutes or until golden brown. Cool on a wire rack. Cut into squares.

NOTE *If using frozen rhubarb, measure rhubarb while still frozen, then thaw completely. Drain in a colander, but do not press liquid out.*

PER SERVING *1 bar equals 145 cal., 5 g fat (3 g sat. fat), 10 mg chol., 126 mg sodium, 24 g carb., 1 g fiber, 2 g pro. Diabetic Exchanges: 1½ starch, 1 fat.*

Swirled Blueberry Frozen Yogurt

My easy frozen treat tastes indulgent, but it's packed with nutrient-rich blueberries and walnuts. A drizzle of white chocolate is the perfect finishing touch.

—CHRISTINA SEREMETIS ROCKLAND, MA

PREP: 30 MIN. + FREEZING
MAKES: 8 SERVINGS

- 1 cup fresh or frozen blueberries
- ⅓ cup sugar
- ⅓ cup finely chopped walnuts
- 1 quart fat-free frozen yogurt, softened

DRIZZLE

- 2½ ounces white baking chocolate, chopped
- 1 tablespoon fat-free milk
- ½ teaspoon vanilla extract

1. In a small bowl, combine the blueberries, sugar and walnuts; let stand for 15 minutes.

2. In a large container, layer a third of the frozen yogurt and half the blueberry mixture. Repeat layers. Top with remaining frozen yogurt. Swirl mixture; freeze until firm.

3. In a small saucepan, combine the chocolate, milk and vanilla. Cook and stir over low heat until chocolate is melted. Serve with frozen yogurt.

PER SERVING *½ cup yogurt with 1½ teaspoons drizzle equals 221 cal., 7 g fat (2 g sat. fat), 3 mg chol., 75 mg sodium, 36 g carb., 1 g fiber, 6 g pro.*

DID YOU KNOW?

Because it contains no cocoa solids, white chocolate technically isn't a chocolate at all. It does contain cocoa butter, which gives white chocolate its rich, buttery texture. Higher-quality white chocolate has a greater percentage of cocoa butter, while imitation chocolate doesn't have any.

Warm Chocolate Melting Cups

These chocolaty custard desserts are surprisingly rich and smooth for less than 200 calories. They'd be ideal for a special dinner party.

—KISSA VAUGHN TROY, TX

PREP: 20 MIN. • **BAKE:** 20 MIN.
MAKES: 10 SERVINGS

- 1¼ cups sugar, divided
- ½ cup baking cocoa
- 2 tablespoons all-purpose flour
- ⅛ teaspoon salt
- ¾ cup water
- ¾ cup plus 1 tablespoon semisweet chocolate chips
- 1 tablespoon brewed coffee
- 1 teaspoon vanilla extract
- 2 large eggs
- 1 large egg white
- 10 fresh strawberry halves, optional

1. In a small saucepan, combine ¾ cup sugar, cocoa, flour and salt. Gradually stir in water. Bring to a boil; cook and stir for 2 minutes or until thickened. Remove from the heat; stir in the chocolate chips, coffee and vanilla until smooth. Transfer to a large bowl.

2. In another bowl, beat eggs and egg white until slightly thickened. Gradually add remaining sugar, beating until the mixture is thick and lemon-colored. Fold into the chocolate mixture.

3. Transfer to ten 4-oz. ramekins coated with cooking spray. Place ramekins in a baking pan; add 1 in. of boiling water to pan. Bake, uncovered, at 350° for 20-25 minutes or just until centers are set. Garnish with strawberry halves if desired. Serve immediately.

PER SERVING *1 dessert equals 197 cal., 6 g fat (3 g sat. fat), 42 mg chol., 51 mg sodium, 37 g carb., 2 g fiber, 3 g pro.*

UPSIDE-DOWN BERRY CAKE

Upside-Down Berry Cake

Here's a summery cake that's delicious warm or cold and served with whipped topping or ice cream. It soaks up loads of flavor from the berries.

—CANDICE SCHOLL WEST SUNBURY, PA

PREP: 20 MIN. • **BAKE:** 30 MIN. + COOLING
MAKES: 15 SERVINGS

- ½ cup chopped walnuts
- 1 cup fresh or frozen blueberries
- 1 cup fresh or frozen raspberries, halved
- 1 cup sliced fresh strawberries
- ¼ cup sugar
- 1 package (3 ounces) raspberry gelatin
- 1 package yellow cake mix (regular size)
- 2 large eggs
- 1¼ cups water
- 2 tablespoons canola oil
- 1½ cups miniature marshmallows

1. In a well-greased 13x9-in. baking pan, layer the walnuts and berries; sprinkle with sugar and gelatin. In a large bowl, combine the cake mix, eggs, water and oil; beat on low speed for 30 seconds. Beat on medium for 2 minutes. Fold in marshmallows. Pour over top.

2. Bake at 350° for 35-40 minutes or until a toothpick inserted near the center comes out clean. Cool for 5 minutes before inverting onto a serving platter. Refrigerate leftovers.

PER SERVING *1 piece equals 276 cal., 7 g fat (2 g sat. fat), 28 mg chol., 249 mg sodium, 51 g carb., 1 g fiber, 3 g pro.*

DOUBLE-NUT STUFFED FIGS

Double-Nut Stuffed Figs

We have a diabetic in the family, so we like desserts that everyone can enjoy guilt-free. These figs are sweet and delicious without compromising on good nutrition. That's why we love the recipe.
—**BOB BAILEY** COLUMBUS, OH

PREP: 20 MIN. • **BAKE:** 30 MIN.
MAKES: 3 DOZEN

- 36 dried Calimyrna figs
- ⅔ cup finely chopped pecans
- ⅔ cup finely chopped walnuts
- 7 tablespoons agave nectar, divided
- 3 tablespoons baking cocoa
- ¼ teaspoon ground cinnamon
- ⅛ teaspoon ground cloves
- ½ cup pomegranate juice
- 4½ teaspoons lemon juice

1. Preheat oven to 350°. Remove stems from figs. Cut an X in the top of each fig, about two-thirds of the way down.
2. In a small bowl, combine pecans, walnuts, 3 tablespoons agave nectar, cocoa, cinnamon and cloves; spoon into figs. Arrange in a 13x9-in. baking dish coated with cooking spray.
3. In a small bowl, mix pomegranate juice, lemon juice and remaining agave nectar; drizzle over figs. Bake, covered, 20 minutes. Bake, uncovered, 8-10 minutes longer or until heated through, basting occasionally with cooking liquid.
PER SERVING *1 stuffed fig equals 98 cal., 3 g fat (trace sat. fat), 0 chol., 3 mg sodium, 17 g carb., 3 g fiber, 1 g pro.* **Diabetic Exchanges:** *1 starch, ½ fat.*

Banana Pudding

I didn't see my son for more than two years after he enlisted in the Marines after high school. When he finally arrived back home, I just grabbed hold of him at the airport and burst out crying. And when we got to our house, the first thing he ate was two bowls of my banana pudding.
—**STEPHANIE HARRIS** MONTPELIER, VA

PREP: 35 MIN. + CHILLING
MAKES: 9 SERVINGS

- ¾ cup sugar
- ¼ cup all-purpose flour
- ¼ teaspoon salt
- 3 cups 2% milk
- 3 large eggs
- 1½ teaspoons vanilla extract
- 8 ounces vanilla wafers (about 60 cookies), divided
- 4 large ripe bananas, cut into ¼-inch slices

1. In a large saucepan, mix sugar, flour and salt. Whisk in milk. Cook and stir over medium heat until thickened and bubbly. Reduce heat to low; cook and stir 2 minutes longer. Remove from heat.
2. In a small bowl, whisk eggs. Whisk a small amount of hot mixture into eggs; return all to the pan, whisking constantly. Bring to a gentle boil; cook and stir 2 minutes. Remove from the heat. Stir in vanilla. Cool 15 minutes, stirring occasionally.
3. In an ungreased 8-in.-square baking dish, layer 25 vanilla wafers, half of the banana slices and half of the pudding. Repeat layers.
4. Press plastic wrap onto surface of pudding. Refrigerate 4 hours or overnight. Just before serving, crush remaining wafers and sprinkle over the top.
PER SERVING *1 serving equals 302 cal., 7 g fat (2 g sat. fat), 80 mg chol., 206 mg sodium, 55 g carb., 2 g fiber, 7 g pro.*

Makeover Red Velvet Cake

I've had my beloved red velvet cake recipe for over 45 years, and it's my family's favorite cake. I asked the cooks at *Taste of Home* to give it a light makeover, and these are the tasty results!

—**BETTY SELCHOW** WHITE BEAR LAKE, MN

PREP: 20 MIN. • **BAKE:** 15 MIN. + COOLING
MAKES: 16 SERVINGS

- ¼ **cup butter, softened**
- 1 **cup sugar**
- 2 **large eggs**
- ¼ **cup unsweetened applesauce**
- 1 **bottle (1 ounce) red food coloring**
- 1 **teaspoon white vinegar**
- 1 **teaspoon vanilla extract**
- 2¼ **cups cake flour**
- 2 **teaspoons baking cocoa**
- 1 **teaspoon baking soda**
- 1 **teaspoon salt**
- 1 **cup buttermilk**

FROSTING

- 4½ **teaspoons all-purpose flour**
- ½ **cup fat-free milk**
- ½ **cup butter, softened**
- ½ **cup sugar**
- ½ **teaspoon vanilla extract**

1. Line two 9-in. round baking pans with parchment paper; coat paper with cooking spray and sprinkle with flour. Set aside. In a large bowl, beat butter and sugar until well blended. Add eggs, one at a time, beating well after each addition. Beat in the applesauce, food coloring, vinegar and vanilla.

2. Combine the flour, cocoa, baking soda and salt. Add to butter mixture alternately with buttermilk. Pour into prepared pans. Bake at 350° for 14-18 minutes or until a toothpick inserted near the center comes out clean. Cool for 10 minutes before removing from pans to wire racks to cool completely.

3. For frosting, in a small saucepan, whisk flour and milk until smooth. Bring to a boil; cook and stir for 2 minutes. Cool to room temperature. In a small bowl, cream butter and sugar until light and fluffy. Beat in flour mixture and vanilla. Spread between layers and over top of cake.

PER SERVING *1 slice equals 241 cal., 9 g fat (6 g sat. fat), 50 mg chol., 315 mg sodium, 36 g carb., trace fiber, 3 g pro.*

THE SKINNY

The original cake batter used ½ cup butter, while the makeover uses ¼ cup each of butter and applesauce. The makeover cake has only two layers instead of four and leaves the sides of the cake unfrosted. This allows the makeover cake to use less frosting than the original, which led to an additional ½ cup of butter saved in the frosting.

ORIGINAL	MAKEOVER
370 Calories	**241** Calories
18g Fat	**9**g Fat
11g Sat. Fat	**6**g Sat. Fat

MAKEOVER RED VELVET CAKE

⑤ INGREDIENTS | FAST FIX ▶
Banana Boats

This recipe, given to me years ago by a good friend, is a favorite with my family when we go camping. It's quick, fun to make and scrumptious!

—**BRENDA LOVELESS** GARLAND, TX

START TO FINISH: 20 MIN.
MAKES: 4 SERVINGS

- 4 **medium unpeeled ripe bananas**
- 4 **teaspoons miniature chocolate chips**
- 4 **tablespoons miniature marshmallows**

1. Cut banana peel lengthwise about ½ in. deep, leaving ½ in. at both ends. Open peel wider to form a pocket. Fill each with 1 teaspoon chocolate chips and 1 tablespoon marshmallows. Crimp and shape four pieces of heavy-duty foil (about 12 in. square) around bananas, forming boats.
2. Grill bananas, covered, over medium heat for 5-10 minutes or until the marshmallows melt and are golden brown.

PER SERVING *1 banana boat equals 136 cal., 2 g fat (1 g sat. fat), 0 chol., 3 mg sodium, 32 g carb., 3 g fiber, 1 g pro.*

CREAM CHEESE
SWIRL BROWNIES

Cream Cheese Swirl Brownies

I'm a chocolate lover, and this treat has satisfied my cravings many times. No one guesses the brownies are lower in fat, because their chewy texture and rich chocolate taste can't be beat.

—**HEIDI JOHNSON** WORLAND, WY

PREP: 20 MIN. • **BAKE:** 25 MIN.
MAKES: 1 DOZEN

- 3 **large eggs**
- 6 **tablespoons reduced-fat butter, softened**
- 1 **cup sugar, divided**
- 3 **teaspoons vanilla extract**
- ½ **cup all-purpose flour**
- ¼ **cup baking cocoa**
- 1 **package (8 ounces) reduced-fat cream cheese**

1. Preheat oven to 350°. Separate two eggs, putting each white in a separate bowl (discard yolks or save for another use); set aside. In a small bowl, beat butter and ¾ cup sugar until crumbly. Beat in the whole egg, one egg white and vanilla until well combined. Combine flour and cocoa; gradually add to egg mixture until blended. Pour into a 9-in.-square baking pan coated with cooking spray; set aside.
2. In a small bowl, beat cream cheese and remaining sugar until smooth. Beat in the second egg white. Drop by rounded tablespoonfuls over the batter; cut through batter with a knife to swirl.
3. Bake 25-30 minutes or until set and edges pull away from sides of pan. Cool on a wire rack.

PER SERVING *1 brownie equals 172 cal., 8 g fat (5 g sat. fat), 36 mg chol., 145 mg sodium, 23 g carb., trace fiber, 4 g pro.* ***Diabetic Exchanges:*** *1½ starch, 1½ fat.*

Grilled Peaches 'n' Berries

Highlight the natural sweetness of peak summertime fruit with brown sugar, butter and a squeeze of lemon juice. Foil packets make this a go-anywhere dessert.

—SHARON BICKETT CHESTER, SC

START TO FINISH: 30 MIN.
MAKES: 2 SERVINGS

- 2 medium ripe peaches, halved and pitted
- ½ cup fresh blueberries
- 1 tablespoon brown sugar
- 2 teaspoons lemon juice
- 4 teaspoons butter

1. Place two peach halves, cut side up, on each of two double thicknesses of heavy-duty foil (12 in. square). Sprinkle each with blueberries, brown sugar and lemon juice; dot with butter. Fold foil around peaches and seal tightly.
2. Grill, covered, over medium-low heat for 18-20 minutes or until tender. Open foil carefully to allow steam to escape.

PER SERVING *1 serving equals 156 cal., 8 g fat (5 g sat. fat), 20 mg chol., 57 mg sodium, 23 g carb., 2 g fiber, 1 g pro.* **Diabetic Exchanges:** *1 fruit, 1 fat, ½ starch.*

APPLE PIE OATMEAL DESSERT

Apple Pie Oatmeal Dessert

This spiced dessert brings back memories of time spent with my family around the kitchen table. I serve it with sweetened whipped cream or a scoop of vanilla ice cream as a topper.

—CAROL GREER EARLVILLE, IL

PREP: 15 MIN. • **COOK:** 4 HOURS
MAKES: 6 SERVINGS

- 1 cup quick-cooking oats
- ½ cup all-purpose flour
- ⅓ cup packed brown sugar
- 2 teaspoons baking powder
- 1½ teaspoons apple pie spice
- ¼ teaspoon salt
- 3 large eggs
- 1⅔ cups 2% milk, divided
- 1½ teaspoons vanilla extract
- 3 medium apples, peeled and finely chopped
  Vanilla ice cream, optional

1. In a large bowl, whisk oats, flour, brown sugar, baking powder, pie spice and salt. In a small bowl, whisk eggs, 1 cup milk and vanilla until blended. Add to oat mixture, stirring just until moistened. Fold in apples.
2. Transfer to a greased 3-qt. slow cooker. Cook, covered, on low for 4-5 hours or until apples are tender and top is set.
3. Stir in remaining milk. Serve warm or cold, with ice cream if desired.

PER SERVING *¾ cup (calculated without ice cream) equals 238 cal., 5 g fat (2 g sat. fat), 111 mg chol., 306 mg sodium, 41 g carb., 3 g fiber, 8 g pro.*

ORANGE DREAM ANGEL FOOD CAKE

Orange Dream Angel Food Cake

Angel food cake becomes a heavenly indulgence with a pretty swirl of orange in every bite. Here's the perfect light summertime dessert. Try it with a small scoop of sherbet for a special treat.

—LAUREN OSBORNE HOLTWOOD, PA

PREP: 25 MIN. • **BAKE:** 30 MIN. + COOLING
MAKES: 16 SERVINGS

- 12 large egg whites
- 1 cup all-purpose flour
- 1¾ cups sugar, divided
- 1½ teaspoons cream of tartar
- ½ teaspoon salt
- 1 teaspoon almond extract
- 1 teaspoon vanilla extract
- 1 teaspoon grated orange peel
- 1 teaspoon orange extract
- 6 drops red food coloring, optional
- 6 drops yellow food coloring, optional

1. Place egg whites in a large bowl; let stand at room temperature for 30 minutes. Sift flour and ¾ cup sugar together twice; set aside.
2. Add the cream of tartar, salt and almond and vanilla extracts to egg whites; beat on medium speed until soft peaks form. Gradually add remaining sugar, about 2 tablespoons at a time, beating on high until stiff glossy peaks form and sugar is dissolved. Gradually fold in flour mixture, about ½ cup at a time.
3. Gently spoon half of batter into an ungreased 10-in. tube pan. To the remaining batter, stir in the orange peel, orange extract and, if desired, food colorings. Gently spoon orange batter over white batter. Cut through both layers with a knife to swirl the orange and remove air pockets.
4. Bake on the lowest oven rack at 375° for 30-35 minutes or until lightly browned and entire top appears dry. Immediately invert pan; cool completely, about 1 hour.
5. Run a knife around side and center tube of pan. Remove cake to a serving plate.

PER SERVING *1 slice equals 130 cal., trace fat (trace sat. fat), 0 chol., 116 mg sodium, 28 g carb., trace fiber, 4 g pro.* **Diabetic Exchange:** *2 starch.*

Lemon-Yogurt Tea Cakes

Light, tender and tangy, these little lemon cakes will be the belle of the brunch. But we also adore them for lunch, supper or snacking.

—RUTH BURRUS ZIONSVILLE, IN

PREP: 20 MIN. • **BAKE:** 20 MIN. + COOLING
MAKES: ABOUT 1 DOZEN

- 2¼ cups all-purpose flour
- 1 cup sugar
- ¾ teaspoon baking powder
- ½ teaspoon baking soda
- ½ teaspoon salt
- ½ cup cold butter
- 1 cup (8 ounces) fat-free plain yogurt
- 3 large egg whites
- 2 tablespoons lemon juice
- 4 teaspoons grated lemon peel
- 1 teaspoon lemon extract

1. In a large bowl, combine the flour, sugar, baking powder, baking soda and salt; cut in butter until mixture resembles coarse crumbs. Whisk the yogurt, egg whites, lemon juice, peel and extract; stir into crumb mixture just until moistened.
2. Fill greased or paper-lined muffin cups three-fourths full. Bake at 350° for 18-22 minutes or until a toothpick inserted near the center comes out clean. Cool for 10 minutes before removing from pan to a wire rack to cool completely.

PER SERVING *1 tea cake equals 232 cal., 8 g fat (5 g sat. fat), 20 mg chol., 255 mg sodium, 37 g carb., 1 g fiber, 4 g pro.*

LEMON-YOGURT TEA CAKES

Cherry Dumplings

This is my mom's recipe. The dumplings are simply out of this world, and they complement the tart cherries.

—**GAIL HALE** FILLMORE, NY

PREP: 10 MIN. • **BAKE:** 30 MIN.
MAKES: 8 SERVINGS

- 1 can (14½ ounces) pitted tart cherries, undrained
- 1 cup sugar, divided
- ½ cup water
- 1 cup all-purpose flour
- 1 teaspoon baking powder
- ½ teaspoon grated lemon peel
  Dash salt
- ⅓ cup milk
- 3 tablespoons butter, melted

1. In a large saucepan, combine the cherries with juice, ¾ cup sugar and the water; bring to a boil. Reduce the heat; cover and simmer.

2. Meanwhile, in a small bowl, combine the flour, baking powder, lemon peel, salt and remaining sugar. Stir in the milk and melted butter just until moistened.

3. Drop by tablespoonfuls onto simmering cherry mixture. Cover and simmer for 20 minutes or until a toothpick inserted in a dumpling comes out clean (do not lift the cover while simmering).

PER SERVING *1 serving equals 216 cal., 5 g fat (3 g sat. fat), 12 mg chol., 107 mg sodium, 42 g carb., 1 g fiber, 2 g pro.*

Lime Coconut Biscotti

Dunk this biscotti into your morning cup of coffee or enjoy as an afternoon snack or after-dinner dessert.

—**DIANA BURRINK** CRETE, IL

PREP: 25 MIN. • **BAKE:** 30 MIN. + COOLING
MAKES: 32 COOKIES

LIME COCONUT BISCOTTI

- ¾ cup sugar
- ¼ cup canola oil
- 2 large eggs
- ¼ cup lime juice
- 1 teaspoon vanilla extract
- ¼ teaspoon coconut extract
- 1¾ cups all-purpose flour
- ⅔ cup cornmeal
- 1½ teaspoons baking powder
- ¼ teaspoon salt
- 1 cup flaked coconut
- 1 teaspoon grated lime peel

1. In a small bowl, beat sugar and oil until blended. Beat in the eggs, lime juice and extracts. Combine the flour, cornmeal, baking powder and salt; gradually add to sugar mixture and mix well (dough will be sticky). Stir in coconut and lime peel.

2. Divide dough in half. With lightly floured hands, shape each half into a 12x2-in. rectangle on a parchment paper-lined baking sheet. Bake at 350° for 20-25 minutes or until set.

3. Place pan on a wire rack. When cool enough to handle, transfer loaves to a cutting board; cut diagonally with a serrated knife into ¾-in. slices. Place cut side down on ungreased baking sheets. Bake for 5-6 minutes on each side or until golden brown. Remove to wire racks to cool. Store in an airtight container.

PER SERVING *1 cookie equals 89 cal., 3 g fat (1 g sat. fat), 13 mg chol., 49 mg sodium, 14 g carb., 1 g fiber, 1 g pro.* **Diabetic Exchanges:** *1 starch, ½ fat.*

HOW TO

CUT BISCOTTI

Once it's cool enough to handle, cut biscotti with a sawing motion, using a serrated knife. Return the  loaf to the oven for a moment if it becomes crumbly or hard to cut. Place slices cut side down on the pan to ensure allover browning and crispness, the signature of classic biscotti.

Fruit & Granola Crisp with Yogurt

Here's an easy dessert you can feel good about serving. Blueberries and peaches are such a delightful flavor combination.

—SUE SCHMIDTKE ORO VALLEY, AZ

START TO FINISH: 10 MIN.
MAKES: 4 SERVINGS

- 3 **cups fresh or frozen sliced peaches, thawed**
- 1 **cup fresh or frozen blueberries, thawed**
- 4 **tablespoons hot caramel ice cream topping**
- 4 **tablespoons granola without raisins**
- 2 **cups low-fat frozen yogurt**

Divide the peaches and blueberries among four 8-oz. ramekins. Top each with caramel and granola. Microwave, uncovered, on high for 1-2 minutes or until bubbly. Top each with a scoop of frozen yogurt.

NOTE *This recipe was tested in a 1,100-watt microwave.*

PER SERVING *1 serving equals 251 cal., 3 g fat (1 g sat. fat), 5 mg chol., 133 mg sodium, 54 g carb., 4 g fiber, 7 g pro.*

PEANUT BUTTER COOKIES

Peanut Butter Cookies

When you bite into one of these yummy cookies, you'll never guess it's low in fat. I like that this recipe makes a small batch.

—MARIA REGAKIS SAUGUS, MA

PREP: 15 MIN. + FREEZING
BAKE: 10 MIN. + COOLING
MAKES: ABOUT 2 DOZEN

- 3 **tablespoons butter**
- 2 **tablespoons reduced-fat peanut butter**
- ½ **cup packed brown sugar**
- ¼ **cup sugar**
- 1 **large egg white**
- 1 **teaspoon vanilla extract**
- 1 **cup all-purpose flour**
- ¼ **teaspoon baking soda**
- ⅛ **teaspoon salt**

1. In a large bowl, cream butter, peanut butter and sugars until light and fluffy. Add egg white; beat until blended. Beat in vanilla. Combine the flour, baking soda and salt; gradually add to creamed mixture and mix well. Shape into an 8-in. roll; wrap in plastic wrap. Freeze 2 hours or until firm.
2. Unwrap and cut into slices, just over ¼ in. thick. Place 2 in. apart on baking sheets coated with cooking spray. Flatten with a fork. Bake at 350° for 6-8 minutes for chewy cookies or 8-10 minutes for crisp cookies. Cool for 1-2 minutes before removing to wire racks; cool completely.

PER SERVING *1 cookie equals 62 cal., 2 g fat (1 g sat. fat), 4 mg chol., 64 mg sodium, 11 g carb., trace fiber, 1 g pro.*
Diabetic Exchanges: *½ starch, ½ fat.*

LIGHT CHEESECAKE

Light Cheesecake

Our family loves cheesecake, but I wanted to serve something healthier. I came up with this lighter version that I make for both holidays and everyday.

—DIANE ROTH ADAMS, WI

PREP: 25 MIN. • **BAKE:** 1 HOUR + CHILLING
MAKES: 12 SERVINGS

- 1¼ cups crushed reduced-fat vanilla wafers (about 40 wafers)
- 2 tablespoons butter, melted
- 1 teaspoon plus 1¼ cups sugar, divided
- 2 packages (8 ounces each) reduced-fat cream cheese
- 1 package (8 ounces) fat-free cream cheese
- 1 cup (8 ounces) reduced-fat sour cream
- 2 tablespoons cornstarch
- 1 teaspoon vanilla extract
- 2 large eggs, lightly beaten
- 2 large egg whites, lightly beaten
- 1 cup sliced fresh strawberries

1. Preheat oven to 350°. In a small bowl, combine wafer crumbs, butter and 1 teaspoon sugar. Press onto the bottom and ½ in. up sides of a greased 9-in. springform pan. Bake 8 minutes. Cool on a wire rack. Reduce oven setting to 325°.

2. In a large bowl, beat cream cheeses and remaining 1¼ cups sugar until smooth. Beat in the sour cream, cornstarch and vanilla. Add eggs and egg whites; beat on low speed just until blended. Pour into crust. Place pan on a baking sheet.

3. Bake 60-65 minutes or until center is almost set. Cool on a wire rack 10 minutes. Loosen sides from pan with a knife. Cool 1 hour longer. Refrigerate overnight, covering when completely cooled.

4. Remove rim from pan. Top cheesecake with strawberries.

PER SERVING *1 slice equals 311 cal., 13 g fat (7 g sat. fat), 74 mg chol., 310 mg sodium, 39 g carb., trace fiber, 10 g pro.*

(5)INGREDIENTS

Frozen Yogurt Fruit Pops

My grandson Patrick, who's now in high school, was Grammy's helper for years. We made these frozen pops for company, and everyone, including the adults, loved them. They're delicious and good for you!

—JUNE DICKENSON PHILIPPI, WV

PREP: 15 MIN. + FREEZING
MAKES: 1 DOZEN

- 2¼ cups (18 ounces) raspberry yogurt
- 2 tablespoons lemon juice
- 2 medium ripe bananas, cut into chunks
- 12 freezer pop molds or 12 paper cups (3 ounces each) and wooden pop sticks

1. Place yogurt, lemon juice and bananas in a blender; cover and process until smooth, stopping to stir if necessary.

2. Pour mixture into molds or paper cups. Top molds with holders. If using cups, top with foil and insert sticks through foil. Freeze until firm.

PER SERVING *1 fruit pop equals 60 cal., 1 g fat (trace sat. fat), 2 mg chol., 23 mg sodium, 13 g carb., 1 g fiber, 2 g pro.* **Diabetic Exchange:** *1 starch.*

Zucchini Chocolate Cake with Orange Glaze

This lightened-up version of a family favorite has rich chocolate flavor, a hint of orange and a crunch from walnuts. Best of all, it's lower in fat thanks to applesauce.

—BARBARA WORREL GRANBURY, TX

PREP: 20 MIN. • **BAKE:** 50 MIN. + COOLING
MAKES: 16 SERVINGS

- ½ cup butter, softened
- 1½ cups sugar
- 2 large eggs
- ¼ cup unsweetened applesauce
- 1 teaspoon vanilla extract
- 2½ cups all-purpose flour
- ½ cup baking cocoa
- 1¼ teaspoons baking powder
- 1 teaspoon salt
- 1 teaspoon ground cinnamon
- ½ teaspoon baking soda
- ½ cup fat-free milk
- 3 cups shredded zucchini
- ½ cup chopped walnuts
- 1 tablespoon grated orange peel

GLAZE
- 1¼ cups confectioners' sugar
- 2 tablespoons orange juice
- 1 teaspoon vanilla extract

1. Coat a 10-in. fluted tube pan with cooking spray and sprinkle with flour.

2. In a bowl, cream butter and sugar until light and fluffy. Add eggs, one at a time, beating well after each addition. Beat in applesauce and vanilla.

3. Combine the flour, cocoa, baking powder, salt, cinnamon and soda; add to creamed mixture alternately with milk, beating well after each addition. Fold in the zucchini, walnuts and orange peel.

4. Transfer to prepared pan. Bake at 350° for 50-60 minutes or until a toothpick inserted near the center comes out clean.

5. Cool 10 minutes before removing from pan to a wire rack to cool completely. Combine the glaze ingredients; drizzle over cake.

PER SERVING *1 slice equals 282 cal., 9 g fat (4 g sat. fat), 42 mg chol., 273 mg sodium, 47 g carb., 2 g fiber, 4 g pro.*

ZUCCHINI CHOCOLATE CAKE WITH ORANGE GLAZE

Devil's Food Snack Cake

My husband and his friends request this cake for their camping trips, but it's perfect for lunch boxes and potlucks, too. No frosting required.

—JULIE DANLER BEL AIRE, KS

PREP: 30 MIN. • **BAKE:** 35 MIN. + COOLING
MAKES: 24 SERVINGS

- 1 cup quick-cooking oats
- 1¾ cups boiling water
- ¼ cup butter, softened
- ½ cup sugar
- ½ cup packed brown sugar
- 2 large eggs
- ⅓ cup buttermilk
- 3 tablespoons canola oil
- 1 teaspoon vanilla extract
- ¾ cup all-purpose flour
- ¾ cup whole wheat flour
- 2 tablespoons dark baking cocoa
- 1 tablespoon instant coffee granules
- 1 teaspoon baking soda
- ⅛ teaspoon salt
- 1 cup (6 ounces) miniature semisweet chocolate chips, divided
- ¾ cup chopped pecans, divided

1. Place oats in a large bowl. Cover with boiling water; let stand for 10 minutes.
2. Meanwhile, in a large bowl, beat butter and sugars until crumbly, about 2 minutes. Add eggs, one at a time, beating well after each addition. Beat in buttermilk, oil and vanilla. Combine the flours, cocoa, coffee granules, baking soda and salt. Gradually add to creamed mixture. Stir in the oat mixture, ½ cup chocolate chips and ⅓ cup pecans.
3. Pour into a 13x9-in. baking pan coated with cooking spray. Sprinkle with remaining chips and pecans. Bake at 350° for 35-40 minutes or until a toothpick inserted near the center comes out clean. Cool on a wire rack before cutting.

PER SERVING *1 piece equals 174 cal., 9 g fat (3 g sat. fat), 23 mg chol., 91 mg sodium, 22 g carb., 2 g fiber, 3 g pro. Diabetic Exchanges: 1½ starch, 1 fat.*

Pumpkin Pie Custard

Instead of pumpkin pie, try my light holiday dessert with only 120 calories. My husband's aunt shared the recipe after she brought this treat to a family party.

—NANCY ZIMMERMAN
CAPE MAY COURT HOUSE, NJ

PREP: 20 MIN. • **BAKE:** 40 MIN. + COOLING
MAKES: 10 SERVINGS

- 2 cups canned pumpkin
- 1 can (12 ounces) fat-free evaporated milk
- 8 large egg whites
- ½ cup fat-free milk
- ¾ cup sugar
- 1 teaspoon ground cinnamon
- ½ teaspoon ground ginger
- ¼ teaspoon salt
- ¼ teaspoon ground cloves
- ¼ teaspoon ground nutmeg
  Fat-free whipped topping, optional

1. In a large bowl, beat the pumpkin, evaporated milk, egg whites and fat-free milk until smooth. Add the sugar, cinnamon, ginger, salt, cloves and nutmeg; mix well.
2. Spoon mixture into ten 6-oz. ramekins or custard cups coated with cooking spray. Place in a 15x10x1-in. baking pan.
3. Bake at 350° for 40-45 minutes or until a knife inserted near the center comes out clean. Cool on a wire rack. Refrigerate until serving. Garnish with whipped topping if desired.

PER SERVING *1 serving (calculated without whipped topping) equals 120 cal., trace fat (trace sat. fat), 2 mg chol., 151 mg sodium, 24 g carb., 2 g fiber, 7 g pro. Diabetic Exchange: 1½ starch.*

VANILLA MERINGUE COOKIES

(5) INGREDIENTS
Blackberry Nectarine Pie

Blackberries are a big crop in my area, so I've made this pretty double-fruit pie many times. I can always tell when my husband wants me to make it because he brings home berries that he picked behind his office.

—**LINDA CHINN** ENUMCLAW, WA

PREP: 25 MIN. + CHILLING
MAKES: 8 SERVINGS

- ¼ cup cornstarch
- 1 can (12 ounces) frozen apple juice concentrate, thawed
- 2 cups fresh blackberries, divided
- 5 medium nectarines, peeled and coarsely chopped
- 1 reduced-fat graham cracker crust (8 inches)
  Reduced-fat whipped topping, optional

1. In a small saucepan, mix the cornstarch and apple juice concentrate until smooth. Bring to a boil. Add ½ cup blackberries; cook and stir 2 minutes or until thickened. Remove from heat.
2. In a large bowl, toss nectarines with remaining blackberries; transfer to crust. Pour apple juice mixture over fruit (crust will be full). Refrigerate, covered, 8 hours or overnight. If desired, serve with whipped topping.
PER SERVING *1 piece (calculated without whipped topping) equals 240 cal., 4 g fat (1 g sat. fat), 0 chol., 106 mg sodium, 50 g carb., 4 g fiber, 3 g pro.*

(5) INGREDIENTS Vanilla Meringue Cookies

My sweet little swirls are light as can be. You can skip the heavy desserts—these are all you need after a big, special dinner.

—**JENNI SHARP** MILWAUKEE, WI

PREP: 20 MIN. • **BAKE:** 40 MIN. + STANDING
MAKES: ABOUT 5 DOZEN

- 3 large egg whites
- 1½ teaspoons clear or regular vanilla extract
- ¼ teaspoon cream of tartar
  Dash salt
- ⅔ cup sugar

1. Place egg whites in a small bowl; let stand at room temperature 30 minutes.
2. Preheat oven to 250°. Add vanilla, cream of tartar and salt to egg whites; beat on medium speed until foamy.

Gradually add sugar, 1 tablespoon at a time, beating on high after each addition until sugar is dissolved. Continue beating until stiff glossy peaks form, about 7 minutes.
3. Cut a small hole in the tip of a pastry bag or in a corner of a food-safe plastic bag; insert a #32 star tip. Transfer meringue to bag. Pipe 1¼-in.-diameter cookies 2 in. apart onto baking sheets that are lined with parchment paper.
4. Bake 40-45 minutes or until firm to the touch. Turn off oven (do not open oven door); leave meringues in oven 1 hour. Remove from oven; cool completely on baking sheets. Remove meringue cookies from parchment paper; store in an airtight container at room temperature.
PER SERVING *1 cookie equals 10 cal., trace fat (0 sat. fat), 0 chol., 5 mg sodium, 2 g carb., 0 fiber, trace pro.* **Diabetic Exchange:** *Free food.*

(5)INGREDIENTS
Old-Fashioned Rice Pudding

This dessert is a wonderful way to end any meal. As a girl, I always waited eagerly for the first heavenly bite. Today, my husband likes to top his with a scoop of ice cream.

—SANDRA MELNYCHENKO GRANDVIEW, MB

PREP: 10 MIN. • **BAKE:** 1 HOUR
MAKES: 6 SERVINGS

- 3½ cups 2% milk
- ½ cup uncooked long grain rice
- ⅓ cup sugar
- ½ teaspoon salt
- ½ cup raisins
- 1 teaspoon vanilla extract
  Ground cinnamon, optional

1. In a large saucepan, combine the milk, rice, sugar and salt. Bring to a boil over medium heat, stirring constantly. Pour into a greased 1½-qt. baking dish.
2. Cover and bake at 325° for 45 minutes, stirring every 15 minutes. Add raisins and vanilla; cover and bake for 15 minutes longer or until rice is tender. Sprinkle with cinnamon if desired. Serve warm or chilled. Store in the refrigerator.

PER SERVING *¾ cup equals 208 cal., 3 g fat (2 g sat. fat), 11 mg chol., 270 mg sodium, 40 g carb., 1 g fiber, 6 g pro.*

Sweet Potato Pudding

I've made this holiday recipe for years. I came up with a low-fat version and nobody noticed the difference. My family prefers this dish served cold, but feel free to try it warm, too.

—TRISHA KRUSE BOISE, ID

PREP: 1¼ HOURS
BAKE: 1¼ HOURS + CHILLING
MAKES: 8 SERVINGS

- 2 pounds sweet potatoes (about 4 medium)
- 1 cup fat-free milk
- ½ cup egg substitute
- ¾ cup packed brown sugar
- ¼ cup all-purpose flour
- ¼ cup raisins
- 2 teaspoons grated orange peel
- 1 teaspoon pumpkin pie spice
- 1 teaspoon vanilla extract
- ⅛ teaspoon salt
- 8 tablespoons fat-free whipped topping in a can

1. Scrub and pierce sweet potatoes. Bake at 350° for 1 to 1¼ hours or until very tender.
2. Cut potatoes in half; scoop out pulp and place in a large bowl. Mash with milk and egg substitute. Stir in the brown sugar, flour, raisins, orange peel, pumpkin pie spice, vanilla and salt until blended.
3. Transfer to a 1½-qt. baking dish coated with cooking spray. Cover and bake at 350° for 1¼-1½ hours or just until top is set. Cool on a wire rack for 1 hour. Refrigerate for at least 2 hours. Serve with whipped topping.

PER SERVING *½ cup pudding with 1 tablespoon whipped topping equals 205 cal., trace fat (trace sat. fat), 1 mg chol., 102 mg sodium, 46 g carb., 2 g fiber, 4 g pro.*

OLD-FASHIONED RICE PUDDING

Slow Cooker Lava Cake

Because I love chocolate, this decadent slow cooker cake has long been a family favorite in our house.

—**ELIZABETH FARRELL** HAMILTON, MT

PREP: 15 MIN.
COOK: 2 HOURS + STANDING
MAKES: 8 SERVINGS

- 1 cup all-purpose flour
- 1 cup packed brown sugar, divided
- 5 tablespoons baking cocoa, divided
- 2 teaspoons baking powder
- ¼ teaspoon salt
- ½ cup fat-free milk
- 2 tablespoons canola oil
- ½ teaspoon vanilla extract
- ⅛ teaspoon ground cinnamon
- 1¼ cups hot water

1. In a large bowl, whisk flour, ½ cup brown sugar, 3 tablespoons cocoa, baking powder and salt. In another bowl, whisk milk, oil and vanilla until blended. Add to flour mixture; stir just until moistened.

2. Spread into a 3-qt. slow cooker coated with cooking spray. In a small bowl, mix cinnamon and the remaining brown sugar and cocoa; stir in hot water. Pour over batter (do not stir).

3. Cook, covered, on high 2-2½ hours or until a toothpick inserted in cake portion comes out clean. Turn off slow cooker; let stand 15 minutes before serving.

PER SERVING *1 serving equals 207 cal., 4 g fat (trace sat. fat), trace chol., 191 mg sodium, 41 g carb., 1 g fiber, 3 g pro.*

Root Beer Float Pie

This is the kind of recipe your kids will look back on and always remember. And the only appliance you need is the refrigerator.

—**CINDY REAMS** PHILIPSBURG, PA

PREP: 15 MIN. + CHILLING
MAKES: 8 SERVINGS

- 1 carton (8 ounces) frozen reduced-fat whipped topping, thawed, divided
- ¾ cup cold diet root beer
- ½ cup fat-free milk
- 1 package (1 ounce) sugar-free instant vanilla pudding mix
- 1 graham cracker crust (9 inches)
  Maraschino cherries, optional

ROOT BEER FLOAT PIE

1. Set aside and refrigerate ½ cup whipped topping for garnish. In a large bowl, whisk the root beer, milk and pudding mix for 2 minutes. Fold in half of the remaining whipped topping. Spread into graham cracker crust.

2. Spread remaining whipped topping over pie. Refrigerate for at least 8 hours or overnight.

3. Dollop reserved whipped topping over each serving; top with a maraschino cherry if desired.

PER SERVING *1 piece equals 185 cal., 8 g fat (4 g sat. fat), trace chol., 275 mg sodium, 27 g carb., trace fiber, 1 g pro.* **Diabetic Exchanges:** *2 starch, 1 fat.*

Hot Fudge Cake

What better way to top off a great meal than with a rich, chocolaty cake? Mom served this dessert with a scoop of ice cream or with cream poured over—and no matter what, I'd always have room for it.

—**VERA REID** LARAMIE, WY

PREP: 20 MIN. • **BAKE:** 35 MIN.
MAKES: 9 SERVINGS

- 1 **cup all-purpose flour**
- ¾ **cup sugar**
- 6 **tablespoons baking cocoa, divided**
- 2 **teaspoons baking powder**
- ¼ **teaspoon salt**
- ½ **cup 2% milk**
- 2 **tablespoons canola oil**
- 1 **teaspoon vanilla extract**
- 1 **cup packed brown sugar**
- 1¾ **cups hot water**
  Ice cream or whipped cream, optional

1. Preheat oven to 350°. In a large bowl, whisk flour, sugar, 2 tablespoons cocoa, baking powder and salt. In another bowl, whisk milk, oil and vanilla until blended. Add to flour mixture; stir just until moistened.
2. Transfer to an ungreased 9-in.-square baking pan. In a small bowl, mix brown sugar and remaining cocoa; sprinkle over batter. Pour hot water over all; do not stir.
3. Bake 35-40 minutes. Serve warm. If desired, top with ice cream.

PER SERVING *1 piece (calculated without whipped cream and ice cream) equals 253 cal., 4 g fat (1 g sat. fat), 2 mg chol., 171 mg sodium, 54 g carb., 1 g fiber, 3 g pro.*

(5) INGREDIENTS

Iced Tea Parfaits

Here's a parfait that's perfect for a garden or patio party. Tea adds a wonderfully unexpected flavor to gelatin. And kids will have fun finding the cherry at the bottom.

—**TEENA PETRUS** JOHNSTOWN, PA

PREP: 15 MIN. + CHILLING
MAKES: 4 SERVINGS

- 2 **cups water**
- 3 **tea bags**
- 1 **package (3 ounces) lemon gelatin**
- 4 **maraschino cherries**
- 1½ **cups whipped topping, divided**
- 4 **lemon slices**

1. In a small saucepan, bring water to a boil. Remove from the heat; add tea bags. Cover and steep for 5 minutes. Discard tea bags. Stir gelatin into tea until completely dissolved. Cool slightly.
2. Pour ¼ cup gelatin mixture into each of four parfait glasses. Place a cherry in each glass; refrigerate until set but not firm, about 1 hour. Transfer remaining gelatin mixture to a small bowl; refrigerate for 1 hour or until soft-set.
3. Whisk the gelatin mixture for 2-3 minutes or until smooth. Stir in ½ cup whipped topping; spoon into parfait glasses. Refrigerate for at least 2 hours. Just before serving, top with remaining whipped topping and garnish with lemon slices.

PER SERVING *1 parfait equals 162 cal., 5 g fat (5 g sat. fat), 0 chol., 48 mg sodium, 27 g carb., 0 fiber, 2 g pro.*
Diabetic Exchanges: *1½ starch, 1 fat.*

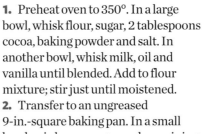

TOP TIP

I am a tea fan, so I have all sorts of teas. You can make these with any flavor you like. I have some berry teas that create amazing colors.

—**RANDCBRUNS** TASTEOFHOME.COM

Arctic Orange Pie

This frosty pie is so easy to make. I have tried lemonade, mango and pineapple juice concentrates instead of orange, and my family loves each one.

—MARIE PRZEPIERSKI ERIE, PA

PREP: 20 MIN. + FREEZING
MAKES: 8 SERVINGS

- 1 **package (8 ounces) fat-free cream cheese**
- 1 **can (6 ounces) frozen orange juice concentrate, thawed**
- 1 **carton (8 ounces) frozen reduced-fat whipped topping, thawed**
- 1 **reduced-fat graham cracker crust (8 inches)**
- 1 **can (11 ounces) mandarin oranges, drained**

In a large bowl, beat cream cheese and orange juice concentrate until smooth. Fold in whipped topping; pour into crust. Cover and freeze for 4 hours or until firm. Remove from the freezer about 10 minutes before cutting. Garnish with oranges.
PER SERVING *1 piece equals 241 cal., 7 g fat (4 g sat. fat), 2 mg chol., 251 mg sodium, 36 g carb., 1 g fiber, 6 g pro.* ***Diabetic Exchanges:*** *1½ fat, 1 starch, 1 fruit.*

STRAWBERRY SORBET SENSATION

Strawberry Sorbet Sensation

On hot days in Colorado, we chill out with slices of this berries-and-cream dessert. The layered effect is so much fun. Use any flavor of sorbet you like.

—KENDRA DOSS COLORADO SPRINGS, CO

PREP: 20 MIN. + FREEZING
MAKES: 8 SERVINGS

- 2 **cups strawberry sorbet, softened if necessary**
- 1 **cup cold fat-free milk**
- 1 **package (1 ounce) sugar-free instant vanilla pudding mix**
- 1 **carton (8 ounces) frozen reduced-fat whipped topping, thawed**
  Sliced fresh strawberries

1. Line an 8x4-in. loaf pan with foil. Spread sorbet onto bottom of pan; place in freezer 15 minutes.
2. In a small bowl, whisk milk and pudding mix 2 minutes. Let stand 2 minutes or until soft-set. Fold whipped topping into pudding; spread over sorbet. Freeze, covered, 4 hours or overnight.
3. Remove dessert from the freezer 10-15 minutes before serving. Unmold onto a serving plate; remove foil. Cut into slices. Serve with strawberries.
PER SERVING *1 slice equals 153 cal., 3 g fat (3 g sat. fat), 1 mg chol., 163 mg sodium, 27 g carb., 2 g fiber, 1 g pro.* ***Diabetic Exchanges:*** *2 starch, ½ fat.*

Apple Oatmeal Cookies

I took these yummy cookies to work and they were gone in seconds. They're a welcome snack that's low in calories.

—NICKI WOODS SPRINGFIELD, MO

PREP: 10 MIN. • **BAKE:** 15 MIN./BATCH
MAKES: ABOUT 5 DOZEN

- 1 package yellow cake mix (regular size)
- 1½ cups quick-cooking oats
- ½ cup packed brown sugar
- 2 teaspoons ground cinnamon
- 1 large egg
- ¾ cup unsweetened applesauce
- 1 cup finely chopped peeled apple
- ½ cup raisins

1. In a large bowl, combine the cake mix, oats, brown sugar and cinnamon. In a small bowl, combine the egg, applesauce, apple and raisins. Stir into oats mixture and mix well.

2. Drop by heaping teaspoonfuls 2 in. apart onto baking sheets coated with cooking spray. Bake at 350° for 12-14 minutes or until golden brown. Let stand for 2 minutes before removing to wire racks to cool.

PER SERVING *1 cookie equals 57 cal., 1 g fat (trace sat. fat), 0 chol., 55 mg sodium, 12 g carb., 1 g fiber, 1 g pro. Diabetic Exchange: 1 starch.*

ORIGINAL	MAKEOVER
317 Calories	208 Calories
16g Fat	6g Fat
8g Sat. Fat	4g Sat. Fat

MAKEOVER DIRT DESSERT

Makeover Dirt Dessert

This lightened-up dessert makes an amazing potluck or reunion treat. Break out the spoons and make sure you get a bite, because this is one dessert that won't be around for long!

—KRISTI LINTON BAY CITY, MI

PREP: 30 MIN. + CHILLING
MAKES: 20 SERVINGS

- 1 package (8 ounces) fat-free cream cheese
- 1 package (3 ounces) cream cheese, softened
- ¾ cup confectioners' sugar
- 3½ cups cold fat-free milk
- 2 packages (1 ounce each) sugar-free instant vanilla pudding mix
- 1 carton (12 ounces) frozen reduced-fat whipped topping, thawed
- 1 package (15½ ounces) reduced-fat Oreo cookies, crushed

1. In a large bowl, beat cream cheeses and confectioners' sugar until smooth. In a large bowl, whisk the milk and pudding mixes for 2 minutes; let stand for 2 minutes or until soft-set. Gradually stir into cream cheese mixture. Fold in whipped topping.

2. Spread 1⅓ cups of crushed cookies into an ungreased 13x9-in. dish. Layer with half of the pudding mixture and half of the remaining cookies. Repeat layers. Refrigerate for at least 1 hour before serving.

PER SERVING *½ cup equals 208 cal., 6 g fat (4 g sat. fat), 6 mg chol., 364 mg sodium, 33 g carb., 1 g fiber, 5 g pro. Diabetic Exchanges: 2 starch, 1 fat.*

Chocolate Hazelnut Soy Pops

I love Nutella, and I'm always looking for ways to use it. These pops help you cool down in the summer, but they also make a cozy treat in the winter.

—BONITA SUTER LAWRENCE, MI

PREP: 10 MIN. + FREEZING
MAKES: 8 POPS

- 1 **cup vanilla soy milk**
- ½ **cup fat-free milk**
- ¾ **cup fat-free vanilla Greek yogurt**
- ⅓ **cup Nutella**
- 8 **freezer pop molds or 8 paper cups (3 ounces each) and wooden pop sticks**

Place milks, yogurt and Nutella in a blender; cover and process until smooth. Pour into molds or paper cups. Top molds with holders. If using cups, top with foil and insert sticks through foil. Freeze until firm.

PER SERVING *1 pop equals 94 cal., 4 g fat (1 g sat. fat), trace chol., 33 mg sodium, 11 g carb., trace fiber, 4 g pro.*
Diabetic Exchanges: 1 starch, ½ fat.

Lemon Angel Cake Roll

Tart and delicious, this pretty cake roll will tickle any lemon lover's fancy. Its feathery angel-food texture is complemented by a light lemon filling.

—TASTE OF HOME TEST KITCHEN

PREP: 30 MIN. • **BAKE:** 15 MIN. + COOLING
MAKES: 10 SERVINGS

- 9 **large egg whites**
- 1½ **teaspoons vanilla extract**
- ¾ **teaspoon cream of tartar**
- 1 **cup plus 2 tablespoons sugar**
- ¾ **cup cake flour**
- 1 **tablespoon confectioners' sugar**

FILLING

- 1 **cup sugar**
- 3 **tablespoons cornstarch**
- 1 **cup water**
- 1 **large egg, lightly beaten**
- ¼ **cup lemon juice**
- 1 **tablespoon grated lemon peel**
  Yellow food coloring, optional
  Additional confectioners' sugar

1. Place the egg whites in a large bowl; let stand at room temperature for 30 minutes. Meanwhile, line a 15x10x1-in. baking pan with waxed paper; lightly coat paper with cooking spray and set aside.

2. Preheat oven to 350°. Add vanilla and cream of tartar to egg whites; beat on medium speed until soft peaks form. Gradually beat in sugar, 2 tablespoons at a time, on high until stiff glossy peaks form and sugar is dissolved. Fold in flour, about ¼ cup at a time.

3. Gently spread batter into prepared pan. Bake 15-20 minutes or until cake springs back when lightly touched. Cool 5 minutes.

4. Turn warm cake onto a kitchen towel dusted with 1 tablespoon confectioners' sugar. Gently peel off waxed paper. Roll up cake in the towel jelly-roll style, starting with a short side. Cool completely on a wire rack.

5. In a large saucepan, combine sugar and cornstarch; stir in water until smooth. Cook and stir over medium-high heat until thickened and bubbly. Reduce heat; cook and stir 2 minutes. Remove from heat. Stir a small amount of hot mixture into egg; return all to the pan, stirring constantly. Bring to a gentle boil; cook and stir 2 minutes.

6. Remove from heat. Gently stir in lemon juice, peel and, if desired, food coloring. Cool to room temperature without stirring.

7. Unroll cake; spread filling to within ½ in. of edges. Roll up again. Place the cake seam side down on a serving plate; sprinkle with additional confectioners' sugar.

PER SERVING *1 slice equals 243 cal., 1 g fat (trace sat. fat), 21 mg chol., 57 mg sodium, 55 g carb., trace fiber, 5 g pro.*

LEMON ANGEL CAKE ROLL

Low-Fat Chocolate Cookies

These soft, cakelike cookies have a mild cocoa flavor and cute chocolate chip topping. Better still, they're ready fast and have just 2 grams of fat!

—MARY HOUCHIN LEBANON, IL

PREP: 15 MIN. + CHILLING
BAKE: 10 MIN./BATCH
MAKES: ABOUT 3½ DOZEN

- ½ cup unsweetened applesauce
- ⅓ cup canola oil
- 3 large egg whites
- ¾ cup sugar
- ¾ cup packed brown sugar
- 2 teaspoons vanilla extract
- 2⅔ cups all-purpose flour
- ½ cup baking cocoa
- 1 teaspoon baking soda
- ½ teaspoon salt
- ¼ cup miniature semisweet chocolate chips

1. In a large bowl, combine the applesauce, oil and egg whites. Beat in sugars and vanilla. Combine the flour, cocoa, baking soda and salt; gradually add to applesauce mixture and mix well. Cover and refrigerate for 2 hours or until slightly firm.

2. Drop dough by rounded teaspoonfuls 2 in. apart onto baking sheets coated with cooking spray. Sprinkle with chocolate chips. Bake at 350° for 8-10 minutes or until set. Remove to wire racks.

PER SERVING *1 cookie equals 78 cal., 2 g fat (trace sat. fat), trace chol., 63 mg sodium, 14 g carb., 1 g fiber, 1 g pro.* **Diabetic Exchange: 1 starch.**

Small Batch Brownies

Here's the perfect chocolaty treat for a small household. For a pretty accent, dust the tops with confectioners' sugar.

—*TASTE OF HOME* TEST KITCHEN

PREP: 15 MIN. • **BAKE:** 15 MIN. + COOLING
MAKES: 6 SERVINGS

- 2 tablespoons butter
- ½ ounce unsweetened chocolate, chopped
- 1 large egg
- ¼ teaspoon vanilla extract
- ⅔ cup sugar
- ⅓ cup all-purpose flour
- ¼ cup baking cocoa
- ¼ teaspoon salt
- ¼ teaspoon confectioners' sugar, optional

1. In a microwave, melt butter and chocolate; stir until smooth. Cool slightly.

2. In a small bowl, whisk egg and vanilla; gradually whisk in sugar. Stir in chocolate mixture. Combine the flour, cocoa and salt; gradually add to chocolate mixture.

3. Transfer to a 9x5-in. loaf pan coated with cooking spray. Bake at 350° for 12-16 minutes or until a toothpick inserted near the center comes out clean. Cool on a wire rack.

Cut into bars. Dust with the confectioners' sugar if desired.

PER SERVING *1 brownie equals 179 cal., 6 g fat (3 g sat. fat), 45 mg chol., 138 mg sodium, 30 g carb., 1 g fiber, 3 g pro.* **Diabetic Exchanges: 2 starch, 1 fat.**

(5) INGREDIENTS
Raspberry Sorbet

With an abundant crop of fresh raspberries from the backyard, I rely on this recipe for a tasty frozen dessert that couldn't be simpler.

—KAREN BAILEY GOLDEN, CO

PREP: 5 MIN. + FREEZING
MAKES: 6 SERVINGS

- ¼ cup plus 1½ teaspoons fresh lemon juice
- 3¾ cups fresh or frozen unsweetened raspberries
- 2¼ cups confectioners' sugar

Place all ingredients in a blender or food processor; cover and process until smooth. Transfer to a freezer container; freeze until firm.

PER SERVING *1 serving equals 216 cal., trace fat (trace sat. fat), 0 chol., 1 mg sodium, 55 g carb., 5 g fiber, 1 g pro.*

RASPBERRY
SORBET

BLACKBERRY COBBLER

Blackberry Cobbler

My husband is from Alabama, so I like to treat him to classic Southern desserts. This cobbler is a must-have treat for us in the summer.

—KIMBERLY DANEK PINKSON
SAN ANSELMO, CA

PREP: 25 MIN. • **BAKE:** 25 MIN.
MAKES: 6 SERVINGS

- 5 **cups fresh blackberries**
- ⅓ **cup turbinado (washed raw) sugar**
- 2 **tablespoons quick-cooking tapioca**
- 1 **tablespoon lemon juice**
- 1½ **teaspoons cornstarch or arrowroot flour**
- 1 **cup all-purpose flour**
- ¼ **cup sugar**
- 1¼ **teaspoons baking powder**
- ¼ **teaspoon salt**
- ¼ **teaspoon ground cinnamon**
- 3 **tablespoons cold butter**
- ⅓ **cup fat-free milk**
  Vanilla ice cream, optional

1. Preheat oven to 375°. In a large bowl, combine first five ingredients. Transfer to a 2-qt. baking dish coated with cooking spray.
2. In a small bowl, combine the flour, sugar, baking powder, salt and cinnamon. Cut in butter until mixture resembles coarse crumbs. Stir in milk just until moistened. Drop by tablespoonfuls onto blackberry mixture.
3. Bake, uncovered, 25-30 minutes or until golden brown. Serve warm, with ice cream if desired.
PER SERVING *1 serving (calculated without ice cream) equals 274 cal., 6 g fat (4 g sat. fat), 15 mg chol., 229 mg sodium, 52 g carb., 7 g fiber, 4 g pro.*

---

(5) INGREDIENTS
Cherry Chocolate Cake

I've had the recipe for this lovely cake for years. It's a chocolate lover's delight! It's so easy to make...and it's easy to take along on potlucks, too. Just spread the second can of pie filling right over the top.

—ANN PURCHASE PANAMA CITY, FL

PREP: 15 MIN. • **BAKE:** 30 MIN. + COOLING
MAKES: 18 SERVINGS

- 1 **package chocolate cake mix (regular size)**
- 3 **large eggs, lightly beaten**
- 1 **teaspoon almond extract**
- 2 **cans (20 ounces each) reduced-sugar cherry pie filling, divided**
- ¾ **teaspoon confectioners' sugar**

1. In a large bowl, combine the cake mix, eggs and almond extract until well blended. Stir in one can of pie filling until blended. Transfer to a 13x9-in. baking pan coated with cooking spray.
2. Bake at 350° for 30-35 minutes or until a toothpick inserted near the center comes out clean. Cool completely on a wire rack. Dust with confectioners' sugar. Top individual servings with remaining pie filling.
PER SERVING *1 piece equals 187 cal., 6 g fat (1 g sat. fat), 35 mg chol., 253 mg sodium, 33 g carb., 1 g fiber, 3 g pro.*
***Diabetic Exchanges:** 1 starch, 1 fruit, 1 fat.*

Plum Crisp

Made with fresh plums and a crunchy oat topping, this crisp is a lighter alternative to classic fruit pie. It goes over well with the women in my church group.

—**DEIDRE KOBEL** BOULDER, CO

PREP: 25 MIN. + STANDING • **BAKE:** 40 MIN.
MAKES: 8 SERVINGS

- ¾ **cup old-fashioned oats**
- ⅓ **cup all-purpose flour**
- ¼ **cup plus 2 tablespoons sugar, divided**
- ¼ **cup packed brown sugar**
- ¼ **teaspoon salt**
- ¼ **teaspoon ground cinnamon**
- ¼ **teaspoon ground nutmeg**
- 3 **tablespoons butter, softened**
- ¼ **cup chopped walnuts**
- 5 **cups sliced fresh plums (about 2 pounds)**
- 1 **tablespoon quick-cooking tapioca**
- 2 **teaspoons lemon juice**

1. In a small bowl, combine the oats, flour, ¼ cup sugar, brown sugar, salt, cinnamon and nutmeg. With clean hands, work butter into sugar mixture until well combined. Add nuts; toss to combine. Refrigerate for 15 minutes.
2. Meanwhile, in a large bowl, combine the plums, tapioca, lemon juice and remaining sugar. Transfer to a greased 9-in. pie plate. Let stand for 15 minutes. Sprinkle topping over plum mixture.
3. Bake at 375° for 40-45 minutes or until topping is golden brown and plums are tender. Serve warm.

PER SERVING *1 serving equals 233 cal., 8 g fat (3 g sat. fat), 11 mg chol., 107 mg sodium, 40 g carb., 3 g fiber, 3 g pro.*

PINEAPPLE UPSIDE-DOWN CAKE FOR TWO

Pineapple Upside-Down Cake for Two

Tender, moist and sweet, these two luscious but lighter cakes are as special as the person you choose to share them with!

—*TASTE OF HOME* TEST KITCHEN

PREP: 15 MIN. • **BAKE:** 20 MIN.
MAKES: 2 SERVINGS

- 4 **teaspoons butter, melted, divided**
- 4 **teaspoons brown sugar**
- 2 **canned unsweetened pineapple slices**
- 2 **maraschino cherries**
- ⅓ **cup all-purpose flour**
- 3 **tablespoons sugar**
- ½ **teaspoon baking powder**
- ⅛ **teaspoon salt**
  Dash ground nutmeg
- 3 **tablespoons fat-free milk**
- ¼ **teaspoon vanilla extract**

1. Pour ½ teaspoon butter into each of two 10-oz. ramekins coated with cooking spray. Sprinkle with brown sugar. Top with a pineapple slice. Place a cherry in the center of each pineapple slice; set aside.
2. In a small bowl, combine the flour, sugar, baking powder, salt and nutmeg. Beat in the milk, vanilla and remaining butter just until combined. Spoon over pineapple.
3. Bake at 350° for 20-25 minutes or until a toothpick inserted near the center comes out clean. Cool for 5 minutes. Run a knife around edges of ramekins; invert onto dessert plates. Serve warm.

PER SERVING *1 serving equals 290 cal., 8 g fat (5 g sat. fat), 21 mg chol., 318 mg sodium, 53 g carb., 1 g fiber, 3 g pro.*

**JACYN SEIBERT'S
CHOCOLATE CHERRY CAKE**
PAGE 304

Holiday Sweets & Treats

Now you can savor **decadent holiday desserts** without the fear of excess calories. In this chapter, you'll discover **lightened-up takes on cherished classics all year long.** Find dozens of mouthwatering **reasons to celebrate** each season!

JESSICA FEIST'S LEMON CURD TARTLETS
PAGE 286

SUSAN WHETZEL'S PATRIOTIC SUGAR COOKIES
PAGE 290

SONYA LABBE'S CRANBERRY TRIFLE
PAGE 299

Dark Chocolate Fondue

Savor all the decadence without a bit of guilt! We kept all the melt-in-your-mouth texture of fudgy fondue in this lusciously lighter version.

—*TASTE OF HOME* **TEST KITCHEN**

START TO FINISH: 20 MIN.
MAKES: 2 CUPS

- 2 **tablespoons all-purpose flour**
- 1½ **cups 2% milk**
- 2 **dark chocolate candy bars (1.55 ounces each), chopped**
- 3 **ounces milk chocolate, chopped**
- 2 **tablespoons light corn syrup**
  Cubed angel food cake and assorted fresh fruit

1. In a small saucepan, combine flour and milk until smooth. Bring to a boil over medium-high heat; cook and stir for 1 minute or until thickened. Reduce heat to low. Stir in chocolate and corn syrup. Cook and stir until melted.
2. Transfer to a small fondue pot and keep warm. Serve with cake cubes and fruit.

PER SERVING *¼ cup (calculated without cake and fruit) equals 154 cal., 7 g fat (5 g sat. fat), 6 mg chol., 29 mg sodium, 21 g carb., 1 g fiber, 2 g pro. Diabetic Exchanges: 1½ fat, 1 starch.*

Sugarless Heart Cookies

Here's a wonderful Valentine's treat, even for those not watching their sugar intake. It's fun to try new tastes by changing the flavor of the gelatin.

—**BECKY JONES** AKRON, OH

PREP: 15 MIN. + CHILLING
BAKE: 10 MIN./BATCH
MAKES: ABOUT 3 DOZEN

- ¾ **cup butter, softened**
- 1 **package (.3 ounce) sugar-free raspberry gelatin**
- ¼ **cup egg substitute**
- 1 **teaspoon vanilla extract**
- 1¾ **cups all-purpose flour**
- ½ **teaspoon baking powder**

1. In a bowl, cream butter and gelatin. Beat in egg substitute and vanilla. Add flour and baking powder; mix well. Chill for 1 hour.
2. Roll out on a lightly floured surface to ¼-in. thickness. Cut with a 1¾-in. heart-shaped cookie cutter. Place on ungreased baking sheets. Bake at 400° for 6-8 minutes or until bottoms are lightly browned and cookies are set. Cool on wire racks.

PER SERVING *1 cookie equals 59 cal., 4 g fat (0 sat. fat), trace chol., 49 mg sodium, 5 g carb., 0 fiber, 1 g pro. Diabetic Exchanges: ½ starch, ½ fat.*

DARK CHOCOLATE FONDUE

Tuxedo Strawberries

Dress up special occasions with these high-fashion treats! The strawberries are actually quite easy to decorate, and they're loved everywhere they go.

—**GISELLA SELLERS** SEMINOLE, FL

PREP: 1 HOUR + CHILLING
MAKES: 1½ DOZEN

- **18 medium fresh strawberries with stems**
- **1 cup white baking chips**
- **3½ teaspoons shortening, divided**
- **1⅓ cups semisweet chocolate chips**

1. Line a tray or baking sheet with waxed paper; set aside. Wash strawberries and pat until completely dry.

2. In a microwave-safe bowl, melt white chips and 1½ teaspoons shortening at 70% power; stir until smooth. Dip each strawberry until two-thirds is coated, forming the tuxedo shirt, allowing excess to drip off. Place on prepared tray; chill for 30 minutes or until set.

3. Melt chocolate chips and remaining shortening. To form the tuxedo jacket, dip each side of berry into chocolate from the tip of the strawberry to the top of vanilla coating. Repeat on the other side, leaving a white V-shape in the center. Set remaining chocolate aside. Chill berries for 30 minutes or until set.

4. Remelt reserved chocolate if necessary. Using melted chocolate and a round pastry tip #2, pipe a bow tie at the top of the white V and three buttons down front of shirt. Chill for 30 minutes or until set. Store in the refrigerator in a covered plastic container for up to 1 day.

PER SERVING *1 strawberry equals 121 cal., 8 g fat (4 g sat. fat), 1 mg chol., 10 mg sodium, 14 g carb., 1 g fiber, 1 g pro.* **Diabetic Exchanges:** *1½ fat, 1 starch.*

TUXEDO STRAWBERRIES

ORIGINAL	MAKEOVER
330 Calories	**164** Calories
13g Fat	**4**g Fat
4g Sat. Fat	**trace** Sat. Fat

MAKEOVER ORANGE CUPCAKES

Makeover Orange Cupcakes

The classic combo of vanilla and orange shines in these cuties. We lightened up the batter and swapped out buttercream icing to save big on fat and calories. And here's a bonus: Now they're lactose-free!

—*TASTE OF HOME* **TEST KITCHEN**

PREP: 30 MIN. • **BAKE:** 20 MIN. + COOLING
MAKES: 2 DOZEN

- 6 **large egg whites**
- 3 **large eggs**
- 1 **cup sugar**
- ¾ **cup vanilla soy milk**
- ⅓ **cup canola oil**
- ⅓ **cup unsweetened applesauce**
- ⅓ **cup plus ¼ cup thawed orange juice concentrate, divided**
- 3 **cups all-purpose flour**
- 1 **tablespoon plus 1½ teaspoons baking powder**
- 1½ **teaspoons salt**
- 1½ **cups confectioners' sugar**
  Assorted sprinkles, optional

1. Preheat oven to 350°. Line 24 muffin cups with paper liners.
2. In a large bowl, beat egg whites, eggs, sugar, soy milk, oil, applesauce and ⅓ cup orange juice concentrate until well blended. In a small bowl, whisk flour, baking powder and salt; gradually beat into egg mixture.
3. Fill prepared cups two-thirds full. Bake 18-22 minutes or until a toothpick inserted in center comes out clean. Cool in pans 10 minutes before removing to wire racks to cool completely.
4. In a small bowl, mix confectioners' sugar and remaining orange juice concentrate until smooth. Dip cupcakes into glaze. If desired, decorate with sprinkles. Let stand until set.
PER SERVING *1 cupcake (calculated without sprinkles) equals 164 cal., 4 g fat (trace sat. fat), 26 mg chol., 249 mg sodium, 29 g carb., trace fiber, 4 g pro. Diabetic Exchanges: 2 starch, 1 fat.*

⑤INGREDIENTS
Lemon Curd Tartlets

Homemade lemon curd is an easy way to set these quick tarts apart. Also try the curd on English muffins, scones or even whole-grain pancakes.

—**JESSICA FEIST** BROOKFIELD, WI

PREP: 35 MIN. + CHILLING
MAKES: 15 TARTLETS

- 3 **large eggs**
- 1 **cup sugar**
- ½ **cup lemon juice**
- 1 **tablespoon grated lemon peel**
- ¼ **cup butter, cubed**
- 1 **package (1.9 ounces) frozen miniature phyllo tart shells, thawed**
  Raspberries, mint leaves and/or whipped cream, optional

1. In a small heavy saucepan over medium heat, whisk the eggs, sugar, lemon juice and peel until blended. Add butter; cook, whisking constantly, until mixture is thickened and coats the back of a metal spoon. Transfer to a small bowl; cool for 10 minutes. Cover and refrigerate until chilled.
2. Just before serving, spoon lemon curd into tart shells. Garnish with raspberries, mint and/or cream if desired. Refrigerate leftovers.
PER SERVING *1 tartlet equals 115 cal., 5 g fat (2 g sat. fat), 50 mg chol., 45 mg sodium, 16 g carb., trace fiber, 2 g pro. Diabetic Exchanges: 1 starch, 1 fat.*

Light & Easy Cheesecake Bars

You'll find fresh hints of lemon in the tender crust and creamy filling.

—PATRICIA NIEH PORTOLA VALLEY, CA

PREP: 20 MIN. • **BAKE:** 30 MIN. + CHILLING
MAKES: 1½ DOZEN

- ⅓ cup butter, softened
- 1 cup sugar, divided
- 4 tablespoons lemon juice, divided
- 1¼ cups all-purpose flour
- ½ teaspoon salt
- 1 package (8 ounces) reduced-fat cream cheese
- 1 package (8 ounces) fat-free cream cheese
- 1 large egg
- 2 teaspoons grated lemon peel
- 18 fresh raspberries, halved

1. Line a 9-in.-square pan with foil; coat with cooking spray and set aside.

2. In a small bowl, beat butter and ¼ cup sugar until smooth, about 2 minutes. Stir in 2 tablespoons lemon juice. Add flour and salt; mix well. Press into prepared pan. Bake at 350° for 14-16 minutes or until edges are golden brown.

3. Meanwhile, in a small bowl, combine cream cheeses and the remaining sugar until smooth. Add egg; beat on low speed just until combined. Stir in lemon peel and remaining lemon juice. Pour over crust. Bake 14-18 minutes longer or until filling is set.

4. Cool on a wire rack for 1 hour. Refrigerate for at least 2 hours. Using foil, lift bars out of pan. Gently peel off foil; cut into bars. Garnish with raspberries.

PER SERVING *1 bar equals 153 cal., 7 g fat (4 g sat. fat), 31 mg chol., 216 mg sodium, 19 g carb., trace fiber, 4 g pro. Diabetic Exchanges: 1½ fat, 1 starch.*

Pastel Tea Cookies

These glazed sugar cookies are perfect for nibbling between sips at a tea party, graduation or shower.

—LORI HENRY ELKHART, IN

PREP: 1 HOUR + CHILLING
BAKE: 10 MIN./BATCH + STANDING
MAKES: 4 DOZEN

- 1 cup butter, softened
- ⅔ cup sugar
- 1 large egg
- 1 teaspoon vanilla extract
- 2½ cups all-purpose flour
- ½ teaspoon salt
- 1¼ cups confectioners' sugar
- 2 teaspoons meringue powder
- 5 teaspoons water
   Pastel food coloring

1. In a large bowl, cream butter and sugar until light and fluffy. Beat in egg and vanilla. Combine flour and salt; gradually add to creamed mixture. Cover and refrigerate 1-2 hours or until dough is easy to handle.

2. Preheat oven to 350°. On a lightly floured surface, roll out dough to ⅛-in. thickness. Cut with floured 2½-in. butterfly or flower cookie cutters. Place 1 in. apart on ungreased baking sheets.

3. Bake 8-10 minutes or until edges are lightly browned. Remove to wire racks to cool.

4. For glaze, in a small bowl, combine confectioners' sugar and meringue powder; stir in water until smooth. Divide among small bowls; tint pastel colors. Spread over cookies; let stand until set.

NOTE *Meringue powder is available from Wilton Industries. Call 800-794-5866 or visit* wilton.com.

PER SERVING *1 cookie equals 82 cal., 4 g fat (2 g sat. fat), 14 mg chol., 54 mg sodium, 11 g carb., trace fiber, 1 g pro. Diabetic Exchanges: 1 starch, ½ fat.*

PASTEL TEA COOKIES

MULTIGRAIN CINNAMON ROLLS

Multigrain Cinnamon Rolls

This simple recipe is sure to become a family favorite. The wholesome cinnamon rolls will fill your kitchen with a warm and wonderful aroma.

—JUDITH EDDY BALDWIN CITY, KS

PREP: 30 MIN. + RISING • **BAKE:** 15 MIN.
MAKES: 1 DOZEN

- 1 **package (¼ ounce) active dry yeast**
- ¾ **cup warm water (110° to 115°)**
- ½ **cup quick-cooking oats**
- ½ **cup whole wheat flour**
- ¼ **cup packed brown sugar**
- 2 **tablespoons butter, melted**
- 1 **large egg**
- 1 **teaspoon salt**
- 1¾ to 2¼ **cups all-purpose flour**

FILLING

- 3 **tablespoons butter, softened**
- ⅓ **cup sugar**
- 2 **teaspoons ground cinnamon**

GLAZE

- 1 **cup confectioners' sugar**
- 6½ **teaspoons half-and-half cream**
- 4½ **teaspoons butter, softened**

1. In a large bowl, dissolve yeast in warm water. Add the oats, whole wheat flour, brown sugar, butter, egg, salt and 1 cup all-purpose flour. Beat on medium speed until smooth. Stir in enough remaining flour to form a soft dough (dough will be sticky).

2. Turn onto a lightly floured surface; knead until smooth and elastic, about 6-8 minutes. Place in a bowl coated with cooking spray, turning once to coat the top. Cover and let rise in a warm place until doubled, about 1 hour.

3. Punch dough down. Roll into an 18x12-in. rectangle; spread with butter. Combine sugar and cinnamon; sprinkle over dough to within ½ in. of edges.

4. Roll up jelly-roll style, starting with a short side; pinch seams to seal. Cut into 12 slices. Place cut side down in a 13x9-in. baking pan coated with cooking spray. Cover and let rise until doubled, about 45 minutes.

5. Bake at 375° for 15-20 minutes or until golden brown. For icing, in a small bowl, beat the confectioners' sugar, cream and butter until smooth. Drizzle over warm rolls.

PER SERVING *1 cinnamon roll equals 240 cal., 7 g fat (4 g sat. fat), 35 mg chol., 251 mg sodium, 40 g carb., 2 g fiber, 4 g pro.*

(5)INGREDIENTS
Chocolate Amaretti

These classic almond paste cookies are like ones you'd find in an Italian bakery. My husband and children are always excited when I include the amaretti in my holiday baking lineup.

—KATHY LONG WHITEFISH BAY, WI

PREP: 15 MIN. • **BAKE:** 20 MIN./BATCH
MAKES: 3 DOZEN

- 1¼ **cups almond paste**
- ¾ **cup sugar**
- 2 **large egg whites**
- ½ **cup confectioners' sugar**
- ¼ **cup baking cocoa**

1. In a large bowl, beat the almond paste, sugar and egg whites until combined. Combine confectioners' sugar and cocoa; gradually add to almond mixture and mix well.

2. Drop by tablespoonfuls 2 in. apart onto parchment paper-lined baking sheets. Bake at 350° for 17-20 minutes or until tops are cracked. Cool for 1 minute before removing from pans to wire racks. Store cookies in an airtight container.

PER SERVING *1 cookie equals 69 cal., 3 g fat (trace sat. fat), 0 chol., 4 mg sodium, 11 g carb., 1 g fiber, 1 g pro.* **Diabetic Exchanges:** *1 starch, ½ fat.*

(5)INGREDIENTS
Chocolate-Dipped Strawberry Meringue Roses

Eat these pretty pink meringues as-is, or crush them into a bowl of strawberries and whipped cream. Readers of my blog, *utry.it*, went nuts when I posted that idea!

—AMY TONG ANAHEIM, CA

PREP: 25 MIN. • **BAKE:** 40 MIN. + COOLING
MAKES: 3½ DOZEN

- **3 large egg whites**
- **¼ cup sugar**
- **¼ cup freeze-dried strawberries**
- **1 package (3 ounces) strawberry gelatin**
- **½ teaspoon vanilla extract, optional**
- **1 cup 60% cacao bittersweet chocolate baking chips, melted**

1. Place egg whites in a large bowl; let stand at room temperature 30 minutes. Preheat oven to 225°.

2. Place sugar and strawberries in a food processor; process until powdery. Add gelatin; pulse to blend.

3. Beat egg whites on medium speed until foamy, adding vanilla if desired. Gradually add gelatin mixture, 1 tablespoon at a time, beating on high until sugar is dissolved. Continue beating until stiff glossy peaks form.

4. Cut a small hole in the tip of a pastry bag or in a corner of a food-safe plastic bag; insert a #1M star tip. Transfer meringue to bag. Pipe 2-in. roses 1½ in. apart onto parchment paper-lined baking sheets.

5. Bake 40-45 minutes or until set and dry. Turn off oven (do not open oven door); leave meringues in oven 1½ hours. Remove from oven; cool completely on baking sheets.

6. Remove meringues from paper. Dip bottoms in melted chocolate; allow excess to drip off. Place on waxed paper; let stand until set, about 45 minutes. Store in an airtight container at room temperature.

PER SERVING *1 cookie equals 33 cal., 1 g fat (1 g sat. fat), 0 chol., 9 mg sodium, 6 g carb., trace fiber, 1 g pro.* ***Diabetic Exchange:*** *½ starch.*

HOW TO

TEST FOR STIFF PEAKS

Stiff peaks are achieved when the whites stand up in points, rather than curling over. If you tilt the bowl, the whites shouldn't move. Sugar is dissolved when the mixture feels silky-smooth between your fingers.

CHOCOLATE-DIPPED STRAWBERRY MERINGUE ROSES

Patriotic Sugar Cookies

One thing I especially love about these sugar cookies is that they're durable and ship well, so they're a wonderful treat to send to the troops overseas. Get a group together to have your own baking-decorating-packing party!

—**SUSAN WHETZEL** PEARISBURG, VA

PREP: 1¼ HOURS + CHILLING
BAKE: 10 MIN./BATCH + COOLING
MAKES: 10 DOZEN

- 1 **cup butter, softened**
- ½ **cup cream cheese, softened**
- 2 **cups sugar**
- 4 **large eggs**
- 1½ **teaspoons vanilla extract**
- 1 **teaspoon lemon extract**
- 5 **cups all-purpose flour**
- 2 **teaspoons baking powder**
- 1 **teaspoon salt**
  Decorating icing and/or colored sugars

1. In a large bowl, cream the butter, cream cheese and sugar until light and fluffy. Beat in eggs and extracts. Combine the flour, baking powder and salt; gradually add to creamed mixture and mix well. Cover and refrigerate for 2 hours or until easy to handle.
2. On a lightly floured surface, roll out dough to ¼-in. thickness. Cut with floured 2- to 3-in. star- and flag-shaped cookie cutters. Place 1 in. apart on ungreased baking sheets. Sprinkle with colored sugars as desired.
3. Bake at 350° for 9-11 minutes or until set. Cool for 2 minutes before removing from pans to wire racks to cool completely. Decorate with icing and additional sugars if desired.
NOTE *If shipping these cookies, consider decorating with royal icing.*
PER SERVING *1 cookie equals 51 cal., 2 g fat (1 g sat. fat), 12 mg chol., 42 mg sodium, 7 g carb., trace fiber, 1 g pro. Diabetic Exchange: ½ starch.*

Cool Watermelon Pops

The kids are going to flip when they see these picture-perfect pops.

—*TASTE OF HOME* TEST KITCHEN

PREP: 20 MIN. + FREEZING
MAKES: 28 POPS

- 2 **cups boiling water**
- 1 **cup sugar**
- 1 **package (3 ounces) watermelon gelatin**
- 1 **envelope unsweetened watermelon cherry Kool-Aid mix**
- 2 **cups refrigerated watermelon juice blend**
- ⅓ **cup miniature semisweet chocolate chips**
- 2 **cups prepared limeade**
- 2 **to 3 teaspoons green food coloring, optional**
- 28 **freezer pop molds or 28 paper cups (3 ounces each) and wooden pop sticks**

1. In a large bowl, combine the water, sugar, gelatin and Kool-Aid mix; stir until sugar is dissolved. Add the watermelon juice. Fill each mold or cup with 3 tablespoons watermelon mixture. Freeze until almost slushy, about 1 hour. Sprinkle with chocolate chips. Top molds with holders. If using cups, top with foil and insert sticks through foil. Freeze.
2. In a small bowl, combine limeade and food coloring if desired. If using freezer molds, remove holders. If using paper cups, remove foil. Pour limeade mixture over tops. Return holders or foil. Freeze until firm.
PER SERVING *1 pop equals 64 cal., 1 g fat (trace sat. fat), 0 chol., 11 mg sodium, 15 g carb., trace fiber, trace pro. Diabetic Exchange: 1 starch.*

PATRIOTIC SUGAR COOKIES

⑤ INGREDIENTS | FAST FIX
Fruity Cereal Bars

With dried apple and cranberries, these crispy cereal bars are perfect for snacks or brown-bag lunches.

—GIOVANNA KRANENBERG

CAMBRIDGE, MN

START TO FINISH: 30 MIN.
MAKES: 20 SERVINGS

- 3 **tablespoons butter**
- 1 **package (10 ounces) large marshmallows**
- 6 **cups crisp rice cereal**
- ½ **cup chopped dried apple**
- ½ **cup dried cranberries**

1. In a large saucepan, combine butter and marshmallows. Cook and stir over medium-low heat until melted. Remove from the heat; stir in the cereal, apples and cranberries.
2. Pat into a 13x9-in. pan coated with cooking spray; cool. Cut into squares.
PER SERVING *1 bar equals 105 cal., 2 g fat (1 g sat. fat), 5 mg chol., 102 mg sodium, 22 g carb., trace fiber, 1 g pro. Diabetic Exchanges: 1½ starch, ½ fat.*

MAKEOVER COOKOUT CARAMEL S'MORES

⑤ INGREDIENTS | FAST FIX
Makeover Cookout Caramel S'mores

These classic treats make a great finish to an informal summertime cookout in the backyard. And toasting the marshmallows extends our after-dinner time together, giving us something fun to do as a family.

—MARTHA HASEMAN HINCKLEY, IL

START TO FINISH: 10 MIN.
MAKES: 4 SERVINGS

- 8 **large marshmallows**
- 4 **whole reduced-fat graham crackers, halved**
- 2 **teaspoons fat-free chocolate syrup**
- 2 **teaspoons fat-free caramel ice cream topping**

Using a long-handled fork, toast marshmallows 6 in. from medium heat until golden brown, turning occasionally. Place two marshmallows on each of four graham cracker halves. Drizzle with chocolate syrup and caramel topping. Top with remaining crackers.
PER SERVING *1 s'more equals 87 cal., 1 g fat (1 g sat. fat), 1 mg chol., 82 mg sodium, 20 g carb., 1 g fiber, 1 g pro. Diabetic Exchange: 1 starch.*

🗨 THE SKINNY

The original s'more used full-fat graham crackers and caramel, as well as half of a chocolate bar per serving. Switching to lighter ingredients—especially the chocolate—saved significant fat and saturated fat.

DECONSTRUCTED RASPBERRY PIE

Snickerdoodles

These irresistible cookies are soft on the inside and crunchy on the outside.

—ASHLEY WISNIEWSKI CHAMPAIGN, IL

PREP: 30 MIN. • **BAKE:** 10 MIN./BATCH
MAKES: 3 DOZEN

- ¼ **cup butter, softened**
- 1 **cup plus 2 tablespoons sugar, divided**
- 1 **large egg**
- 1 **tablespoon agave nectar**
- 1 **teaspoon vanilla extract**
- 1¾ **cups white whole wheat flour**
- ½ **teaspoon baking soda**
- ½ **teaspoon cream of tartar**
- 2 **teaspoons ground cinnamon**

1. In a bowl, cream butter and 1 cup sugar until blended. Beat in egg, agave nectar and vanilla. Combine the flour, baking soda and cream of tartar; gradually beat into creamed mixture.
2. In a small bowl, combine cinnamon and remaining sugar. Shape dough into 1-in. balls; roll in cinnamon-sugar. Place 2 in. apart on greased baking sheets. Bake at 375° for 9-11 minutes or until lightly browned. Cool 2 minutes before removing from pans to wire racks.
PER SERVING *1 cookie equals 52 cal., 1 g fat (1 g sat. fat), 8 mg chol., 24 mg sodium, 10 g carb., 1 g fiber, 1 g pro.* **Diabetic Exchange:** *½ starch.*

Deconstructed Raspberry Pie

It took us a couple of tries to get the crumb crust just right in this fun-to-make, fun-to-eat dessert. Try it with fresh strawberries or blueberries if you like.

—TASTE OF HOME TEST KITCHEN

PREP: 15 MIN. • **BAKE:** 5 MIN. + COOLING
MAKES: 4 SERVINGS

- 2⅔ **cups fresh raspberries**
- 2 **teaspoons sugar**
- ½ **cup graham cracker crumbs**
- 2 **tablespoons butter, melted**
- 4 **tablespoons whipped cream**
- ¼ **teaspoon baking cocoa**

1. In a small bowl, combine the raspberries and sugar; set aside.
2. In another small bowl, combine cracker crumbs and butter. Press into an 8x6-in. rectangle on an ungreased baking sheet. Bake at 350° for 5-6 minutes or until lightly browned. Cool completely on a wire rack. Break into large pieces.
3. To assemble, divide half of graham cracker pieces among four dessert plates; top with ⅓ cup raspberries. Repeat layers. Top each with 1 tablespoon whipped cream and dust with cocoa.
PER SERVING *1 serving equals 153 cal., 8 g fat (4 g sat. fat), 18 mg chol., 109 mg sodium, 20 g carb., 6 g fiber, 2 g pro.* **Diabetic Exchanges:** *1½ fat, 1 fruit, ½ starch.*

(5) INGREDIENTS FAST FIX >

Sweet Pineapple Cider

The best thing about this recipe? You can make it hours ahead so you can spend more time with your guests. And you can keep it warm on the stovetop or in a slow cooker throughout the party.

—**MARY PRICE** YOUNGSTOWN, OH

START TO FINISH: 30 MIN.
MAKES: 12 SERVINGS (¾ CUP EACH)

- 2 small apples, divided
- 10 whole cloves
- 1 bottle (48 ounces) unsweetened apple juice
- 4 cans (6 ounces each) unsweetened pineapple juice
- 2 cinnamon sticks (3 inches)

1. Core and cut one apple into 10 slices. Insert one clove into each slice. In a Dutch oven, combine juices. Add apple slices and cinnamon sticks. Bring to a boil. Reduce heat; simmer, uncovered, for 15-20 minutes or until flavors are blended.

2. Discard the apple slices and cinnamon sticks. Core and cut remaining apple into 12 slices. Ladle cider into mugs; garnish with apple slices. Serve warm.

PER SERVING *¾ cup equals 93 cal., trace fat (trace sat. fat), 0 chol., 5 mg sodium, 23 g carb., trace fiber, trace pro.* **Diabetic Exchange:** *1½ fruit.*

FAST FIX >

Caramel Corn Treats

These treats, a funky-fun version of Rice Krispie squares, are a cinch to make and will delight the kiddies.

—**CATHY TANG** REDMOND, WA

START TO FINISH: 15 MIN.
MAKES: 2 DOZEN

- 5 cups caramel corn
- 2 cups miniature pretzels
- 1 cup miniature cheddar cheese fish-shaped crackers
- 1¼ cups Reese's pieces, divided
- 1 package (10½ ounces) miniature marshmallows
- ¼ cup butter, cubed
- ¼ teaspoon vanilla extract

1. In a large bowl, combine the caramel corn, pretzels, crackers and 1 cup Reese's pieces. In a large microwave-safe bowl, melt marshmallows and butter; add vanilla and stir until smooth. Pour over pretzel mixture; stir until well coated.

2. Press into a greased 13x9-in. pan. Sprinkle with remaining Reese's pieces; press lightly. Let stand until set. Cut into bars.

PER SERVING *1 bar equals 161 cal., 5 g fat (3 g sat. fat), 6 mg chol., 128 mg sodium, 28 g carb., 1 g fiber, 2 g pro.* **Diabetic Exchanges:** *1½ starch, 1 fat.*

CARAMEL CORN TREATS

BLACK CAT DIPPERS
WITH PUMPKIN PIE DIP

Black Cat Dippers with Pumpkin Pie Dip

Here's an easy recipe sure to impress party guests. The black cat cutouts that accompany the in-a-dash dip are prepared with convenient refrigerated pie pastry.

—**DIANE TURNER** BRUNSWICK, OH

PREP: 20 MIN. • **BAKE:** 10 MIN./BATCH
MAKES: 2½ DOZEN BLACK CATS (3 CUPS DIP)

- 1 package (8 ounces) cream cheese, softened
- 1 can (15 ounces) solid-pack pumpkin
- 1 cup confectioners' sugar
- 1 tablespoon pumpkin pie spice
- 1 tablespoon honey
- 1 package (15 ounces) refrigerated pie pastry
- 1 large egg
- 1 tablespoon milk
  Black paste food coloring
- ¼ cup sugar
- ½ teaspoon ground cinnamon

1. In a large bowl, beat cream cheese until fluffy. Add the pumpkin, confectioners' sugar, pie spice and honey; beat until smooth. Cover and refrigerate until serving.

2. Roll out each pie pastry directly on an ungreased baking sheet to ⅛-in. thickness. Cut with a floured 2-in. cat-shaped cookie cutter, leaving at least 1 in. between cutouts. Remove excess dough and reroll scraps if desired. Beat the egg, milk and food coloring; brush over cutouts. Combine sugar and cinnamon; sprinkle over cutouts.

3. Bake at 400° for 6-7 minutes or until edges begin to brown. Remove to wire racks to cool. Serve with pumpkin dip.

PER SERVING *1 black cat with 2 tablespoons dip equals 152 cal., 8 g fat (4 g sat. fat), 18 mg chol., 97 mg sodium, 18 g carb., 1 g fiber, 2 g pro.* *Diabetic Exchanges: 1½ fat, 1 starch.*

BOO-RRIFIC KISSES

Boo-rrific Kisses

These cute meringue cookies look like tiny ghosts. And with just 15 calories apiece, each little treat can be enjoyed guilt-free!

—**PHYLLIS SCHMALZ** KANSAS CITY, KS

PREP: 20 MIN. • **BAKE:** 40 MIN. + STANDING
MAKES: 2½ DOZEN

- 2 large egg whites
- ½ teaspoon vanilla extract
- ¼ teaspoon almond extract
- ⅛ teaspoon cider vinegar
- ½ cup sugar
  Orange food coloring, optional
- 1½ teaspoons miniature semisweet chocolate chips

1. Place egg whites in a small bowl; let stand at room temperature for 30 minutes. Add extracts and vinegar; beat on medium speed until soft peaks form. Gradually beat in sugar, 1 tablespoon at a time, on high until stiff glossy peaks form and sugar is dissolved, about 6 minutes. Beat in food coloring if desired.

2. Cut a small hole in the corner of a pastry or plastic bag; insert a #10 round pastry tip. Fill bag with egg white mixture. Pipe 1½-in.-diameter ghosts onto parchment paper-lined baking sheets. Add two chips on each for eyes.

3. Bake at 250° for 40-45 minutes or until set and dry. Turn oven off; leave cookies in oven for 1 hour. Carefully remove from parchment paper. Store in an airtight container.

PER SERVING *1 cookie equals 15 cal., trace fat (trace sat. fat), 0 chol., 4 mg sodium, 3 g carb., trace fiber, trace pro.* *Diabetic Exchange: Free food.*

TOP TIP

These are amazing! Some of my variations are adding orange extract, apple pie seasoning, or instant hazelnut coffee granules. That's the best! My mom and I love them.

—**LJOBERLE** TASTEOFHOME.COM

ORIGINAL	MAKEOVER
542 Calories	**363** Calories
27g Fat	**17**g Fat
8g Sat. Fat	**5**g Sat. Fat

MAKEOVER SWEET POTATO PECAN PIE

Makeover Sweet Potato Pecan Pie

Taste of Home lightened up my cherished pie recipe and kept all the festive fall flavors.
—**MARGIE WILLIAMS** MOUNT JULIET, TN

PREP: 25 MIN. • **BAKE:** 45 MIN. + CHILLING
MAKES: 8 SERVINGS

- 1 **sheet refrigerated pie pastry**
- 1½ **cups mashed sweet potatoes**
- ⅓ **cup 2% milk**
- ¼ **cup packed dark brown sugar**
- 1 **tablespoon reduced-fat butter, melted**
- ½ **teaspoon vanilla extract**
- ¼ **teaspoon salt**
- ½ **teaspoon ground cinnamon**
- ¼ **teaspoon ground allspice**
- ¼ **teaspoon ground nutmeg**

PECAN LAYER
- 1 **large egg**
- ⅓ **cup packed dark brown sugar**
- ⅓ **cup corn syrup**
- 1 **tablespoon reduced-fat butter, melted**
- ¼ **teaspoon vanilla extract**
- ⅔ **cup chopped pecans**

1. On a lightly floured surface, unroll pastry. Transfer to a 9-in. pie plate. Trim pastry to ½ in. beyond edge of plate; flute edges.
2. In a small bowl, combine the sweet potatoes, milk, brown sugar, butter, vanilla, salt and spices. Spread evenly into pastry shell.
3. For pecan layer, in another small bowl, whisk egg and brown sugar until blended. Add the corn syrup, butter and vanilla; mix well. Stir in pecans. Pour over sweet potato mixture.
4. Bake at 350° for 45-55 minutes or until a knife inserted near the center comes out clean. Cool completely on a wire rack. Refrigerate for at least 3 hours before serving.
PER SERVING *1 piece equals 363 cal., 17 g fat (5 g sat. fat), 36 mg chol., 255 mg sodium, 53 g carb., 3 g fiber, 4 g pro.*

Pumpkin Pecan Custard

My family loves pumpkin pie, but this is a delicious, creamy, healthier alternative, and we don't miss the crust at all.
—**ABBY BOOTH** COWETA, OK

PREP: 20 MIN. • **BAKE:** 35 MIN. + CHILLING
MAKES: 8 SERVINGS

- 1 **can (15 ounces) solid-pack pumpkin**
- 1 **can (12 ounces) reduced-fat evaporated milk**
- ¾ **cup egg substitute**
- ⅓ **cup packed brown sugar**
- 1½ **teaspoons vanilla extract**
- 1 **teaspoon ground cinnamon**
- ½ **teaspoon ground ginger**
- ¼ **teaspoon ground cloves**
- ⅛ **teaspoon salt**

TOPPING
- 3 **tablespoons all-purpose flour**
- 3 **tablespoons brown sugar**
- ½ **teaspoon ground cinnamon**
- 2 **tablespoons cold butter**
- ½ **cup chopped pecans**

1. In a large bowl, combine the first nine ingredients. Transfer to eight 6-oz. ramekins or custard cups. Place in a baking pan; add 1 in. of boiling water to pan. Bake, uncovered, at 325° for 20 minutes.
2. Meanwhile, for topping, in a small bowl, combine the flour, brown sugar and cinnamon. Cut in butter until crumbly. Stir in pecans. Sprinkle over custards. Bake 15-20 minutes longer or until a knife inserted near the center comes out clean.
3. Remove ramekins from water bath; cool for 10 minutes. Cover and refrigerate for at least 4 hours.
PER SERVING *1 custard equals 213 cal., 9 g fat (3 g sat. fat), 11 mg chol., 160 mg sodium, 27 g carb., 3 g fiber, 7 g pro.* **Diabetic Exchanges:** *2 starch, 1½ fat.*

Cranberry-Pumpkin Spice Cake

Even though this cake is light, my kids love it! I stock up on canned pumpkin in the fall when it's on sale so I can make it all year.

—**CAMI LAFORGE** MURRAY, UT

PREP: 20 MIN. • **BAKE:** 20 MIN. + COOLING
MAKES: 9 SERVINGS

- 1 large egg
- 1 large egg white
- ½ cup canned pumpkin
- 2 tablespoons butter, melted
- 1 tablespoon canola oil
- 1 teaspoon vanilla extract
- 1 cup all-purpose flour
- ¾ cup packed brown sugar
- 1 teaspoon baking powder
- ½ teaspoon ground cinnamon
- ¼ teaspoon baking soda
- ¼ teaspoon salt
- ⅓ cup dried cranberries
- ¼ cup chopped walnuts
- 2 teaspoons grated orange peel
- 1 teaspoon confectioners' sugar

1. Preheat oven to 350°. Meanwhile, coat a 9-in.-square baking pan with cooking spray.

2. In a large bowl, beat egg and egg white until foamy. Add pumpkin, melted butter, oil and vanilla; beat until well blended. In another bowl, whisk flour, brown sugar, baking powder, cinnamon, baking soda and salt; stir into egg mixture. Stir in cranberries, walnuts and orange peel. Transfer to prepared pan.

3. Bake 20-25 minutes or until a toothpick inserted in center comes out clean. Cool completely in pan on a wire rack. Sprinkle with confectioners' sugar before serving.

PER SERVING *1 piece equals 208 cal., 7 g fat (2 g sat. fat), 30 mg chol., 192 mg sodium, 34 g carb., 1 g fiber, 4 g pro. **Diabetic Exchanges:** 2 starch, 1½ fat.*

Pear-Cranberry Gingerbread Cake

I love the warm, spicy flavors and festive fall fruits in this upside-down gingerbread cake. It could have a special place at any holiday buffet.

—**CHRISTINA METKE** CALGARY, AB

PREP: 25 MIN. • **BAKE:** 35 MIN. + COOLING
MAKES: 24 SERVINGS

- ¾ cup butter, melted, divided
- ⅔ cup packed brown sugar, divided
- 3 medium pears, sliced
- 2 cups fresh or frozen cranberries, thawed
- ¾ cup brewed chai tea
- ½ cup sugar
- ½ cup molasses
- 1 large egg
- 2 cups all-purpose flour
- 1 teaspoon ground ginger
- 1 teaspoon ground cinnamon
- ½ teaspoon salt
- ½ teaspoon baking soda
- ½ teaspoon ground cloves
- ¼ teaspoon ground nutmeg

1. Pour ¼ cup melted butter into a 13x9-in. baking dish; sprinkle with ⅓ cup brown sugar. Arrange pears and cranberries in a single layer over brown sugar.

2. In a small bowl, beat the brewed tea, sugar, molasses, egg and remaining butter and brown sugar until well blended. Combine the remaining ingredients; gradually beat into tea mixture until blended.

3. Spoon over pears. Bake at 350° for 35-45 minutes or until a toothpick inserted near the center comes out clean. Cool for 10 minutes before inverting onto a serving plate. Serve warm.

PER SERVING *1 piece equals 166 cal., 6 g fat (4 g sat. fat), 24 mg chol., 124 mg sodium, 27 g carb., 1 g fiber, 2 g pro. **Diabetic Exchanges:** 1½ starch, 1 fat.*

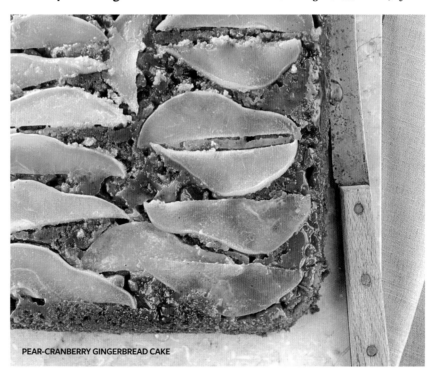

PEAR-CRANBERRY GINGERBREAD CAKE

Gluten-Free Kahlua Dessert

Whether you follow a gluten-free diet or not, you'll delight in every bite of this creamy treat. It's accented with subtle notes of Kahlua.

—**MELISSA MCCRADY** WAUWATOSA, WI

PREP: 30 MIN. + CHILLING
MAKES: 12 SERVINGS

- 1 **cup gluten-free cornflakes, crushed**
- 2 **tablespoons butter, melted**
- 2 **teaspoons unflavored gelatin**
- ¼ **cup cold water**
- 12 **ounces reduced-fat cream cheese**
- 2 **tablespoons sugar**
- ⅔ **cup fat-free sweetened condensed milk**
- ¼ **cup Kahlua (coffee liqueur)**
- 2 **cups fat-free whipped topping**
- 2 **ounces dark chocolate candy bar, melted**
  Fresh raspberries and mint leaves, optional

1. Combine cornflake crumbs and butter; press onto the bottom of a 9-in.-square pan coated with cooking spray. Refrigerate for 10 minutes.

2. Meanwhile, in a small saucepan, sprinkle gelatin over cold water; let stand 1 minute. Heat over low heat, stirring until gelatin is completely dissolved. Remove from the heat and set aside.

3. In a large bowl, beat cream cheese and sugar until smooth. Beat in the milk, Kahlua and gelatin mixture until blended. Gently fold in whipped topping; pour over crust. Refrigerate for at least 4 hours or until firm.

4. Drizzle with melted chocolate; garnish with raspberries and mint leaves if desired.

NOTE *Read all ingredient labels for possible gluten content prior to use. Ingredient formulas can change, and production facilities vary among brands. If you're concerned that your brand may contain gluten, contact the company.*

PER SERVING *1 piece (calculated without raspberries) equals 217 cal., 9 g fat (6 g sat. fat), 28 mg chol., 176 mg sodium, 25 g carb., 1 g fiber, 5 g pro. Diabetic Exchanges: 2 fat, 1½ starch.*

Cutout Sugar Cookies

We dreamed up these chewy sugar cookies that are surprisingly low in fat. Decorated for the holidays with colored sugar, sprinkles or frosting, they won't last long...so make sure you stash some away for Santa!

—*TASTE OF HOME* TEST KITCHEN

PREP: 25 MIN. + CHILLING
BAKE: 10 MIN./BATCH
MAKES: 2½ DOZEN

- 6 **tablespoons butter, softened**
- ½ **cup sugar**
- ½ **cup packed brown sugar**
- 1 **large egg**
- 1 **teaspoon vanilla extract**
- 2 **tablespoons vegetable oil**
- 1 **tablespoon light corn syrup**
- 1½ **cups all-purpose flour**
- ¼ **cup cornmeal**
- ½ **teaspoon baking powder**
- ½ **teaspoon salt**
- 1¼ **cups colored sugar of your choice**

1. In a large bowl, beat butter and sugars until creamy. Beat in egg and vanilla. Beat in oil and corn syrup. Combine the flour, cornmeal, baking powder and salt. Add to creamed mixture just until blended. Divide in half; wrap each portion in plastic wrap. Refrigerate for at least 2 hours.

2. On a lightly floured surface, roll dough out to ¼-in. thickness. Cut out dough with lightly floured 2½-in. cookie cutters. Place 2 in. apart on baking sheets coated with cooking spray. Sprinkle each cutout with 2 teaspoons colored sugar. Bake at 350° for 7-9 minutes or until set and bottoms are lightly browned. Cool for 2 minutes before removing to wire racks to cool completely.

PER SERVING *1 cookie equals 117 cal., 3 g fat (2 g sat. fat), 13 mg chol., 98 mg sodium, 21 g carb., trace fiber, 1 g pro. Diabetic Exchange: 1½ starch.*

Cranberry Pomegranate Margaritas

I came up with this beverage to serve at holiday celebrations for a different kind of margarita. It's light, refreshing, and looks beautiful with sugar crystals on glass rims.

—MINDIE HILTON SUSANVILLE, CA

START TO FINISH: 5 MIN.
MAKES: 12 SERVINGS (¾ CUP EACH)

- 4½ cups diet lemon-lime soda, chilled
- 1½ cups tequila
- 1½ cups cranberry juice, chilled
- 1½ cups pomegranate juice, chilled
  Pomegranate slices and frozen cranberries, optional

In a pitcher, combine the soda, tequila and juices. Serve in chilled glasses. Garnish with pomegranate and cranberries if desired.

PER SERVING *¾ cup equals 97 cal., trace fat (trace sat. fat), 0 chol., 13 mg sodium, 8 g carb., trace fiber, trace pro.*

CRANBERRY TRIFLE

Cranberry Trifle

You'd never guess that this stunning trifle has been lightened up. It boasts all of the original's festive flavor, but has only half the fat and far fewer calories!

—SONYA LABBE WEST HOLLYWOOD, CA

PREP: 25 MIN. + CHILLING
MAKES: 15 SERVINGS

- 1 package (16 ounces) frozen unsweetened strawberries, thawed
- 1 package (12 ounces) fresh or frozen cranberries
- 1 cup sugar
- ½ cup water
- 4 teaspoons grated orange peel
- 1 package (8 ounces) reduced-fat cream cheese
- ¼ cup packed light brown sugar
- ½ teaspoon vanilla extract
- 1 carton (8 ounces) frozen whipped topping, thawed
- 2 loaves (10¾ ounces each) frozen reduced-fat pound cake, thawed and cubed

1. In a large saucepan, combine the first five ingredients. Cook over medium heat until the berries pop, about 15 minutes. Cool completely.
2. Meanwhile, in a large bowl, beat the cream cheese, brown sugar and vanilla until smooth. Fold in the whipped topping.
3. Place a third of the cake cubes in a 3-qt. trifle bowl; top with a third of the cranberry mixture and a third of the cream cheese mixture. Repeat layers twice. Cover and refrigerate for at least 2 hours before serving.

PER SERVING *1 cup equals 316 cal., 12 g fat (6 g sat. fat), 33 mg chol., 254 mg sodium, 49 g carb., 2 g fiber, 4 g pro.*

ORIGINAL	MAKEOVER
584 Calories	426 Calories
33g Fat	13g Fat
17g Sat. Fat	7g Sat. Fat

(5)INGREDIENTS FAST FIX ▶

Spiced Coffee

This is a great drink to fix on a chilly night. I love to experiment with flavored coffees and this one is definitely worth trying.

—JILL GARN CHARLOTTE, MI

START TO FINISH: 20 MIN.
MAKES: 2 SERVINGS

- 2 **cups water**
- 5 **teaspoons instant coffee granules**
- ½ **cinnamon stick (3 inches)**
- 4 **whole cloves**
- 5 **teaspoons sugar**
  Whipped topping, optional

In a small saucepan, combine the water, coffee granules, cinnamon stick and cloves. Bring to a boil. Remove from the heat; cover and let stand for 5-8 minutes. Strain and discard spices. Stir in sugar until dissolved. Ladle into mugs. Serve with whipped topping if desired.

PER SERVING *1 cup (calculated without whipped topping) equals 46 cal., trace fat (trace sat. fat), 0 chol., 1 mg sodium, 11 g carb., 0 fiber, trace pro.* **Diabetic Exchange:** *½ starch.*

Makeover Cherry Almond Mousse Pie

With less than half the fat of the original pie, this makeover is a win! Everybody loves the festive chocolate-cherry flavors.

—JULIE HIEGGELKE GRAYSLAKE, IL

PREP: 25 MIN. + CHILLING
MAKES: 8 SERVINGS

- 1 **can (14 ounces) fat-free sweetened condensed milk, divided**
- 1 **ounce unsweetened chocolate, chopped**
- ½ **teaspoon almond extract, divided**
- 1 **frozen pie shell, baked**
- 1 **jar (10 ounces) maraschino cherries, drained**

MAKEOVER CHERRY ALMOND MOUSSE PIE

- 1 **package (8 ounces) fat-free cream cheese**
- ¾ **cup cold water**
- 1 **package (1 ounce) sugar-free instant vanilla pudding mix**
- 2 **cups reduced-fat whipped topping**
- ¼ **cup chopped almonds, toasted**
  Chocolate curls, optional

1. In a small saucepan over low heat, cook and stir ½ cup milk and chocolate for 4-5 minutes or until the chocolate is melted. Stir in ¼ teaspoon extract. Pour into pie shell; set aside.

2. Set aside eight whole cherries for garnish. Chop the remaining cherries; set aside. In a large bowl, beat cream cheese until smooth. Gradually beat in water and remaining milk. Add pudding mix and remaining extract; mix well. Fold in whipped topping.

Stir in almonds and reserved chopped cherries.

3. Pour over the pie. Refrigerate for 4 hours or until set. Garnish with whole cherries and chocolate curls if desired.

PER SERVING *1 piece (calculated without chocolate curls) equals 426 cal., 13 g fat (7 g sat. fat), 14 mg chol., 453 mg sodium, 69 g carb., 1 g fiber, 10 g pro.*

THE SKINNY

The original recipe used regular sweetened condensed milk and full-fat cream cheese. Switching to the fat-free versions saved a whopping 14 grams of fat and 9 grams of saturated fat per slice!

Creamy Eggnog

I have been making this velvety-smooth eggnog on Christmas Day for about 40 years. My family always looks forward to this traditional treat. Feel free to add a little coffee-flavored liqueur.

—**BARBARA SMITH** CHIPLEY, FL

PREP: 20 MIN. + CHILLING • **COOK:** 25 MIN.
MAKES: 8 SERVINGS

- 2 **large eggs, separated**
- 1 **can (14 ounces) fat-free sweetened condensed milk**
- ¼ **teaspoon salt**
- 4 **cups 2% milk, divided**
- 1 **teaspoon vanilla extract**
- ⅛ **teaspoon ground nutmeg**
- 2 **tablespoons sugar**
- ⅛ **teaspoon cream of tartar**
  Additional ground nutmeg, optional

1. In a small heavy saucepan, whisk the egg yolks, sweetened condensed milk and salt until blended. Stir in 2 cups milk. Cook over medium-low heat for 20-30 minutes or until bubbles form around sides of pan and a thermometer reads at least 160°, stirring constantly. (Do not boil.) Immediately remove from heat.

2. Pour into a large bowl. Place bowl in an ice-water bath, stirring frequently until cooled. Stir in the vanilla, nutmeg and remaining milk. Refrigerate until cold.

3. In a small heavy saucepan, combine the egg whites, sugar and cream of tartar. With a hand mixer, beat on low speed for 1 minute. Continue beating over low heat until egg mixture reaches 160°, about 4 minutes.

4. Transfer to a bowl. Beat until stiff glossy peaks form and the sugar is dissolved. Gently stir into the milk mixture until blended. Sprinkle each serving with nutmeg if desired.

PER SERVING *¾ cup equals 232 cal., 4 g fat (2 g sat. fat), 68 mg chol., 203 mg sodium, 40 g carb., trace fiber, 9 g pro.*

Sunshine Crepes

My family wanted coffee and something light for a special breakfast, so I whipped up these sweet and fruity crepes. They were a big hit with everyone!

—**MARY HOBBS** CAMPBELL, MO

PREP: 15 MIN. + CHILLING • **COOK:** 15 MIN.
MAKES: 6 SERVINGS

- ⅔ **cup milk**
- 2 **large eggs**
- 1 **tablespoon canola oil**
- ½ **cup all-purpose flour**
- 1 **teaspoon sugar**
- ¼ **teaspoon salt**

FILLING
- 1 **can (20 ounces) crushed pineapple, drained**
- 1 **can (11 ounces) mandarin oranges, drained**
- 1 **teaspoon vanilla extract**
- 1 **carton (8 ounces) frozen whipped topping, thawed**
  Confectioners' sugar

1. In a large bowl, beat the milk, eggs and oil. Combine the flour, sugar and salt; add to milk mixture and mix well. Cover and refrigerate for 1 hour.

2. Coat an 8-in. nonstick skillet with cooking spray; heat over medium heat. Stir crepe batter; pour 2 tablespoons into center of skillet. Lift and tilt pan to coat bottom evenly. Cook until top appears dry; turn and cook 15-20 seconds longer. Remove to a wire rack. Repeat with remaining batter, coating skillet as needed. When cool, stack crepes with waxed paper or paper towels in between.

3. For filling, in a large bowl, combine the pineapple, oranges and vanilla; fold in whipped topping. Spoon ⅓ cup down the center of each crepe; roll up. Dust with confectioners' sugar.

PER SERVING *2 crepes equals 302 cal., 11 g fat (8 g sat. fat), 75 mg chol., 136 mg sodium, 43 g carb., 1 g fiber, 5 g pro.* **Diabetic Exchanges:** *2 starch, 2 fat, 1 fruit.*

SUNSHINE CREPES

Gluten-Free Peanut Butter Kiss Cookies

Serve these chocolate-topped cookies, and everyone will want to kiss the cook! For a change of pace, try them with chunky peanut butter, too.

—CANADA60

TASTE OF HOME ONLINE COMMUNITY

PREP: 20 MIN. + CHILLING
BAKE: 10 MIN./BATCH
MAKES: 4 DOZEN

- ¼ cup butter-flavored shortening
- 1¼ cups packed brown sugar
- ¾ cup creamy peanut butter
- 1 large egg
- ¼ cup unsweetened applesauce
- 3 teaspoons vanilla extract
- 1 cup white rice flour
- ½ cup potato starch
- ¼ cup tapioca flour
- 1 teaspoon baking powder
- ¾ teaspoon baking soda
- ¼ teaspoon salt
- 48 milk chocolate kisses, unwrapped

1. In a large bowl, beat shortening, brown sugar and peanut butter until blended. Beat in egg, applesauce and vanilla (mixture will appear curdled). In another bowl, whisk rice flour, potato starch, tapioca flour, baking powder, baking soda and salt; gradually beat into creamed mixture. Refrigerate, covered, 1 hour.

2. Preheat oven to 375°. Shape dough into forty-eight 1-in. balls; place 2 in. apart on ungreased baking sheets. Bake 9-11 minutes or until slightly cracked. Immediately press a chocolate kiss into center of each cookie. Cool on pans 2 minutes. Remove to wire racks to cool.

NOTE *Read all ingredient labels for possible gluten content prior to use. Ingredient formulas can change, and production facilities vary among brands. If you're concerned that your brand may contain gluten, contact the company.*

PER SERVING *1 cookie equals 98 cal., 5 g fat (2 g sat. fat), 5 mg chol., 67 mg sodium, 13 g carb., trace fiber, 2 g pro. Diabetic Exchanges: 1 starch, 1 fat.*

Peppermint Swirl Fudge

Indulge your sweet tooth with these rich swirled squares. For Christmasy color, I add crushed peppermint candies and red food coloring.

—SUZETTE JURY KEENE, CA

PREP: 15 MIN. + CHILLING
MAKES: ABOUT 1½ POUNDS

- 1 teaspoon butter
- 1 package (10 to 12 ounces) white baking chips
- 1 can (16 ounces) vanilla frosting
- ½ teaspoon peppermint extract
- 8 drops red food coloring
- 2 tablespoons crushed peppermint candies

1. Line a 9-in.-square pan with foil and grease the foil with butter; set aside.

2. In a small saucepan, melt chips; stir until smooth. Remove from the heat. Stir in frosting and extract. Spread into prepared pan.

3. Randomly place drops of food coloring over fudge; cut through fudge with a knife to swirl. Sprinkle with the peppermint candies. Refrigerate for 1 hour or until set.

4. Using foil, lift fudge out of pan. Gently peel off foil; cut fudge into 1-in. squares. Store in an airtight container.

PER SERVING *1 piece equals 45 cal., 3 g fat (1 g sat. fat), 1 mg chol., 17 mg sodium, 6 g carb., 0 fiber, trace pro. Diabetic Exchange: 1 starch.*

Cranberry-Grape Spritzer

Here's a festive alcohol-free drink that's easy on the waistline. A splash of club soda gives it sparkle.

—KAREN SCHWABENLENDER WAXHAW, NC

START TO FINISH: 5 MIN.
MAKES: 1 SERVING

- ½ cup cranberry-apple juice
- ½ cup grape juice
- ¼ cup club soda
  Lemon slice

Combine juices and club soda in a tall glass; add ice. Garnish with lemon.
PER SERVING *1¼ cups (calculated without lemon slice) equals 134 cal., trace fat (trace sat. fat), 0 chol., 37 mg sodium, 33 g carb., trace fiber, 1 g pro.*

Makeover White Fruitcake

I remember my mother making this recipe every Christmas, and it just wouldn't be Christmas in our home without it, either. The cooks at *Taste of Home* gave it a much-needed makeover so we can enjoy it without the guilt.

—JUDY GREBETZ RACINE, WI

PREP: 20 MIN. + STANDING
BAKE: 1½ HOURS + COOLING
MAKES: 20 SERVINGS

- ¾ cup red candied cherries
- ¾ cup green candied cherries
- 1¼ cups brandy, divided
- 6 large eggs, separated
- 2 large egg whites
- ½ cup butter, softened
- 1½ cups sugar
- 4 cups all-purpose flour
- ½ cup unsweetened applesauce
- 1½ cups sliced almonds
- 1½ cups golden raisins
- ¾ cup flaked coconut

ORIGINAL	MAKEOVER
537 Calories	**352** Calories
30g Fat	**11g** Fat
14g Sat. Fat	**5g** Sat. Fat

MAKEOVER WHITE FRUITCAKE

1. In a small bowl, combine cherries and ¼ cup brandy; let stand overnight. Place eight egg whites in a large bowl; let stand at room temperature for 30 minutes.

2. In a large bowl, cream butter and sugar until well blended. Add egg yolks, one at a time, beating well after each addition. Beat in remaining brandy. Gradually add flour to the creamed mixture alternately with the applesauce.

3. With clean beaters, beat egg whites until stiff peaks form; fold into batter.

Fold in the cherry mixture, almonds, raisins and coconut. Gently spoon into a 10-in. tube pan with removable bottom coated with cooking spray. Bake at 300° for 1½-1¾ hours or until a toothpick inserted near the center comes out clean.

4. Cool fruitcake for 10 minutes before removing from pan to a wire rack to cool completely.
PER SERVING *1 slice equals 352 cal., 11 g fat (5 g sat. fat), 75 mg chol., 80 mg sodium, 56 g carb., 2 g fiber, 7 g pro.*

Chocolate Cherry Cake

You can have your cake and eat it too with this lower-calorie treat. The rich chocolate cake is draped with a fantastic cherry-port sauce.

—JACYN SIEBERT SAN FRANCISCO, CA

PREP: 30 MIN. • **BAKE:** 15 MIN. + COOLING
MAKES: 14 SERVINGS

- 2 large eggs
- 2 large egg whites
- ½ cup buttermilk
- ⅓ cup strong brewed coffee
- 3 tablespoons canola oil
- 1 teaspoon vanilla extract
- 1 cup all-purpose flour
- ⅔ cup baking cocoa
- ½ cup packed brown sugar
- 1½ teaspoons baking powder
- ¼ teaspoon baking soda
- ¼ teaspoon salt
- **CHERRY TOPPING**
- ½ cup cherry juice blend
- ½ cup port wine or additional cherry juice blend
- ⅔ cup dried tart cherries
- 2 tablespoons honey
  Dash salt
- 1 package (12 ounces) frozen pitted dark sweet cherries, thawed and halved
- 1 tablespoon cornstarch
- 2 tablespoons cold water
- ½ teaspoon almond extract
- 1 cup sweetened whipped cream

1. Coat a 9-in. round baking pan with cooking spray and sprinkle with flour. In a large bowl, beat the eggs, egg whites, buttermilk, coffee, oil and vanilla until well blended. Combine the flour, cocoa, brown sugar, baking powder, baking soda and salt; gradually beat into egg mixture until blended.
2. Transfer to prepared pan. Bake at 350° for 15-20 minutes or until a toothpick inserted near the center comes out clean. Cool for 10 minutes before removing from pan to a wire rack. Cool completely.
3. In a large saucepan, combine the cherry juice, wine, dried cherries, honey and salt. Bring to a boil. Reduce heat; simmer, uncovered, 8-11 minutes or until liquid is reduced by half. Add the dark cherries; cook and stir for 2 minutes.
4. Combine cornstarch and water; whisk into cherry mixture. Cook and stir for 1-2 minutes or until thickened. Remove from the heat; stir in extract. Cool.
5. Serve cake with cherry topping; garnish with whipped cream.
PER SERVING *1 slice cake with 2 tablespoons topping and 1 tablespoon whipped cream equals 213 cal., 8 g fat (3 g sat. fat), 42 mg chol., 153 mg sodium, 31 g carb., 2 g fiber, 4 g pro.* **Diabetic Exchanges:** *2 starch, 1½ fat.*

Basil Citrus Cocktail

This irresistible cocktail is fruity, fantastic and low in calories!

—TASTE OF HOME TEST KITCHEN

START TO FINISH: 10 MIN.
MAKES: 1 SERVING.

- 6 fresh basil leaves
- 1½ to 2 cups ice cubes
- 2 ounces white grapefruit juice
- 2 ounces freshly squeezed mandarin orange juice
- ¾ ounce gin
- ½ ounce Domaine de Canton ginger liqueur

1. In a cocktail shaker, muddle the basil leaves.
2. Fill shaker three-fourths full with ice. Add the juices, gin and ginger liqueur; cover and shake for 10-15 seconds or until condensation forms on outside of shaker. Strain into a chilled cocktail glass.
PER SERVING *1 serving equals 136 cal., trace fat (trace sat. fat), 0 chol., trace sodium, 14 g carb., trace fiber, 1 g pro.*

(5) INGREDIENTS Jellied Champagne Dessert

This refreshing dessert looks just like a glass of bubbling champagne.
—**JAMES SCHEND** PLEASANT PRAIRIE, WI

PREP: 20 MIN. + CHILLING
MAKES: 8 SERVINGS

- 1 tablespoon unflavored gelatin
- 2 cups cold white grape juice, divided
- 2 tablespoons sugar
- 2 cups champagne or club soda
- 8 fresh strawberries, hulled

1. In a small saucepan, sprinkle gelatin over 1 cup cold grape juice; let stand for 1 minute. Heat over low heat, stirring until gelatin is completely dissolved. Stir in sugar. Remove from the heat; stir in remaining grape juice. Cool to room temperature.

2. Transfer gelatin mixture to a large bowl. Slowly stir in champagne. Pour half of the mixture into eight champagne or parfait glasses. Add one strawberry to each glass. Chill glasses and remaining gelatin mixture until almost set, about 1 hour.

3. Place the reserved gelatin mixture in a blender; cover and process until foamy. Pour into glasses. Chill for 3 hours or until set.

PER SERVING *1/2 cup equals 96 cal., trace fat (trace sat. fat), 0 chol., 9 mg sodium, 13 g carb., trace fiber, 1 g pro.* **Diabetic Exchange:** *1 starch.*

Chocolate-Dipped Phyllo Sticks

Looking for something light and special to bake up for the holidays? Try these crunchy treats. They're great with coffee or alongside sorbet and sherbet.
—**PEGGY WOODWARD** EAST TROY, WI

PREP: 35 MIN. • **BAKE:** 5 MIN./BATCH
MAKES: 20 STICKS

- 4 sheets phyllo dough (14x9-inch size)
- 2 tablespoons butter, melted
- 1 tablespoon sugar
- 1/4 teaspoon ground cinnamon
  Cooking spray
- 2 ounces semisweet chocolate, finely chopped
- 1/2 teaspoon shortening
- 1/2 ounce white baking chocolate, melted

1. Preheat oven to 425°. Place one sheet of phyllo dough on a work surface; brush with butter. Cover with a second sheet of phyllo; brush with butter. (Keep remaining phyllo dough covered with plastic wrap and a damp towel to prevent it from drying out.) Cut phyllo in half lengthwise. Cut each half into five 4 1/2x2 3/4-in. rectangles. Tightly roll each rectangle from one long side, forming a 4 1/2-in.-long stick.

2. Combine sugar and cinnamon. Coat sticks with cooking spray; sprinkle with cinnamon-sugar. Place on an ungreased baking sheet. Bake at 425° for 3-5 minutes or until lightly browned. Remove to a wire rack to cool. Repeat with remaining phyllo dough, butter and cinnamon-sugar.

3. In a microwave, melt semisweet chocolate and shortening; stir until smooth. Dip one end of phyllo sticks in chocolate; allow extra to drip off. Place on waxed paper; let stand until set. Drizzle with white chocolate.

PER SERVING *1 phyllo stick equals 38 cal., 2 g fat (1 g sat. fat), 3 mg chol., 18 mg sodium, 4 g carb., trace fiber, trace pro.*

CHOCOLATE-DIPPED PHYLLO STICKS

General Recipe Index

Alphabetical Recipe Index